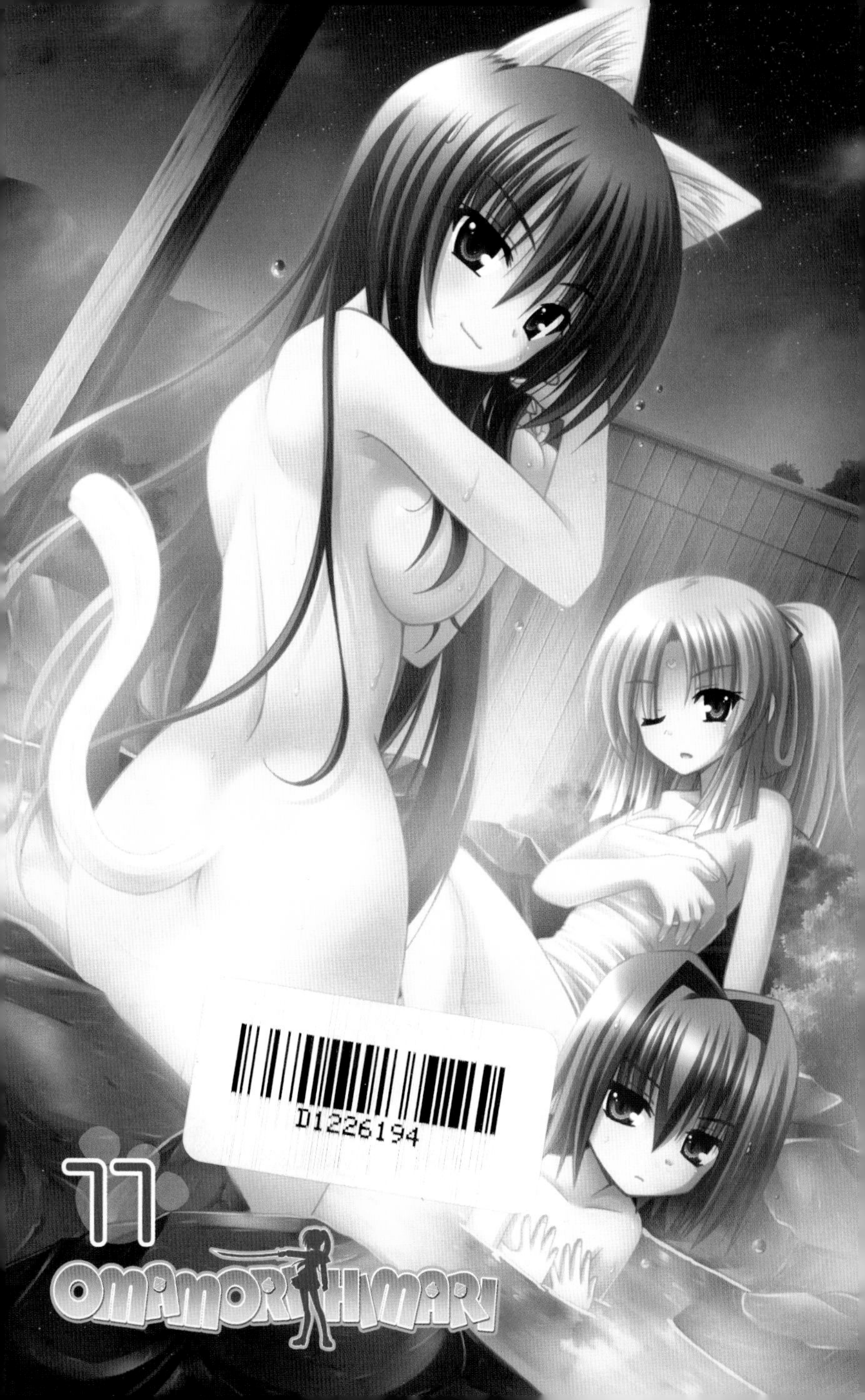
11
OMAMORI HIMARI

CONTENTS

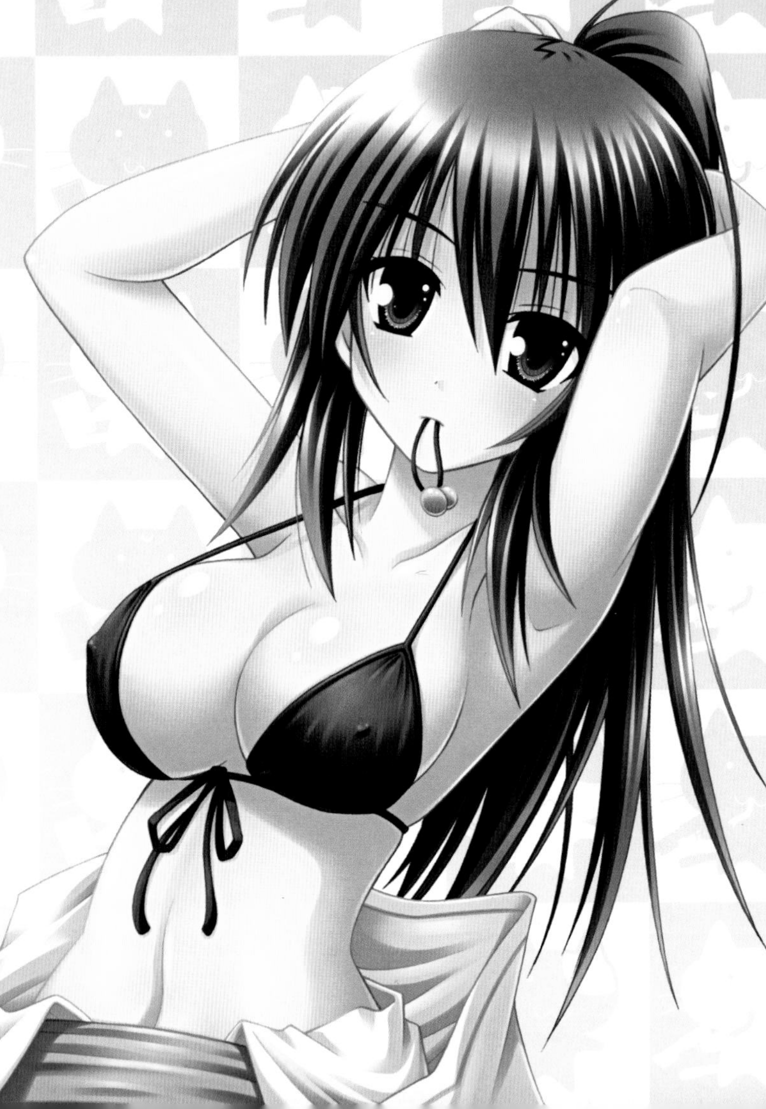

OMAMORI HIMARI ⑪

MILAN MATRA

Translation: Christine Dashiell • Lettering: Stephanie Lee

This book is a work of fiction. Names, characters, places, and incidents are the product of the author's imagination or are used fictitiously. Any resemblance to actual events, locales, or persons, living or dead, is coincidental.

OMAMORI HIMARI Volume 11 © MATRA MILAN 2013. Edited by FUJIMISHOBO. First published in Japan in 2013 by KADOKAWA CORPORATION, Tokyo. English translation rights arranged with KADOKAWA CORPORATION, Tokyo, through TUTTLE-MORI AGENCY, INC., Tokyo.

Translation © 2014 by Hachette Book Group, Inc.

All rights reserved. In accordance with the U.S. Copyright Act of 1976, the scanning, uploading, and electronic sharing of any part of this book without the permission of the publisher is unlawful piracy and theft of the author's intellectual property. If you would like to use material from the book (other than for review purposes), prior written permission must be obtained by contacting the publisher at permissions@hbgusa.com. Thank you for your support of the author's rights.

Yen Press
Hachette Book Group
237 Park Avenue, New York, NY 10017

www.HachetteBookGroup.com
www.YenPress.com

Yen Press is an imprint of Hachette Book Group, Inc. The Yen Press name and logo are trademarks of Hachette Book Group, Inc.

First Yen Press Edition: January 2014

ISBN: 978-0-316-36900-8

10 9 8 7 6 5 4 3 2 1

BVG

Printed in the United States of America

IN VOLUME 11, THE FIELD OF VISION IS NARROWED AND LINGERS IN THE BRAIN. ALL OF A SUDDEN, KUESU'S BACK FROM THE DEAD. I'VE EMPLOYED THIS KIND OF PATTERN OF SUDDEN DEATH BEING IMMEDIATELY FOLLOWED BY SPEEDY RECOVERY IN MY PAST WORKS TOO, SO I WROTE THE AFTERWORD IN THE LAST VOLUME REALLY SOBER SO AS TO NOT GIVE AWAY WHAT WAS IN STORE. I'M SO PROUD OF MYSELF (HEH).
EVERY CHAPTER HAS BOOBIES AND PANTIES GALORE, BUT THE CHARACTERS ARE IN A REAL PINCH NOW.
...SINCE THE BASIC STORY'S SO RAUNCHY, YOU CAN'T EXPECT ME TO CHANGE IT. CAN YOU?
BUT NOW IT'S HIMARI WHO'S IN TROUBLE. THE FINAL BOOK IS AT HAND!

JANUARY 2013 MATRA MILAN

SPECIAL THANKS TO: STUDIO HIBARI-SAMA, YUKI MATSUOKA-SAMA, YUNA KAGEZAKI-SAMA, SHOUYOU SAIJOU-SAMA, TZAWA-SAMA (ICHIJINSHA)

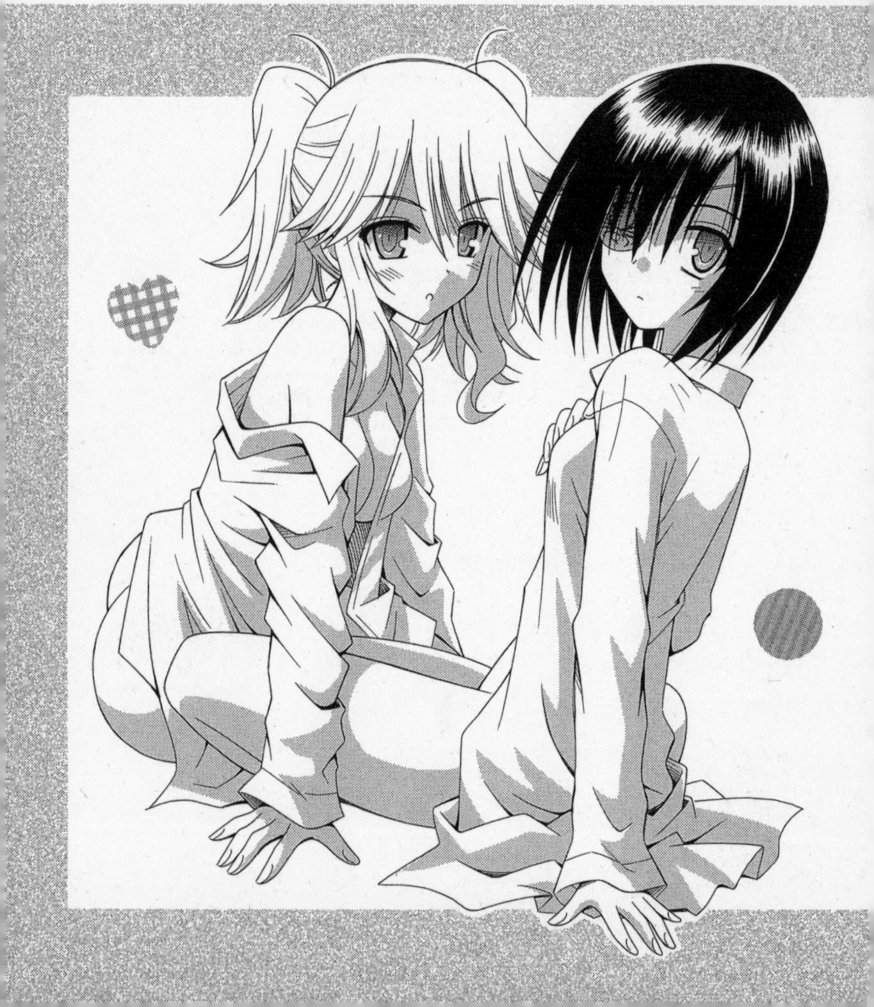

CAST OF CHARACTERS

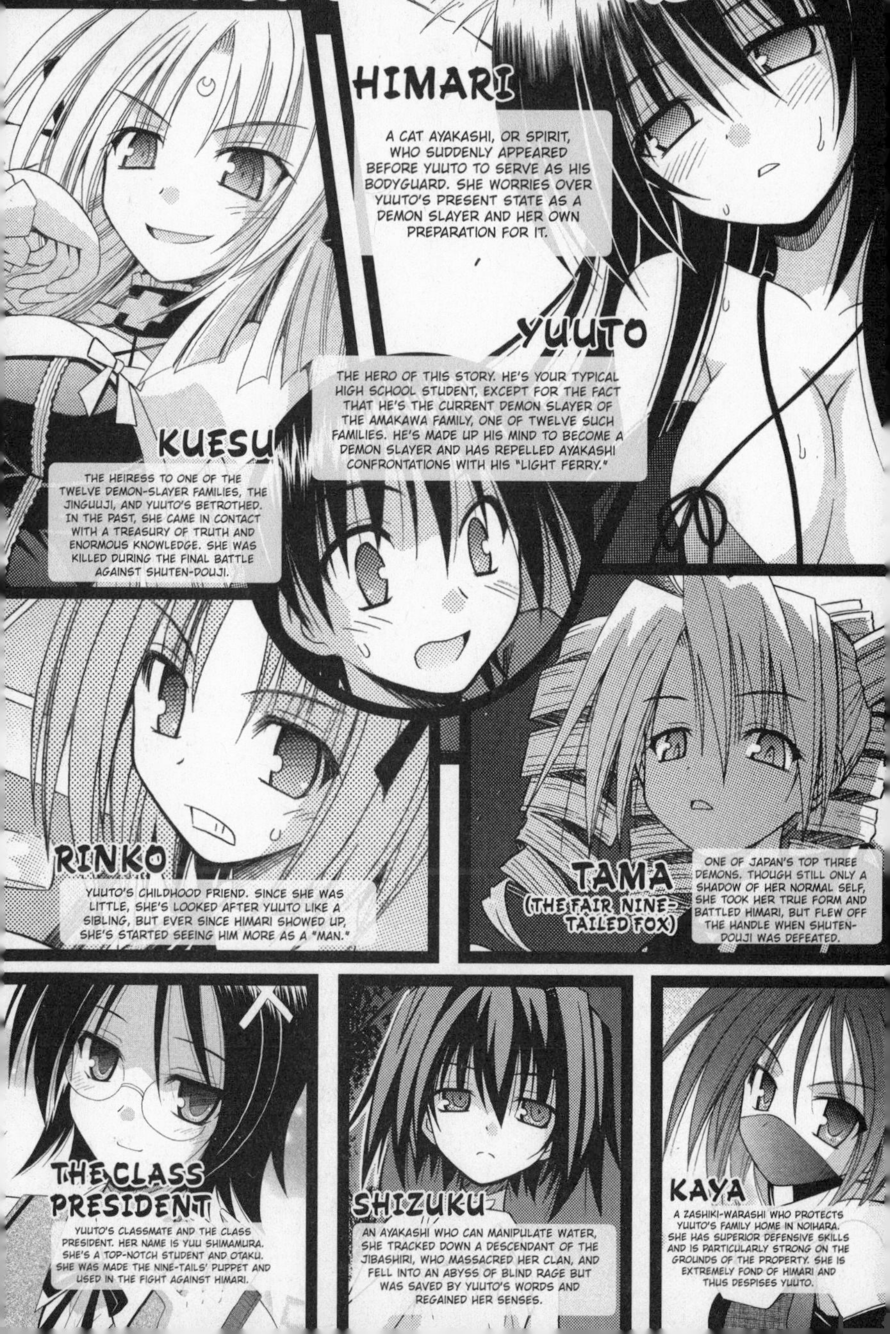
HIMARI
A CAT AYAKASHI, OR SPIRIT, WHO SUDDENLY APPEARED BEFORE YUUTO TO SERVE AS HIS BODYGUARD. SHE WORRIES OVER YUUTO'S PRESENT STATE AS A DEMON SLAYER AND HER OWN PREPARATION FOR IT.
YUUTO
THE HERO OF THIS STORY. HE'S YOUR TYPICAL HIGH SCHOOL STUDENT, EXCEPT FOR THE FACT THAT HE'S THE CURRENT DEMON SLAYER OF THE AMAKAWA FAMILY, ONE OF TWELVE SUCH FAMILIES. HE'S MADE UP HIS MIND TO BECOME A DEMON SLAYER AND HAS REPELLED AYAKASHI CONFRONTATIONS WITH HIS "LIGHT FERRY."
KUESU
THE HEIRESS TO ONE OF THE TWELVE DEMON-SLAYER FAMILIES, THE JINGUUJI, AND YUUTO'S BETROTHED. IN THE PAST, SHE CAME IN CONTACT WITH A TREASURY OF TRUTH AND ENORMOUS KNOWLEDGE. SHE WAS KILLED DURING THE FINAL BATTLE AGAINST SHUTEN-DOUJI.
TAMA (THE FAIR NINE-TAILED FOX)
ONE OF JAPAN'S TOP THREE DEMONS. THOUGH STILL ONLY A SHADOW OF HER NORMAL SELF, SHE TOOK HER TRUE FORM AND BATTLED HIMARI, BUT FLEW OFF THE HANDLE WHEN SHUTEN-DOUJI WAS DEFEATED.
RINKO
YUUTO'S CHILDHOOD FRIEND. SINCE SHE WAS LITTLE, SHE'S LOOKED AFTER YUUTO LIKE A SIBLING, BUT EVER SINCE HIMARI SHOWED UP, SHE'S STARTED SEEING HIM MORE AS A "MAN."
KAYA
A ZASHIKI-WARASHI WHO PROTECTS YUUTO'S FAMILY HOME IN NOIHARA. SHE HAS SUPERIOR DEFENSIVE SKILLS AND IS PARTICULARLY STRONG ON THE GROUNDS OF THE PROPERTY. SHE IS EXTREMELY FOND OF HIMARI AND THUS DESPISES YUUTO.
SHIZUKU
AN AYAKASHI WHO CAN MANIPULATE WATER, SHE TRACKED DOWN A DESCENDANT OF THE JIBASHIRI, WHO MASSACRED HER CLAN, AND FELL INTO AN ABYSS OF BLIND RAGE BUT WAS SAVED BY YUUTO'S WORDS AND REGAINED HER SENSES.
THE CLASS PRESIDENT
YUUTO'S CLASSMATE AND THE CLASS PRESIDENT. HER NAME IS YUU SHIMAMURA. SHE'S A TOP-NOTCH STUDENT AND OTAKU. SHE WAS MADE THE NINE-TAILS' PUPPET AND USED IN THE FIGHT AGAINST HIMARI.

❖THE❖STORY❖SO❖FAR❖

YUUTO AMAKAWA IS A HIGH SCHOOLER WITH A SEVERE ALLERGY TO CATS. WHO SHOULD APPEAR BEFORE HIM ONE DAY OTHER THAN A FELINE AYAKASHI, HIMARI?

"I WILL PROTECT YOU, YOUNG LORD."

SUCH IS THE PROCLAMATION MADE BY HIMARI, HAVING BEEN GIVEN THE DUTY OF PROTECTING YUUTO, THANKS TO A PLEDGE MADE LONG AGO. BUT YUUTO ALSO HAS TO DEAL WITH HIS NEIGHBOR AND CHILDHOOD FRIEND, RINKO, AS WELL AS THE AYAKASHI SHIZUKU, WHO WAS SWAYED BY YUUTO'S KINDNESS AND DECIDED TO LIVE WITH HIM. WITH ALL THESE GIRLS IN HIS LIFE, YUUTO'S DAYS QUICKLY BECOME OFF-THE-WALL AND FULL OF FUN WITH NO END OF SURPRISES.

AFTER SUFFERING THE SURPRISE ATTACK LAUNCHED BY THE NINE-TAILS WHO IS USING THE CLASS PRESIDENT AS HER PAWN, HIMARI IS FORCED INTO A HARD FIGHT. AS SOON AS SHIZUKU ERECTS THE STRAY HOUSE...

"THERE IS NO TOMORROW FOR YOU."

NO LONGER CURBING HER POWERS, HIMARI'S EXPRESSION CHANGES COMPLETELY, AND THE HUNT BEGINS.

MEANWHILE, KUESU GOES TO YUUTO, URGES HIM TO TAKE ACTION, AND GOES TO FIGHT SHUTEN-DOUJI ON HER OWN.

"I DID STEAL A GOOD LUCK CHARM...WITH MY LIPS, YUU-CHAN."

HOWEVER, WHILE TRYING TO PROTECT SHIZUKU WHO HAS ERECTED THE STRAY HOUSE AND IS THEREFORE DEFENSELESS, SHE TURNS HER BACK ON SHUTEN-DOUJI FOR A MOMENT AND SUFFERS A CRUSHING BLOW FROM HIM FOR IT.

"DESTRUCTIVE BACKSTABBING MAGIC STAFF! GHOST SWORD REPRODUCTION 'LÆVATEINN'!!!"

CALLING FORTH THE LAST OF HER POWERS, SHE DEFEATS SHUTEN-DOUJI AND THEN COLLAPSES LIFELESS IN YUUTO'S ARMS.

"CAT...YOUR WHITE LIGHT AS A BODYGUARD MUST SHINE ON."

HIMARI TAKES HER WORDS TO HEART AND IS ROUSED INTO ACTION, ONLY TO GIVE CHASE AND FIND HERSELF OUTNUMBERED. THAT'S WHEN YUUTO STEPS IN AND CHALLENGES THE NINE-TAILS ON HIS OWN AT LAST.

"YOUNG LORD, IF YOU DIE, I SHALL BE MOST ENRAGED. I SHALL BE A SOBBING MASS OF RAGE."

THE NINE-TAILS LOSES SELF-CONTROL WHEN SHE SEES THAT SHUTEN-DOUJI'S BEEN DEFEATED AND BITES ONTO YUUTO, BUT HIMARI CHOMPS ONTO HER WINDPIPE IN TURN!!

MENAGERIE 63: THE FELINE AYAKASHI'S FANGS SINK DEEP

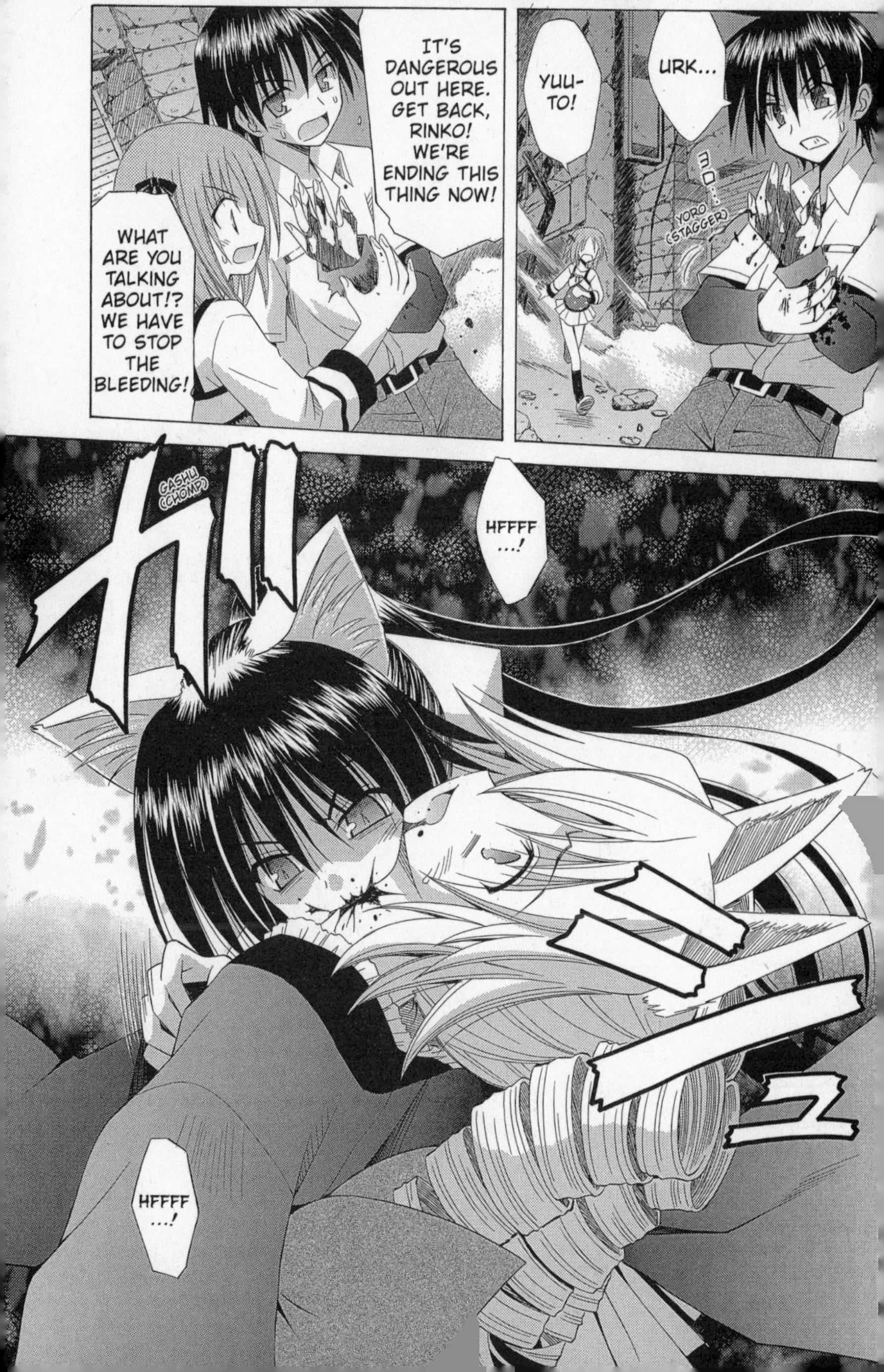
URK...
YUU-TO!
YORO (STAGGER)
IT'S DANGEROUS OUT HERE. GET BACK, RINKO! WE'RE ENDING THIS THING NOW!
WHAT ARE YOU TALKING ABOUT!? WE HAVE TO STOP THE BLEEDING!
HFFFF ...!
GASHU (CHOMP)
HFFFF ...!

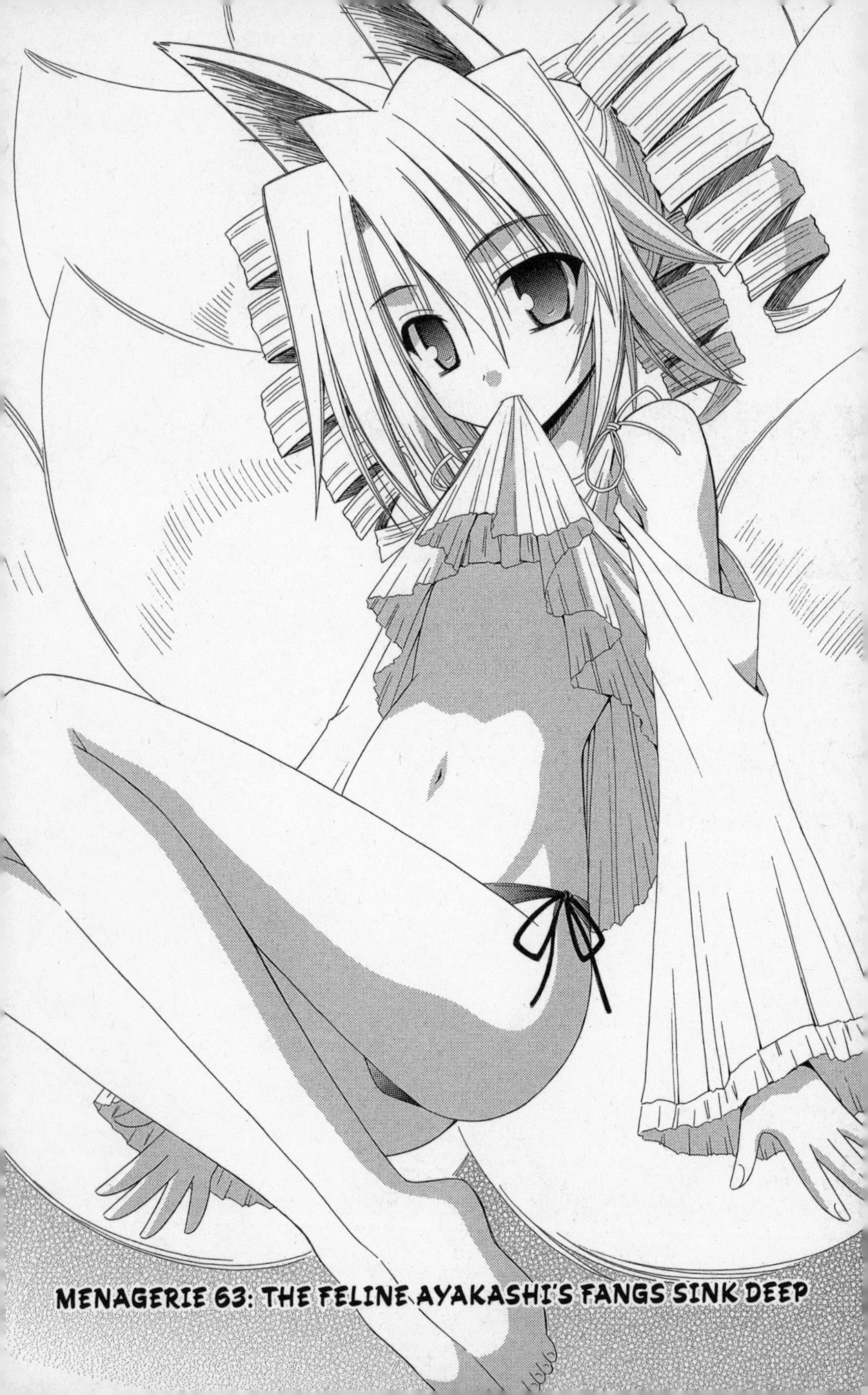
MENAGERIE 63: THE FELINE AYAKASHI'S FANGS SINK DEEP

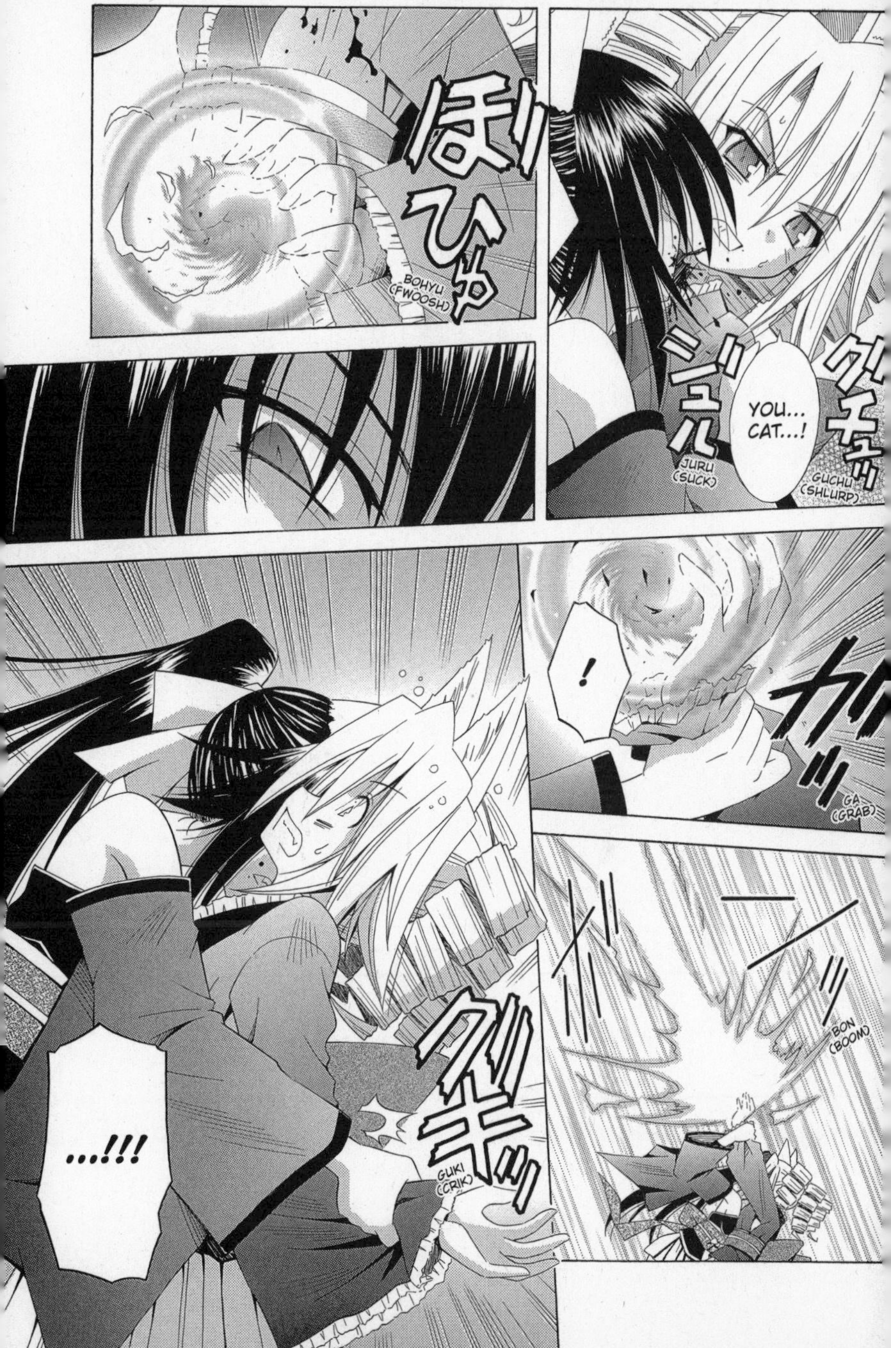
グチュッ
GUCHU (SHLURP)
YOU... CAT...!
ジュル
JURU (SUCK)
ぼひゅ
BOHYU (FWOOSH)
!
ガッ
GA (GRAB)
ボンッ
BON (BOOM)
...!!!
グキッ
GUKI (CRIK)

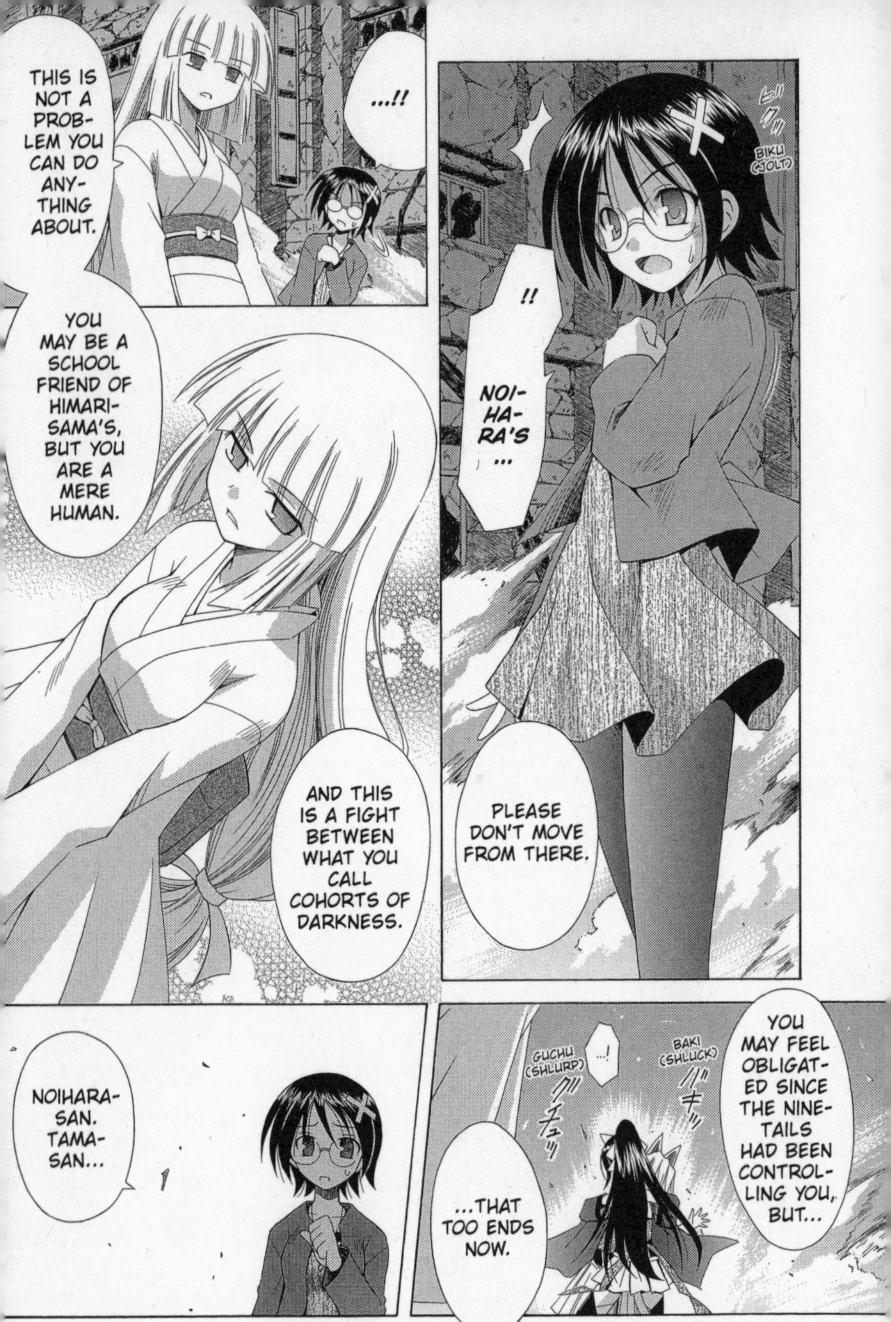
BIKU (JOLT)
!!
NOIHARA'S...
PLEASE DON'T MOVE FROM THERE.
THIS IS NOT A PROBLEM YOU CAN DO ANYTHING ABOUT.
...!!
YOU MAY BE A SCHOOL FRIEND OF HIMARI-SAMA'S, BUT YOU ARE A MERE HUMAN.
AND THIS IS A FIGHT BETWEEN WHAT YOU CALL COHORTS OF DARKNESS.
YOU MAY FEEL OBLIGATED SINCE THE NINE-TAILS HAD BEEN CONTROLLING YOU, BUT...
BAKI (SHLUCK)
...!
GUCHU (SHLURP)
...THAT TOO ENDS NOW.
NOIHARA-SAN. TAMA-SAN...

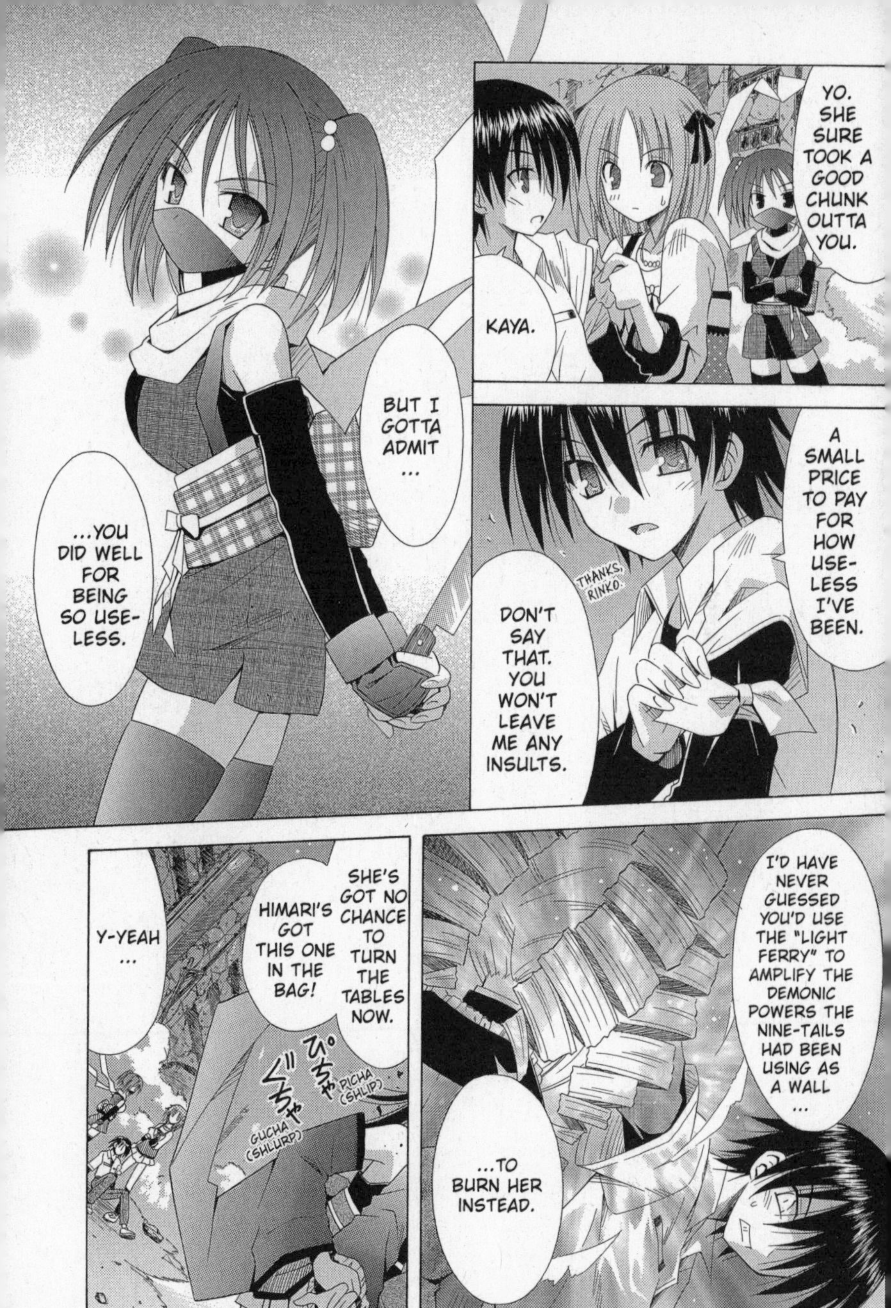
YO. SHE SURE TOOK A GOOD CHUNK OUTTA YOU.
KAYA.
A SMALL PRICE TO PAY FOR HOW USE-LESS I'VE BEEN.
THANKS, RINKO.
DON'T SAY THAT. YOU WON'T LEAVE ME ANY INSULTS.
BUT I GOTTA ADMIT...
...YOU DID WELL FOR BEING SO USE-LESS.
I'D HAVE NEVER GUESSED YOU'D USE THE "LIGHT FERRY" TO AMPLIFY THE DEMONIC POWERS THE NINE-TAILS HAD BEEN USING AS A WALL...
...TO BURN HER INSTEAD.
SHE'S GOT NO CHANCE TO TURN THE TABLES NOW.
HIMARI'S GOT THIS ONE IN THE BAG!
Y-YEAH...
ぴちゃ
PICHA (SHLIP)
ぐちゃ
GUCHA (SHLURP)

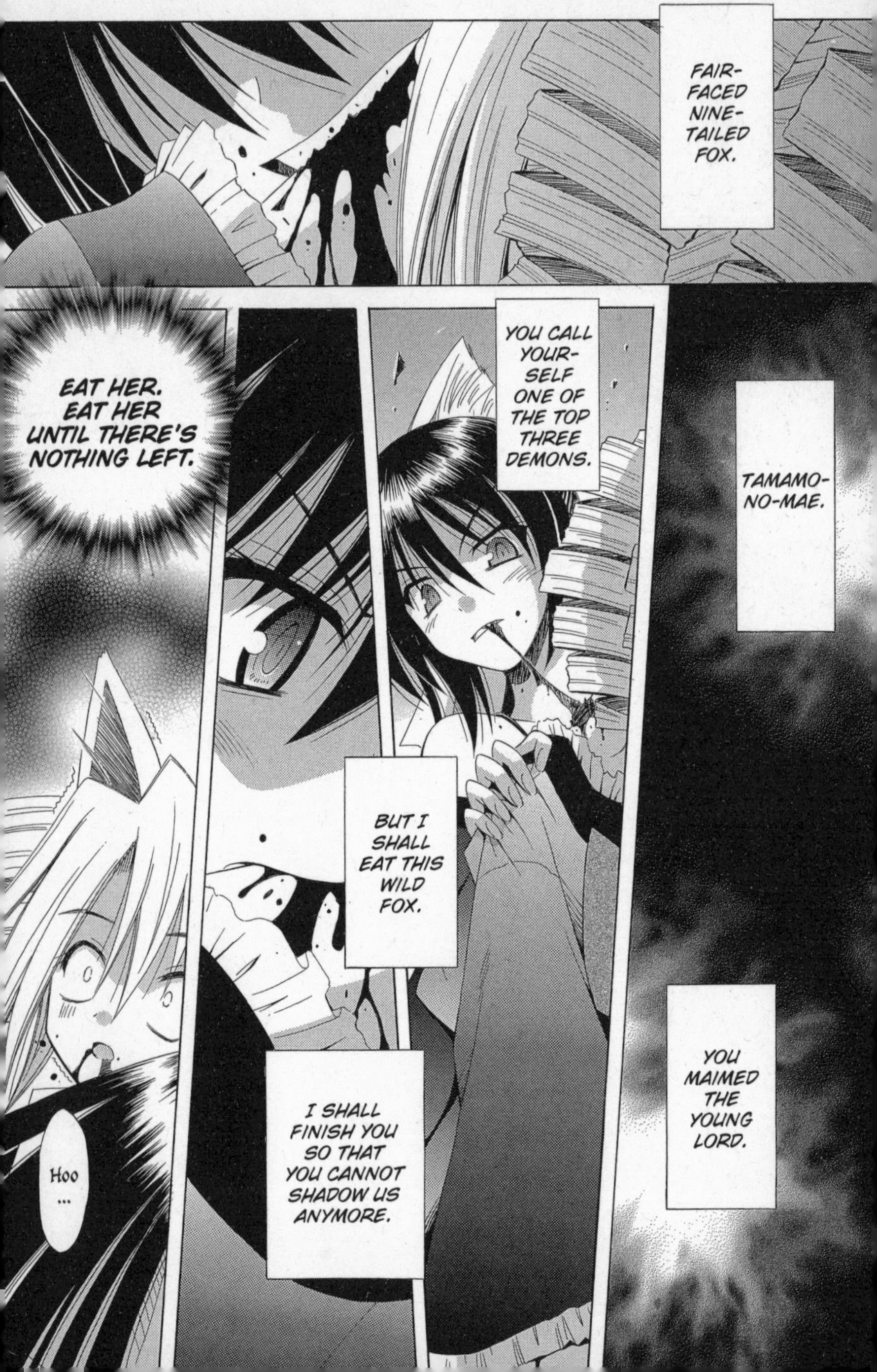
FAIR-FACED NINE-TAILED FOX.
TAMAMO-NO-MAE.
YOU CALL YOURSELF ONE OF THE TOP THREE DEMONS.
YOU MAIMED THE YOUNG LORD.
BUT I SHALL EAT THIS WILD FOX.
I SHALL FINISH YOU SO THAT YOU CANNOT SHADOW US ANYMORE.
EAT HER. EAT HER UNTIL THERE'S NOTHING LEFT.
Hoo ...

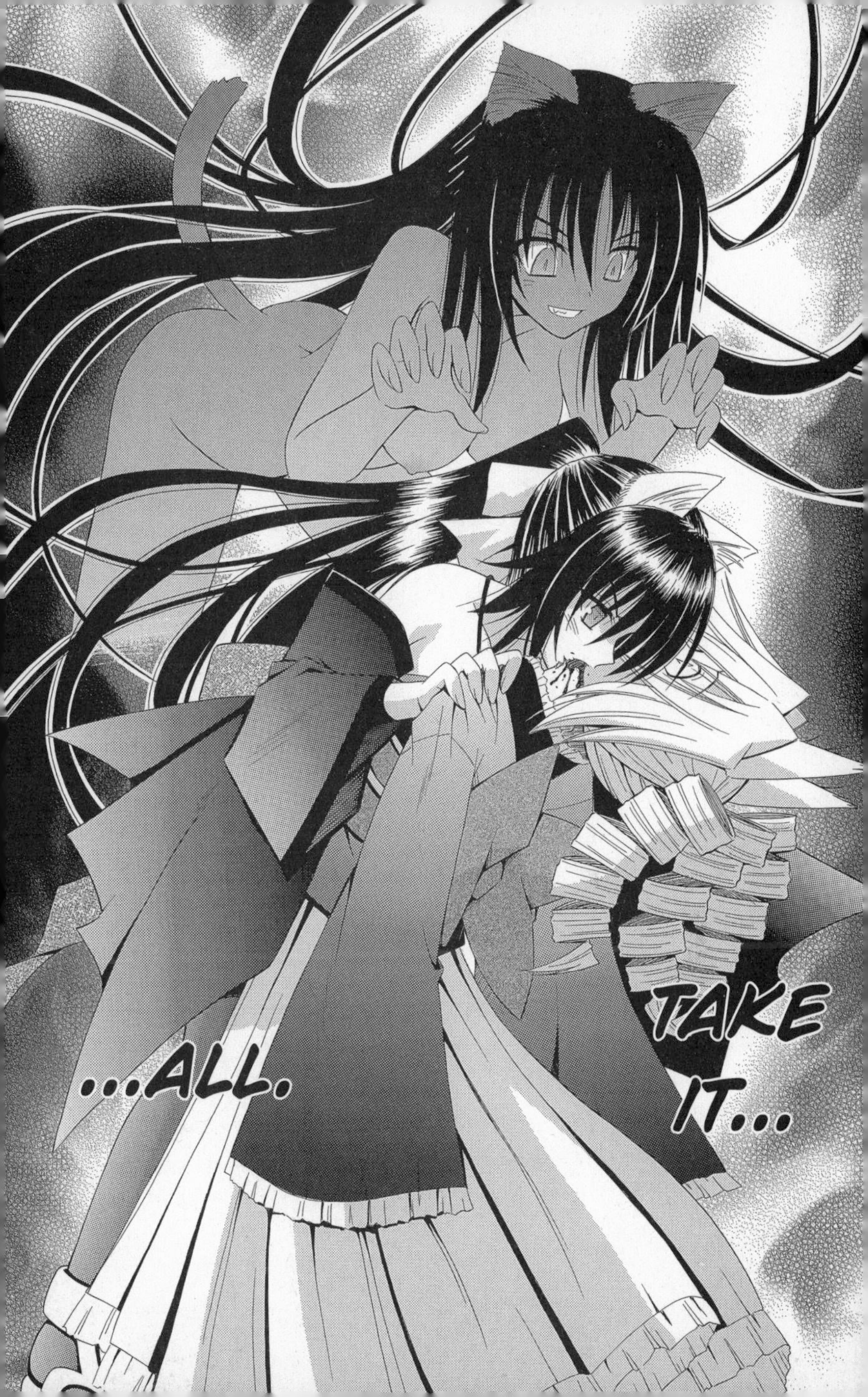
TAKE IT...
...ALL.

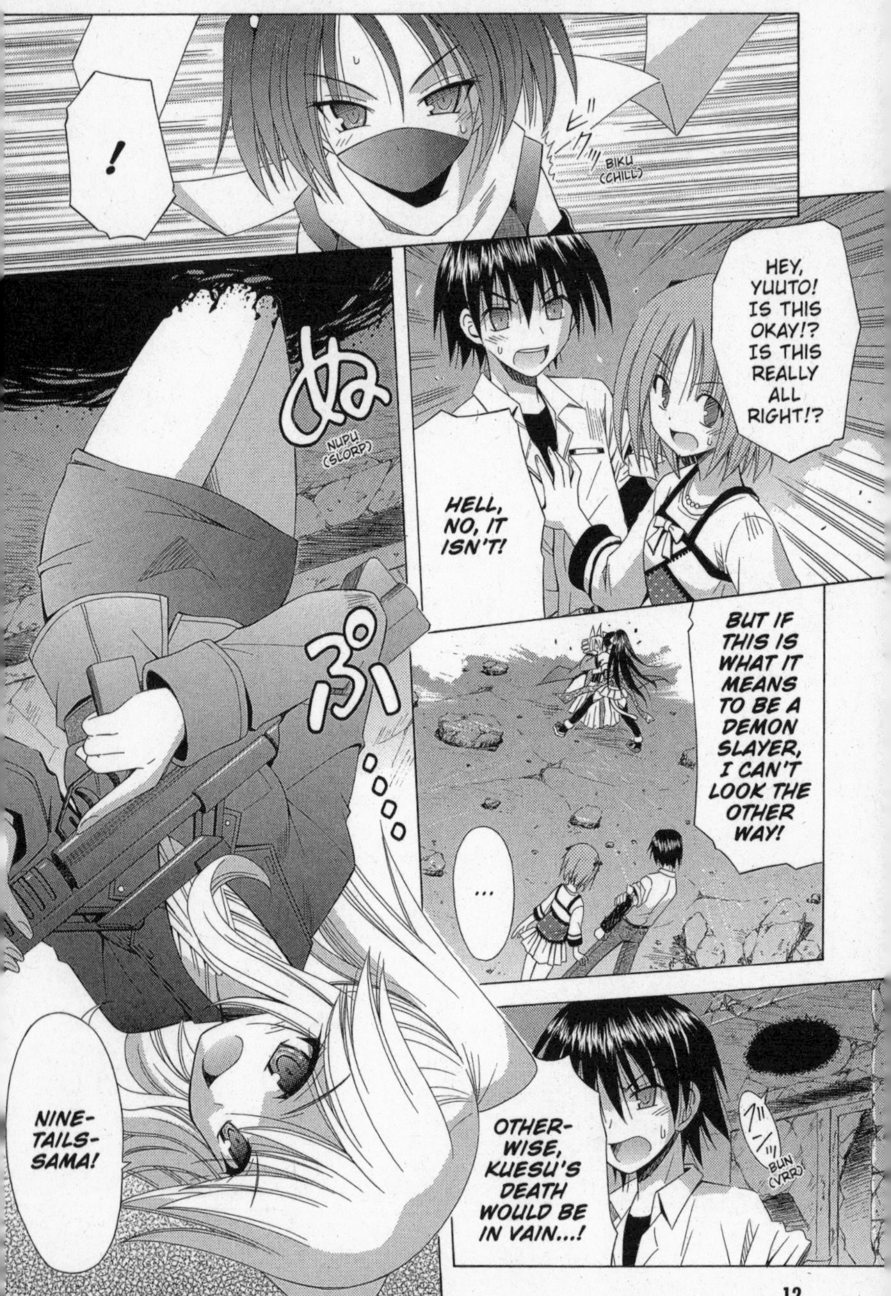

!
BIKU (CHILL)
HEY, YUUTO! IS THIS OKAY!? IS THIS REALLY ALL RIGHT!?
HELL, NO, IT ISN'T!
BUT IF THIS IS WHAT IT MEANS TO BE A DEMON SLAYER, I CAN'T LOOK THE OTHER WAY!
...
OTHER-WISE, KUESU'S DEATH WOULD BE IN VAIN...!
BUN (VRR)
ぬ
NUPU (SLORP)
ぷ
NINE-TAILS-SAMA!

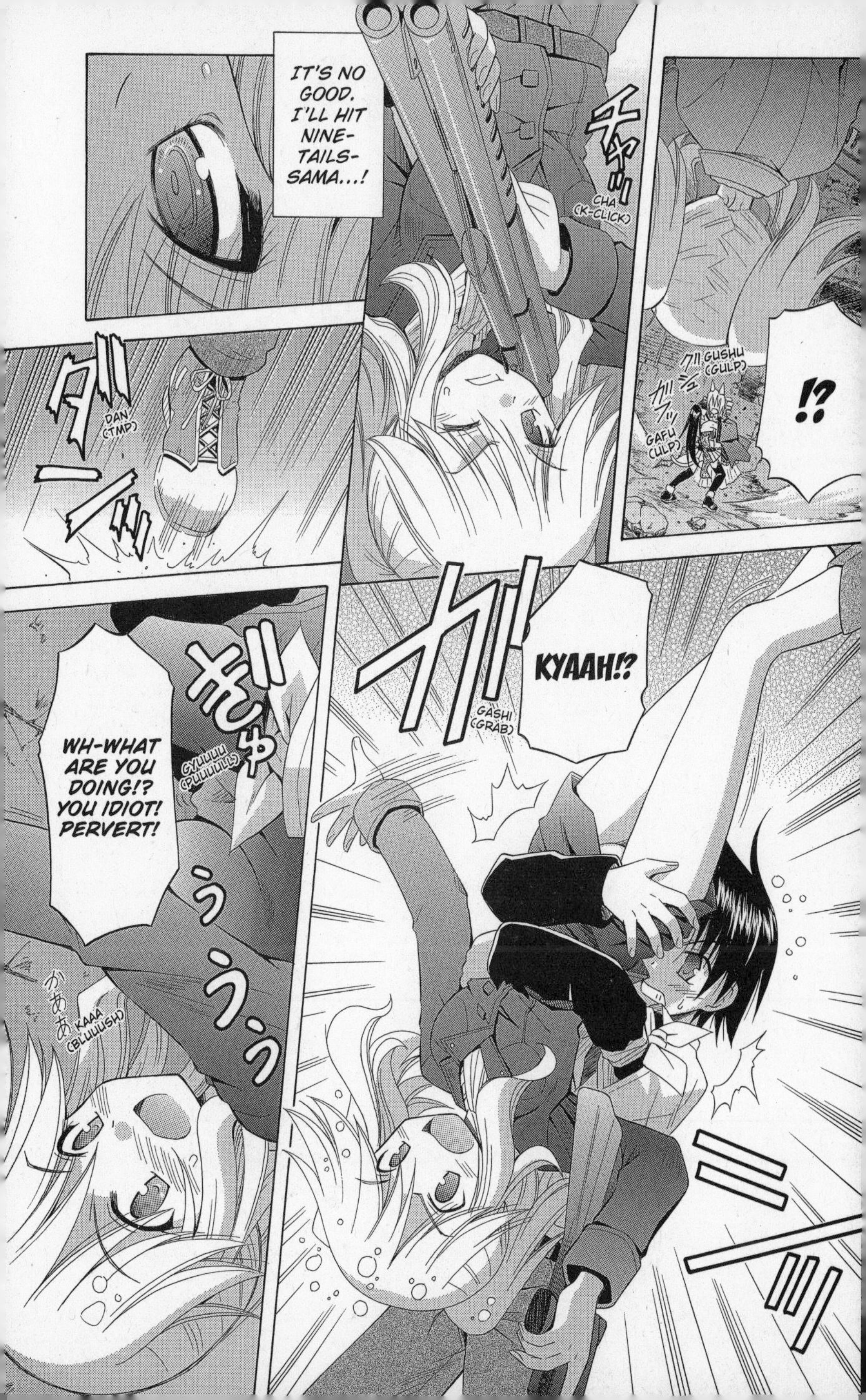

!?
GUSHU (GULP)
GAFU (GULP)
CHA (K-CLICK)
IT'S NO GOOD. I'LL HIT NINE-TAILS-SAMA...!
DAN (TMP)
GASHI (GRAB)
KYAAH!?
WH-WHAT ARE YOU DOING!? YOU IDIOT! PERVERT!
GYUUUU (PUUUULL)
KAAA (BLUUUSH)

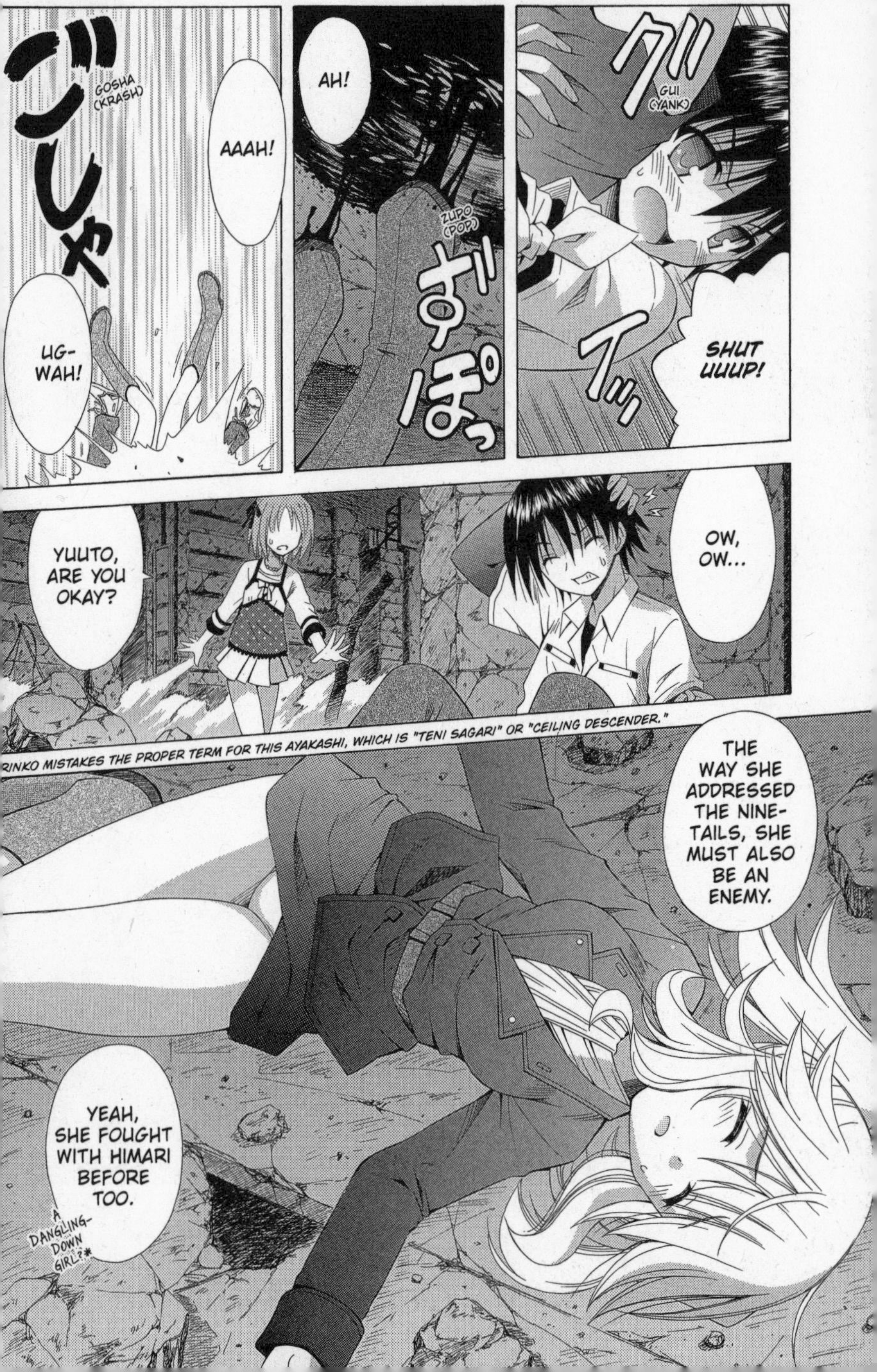
GUI (YANK)
SHUT UUUP!
AH!
ZUPO (POP)
AAAH!
GOSHA (KRASH)
UG-WAH!
OW, OW...
YUUTO, ARE YOU OKAY?
*RINKO MISTAKES THE PROPER TERM FOR THIS AYAKASHI, WHICH IS "TENI SAGARI" OR "CEILING DESCENDER."
THE WAY SHE ADDRESSED THE NINE-TAILS, SHE MUST ALSO BE AN ENEMY.
YEAH, SHE FOUGHT WITH HIMARI BEFORE TOO.
A DANGLING-DOWN GIRL?*

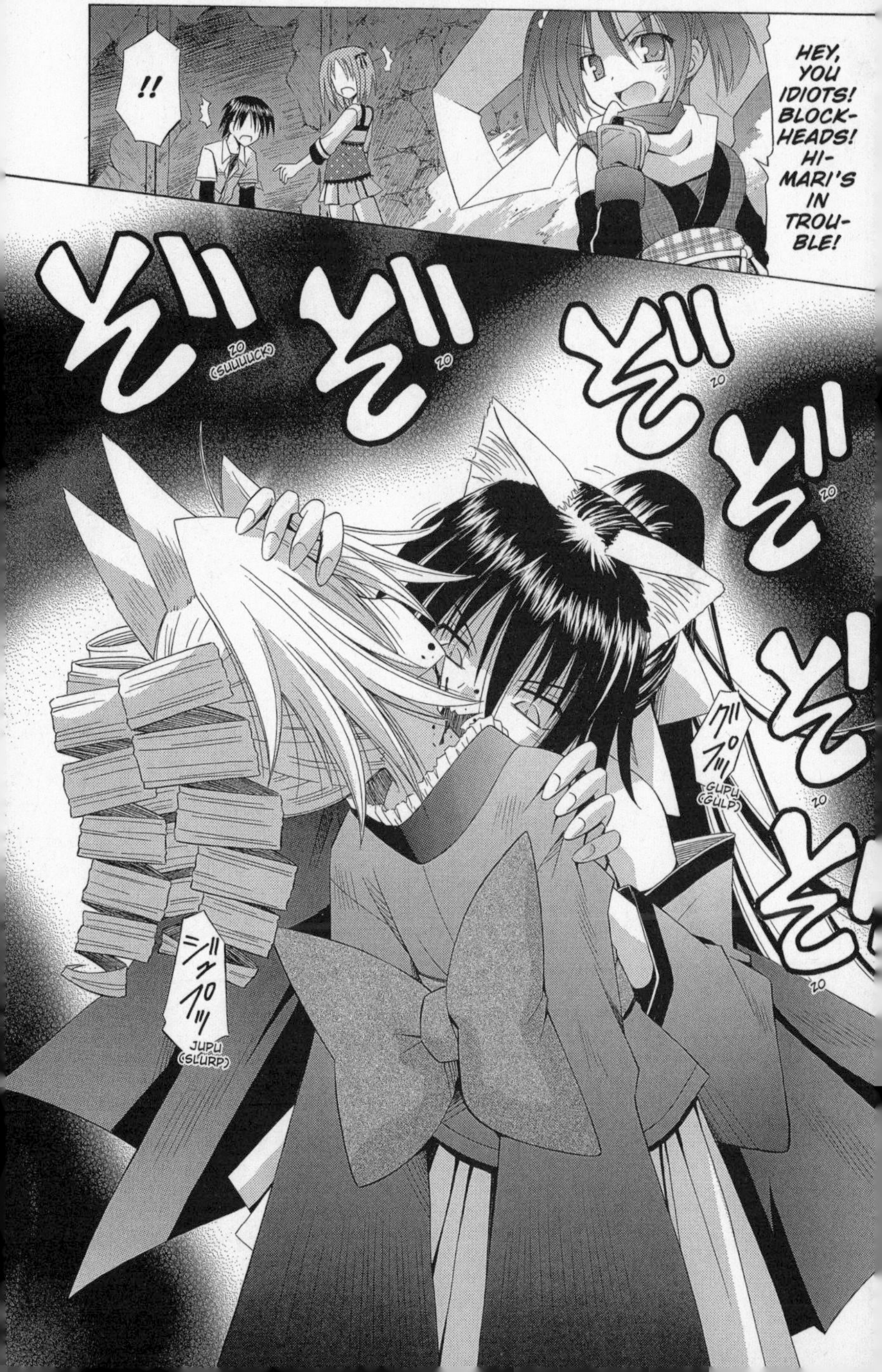
HEY, YOU IDIOTS! BLOCKHEADS! HIMARI'S IN TROUBLE!
!!
ZO (SUUUUCK)
ZO
ZO
ZO
GUPU (GULP)
ZO
ZO
JUPU (SLURP)

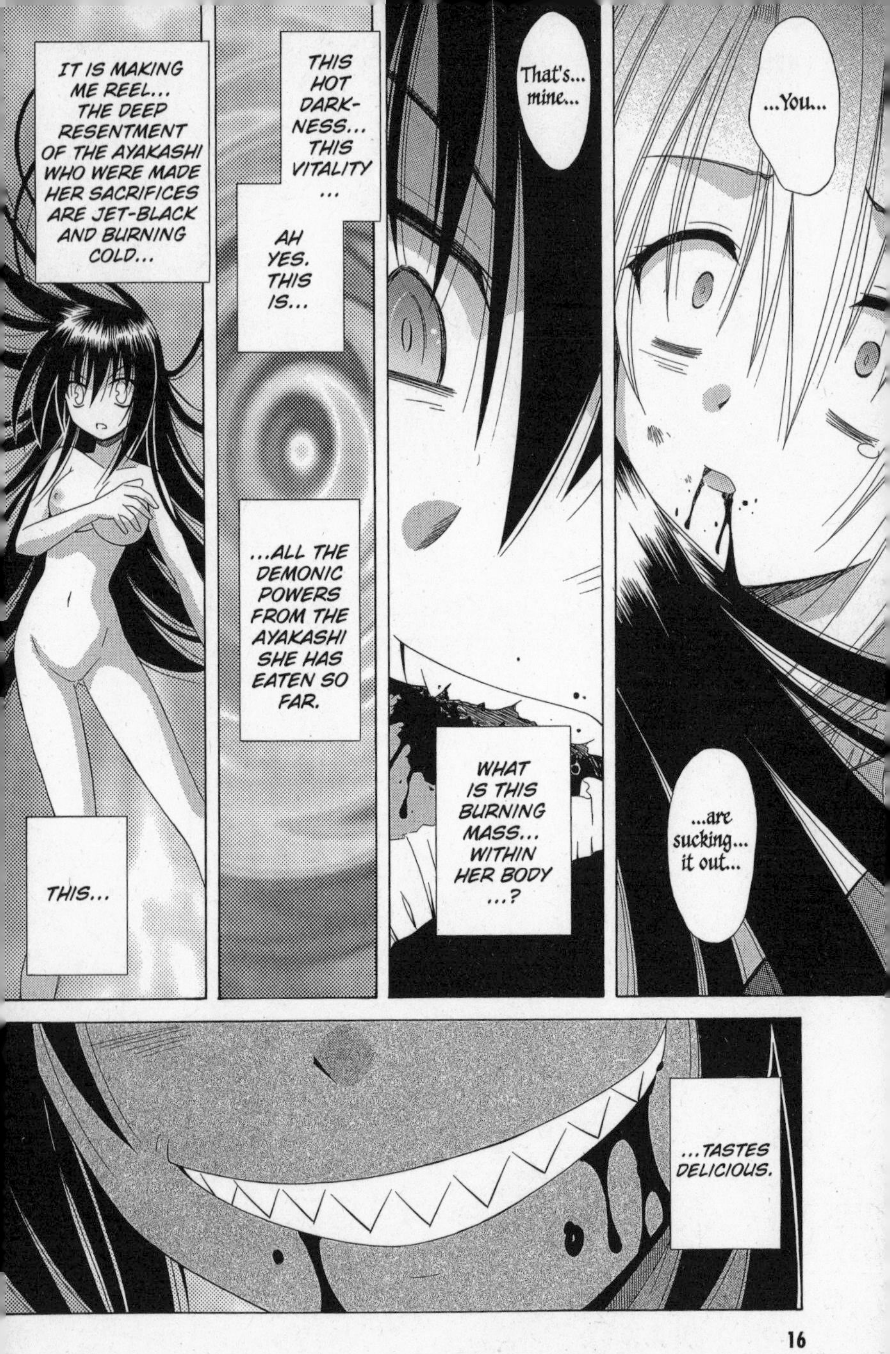
...You...
...are sucking... it out...
That's... mine...
WHAT IS THIS BURNING MASS... WITHIN HER BODY ...?
THIS HOT DARKNESS... THIS VITALITY ...
AH YES. THIS IS...
...ALL THE DEMONIC POWERS FROM THE AYAKASHI SHE HAS EATEN SO FAR.
IT IS MAKING ME REEL... THE DEEP RESENTMENT OF THE AYAKASHI WHO WERE MADE HER SACRIFICES ARE JET-BLACK AND BURNING COLD...
THIS...
...TASTES DELICIOUS.

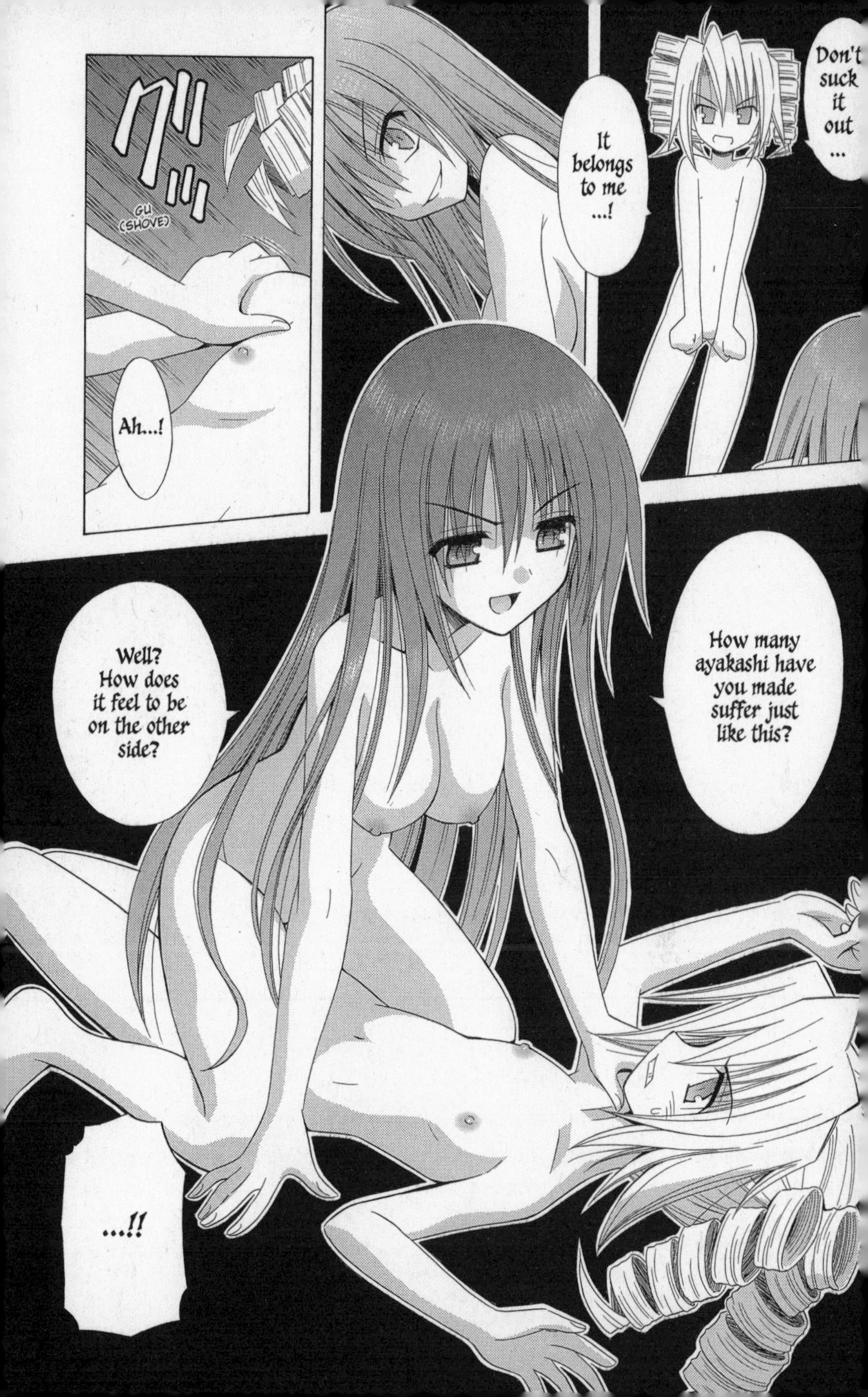
Don't suck it out ...
It belongs to me ...!
GU (SHOVE)
Ah...!
How many ayakashi have you made suffer just like this?
Well? How does it feel to be on the other side?
...!!

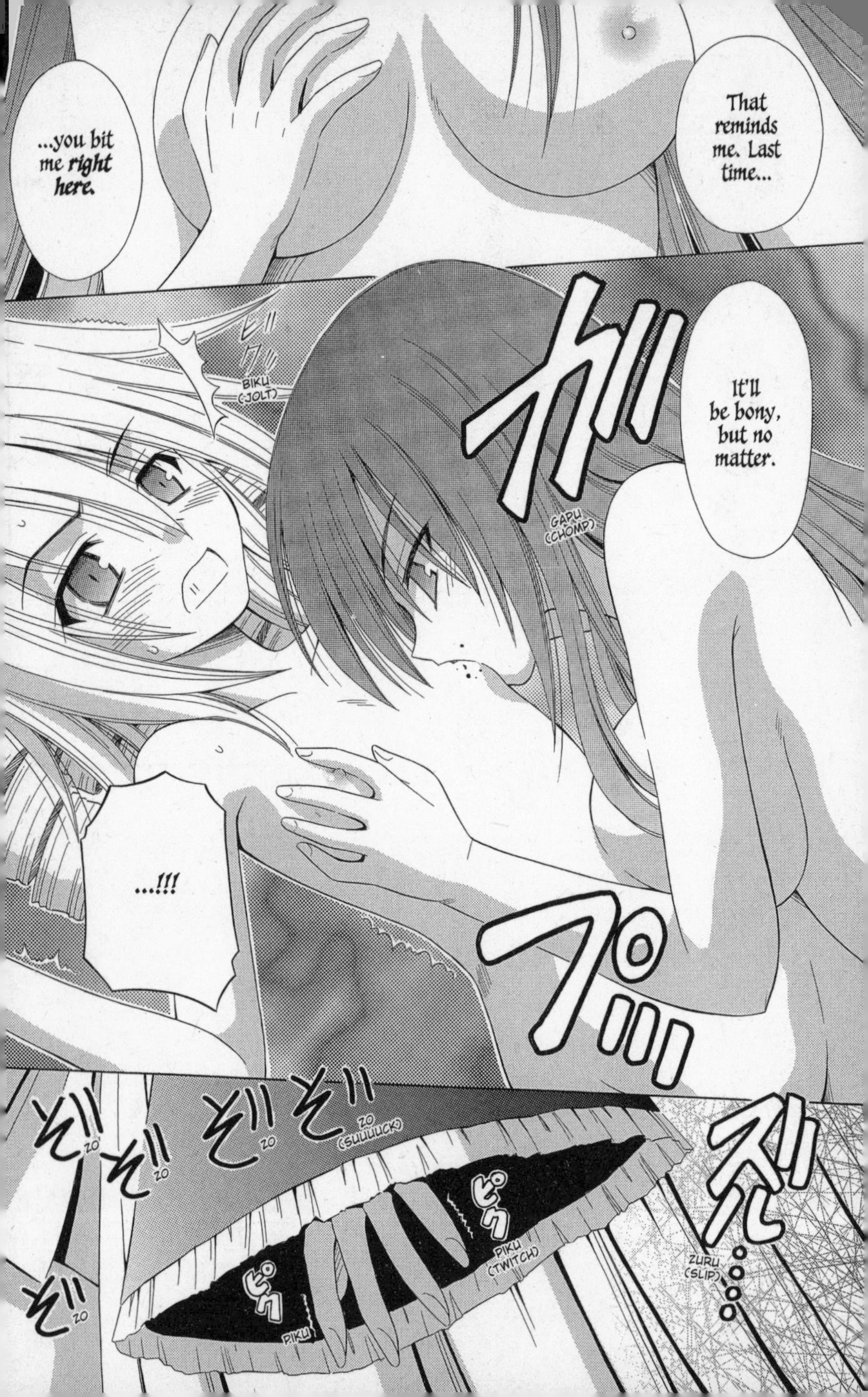
That reminds me. Last time...
...you bit me ***right here.***
It'll be bony, but no matter.
GAPU (CHOMP)
BIKU (JOLT)
...!!!
ZURU (SLIP)
PIKU (TWITCH)
PIKU
ZO (SUUUUCK)
ZO
ZO
ZO
ZO

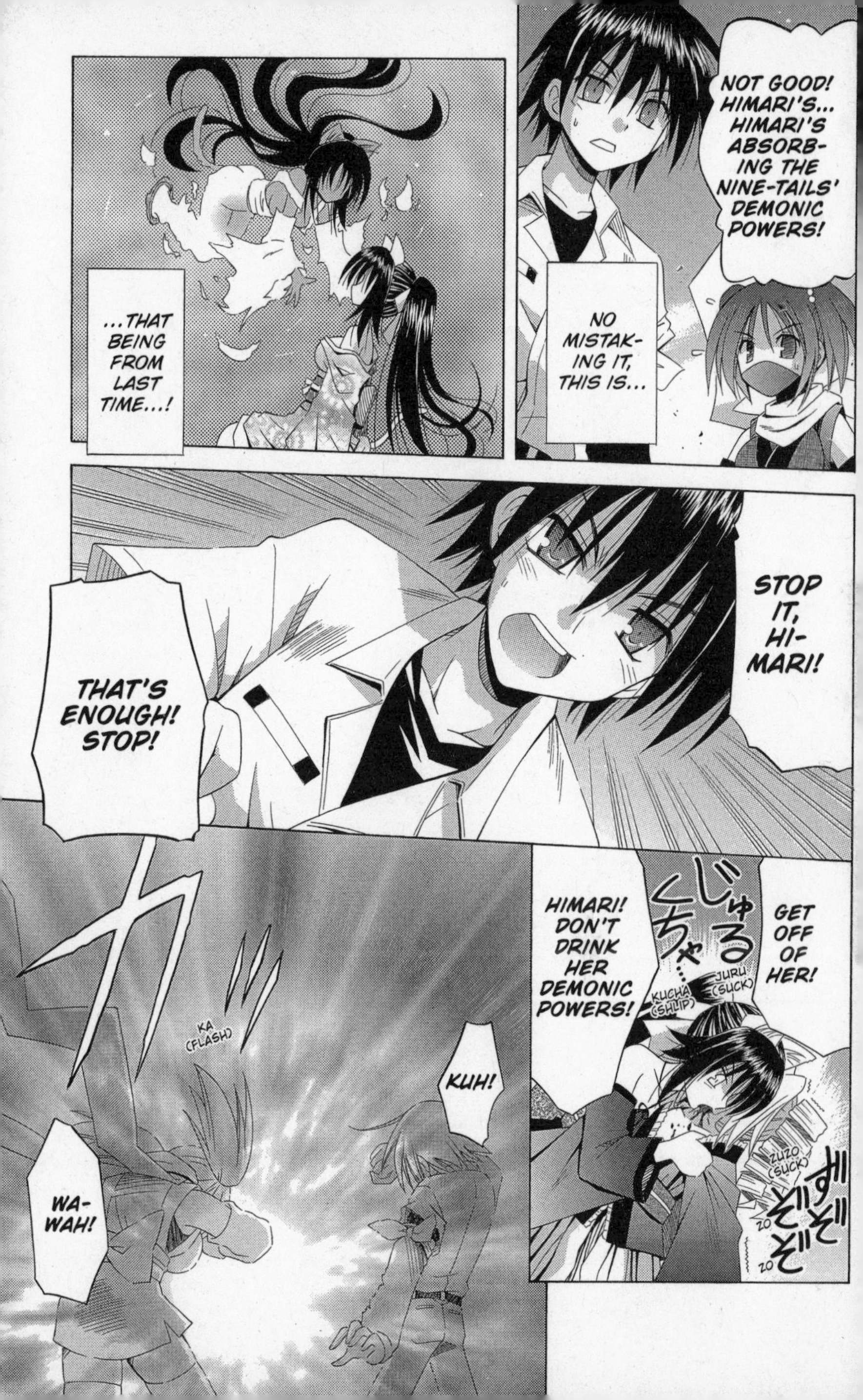
NOT GOOD! HIMARI'S... HIMARI'S ABSORBING THE NINE-TAILS' DEMONIC POWERS!
NO MISTAKING IT, THIS IS...
...THAT BEING FROM LAST TIME...!
STOP IT, HIMARI!
THAT'S ENOUGH! STOP!
GET OFF OF HER!
じゅる
JURU (SUCK)
くちゃ...
KUCHA (SHLIP)
HIMARI! DON'T DRINK HER DEMONIC POWERS!
ずぞぞぞ
ZUZO (SUCK)
ZO
ZO
KA (FLASH)
KUH!
WA-WAH!

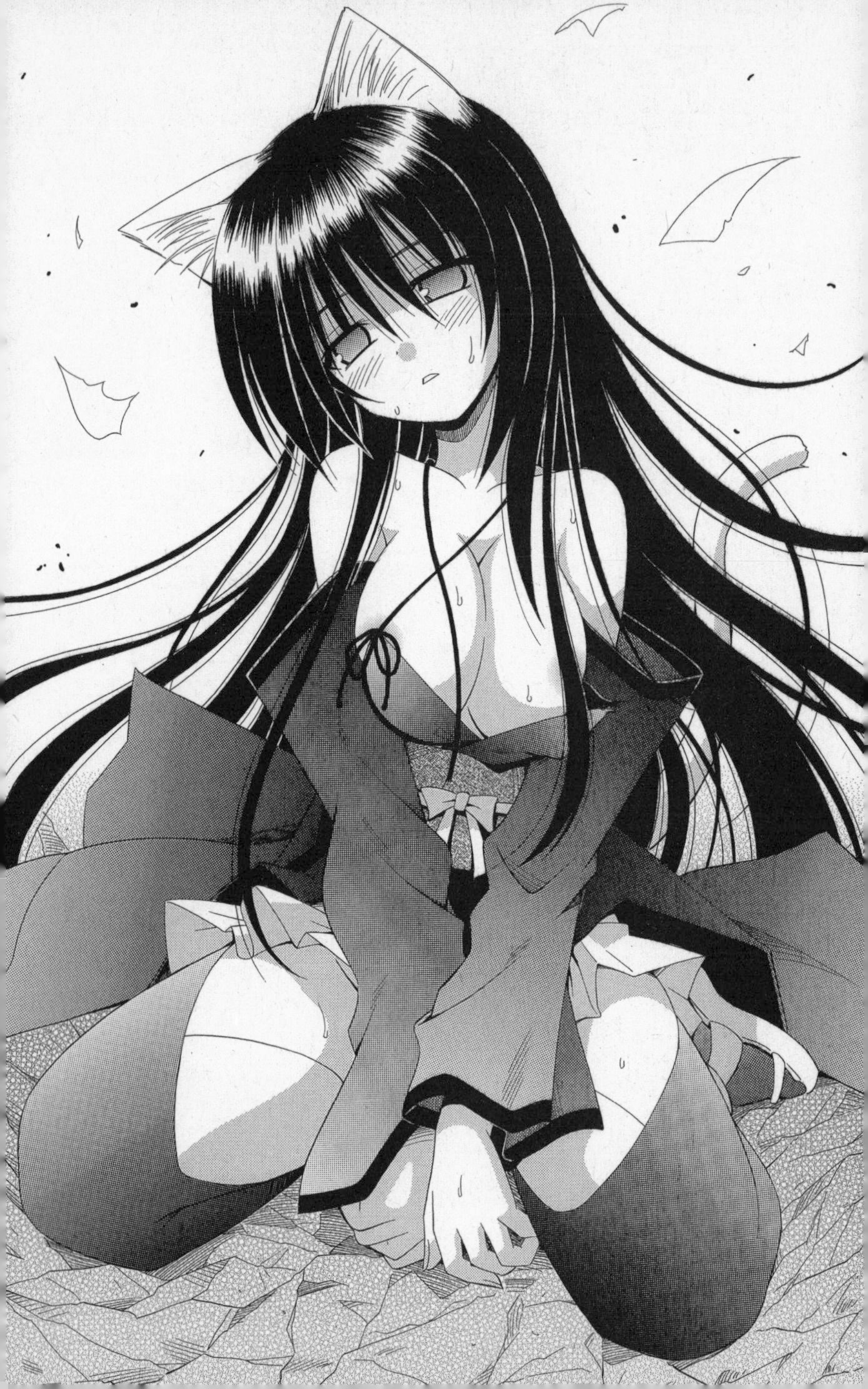

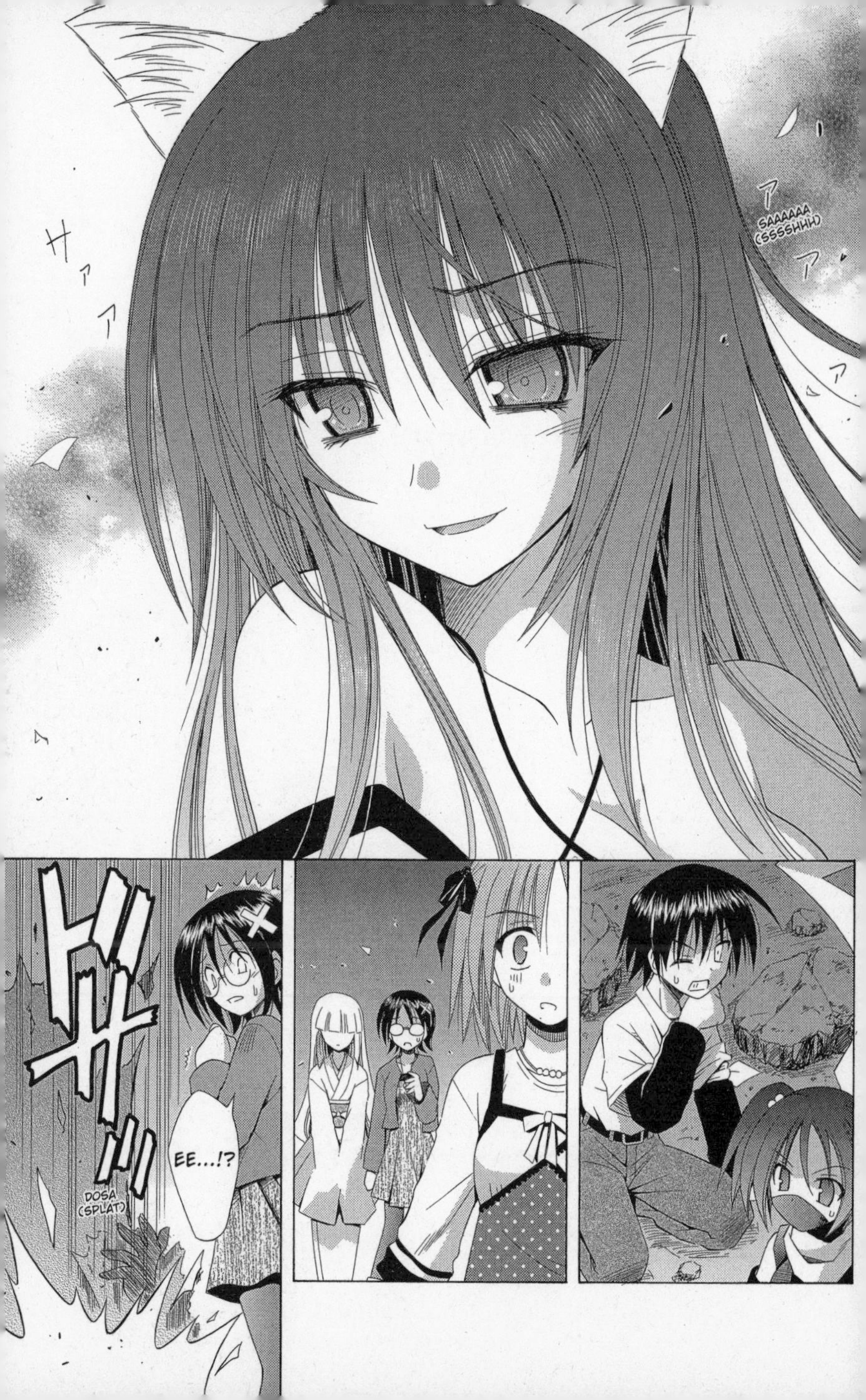
SAAAAAA (SSSSHHH)
DOSA (SPLAT)
EE...!?

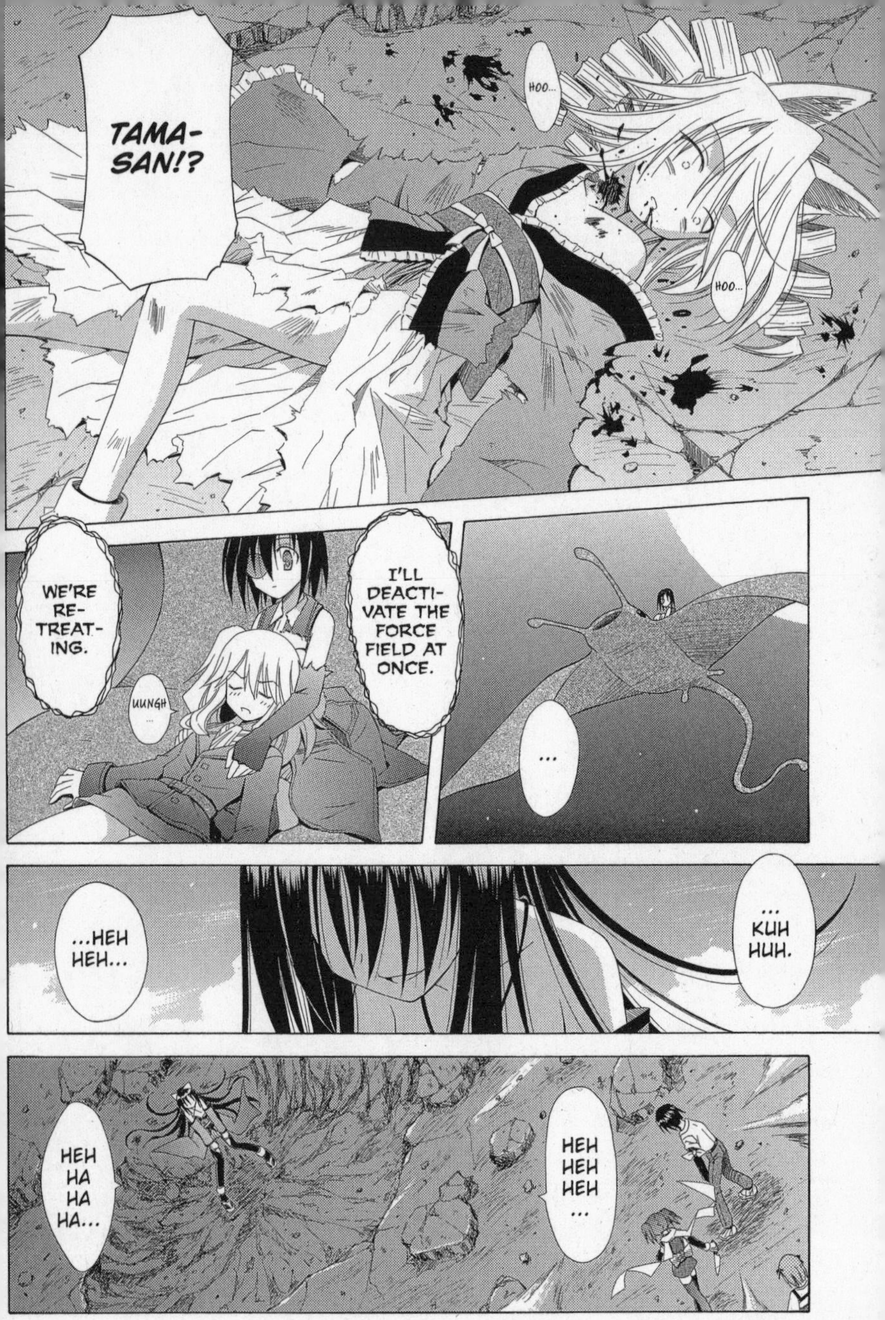
HOO...
HOO...
TAMA-SAN!?
...
I'LL DEACTIVATE THE FORCE FIELD AT ONCE.
WE'RE RE-TREATING.
UUNGH ...
... KUH HUH.
...HEH HEH...
HEH HEH HEH ...
HEH HA HA HA...

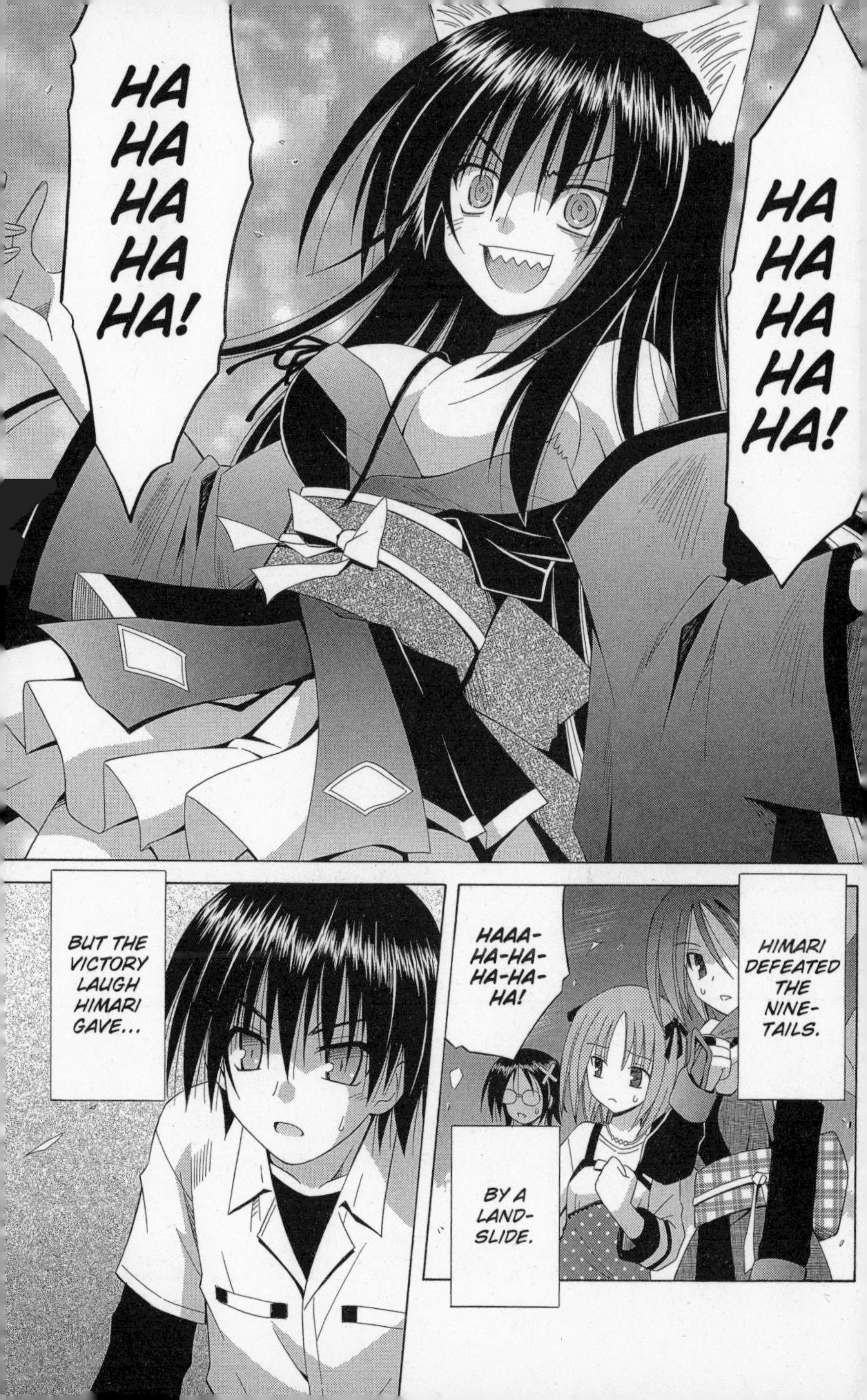
HA HA HA HA HA!
HA HA HA HA HA!
HIMARI DEFEATED THE NINE-TAILS.
HAAA-HA-HA-HA-HA-HA!
BY A LAND-SLIDE.
BUT THE VICTORY LAUGH HIMARI GAVE...

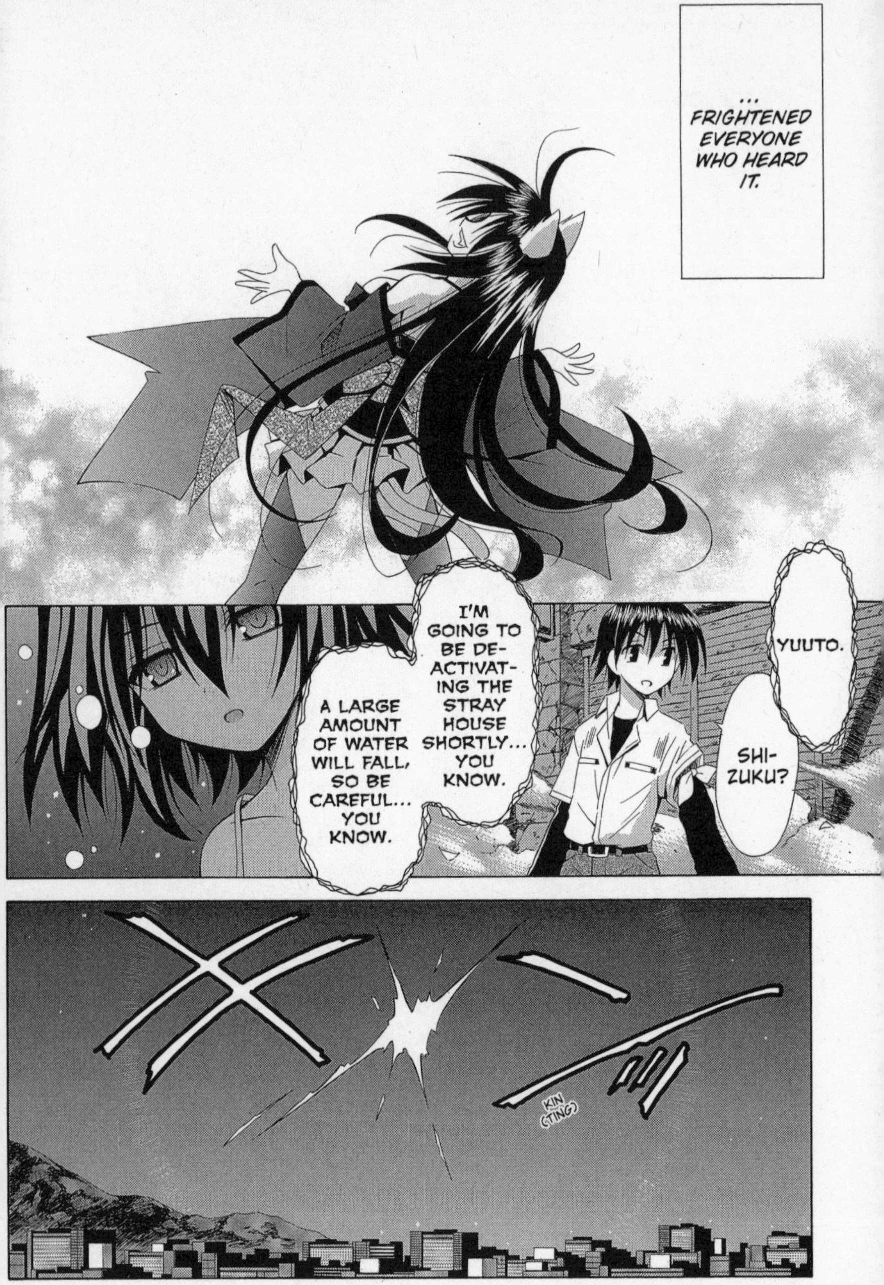
...FRIGHTENED EVERYONE WHO HEARD IT.
YUUTO.
SHI-ZUKU?
I'M GOING TO BE DE-ACTIVAT-ING THE STRAY HOUSE SHORTLY... YOU KNOW.
A LARGE AMOUNT OF WATER WILL FALL, SO BE CAREFUL... YOU KNOW.
KIN (TING)

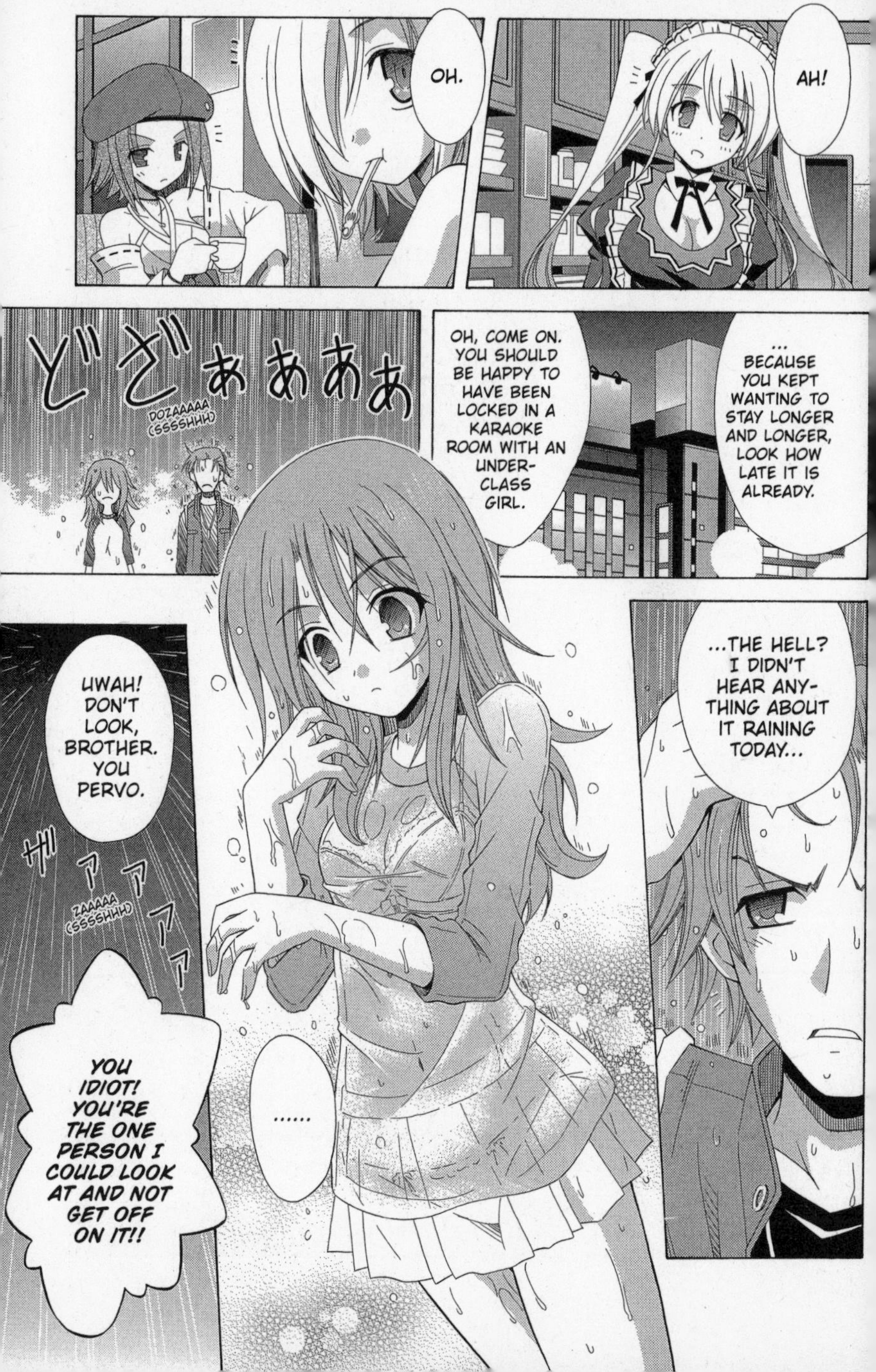
AH!
OH.
...BECAUSE YOU KEPT WANTING TO STAY LONGER AND LONGER, LOOK HOW LATE IT IS ALREADY.
OH, COME ON. YOU SHOULD BE HAPPY TO HAVE BEEN LOCKED IN A KARAOKE ROOM WITH AN UNDER-CLASS GIRL.
どざぁぁぁぁ
DOZAAAAA (SSSSHHH)
...THE HELL? I DIDN'T HEAR ANY-THING ABOUT IT RAINING TODAY...
......
UWAH! DON'T LOOK, BROTHER. YOU PERVO.
ザァァァ
ZAAAAA (SSSSHHH)
YOU IDIOT! YOU'RE THE ONE PERSON I COULD LOOK AT AND NOT GET OFF ON IT!!

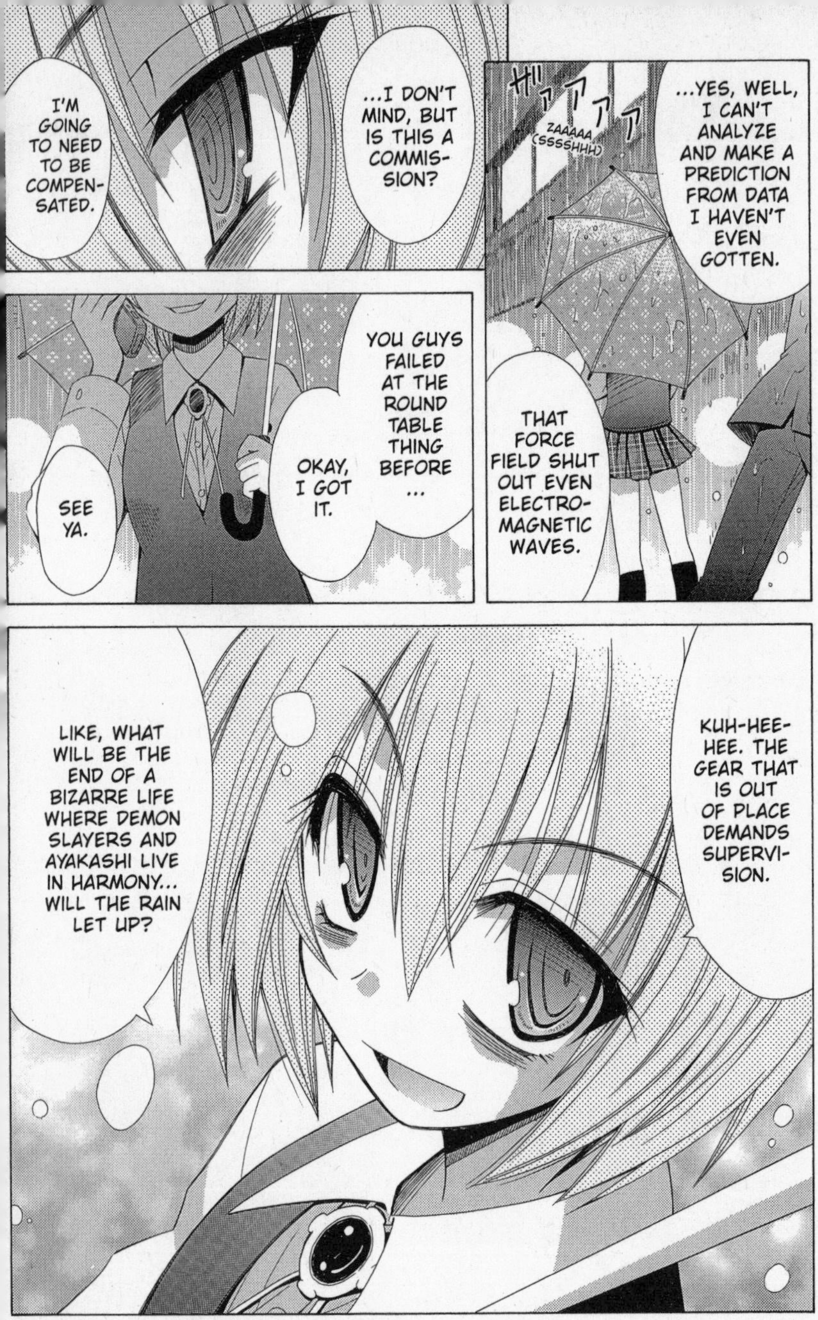
ザァァァ
ZAAAAA (SSSSHHH)
...YES, WELL, I CAN'T ANALYZE AND MAKE A PREDICTION FROM DATA I HAVEN'T EVEN GOTTEN.
THAT FORCE FIELD SHUT OUT EVEN ELECTRO-MAGNETIC WAVES.
...I DON'T MIND, BUT IS THIS A COMMIS-SION?
I'M GOING TO NEED TO BE COMPEN-SATED.
YOU GUYS FAILED AT THE ROUND TABLE THING BEFORE ...
OKAY, I GOT IT.
SEE YA.
KUH-HEE-HEE. THE GEAR THAT IS OUT OF PLACE DEMANDS SUPERVI-SION.
LIKE, WHAT WILL BE THE END OF A BIZARRE LIFE WHERE DEMON SLAYERS AND AYAKASHI LIVE IN HARMONY... WILL THE RAIN LET UP?

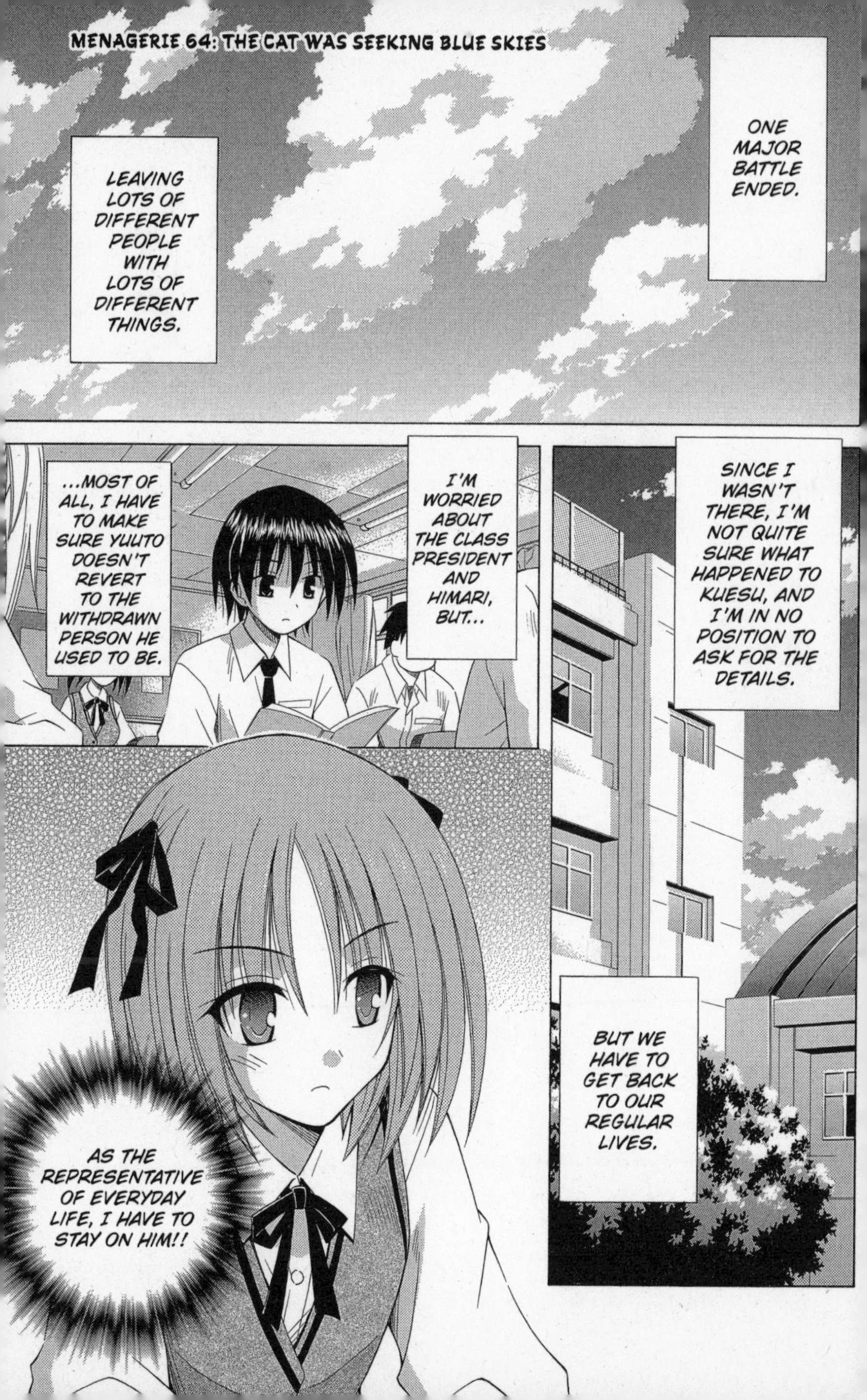
MENAGERIE 64: THE CAT WAS SEEKING BLUE SKIES
ONE MAJOR BATTLE ENDED.
LEAVING LOTS OF DIFFERENT PEOPLE WITH LOTS OF DIFFERENT THINGS.
SINCE I WASN'T THERE, I'M NOT QUITE SURE WHAT HAPPENED TO KUESU, AND I'M IN NO POSITION TO ASK FOR THE DETAILS.
BUT WE HAVE TO GET BACK TO OUR REGULAR LIVES.
I'M WORRIED ABOUT THE CLASS PRESIDENT AND HIMARI, BUT...
...MOST OF ALL, I HAVE TO MAKE SURE YUUTO DOESN'T REVERT TO THE WITHDRAWN PERSON HE USED TO BE.
AS THE REPRESENTATIVE OF EVERYDAY LIFE, I HAVE TO STAY ON HIM!!

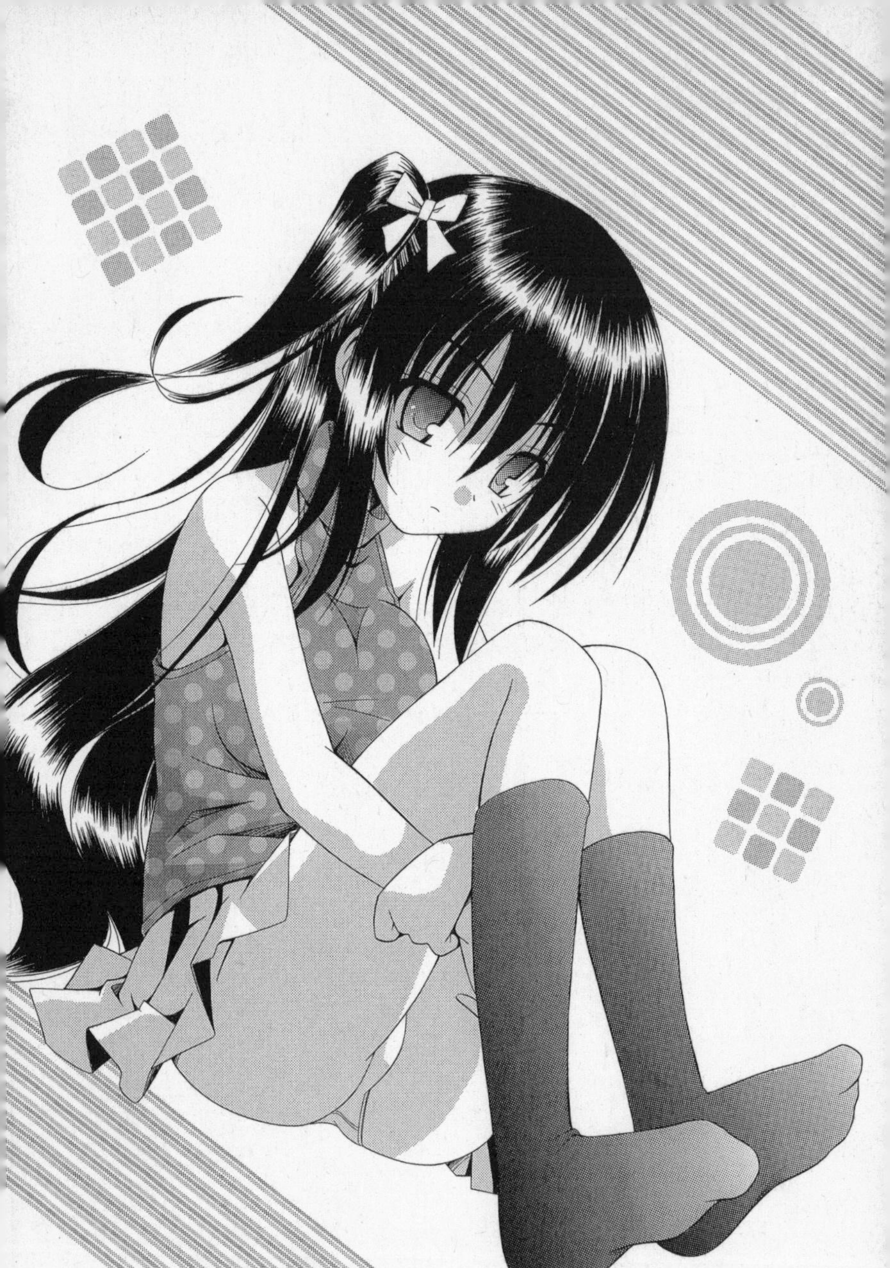

MENAGERIE 64: THE CAT WAS SEEKING BLUE SKIES

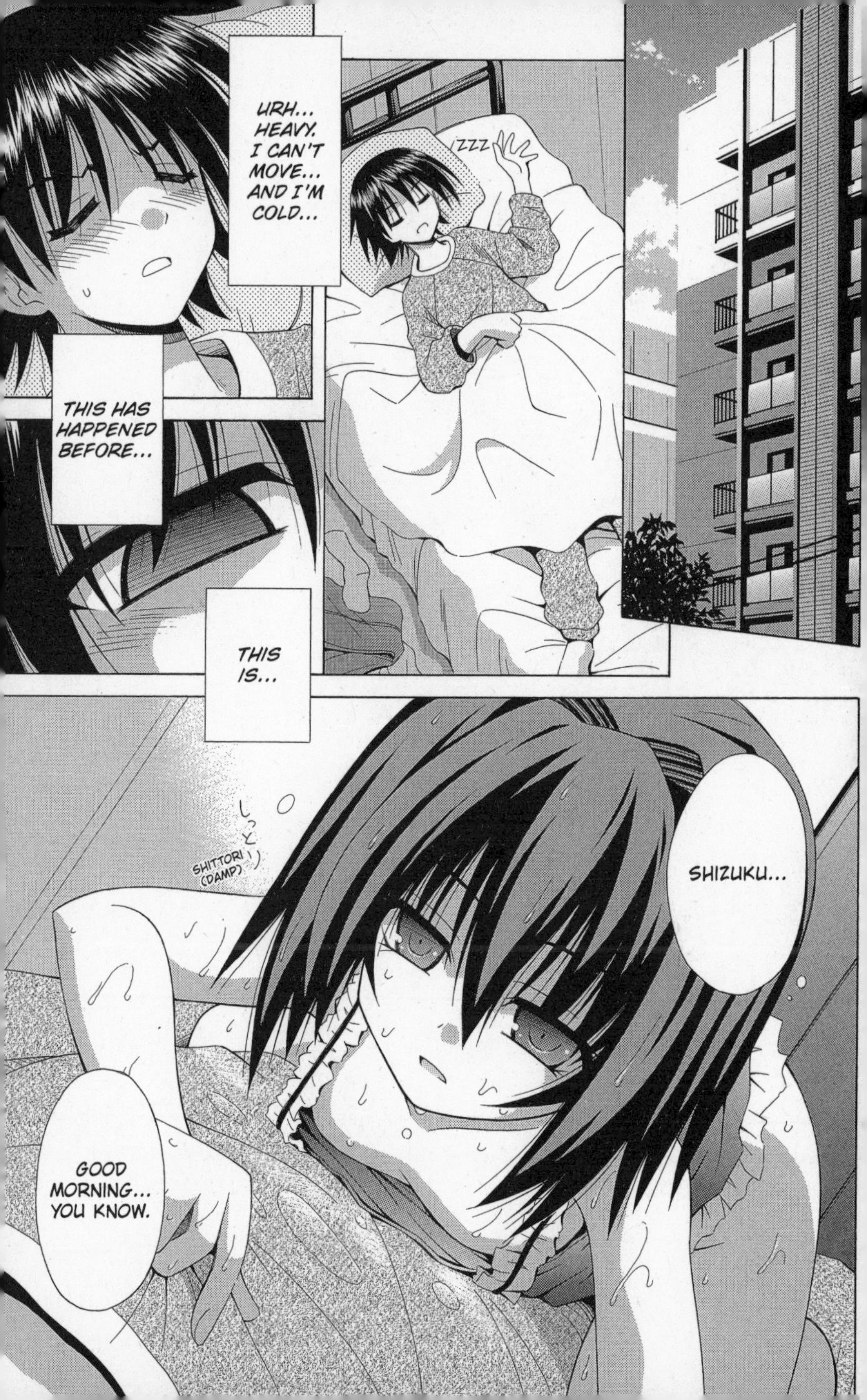
ZZZ
URH... HEAVY. I CAN'T MOVE... AND I'M COLD...
THIS HAS HAPPENED BEFORE...
THIS IS...
SHIZUKU...
しっとり
SHITTORI (DAMP)
GOOD MORNING... YOU KNOW.

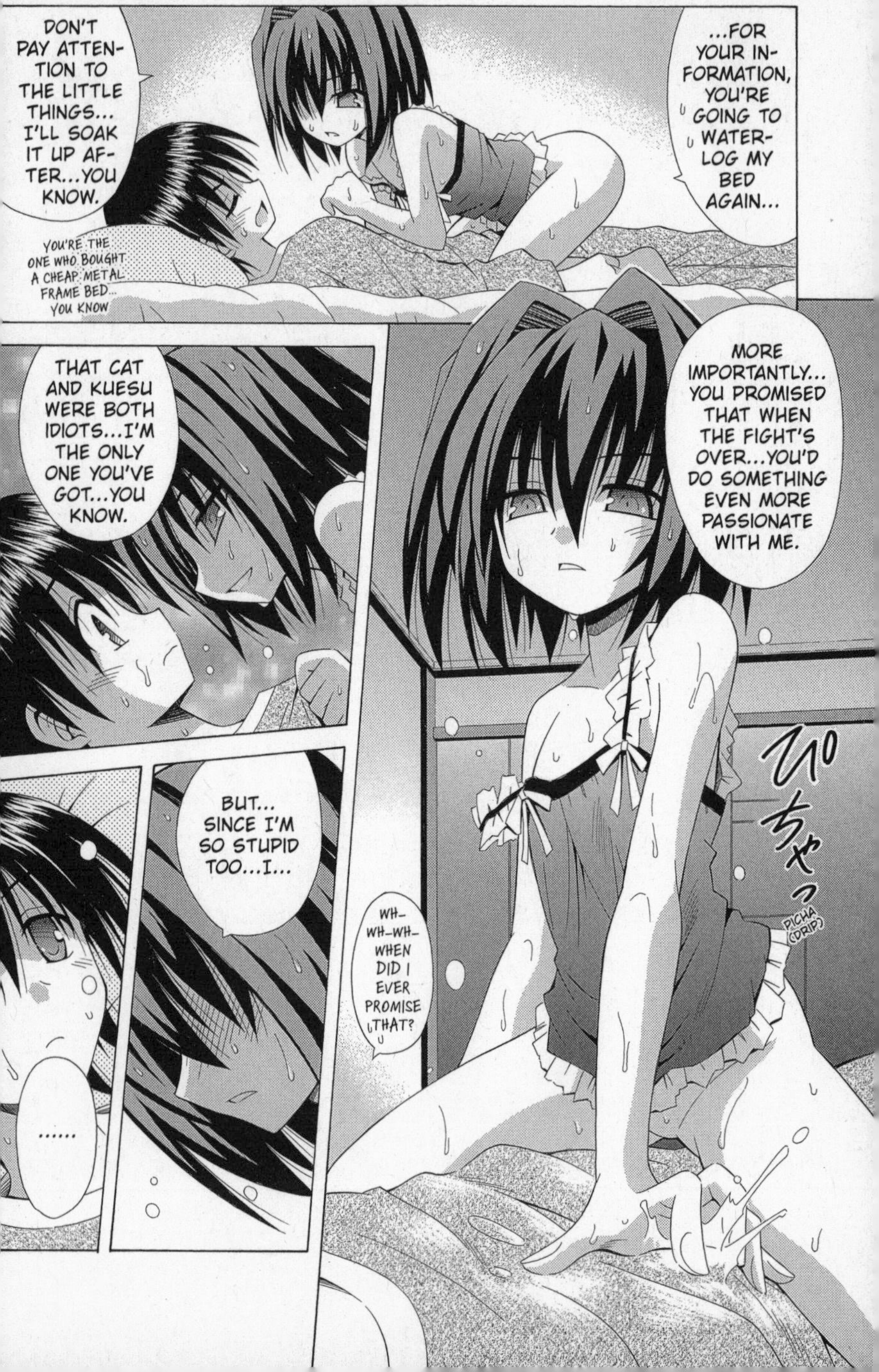
...FOR YOUR INFORMATION, YOU'RE GOING TO WATERLOG MY BED AGAIN...
DON'T PAY ATTENTION TO THE LITTLE THINGS... I'LL SOAK IT UP AFTER...YOU KNOW.
YOU'RE THE ONE WHO BOUGHT A CHEAP METAL FRAME BED... YOU KNOW
MORE IMPORTANTLY... YOU PROMISED THAT WHEN THE FIGHT'S OVER...YOU'D DO SOMETHING EVEN MORE PASSIONATE WITH ME.
ぴちゃっ
PICHA (DRIP)
WH-WH-WH-WHEN DID I EVER PROMISE THAT?
THAT CAT AND KUESU WERE BOTH IDIOTS...I'M THE ONLY ONE YOU'VE GOT...YOU KNOW.
BUT... SINCE I'M SO STUPID TOO...I...
......

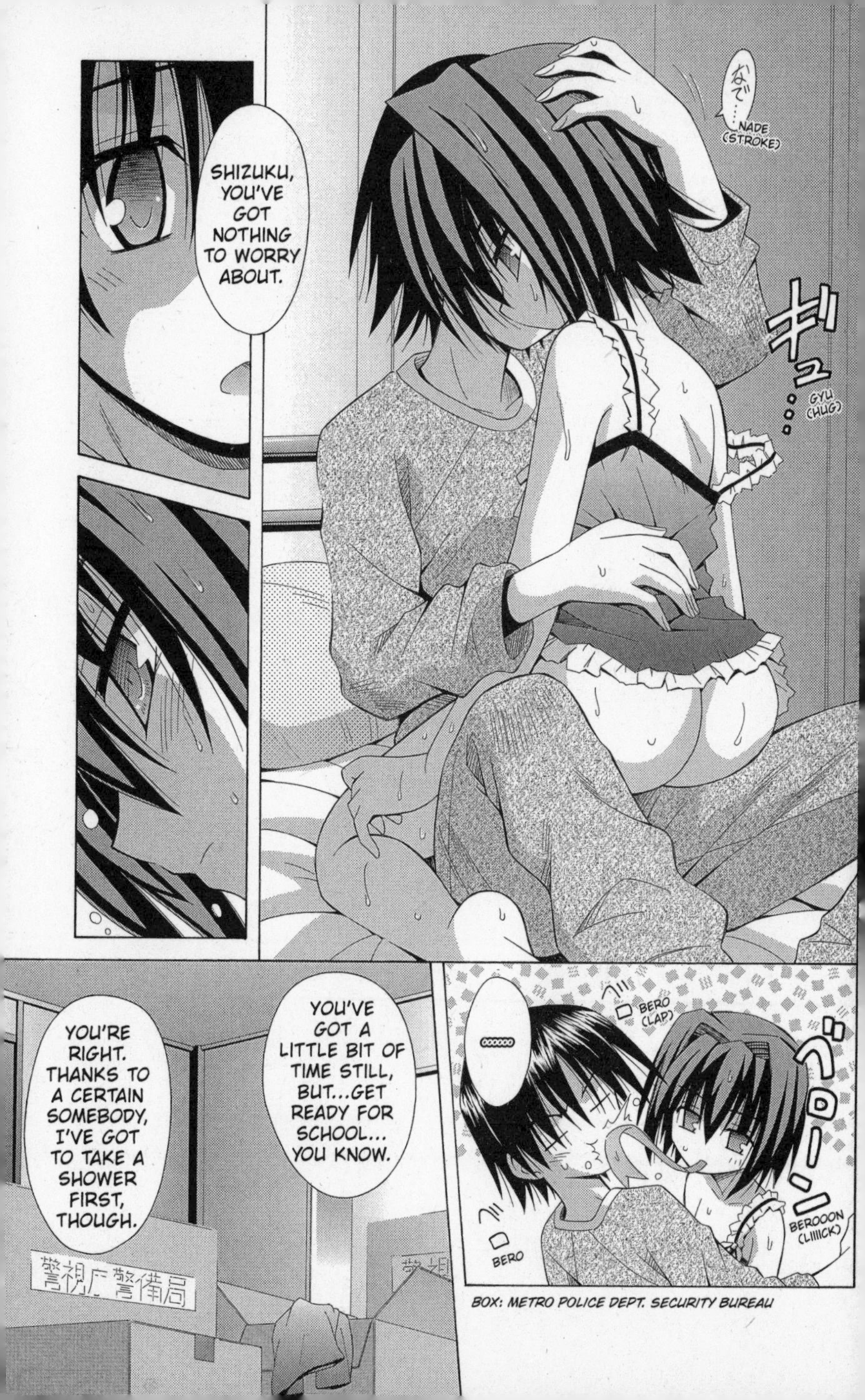
なで…
NADE (STROKE)
ギュ…
GYU (HUG)
SHIZUKU, YOU'VE GOT NOTHING TO WORRY ABOUT.
……
ベロ
BERO (LAP)
べローン
BEROOON (LIIIIICK)
ベロ
BERO
YOU'VE GOT A LITTLE BIT OF TIME STILL, BUT...GET READY FOR SCHOOL... YOU KNOW.
YOU'RE RIGHT. THANKS TO A CERTAIN SOMEBODY, I'VE GOT TO TAKE A SHOWER FIRST, THOUGH.
警視庁警備局

BOX: METRO POLICE DEPT. SECURITY BUREAU

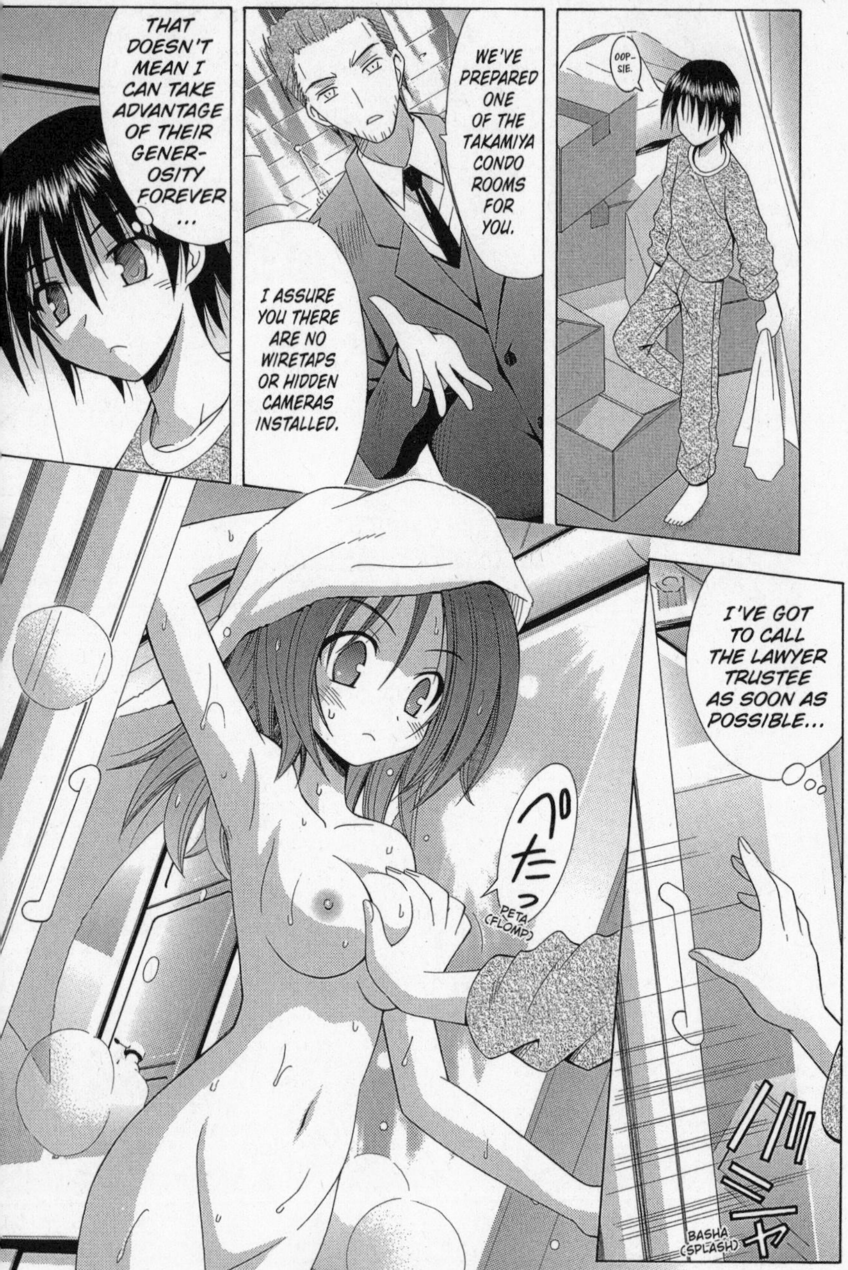
OOP-SIE.
WE'VE PREPARED ONE OF THE TAKAMIYA CONDO ROOMS FOR YOU.
I ASSURE YOU THERE ARE NO WIRETAPS OR HIDDEN CAMERAS INSTALLED.
THAT DOESN'T MEAN I CAN TAKE ADVANTAGE OF THEIR GENER-OSITY FOREVER ...
I'VE GOT TO CALL THE LAWYER TRUSTEE AS SOON AS POSSIBLE...
ぺたっ
PETA (FLOMP)
BASHA (SPLASH)

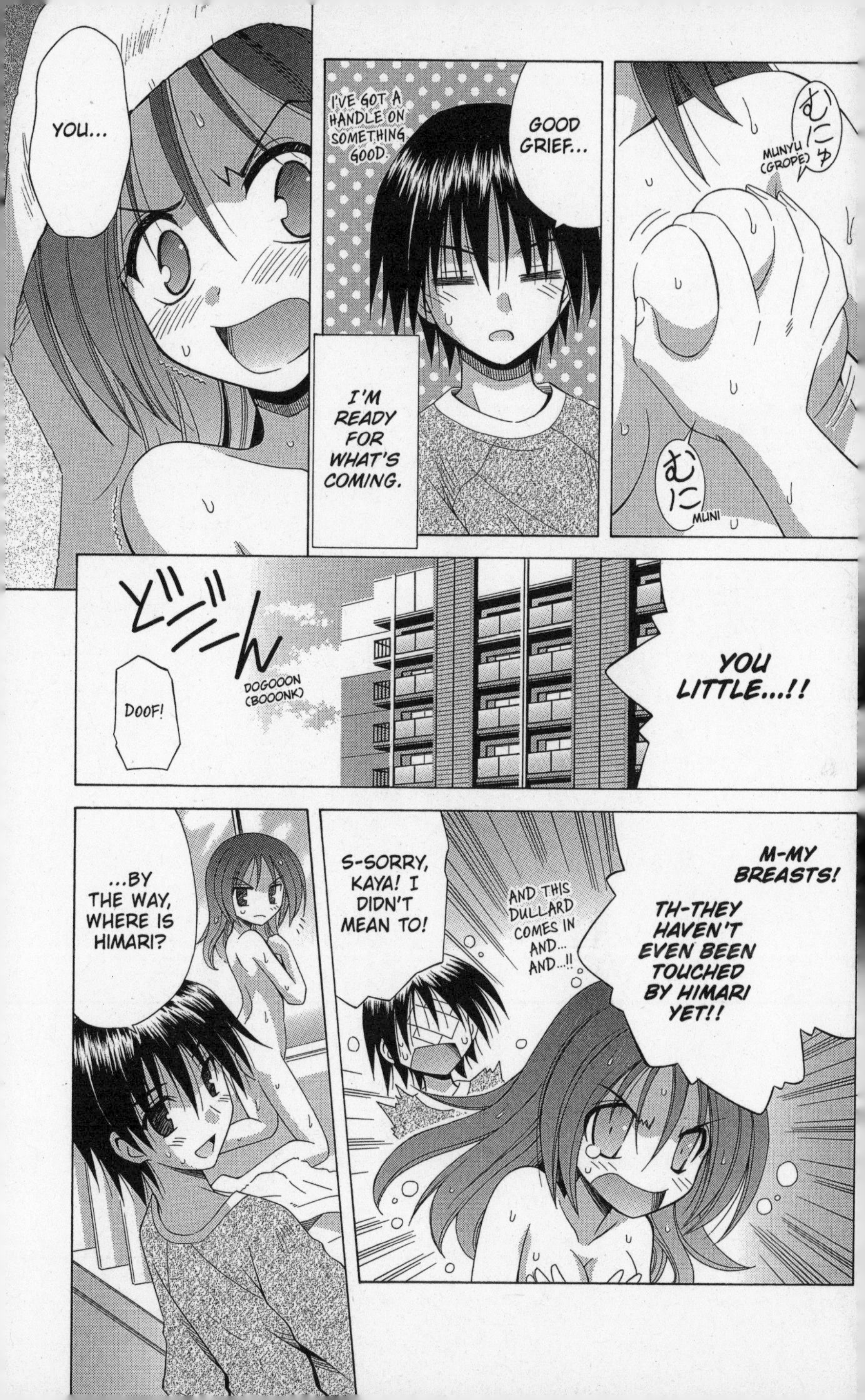

むにゅ
MUNYU (GROPE)
むに
MUNI
GOOD GRIEF...
I'VE GOT A HANDLE ON SOMETHING GOOD.
I'M READY FOR WHAT'S COMING.
YOU...
YOU LITTLE...!!
どごーん
DOGOOON (BOOONK)
DOOF!
M-MY BREASTS!
TH-THEY HAVEN'T EVEN BEEN TOUCHED BY HIMARI YET!!
AND THIS DULLARD COMES IN AND... AND...!!
S-SORRY, KAYA! I DIDN'T MEAN TO!
...BY THE WAY, WHERE IS HIMARI?

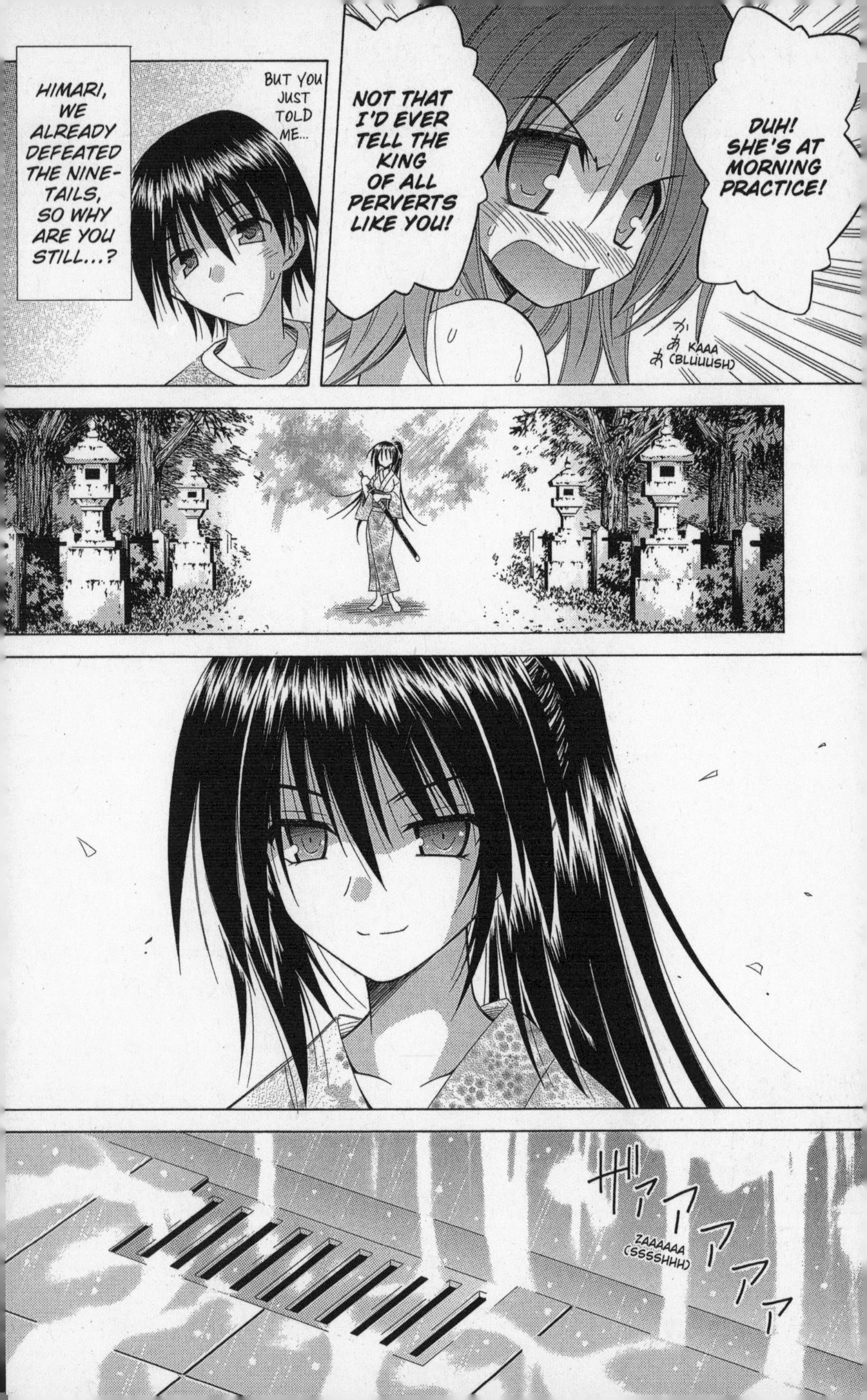

DUH! SHE'S AT MORNING PRACTICE!
NOT THAT I'D EVER TELL THE KING OF ALL PERVERTS LIKE YOU!
かああ KAAA (BLUUUSH)
BUT YOU JUST TOLD ME...
HIMARI, WE ALREADY DEFEATED THE NINE-TAILS, SO WHY ARE YOU STILL...?
ZAAAAAA (SSSSHHH)

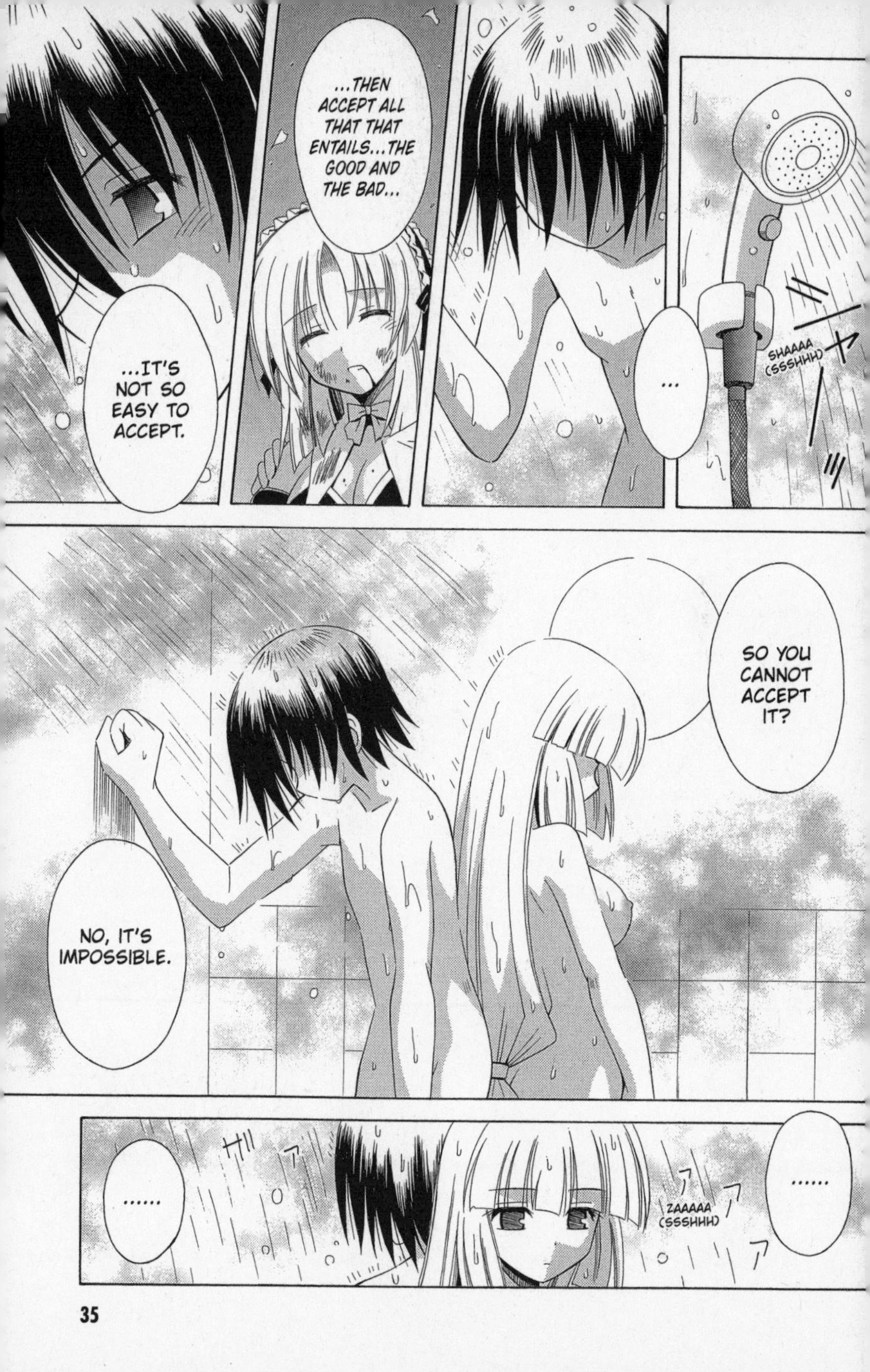
SHAAAA (SSSHHH)
...
...THEN ACCEPT ALL THAT THAT ENTAILS...THE GOOD AND THE BAD...
...IT'S NOT SO EASY TO ACCEPT.
SO YOU CANNOT ACCEPT IT?
NO, IT'S IMPOSSIBLE.
......
ZAAAAA (SSSHHH)
......

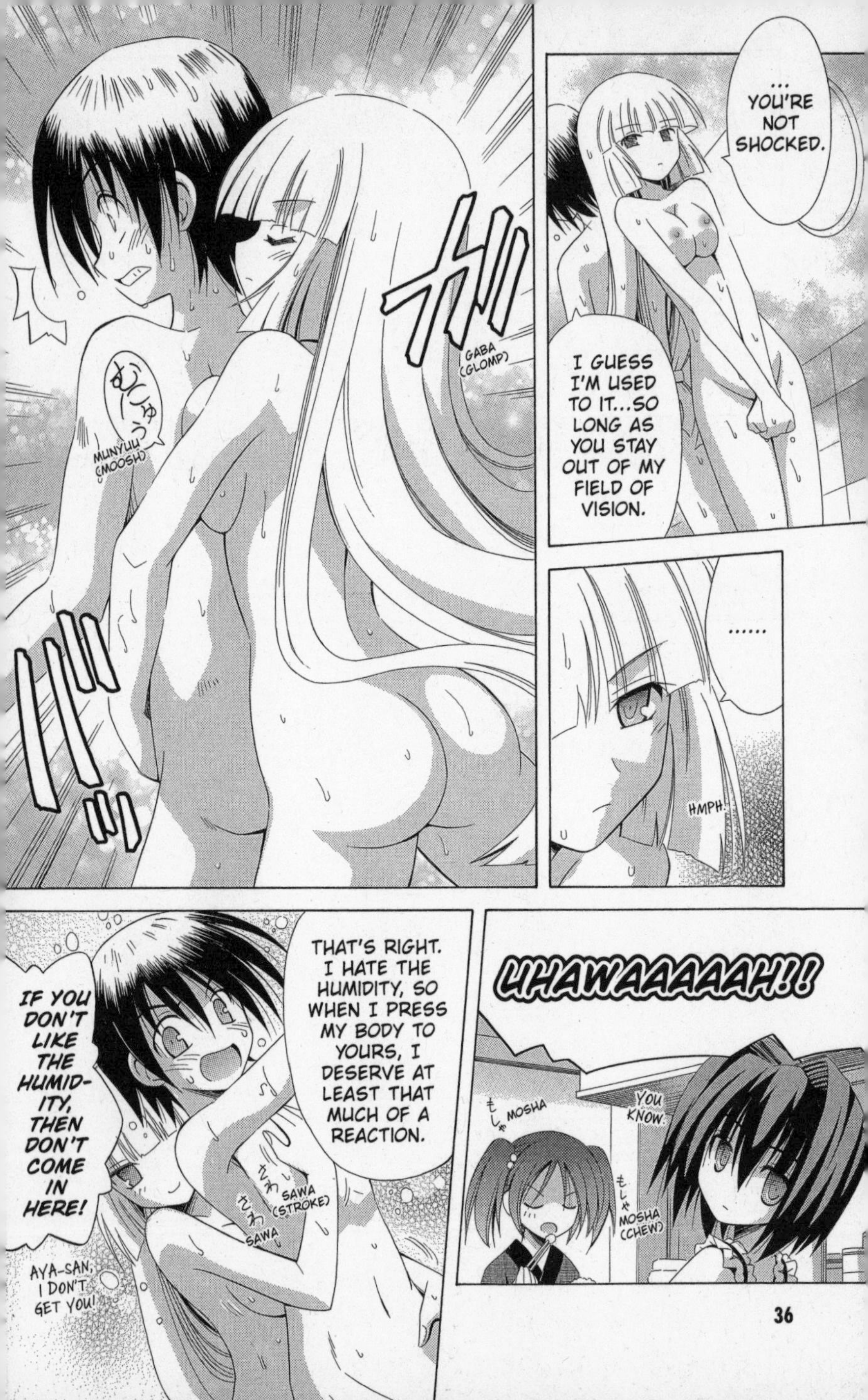

... YOU'RE NOT SHOCKED.
I GUESS I'M USED TO IT...SO LONG AS YOU STAY OUT OF MY FIELD OF VISION.
......
HMPH!
GABA (GLOMP)
むにゅう
MUNYUU (MOOSH)
UHAWAAAAAAH!!
もしゃ MOSHA
YOU KNOW.
もしゃ MOSHA (CHEW)
THAT'S RIGHT. I HATE THE HUMIDITY, SO WHEN I PRESS MY BODY TO YOURS, I DESERVE AT LEAST THAT MUCH OF A REACTION.
IF YOU DON'T LIKE THE HUMIDITY, THEN DON'T COME IN HERE!
さわ SAWA (STROKE)
さわ SAWA
AYA-SAN, I DON'T GET YOU!

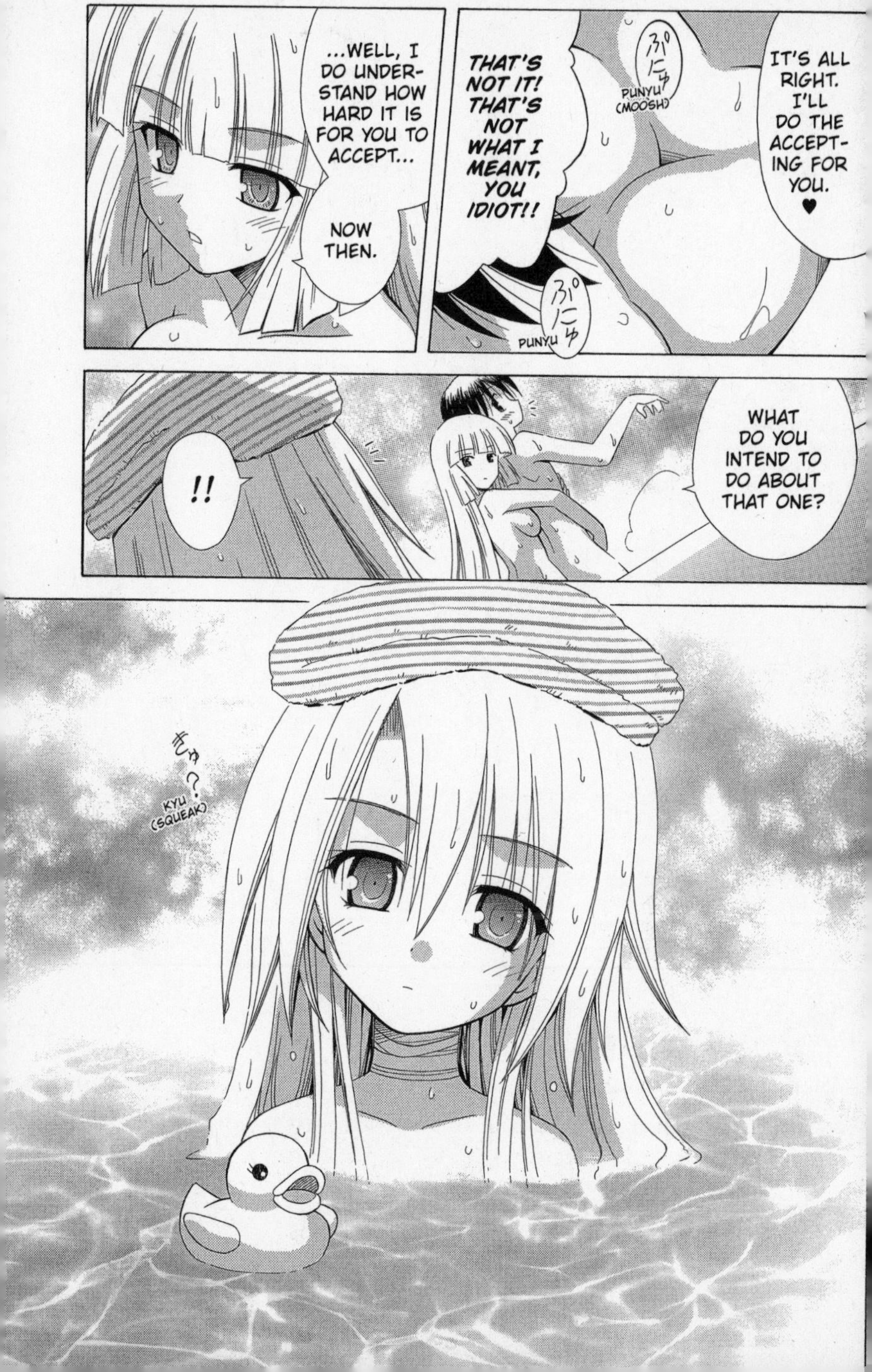

IT'S ALL RIGHT. I'LL DO THE ACCEPTING FOR YOU. ♥
ぷにゅ
PUNYU (MOOSH)
THAT'S NOT IT! THAT'S NOT WHAT I MEANT, YOU IDIOT!!
ぷにゅ
PUNYU
...WELL, I DO UNDERSTAND HOW HARD IT IS FOR YOU TO ACCEPT...
NOW THEN.
WHAT DO YOU INTEND TO DO ABOUT THAT ONE?
!!
きゅ?
KYU (SQUEAK)

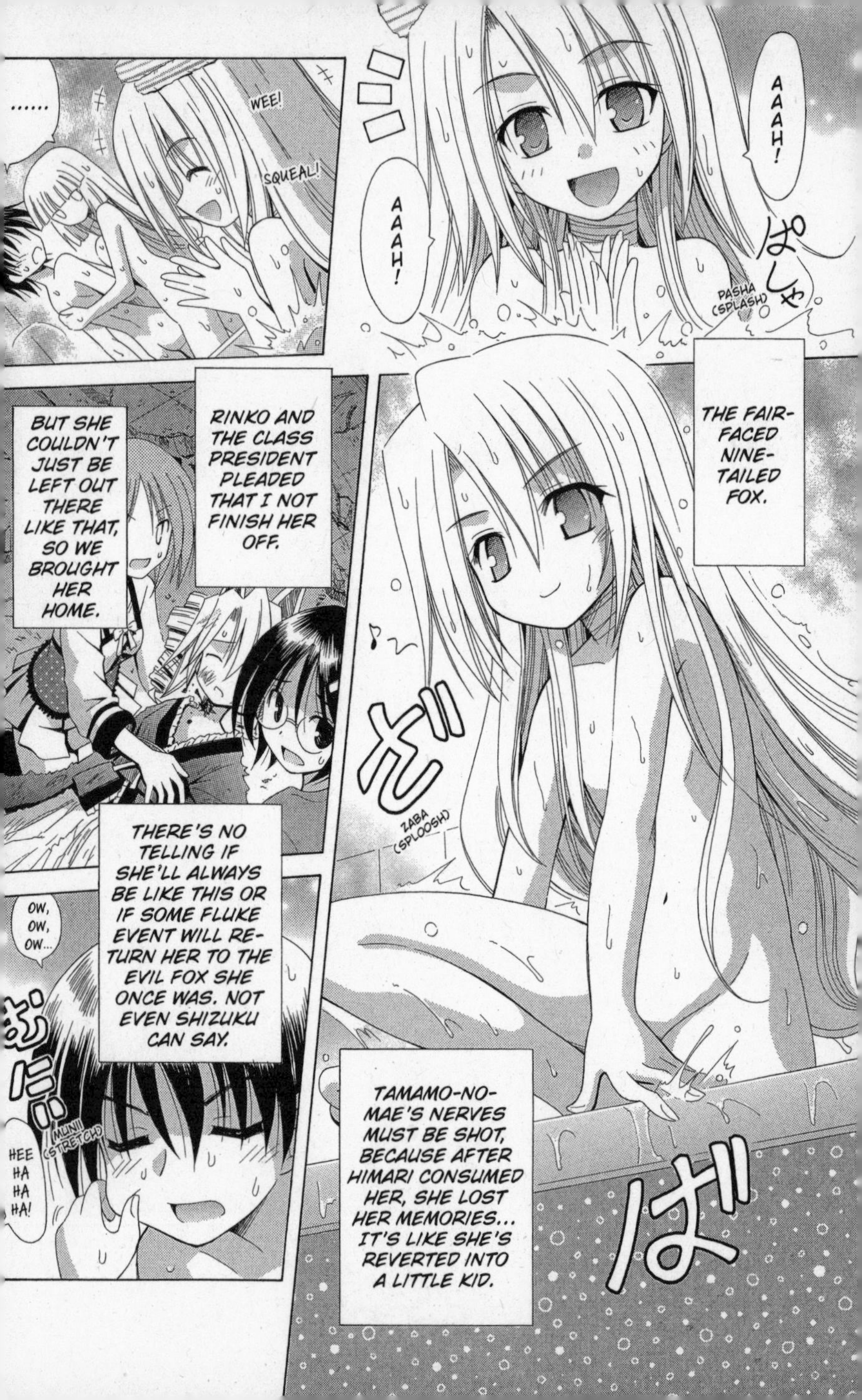
AAAH!
AAAH!
ぱしゃ
PASHA (SPLASH)
......
WEE!
SQUEAL!
THE FAIR-FACED NINE-TAILED FOX.
ざ
ZABA (SPLOOSH)
TAMAMO-NO-MAE'S NERVES MUST BE SHOT, BECAUSE AFTER HIMARI CONSUMED HER, SHE LOST HER MEMORIES... IT'S LIKE SHE'S REVERTED INTO A LITTLE KID.
ば
RINKO AND THE CLASS PRESIDENT PLEADED THAT I NOT FINISH HER OFF.
BUT SHE COULDN'T JUST BE LEFT OUT THERE LIKE THAT, SO WE BROUGHT HER HOME.
THERE'S NO TELLING IF SHE'LL ALWAYS BE LIKE THIS OR IF SOME FLUKE EVENT WILL RE-TURN HER TO THE EVIL FOX SHE ONCE WAS. NOT EVEN SHIZUKU CAN SAY.
OW, OW, OW...
むに
MUNII (STRETCH)
HEE HA HA HA!

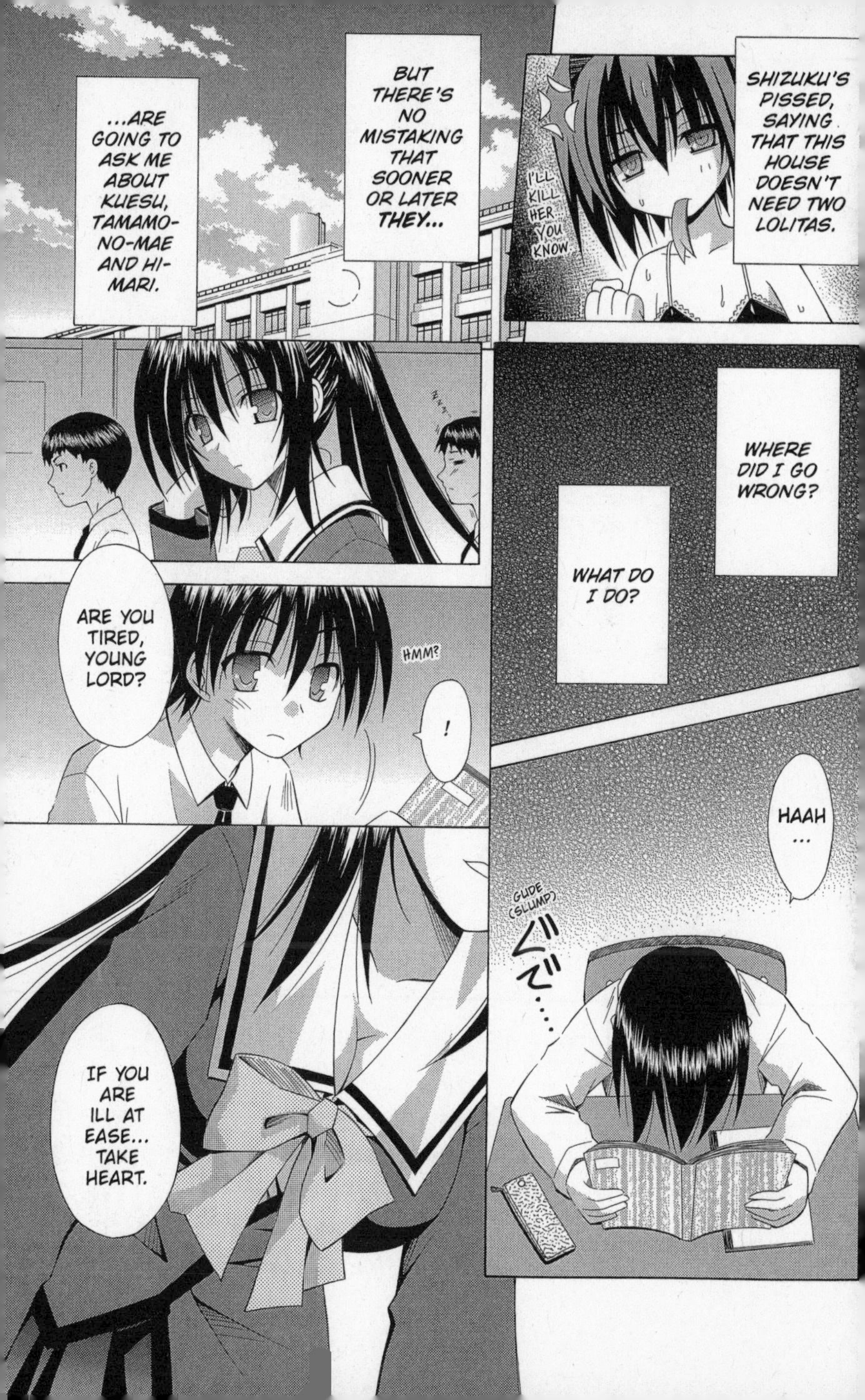
SHIZUKU'S PISSED, SAYING THAT THIS HOUSE DOESN'T NEED TWO LOLITAS.
I'LL KILL HER YOU KNOW
BUT THERE'S NO MISTAKING THAT SOONER OR LATER THEY...
...ARE GOING TO ASK ME ABOUT KUESU, TAMAMO-NO-MAE AND HI-MARI.
WHERE DID I GO WRONG?
WHAT DO I DO?
HAAH...
GUDE (SLUMP)
ぐで…
ARE YOU TIRED, YOUNG LORD?
HMM?
!
IF YOU ARE ILL AT EASE... TAKE HEART.

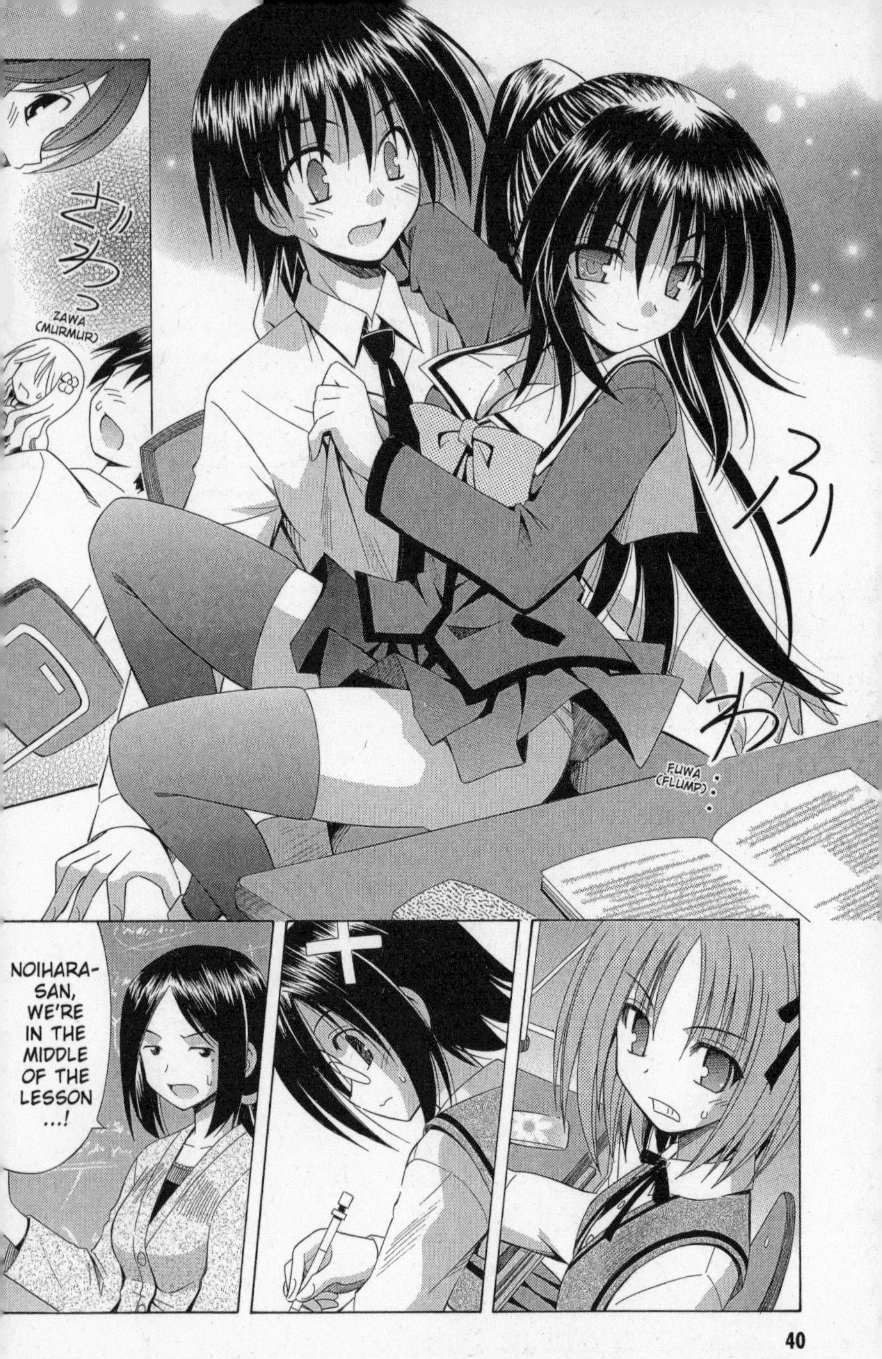
FUWA (FLUMP)
ZAWA (MURMUR)
NOIHARA-SAN, WE'RE IN THE MIDDLE OF THE LESSON ...!

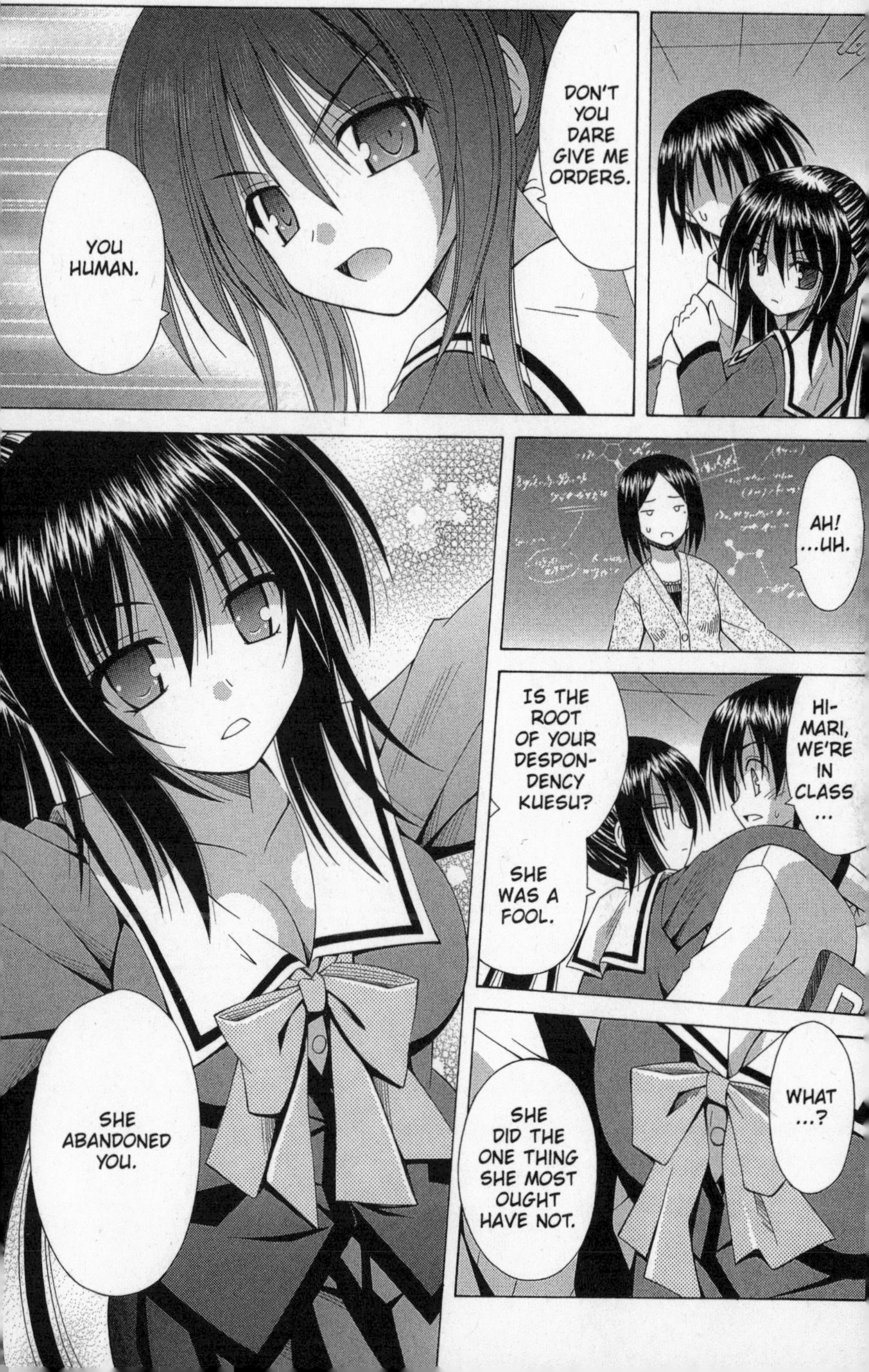
DON'T YOU DARE GIVE ME ORDERS.
YOU HUMAN.
AH! ...UH.
HI-MARI, WE'RE IN CLASS...
IS THE ROOT OF YOUR DESPON-DENCY KUESU?
SHE WAS A FOOL.
WHAT...?
SHE DID THE ONE THING SHE MOST OUGHT HAVE NOT.
SHE ABANDONED YOU.

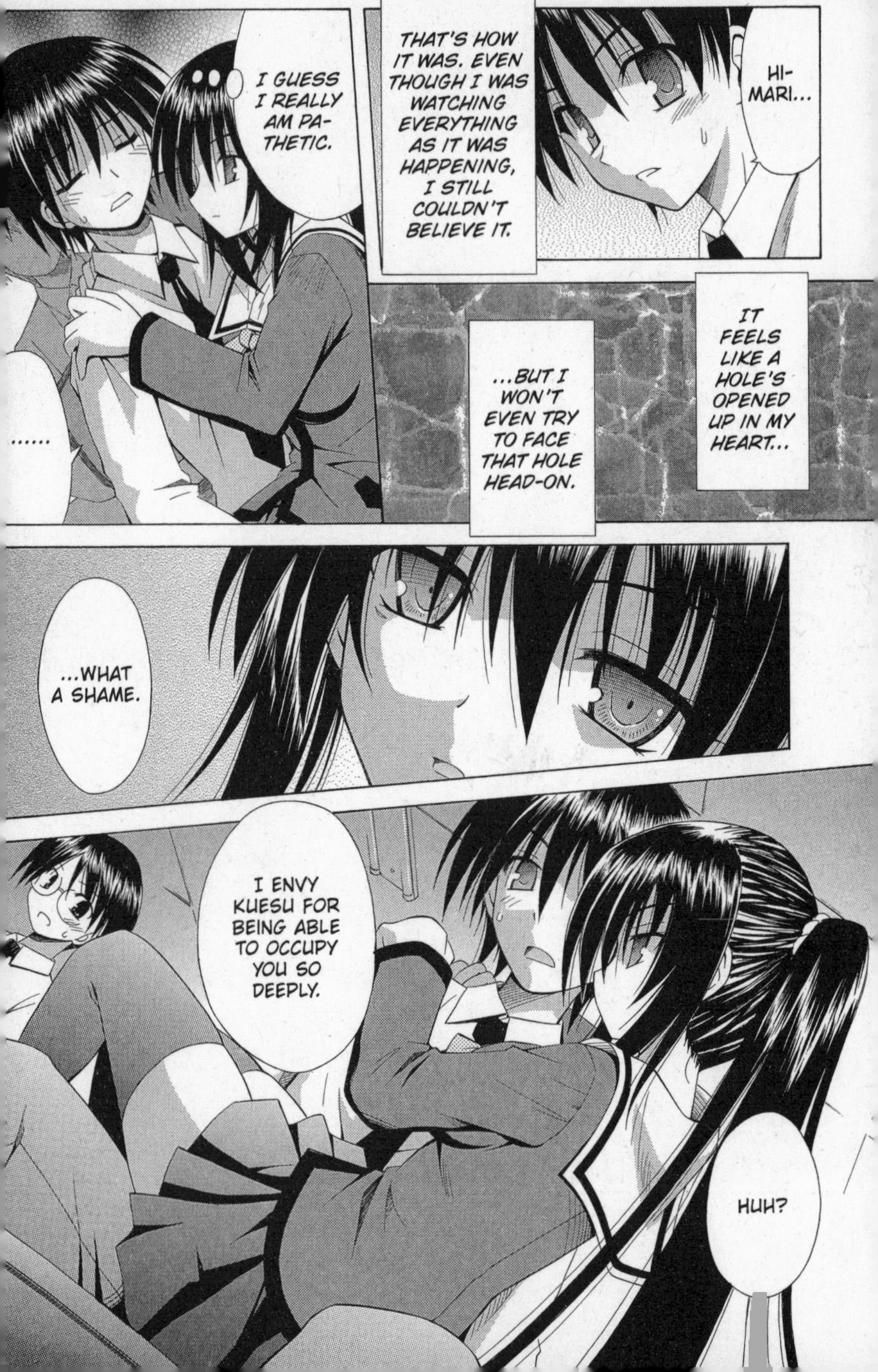
HI-MARI...
THAT'S HOW IT WAS. EVEN THOUGH I WAS WATCHING EVERYTHING AS IT WAS HAPPENING, I STILL COULDN'T BELIEVE IT.
IT FEELS LIKE A HOLE'S OPENED UP IN MY HEART...
...BUT I WON'T EVEN TRY TO FACE THAT HOLE HEAD-ON.
I GUESS I REALLY AM PA-THETIC.
......
...WHAT A SHAME.
I ENVY KUESU FOR BEING ABLE TO OCCUPY YOU SO DEEPLY.
HUH?

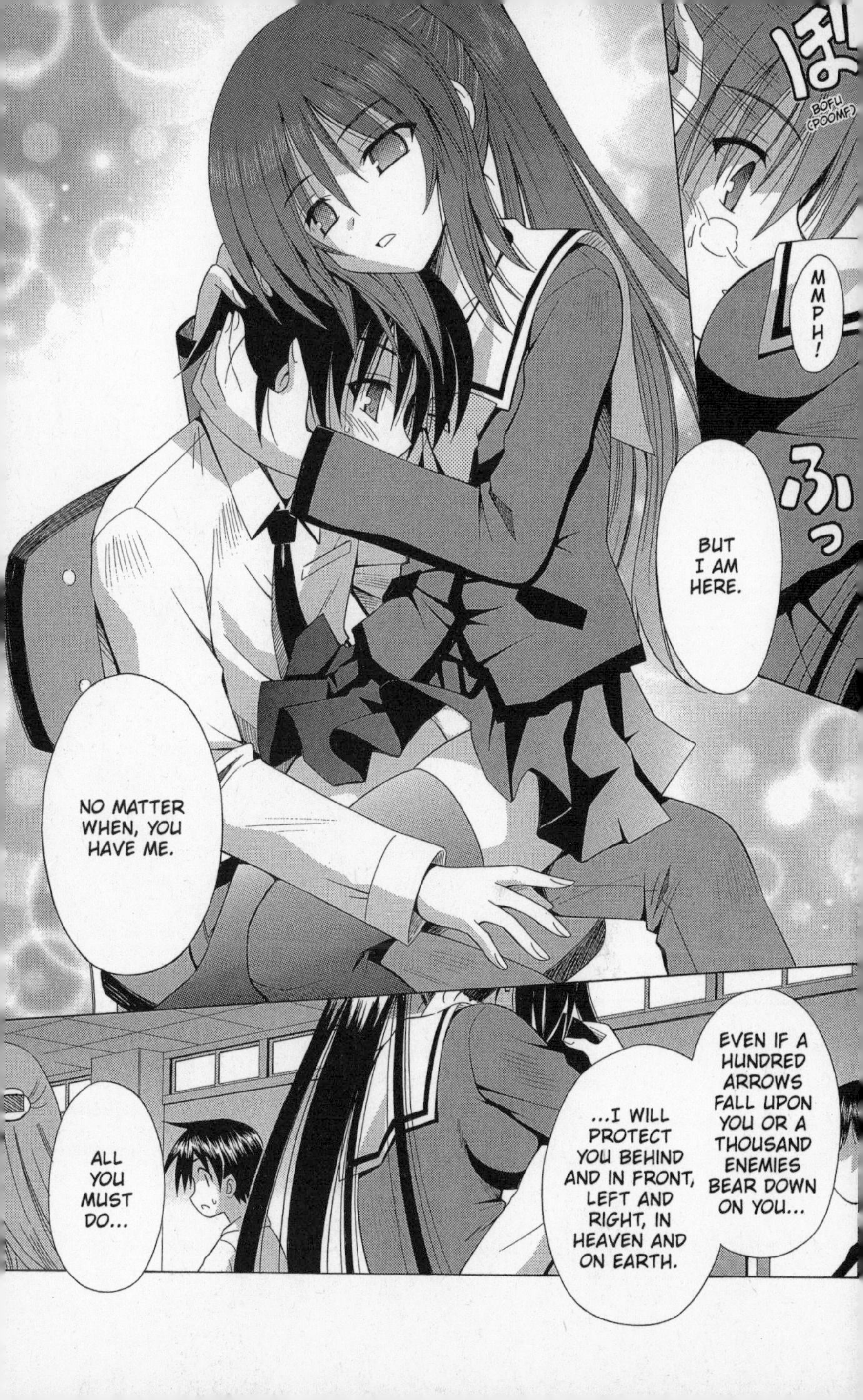
BOFU (POOMF)
MMPH!
ふっ
BUT I AM HERE.
NO MATTER WHEN, YOU HAVE ME.
EVEN IF A HUNDRED ARROWS FALL UPON YOU OR A THOUSAND ENEMIES BEAR DOWN ON YOU...
...I WILL PROTECT YOU BEHIND AND IN FRONT, LEFT AND RIGHT, IN HEAVEN AND ON EARTH.
ALL YOU MUST DO...

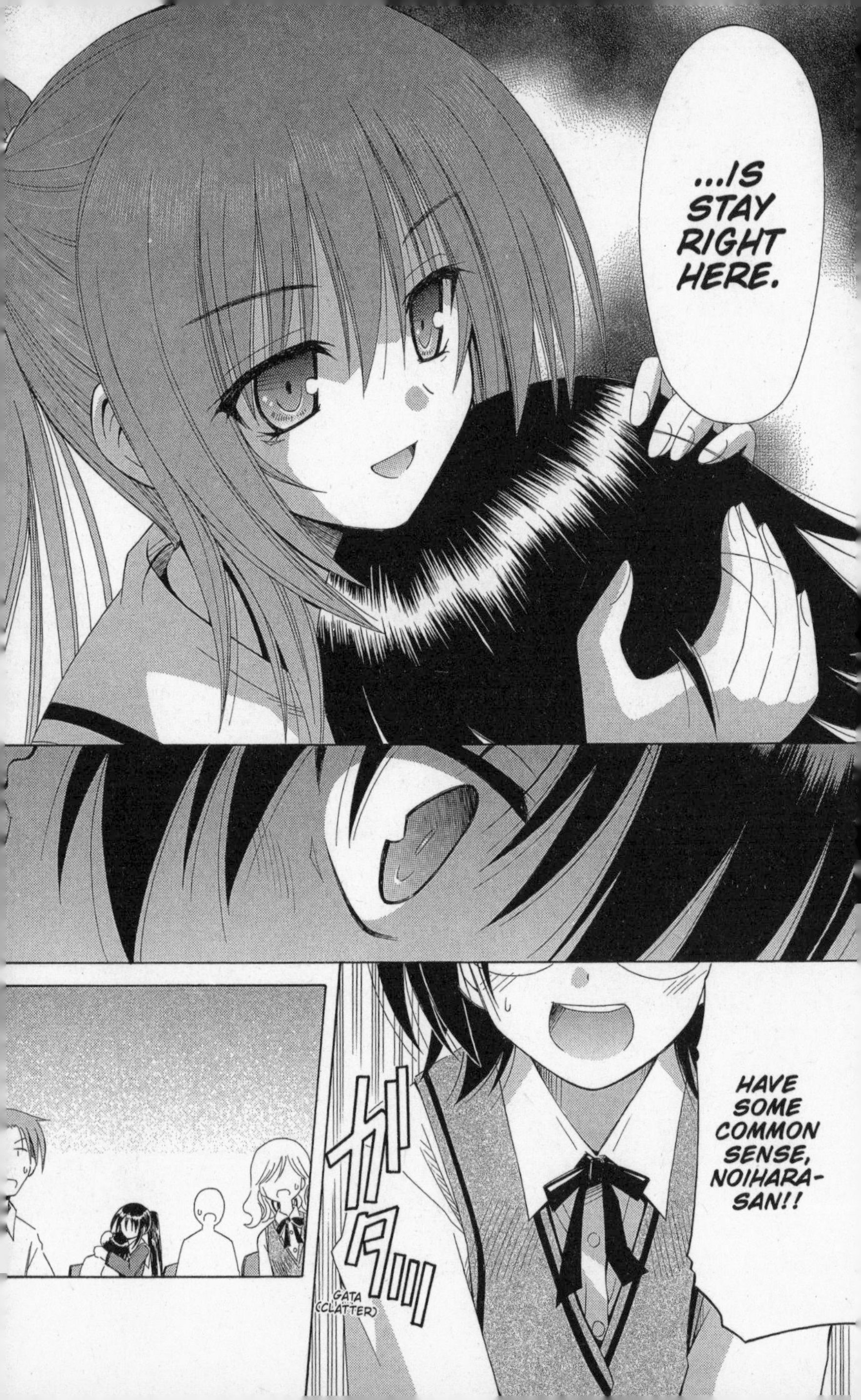
...IS STAY RIGHT HERE.
HAVE SOME COMMON SENSE, NOIHARA-SAN!!
ガタ
GATA (CLATTER)

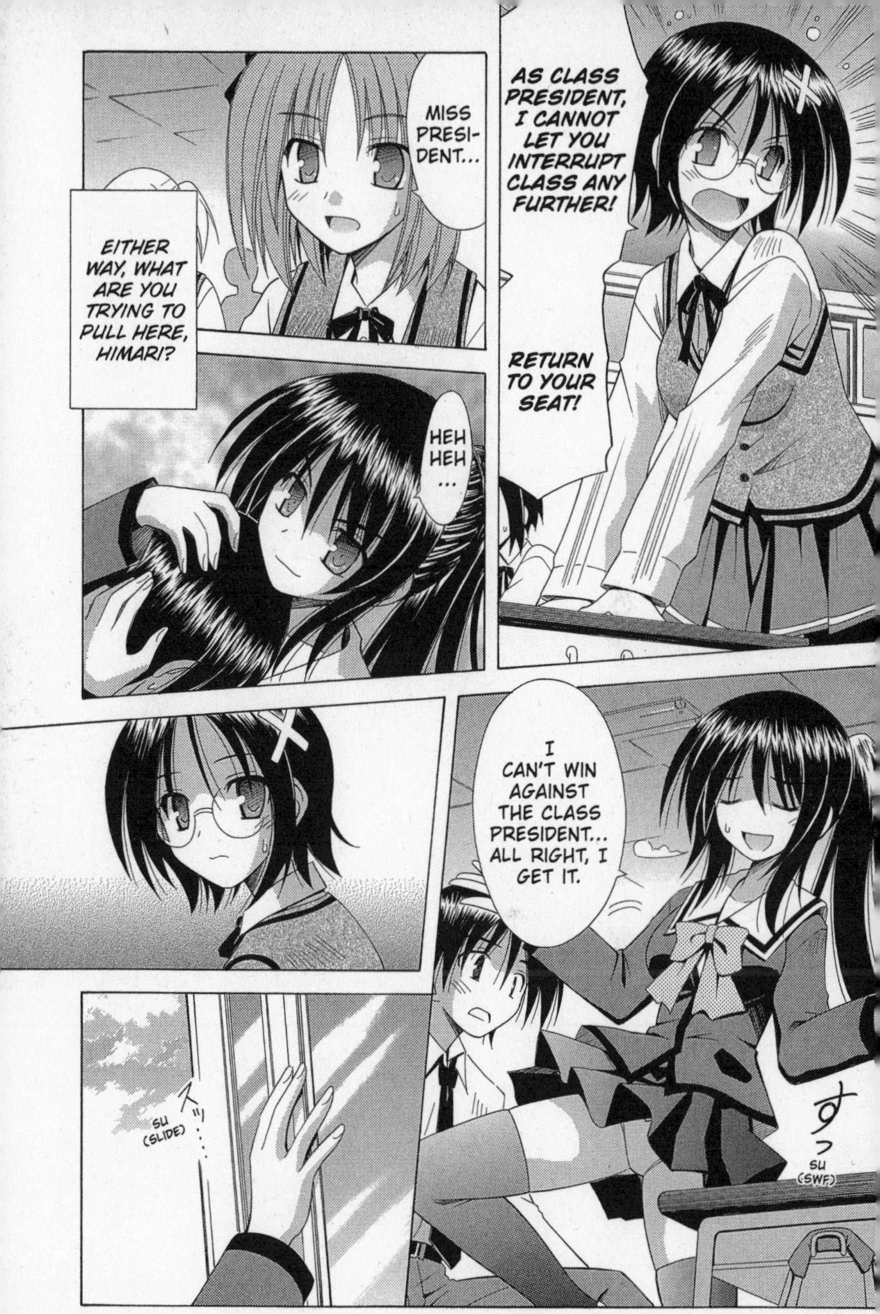
AS CLASS PRESIDENT, I CANNOT LET YOU INTERRUPT CLASS ANY FURTHER!
RETURN TO YOUR SEAT!
MISS PRESIDENT...
EITHER WAY, WHAT ARE YOU TRYING TO PULL HERE, HIMARI?
HEH HEH ...
I CAN'T WIN AGAINST THE CLASS PRESIDENT... ALL RIGHT, I GET IT.
すっ
SU (SWF)
スッ…
SU (SLIDE)

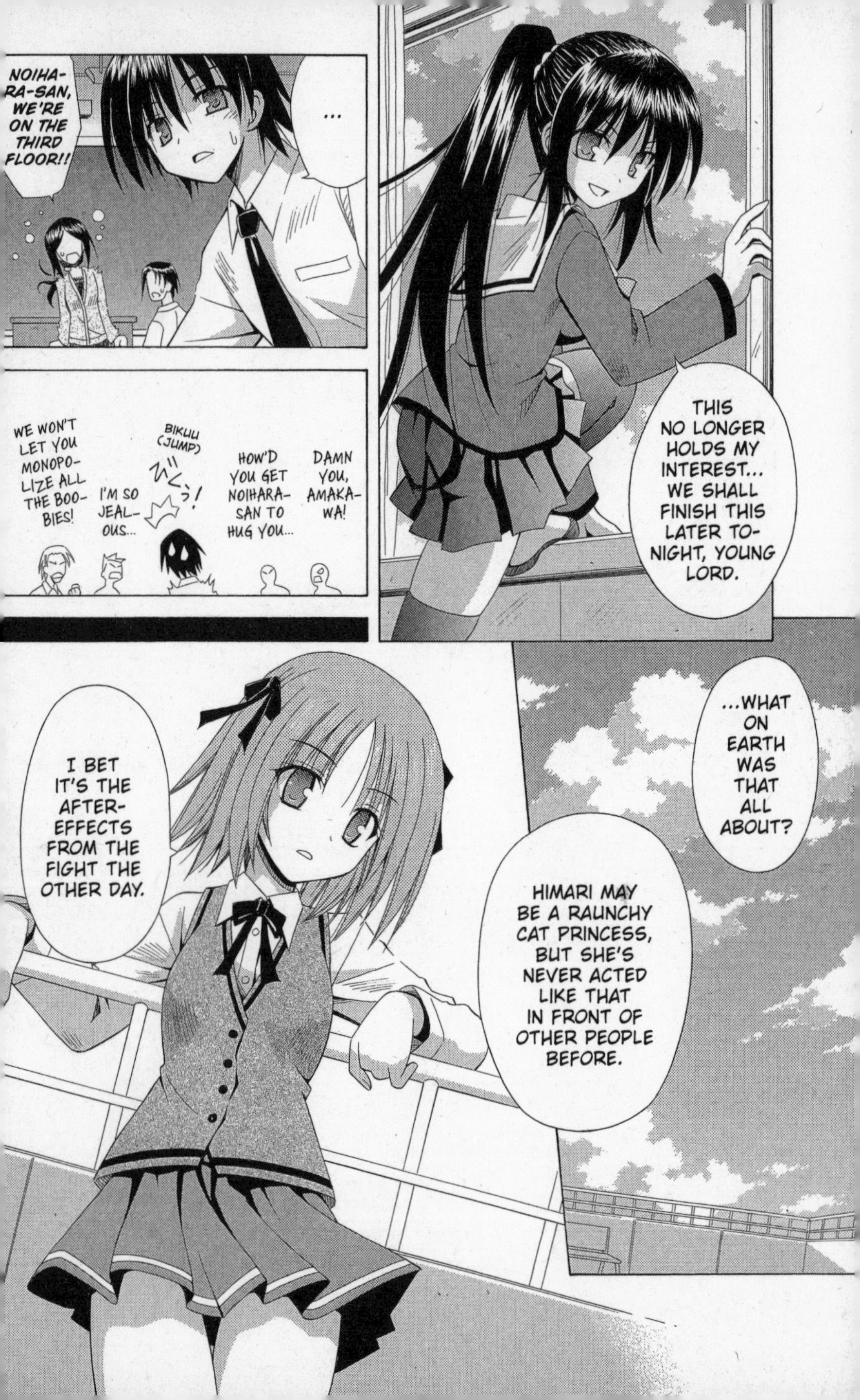
THIS NO LONGER HOLDS MY INTEREST... WE SHALL FINISH THIS LATER TO-NIGHT, YOUNG LORD.
...
NOIHARA-SAN, WE'RE ON THE THIRD FLOOR!!
DAMN YOU, AMAKAWA!
HOW'D YOU GET NOIHARA-SAN TO HUG YOU...
BIKUU (JUMP)
I'M SO JEALOUS...
WE WON'T LET YOU MONOPOLIZE ALL THE BOOBIES!
...WHAT ON EARTH WAS THAT ALL ABOUT?
HIMARI MAY BE A RAUNCHY CAT PRINCESS, BUT SHE'S NEVER ACTED LIKE THAT IN FRONT OF OTHER PEOPLE BEFORE.
I BET IT'S THE AFTER-EFFECTS FROM THE FIGHT THE OTHER DAY.

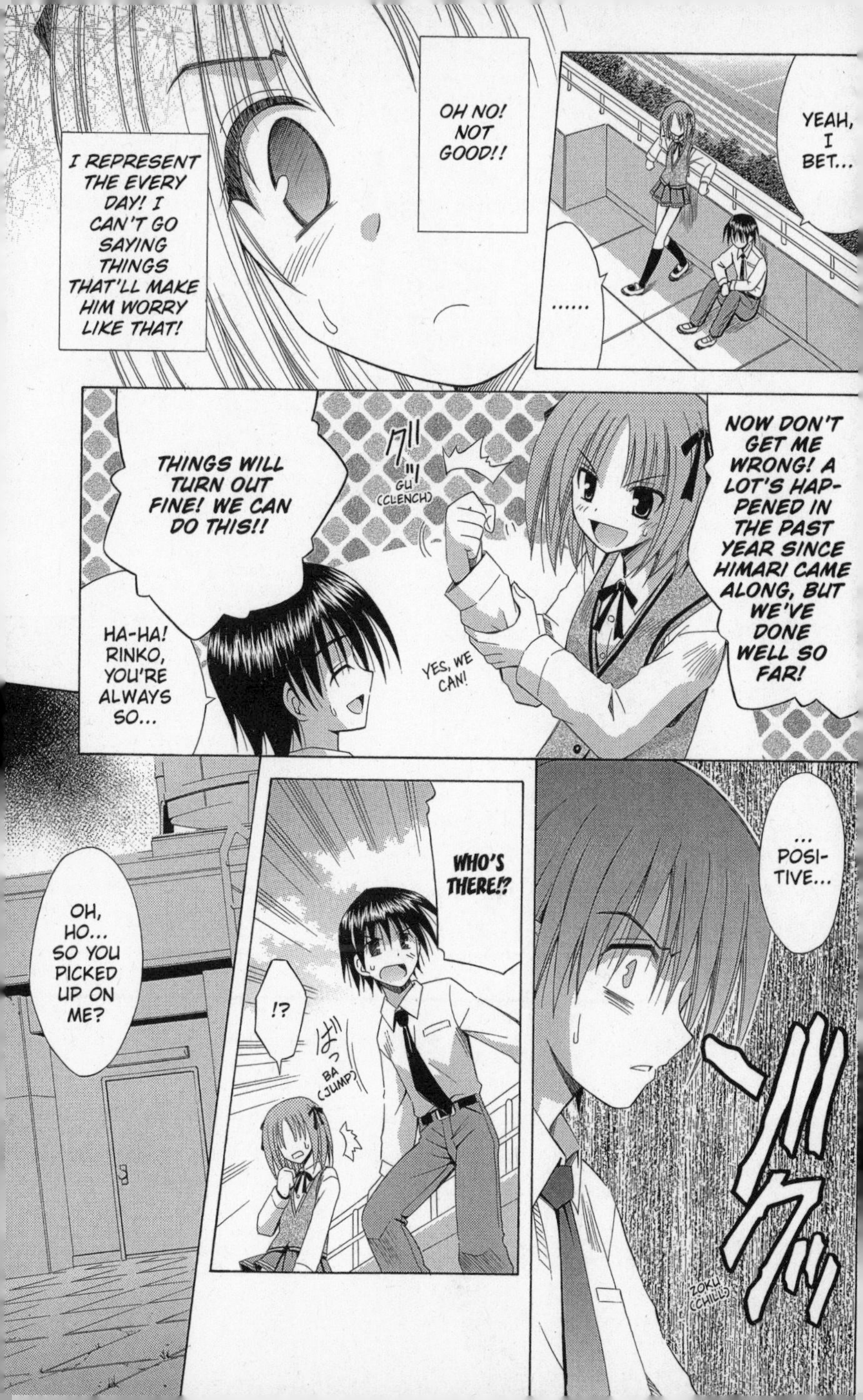
YEAH, I BET...
......
OH NO! NOT GOOD!!
I REPRESENT THE EVERY DAY! I CAN'T GO SAYING THINGS THAT'LL MAKE HIM WORRY LIKE THAT!
NOW DON'T GET ME WRONG! A LOT'S HAP-PENED IN THE PAST YEAR SINCE HIMARI CAME ALONG, BUT WE'VE DONE WELL SO FAR!
GU (CLENCH)
THINGS WILL TURN OUT FINE! WE CAN DO THIS!!
YES, WE CAN!
HA-HA! RINKO, YOU'RE ALWAYS SO...
... POSI-TIVE...
ZOKU (CHILL)
WHO'S THERE!?
!?
BA (JUMP)
OH, HO... SO YOU PICKED UP ON ME?

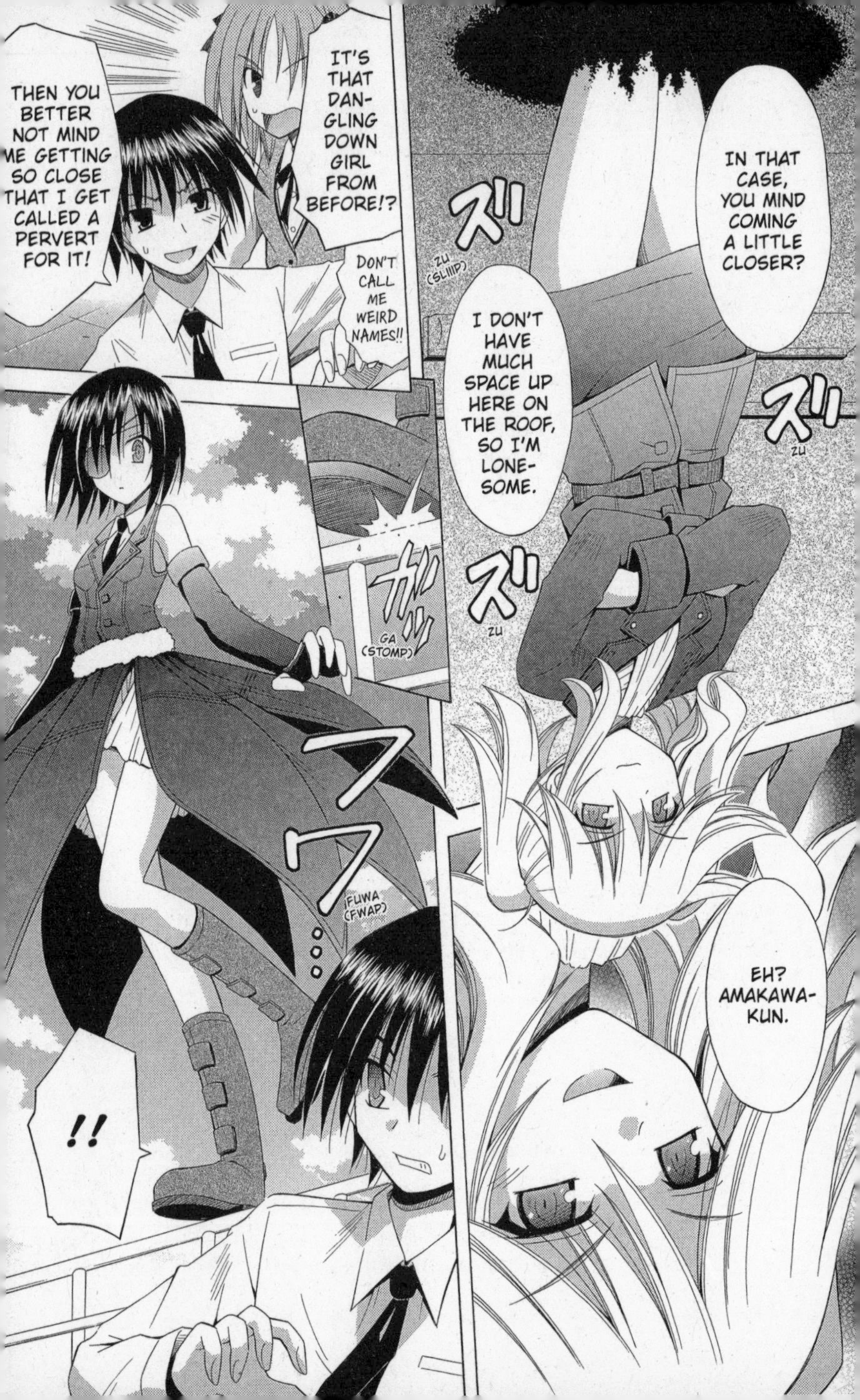
IN THAT CASE, YOU MIND COMING A LITTLE CLOSER?
ZU (SLIIIP)
I DON'T HAVE MUCH SPACE UP HERE ON THE ROOF, SO I'M LONESOME.
ZU
ZU
EH? AMAKAWA-KUN.
IT'S THAT DANGLING DOWN GIRL FROM BEFORE!?
DON'T CALL ME WEIRD NAMES!!
THEN YOU BETTER NOT MIND ME GETTING SO CLOSE THAT I GET CALLED A PERVERT FOR IT!
GA (STOMP)
FUWA (FWAP)
!!

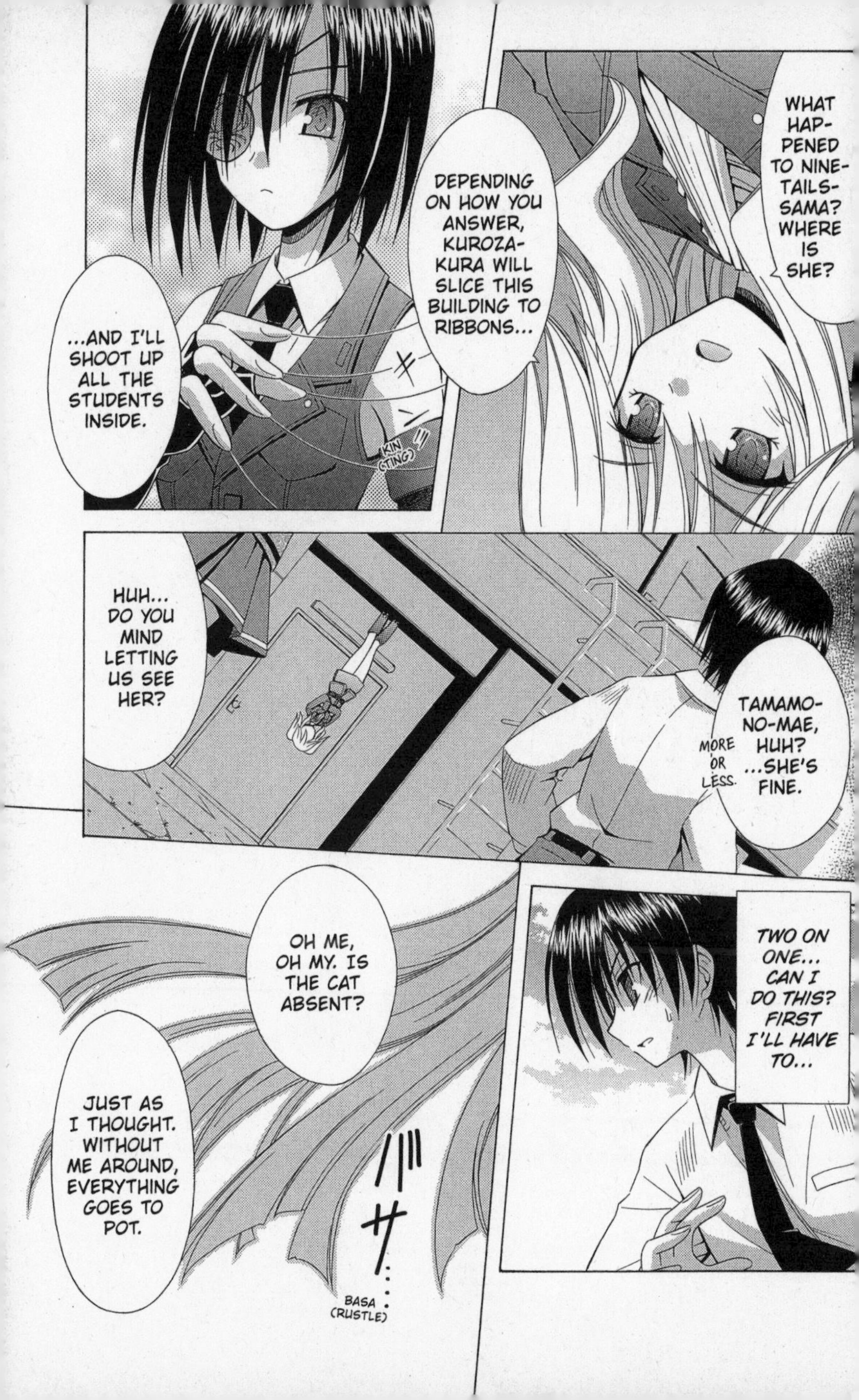
WHAT HAP-PENED TO NINE-TAILS-SAMA? WHERE IS SHE?
DEPENDING ON HOW YOU ANSWER, KUROZA-KURA WILL SLICE THIS BUILDING TO RIBBONS...
KIN (TING)
...AND I'LL SHOOT UP ALL THE STUDENTS INSIDE.
TAMAMO-NO-MAE, HUH? ...SHE'S FINE.
MORE OR LESS.
HUH... DO YOU MIND LETTING US SEE HER?
TWO ON ONE... CAN I DO THIS? FIRST I'LL HAVE TO...
OH ME, OH MY. IS THE CAT ABSENT?
JUST AS I THOUGHT. WITHOUT ME AROUND, EVERYTHING GOES TO POT.
BASA (RUSTLE)

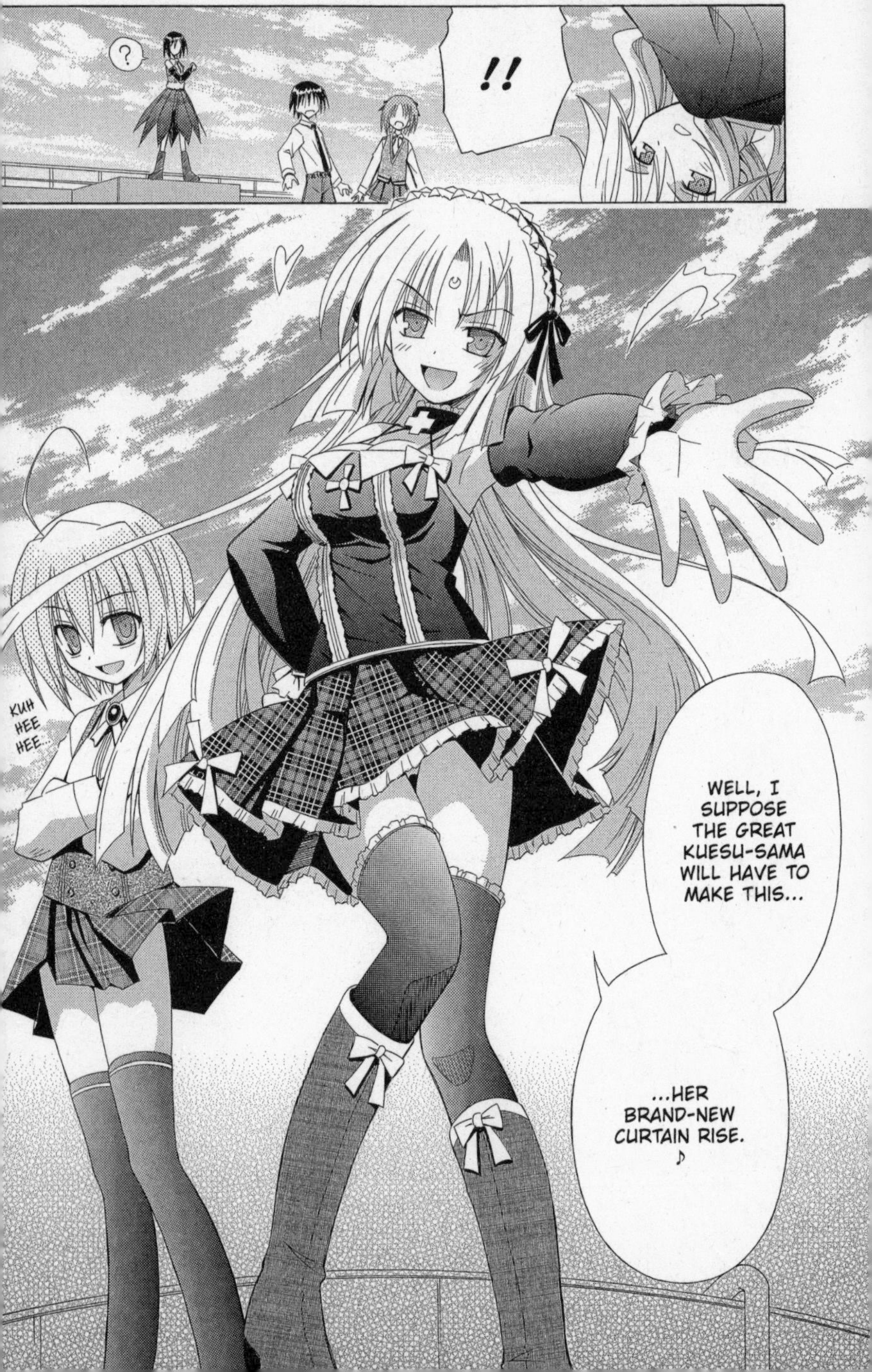
!!
?
WELL, I SUPPOSE THE GREAT KUESU-SAMA WILL HAVE TO MAKE THIS...
...HER BRAND-NEW CURTAIN RISE. ♪
KUH HEE HEE...

MENAGERIE 65: THE UNCHANGING WITCH, THE CAT'S MOMENT

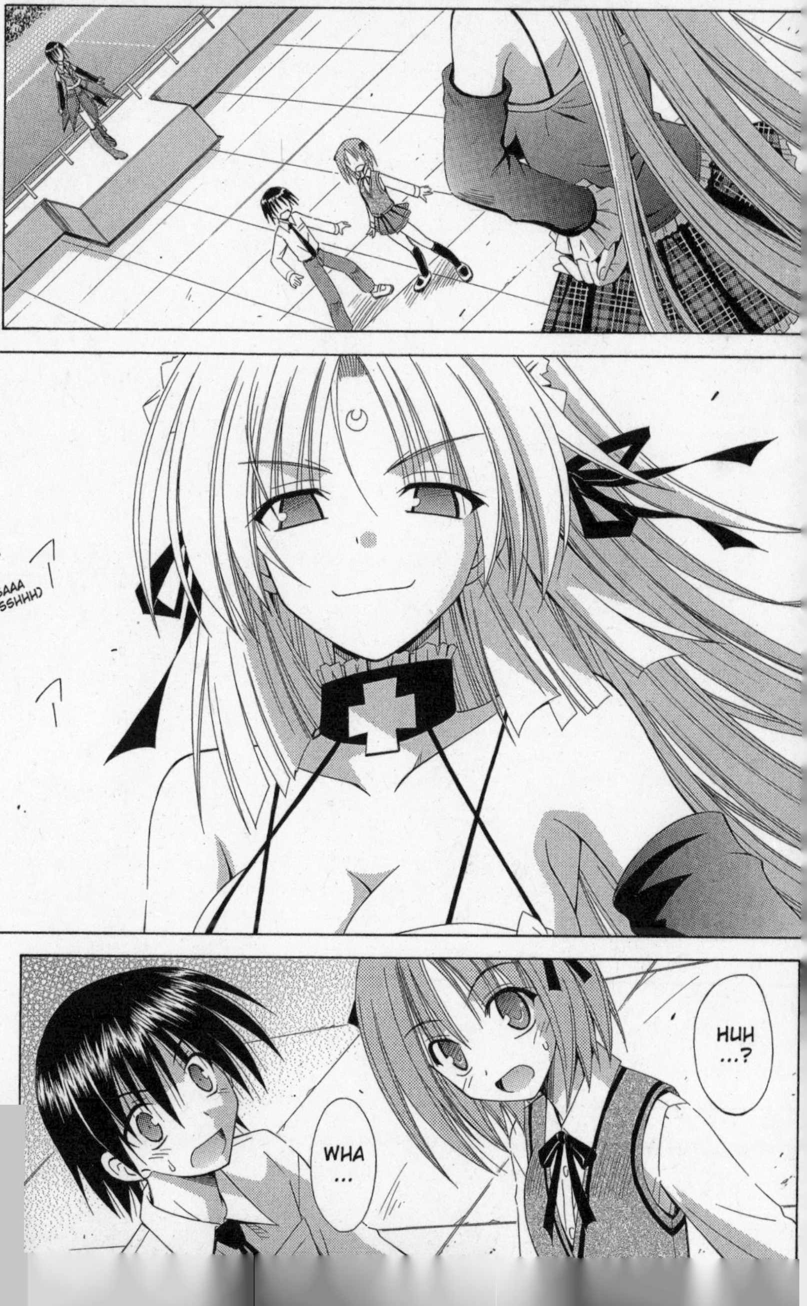
SAAA (SSSHHH)
HUH ...?
WHA ...

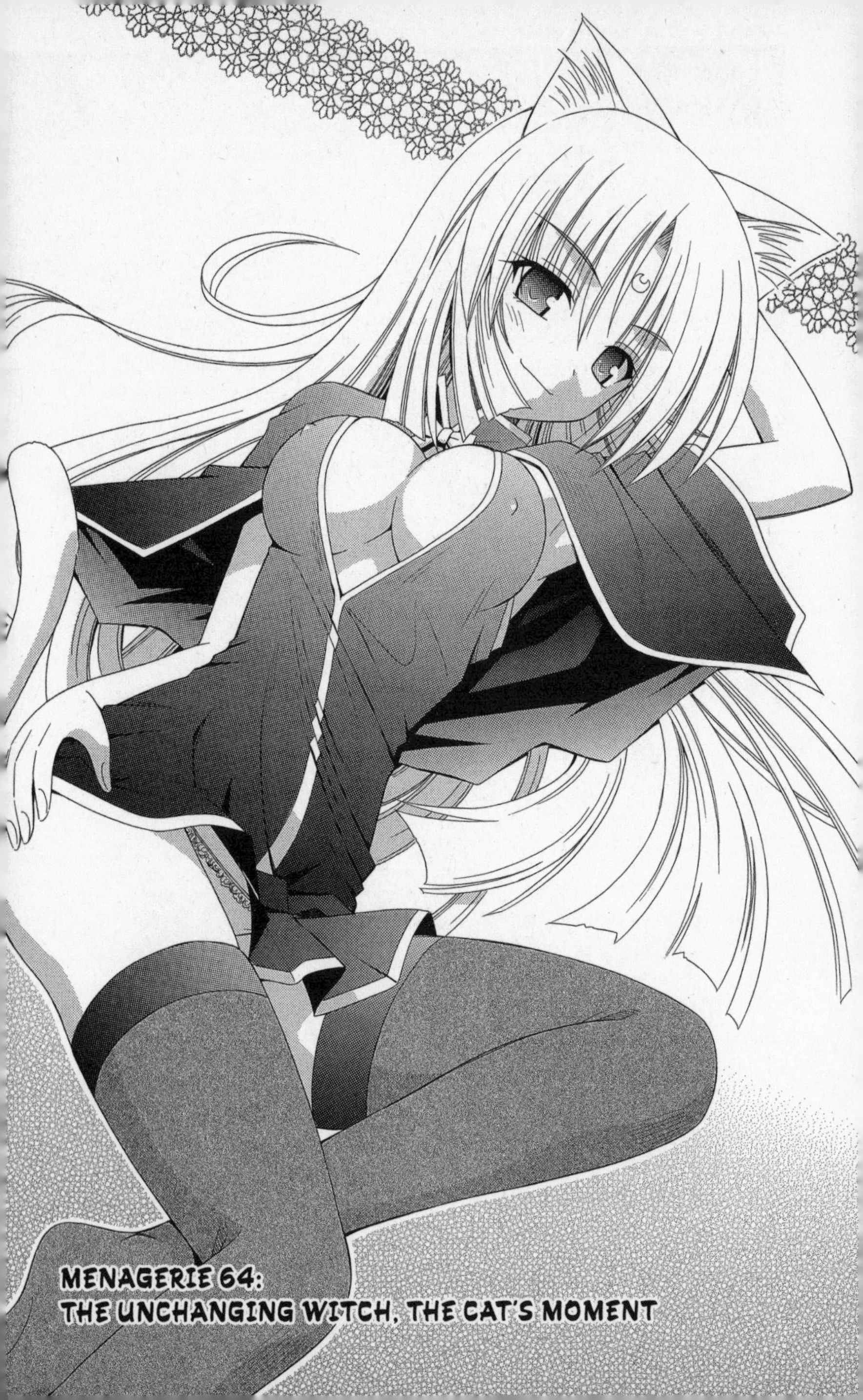

MENAGERIE 64:
THE UNCHANGING WITCH, THE CAT'S MOMENT

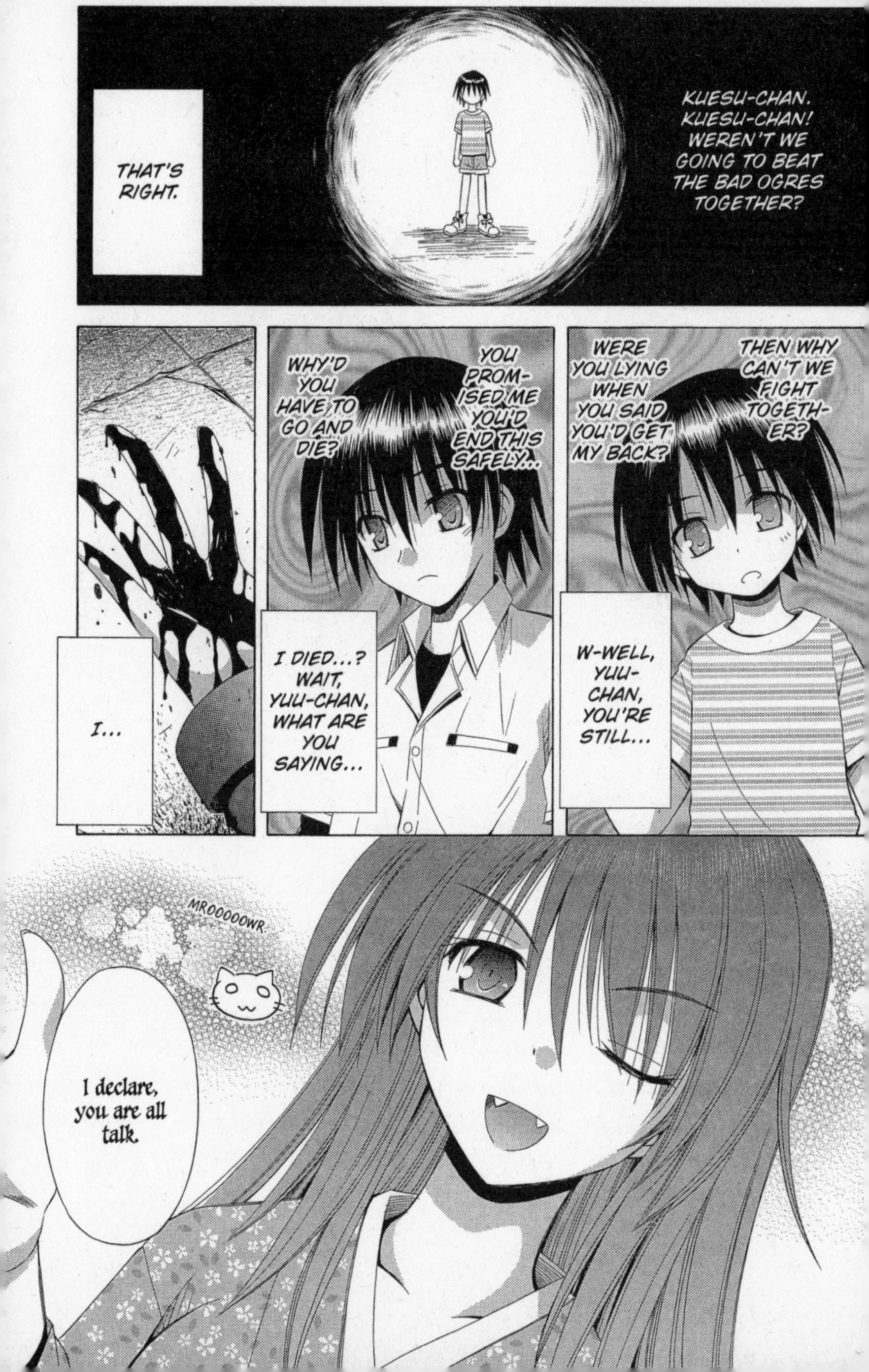
KUESU-CHAN. KUESU-CHAN! WEREN'T WE GOING TO BEAT THE BAD OGRES TOGETHER?
THAT'S RIGHT.
THEN WHY CAN'T WE FIGHT TOGETH-ER?
WERE YOU LYING WHEN YOU SAID YOU'D GET MY BACK?
W-WELL, YUU-CHAN, YOU'RE STILL...
YOU PROM-ISED ME YOU'D END THIS SAFELY...
WHY'D YOU HAVE TO GO AND DIE?
I DIED...? WAIT, YUU-CHAN, WHAT ARE YOU SAYING...
I...
MROOOOOWR.
I declare, you are all talk.

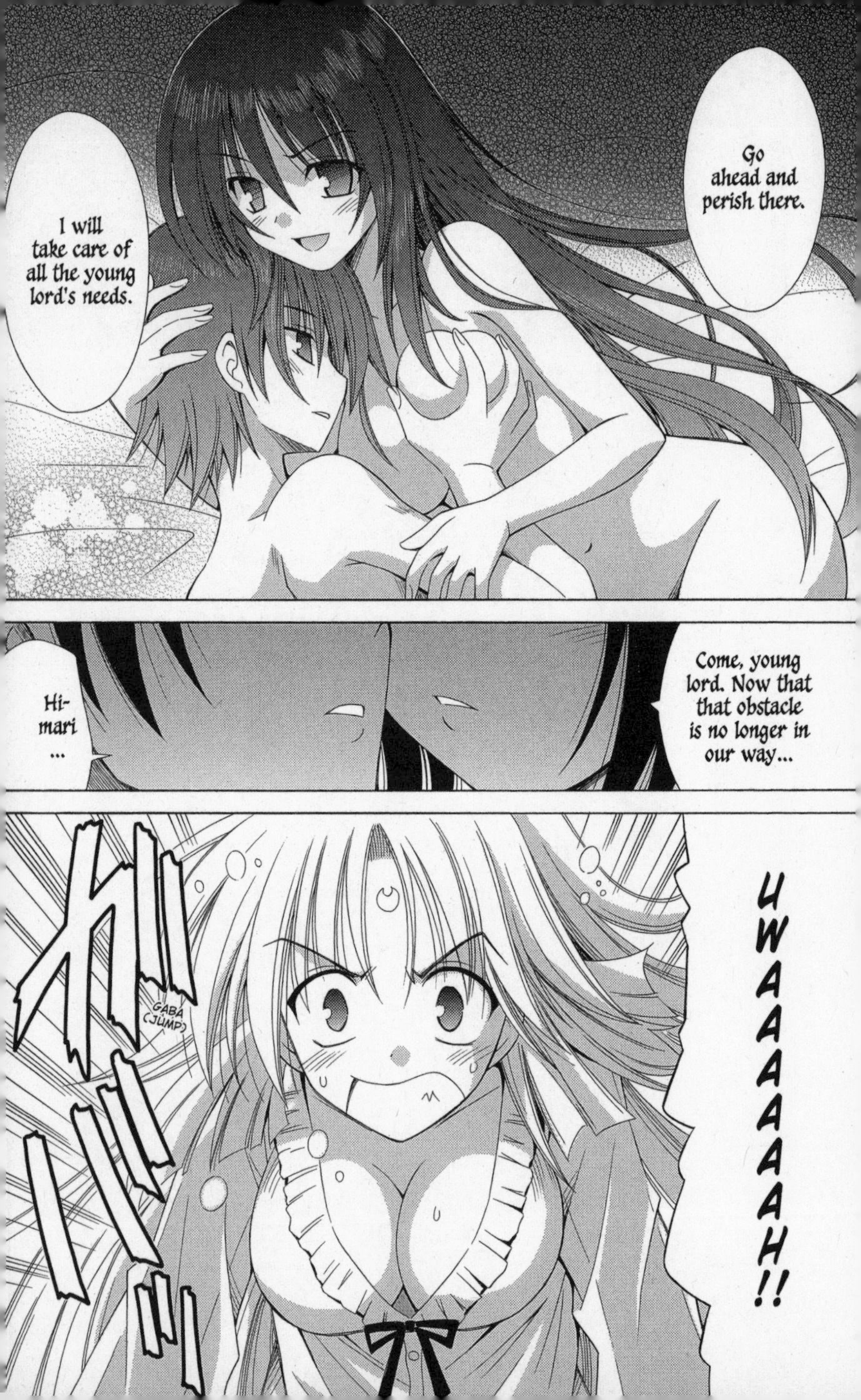
Go ahead and perish there.
I will take care of all the young lord's needs.
Come, young lord. Now that that obstacle is no longer in our way...
Hi-mari ...
UWAAAAAAH!!
GABA (JUMP)

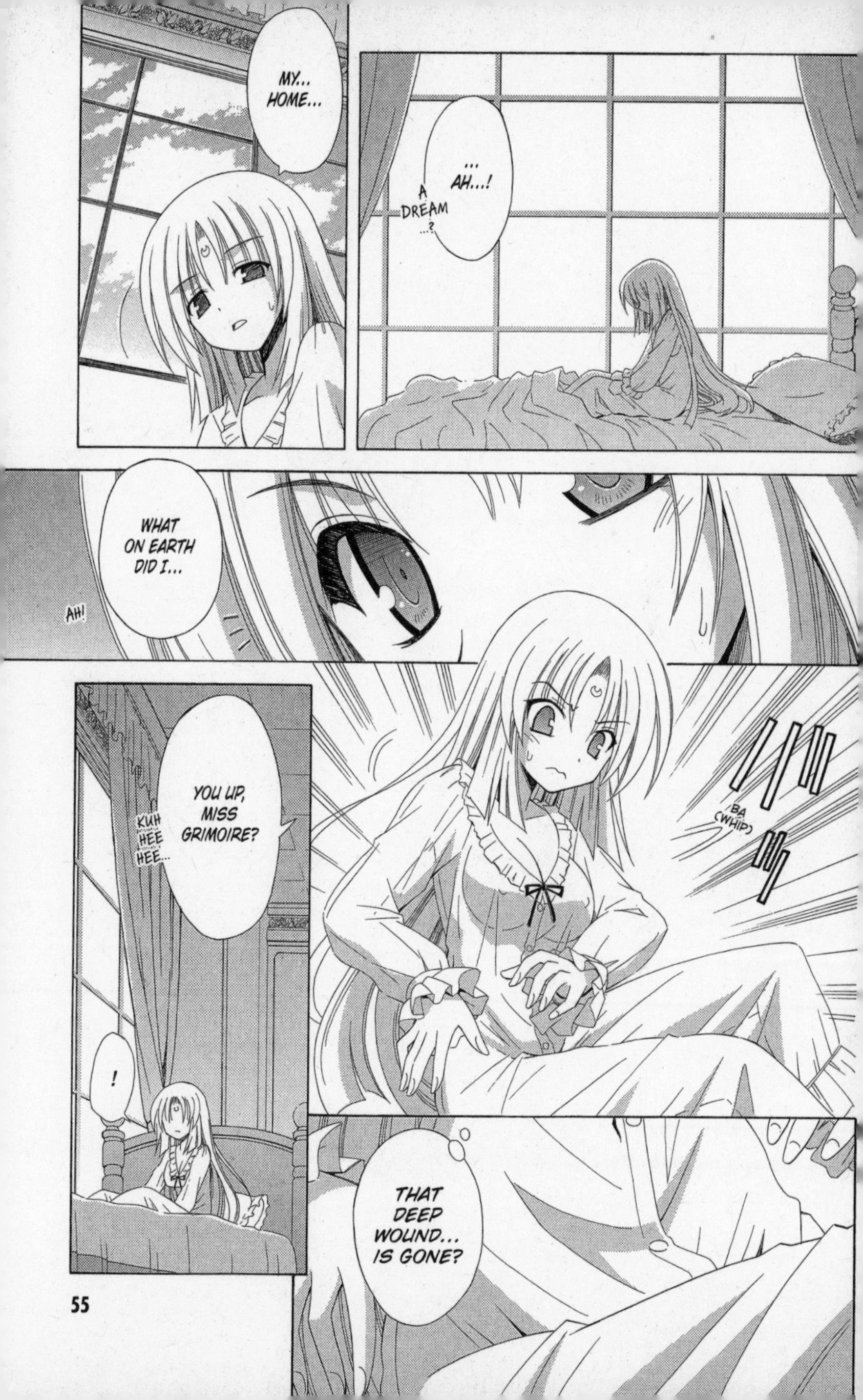
... AH...!
A DREAM ...?
MY... HOME...
WHAT ON EARTH DID I...
AH!
BA (WHIP)
THAT DEEP WOUND... IS GONE?
YOU UP, MISS GRIMOIRE?
KUH HEE HEE...
!

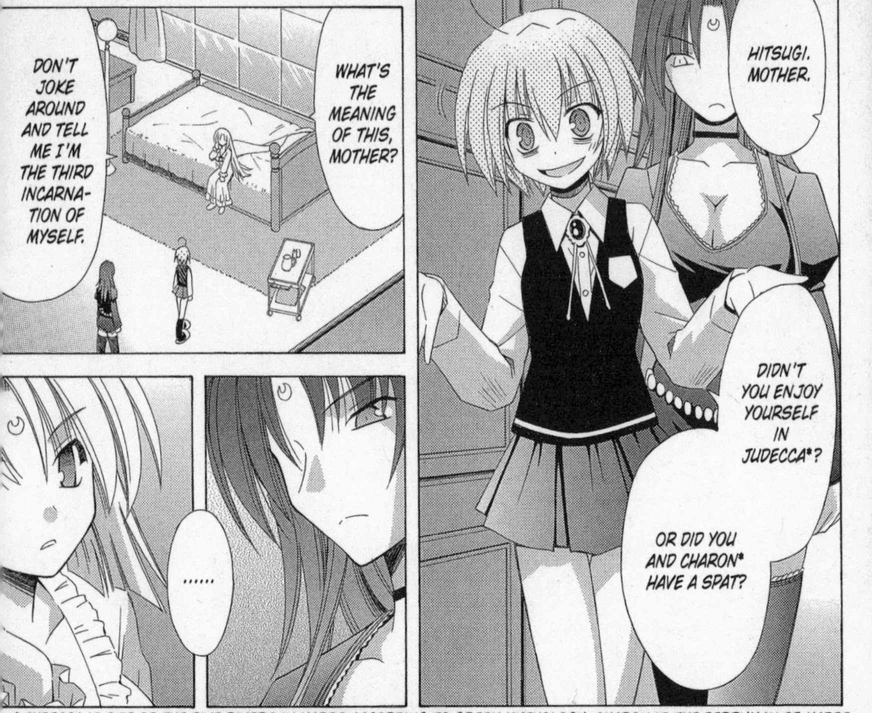
HITSUGI. MOTHER.
DIDN'T YOU ENJOY YOURSELF IN JUDECCA*?
OR DID YOU AND CHARON* HAVE A SPAT?
WHAT'S THE MEANING OF THIS, MOTHER?
DON'T JOKE AROUND AND TELL ME I'M THE THIRD INCARNATION OF MYSELF.
......

*JUDECCA IS ONE OF THE FIVE RIVERS IN HADES ACCORDING TO GREEK MYTHOLOGY; CHARON IS THE FERRYMAN OF HADES.

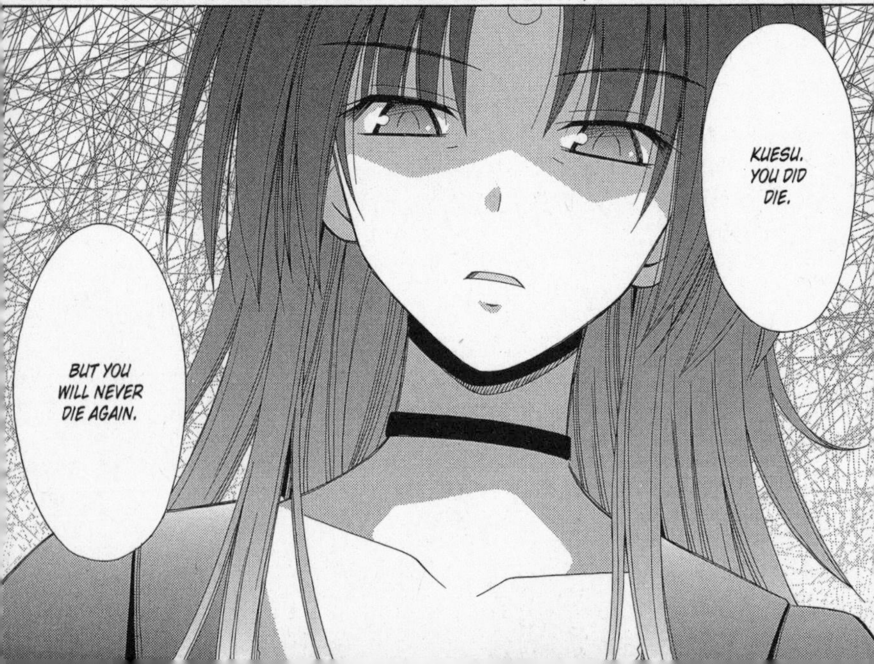
KUESU. YOU DID DIE.
BUT YOU WILL NEVER DIE AGAIN.

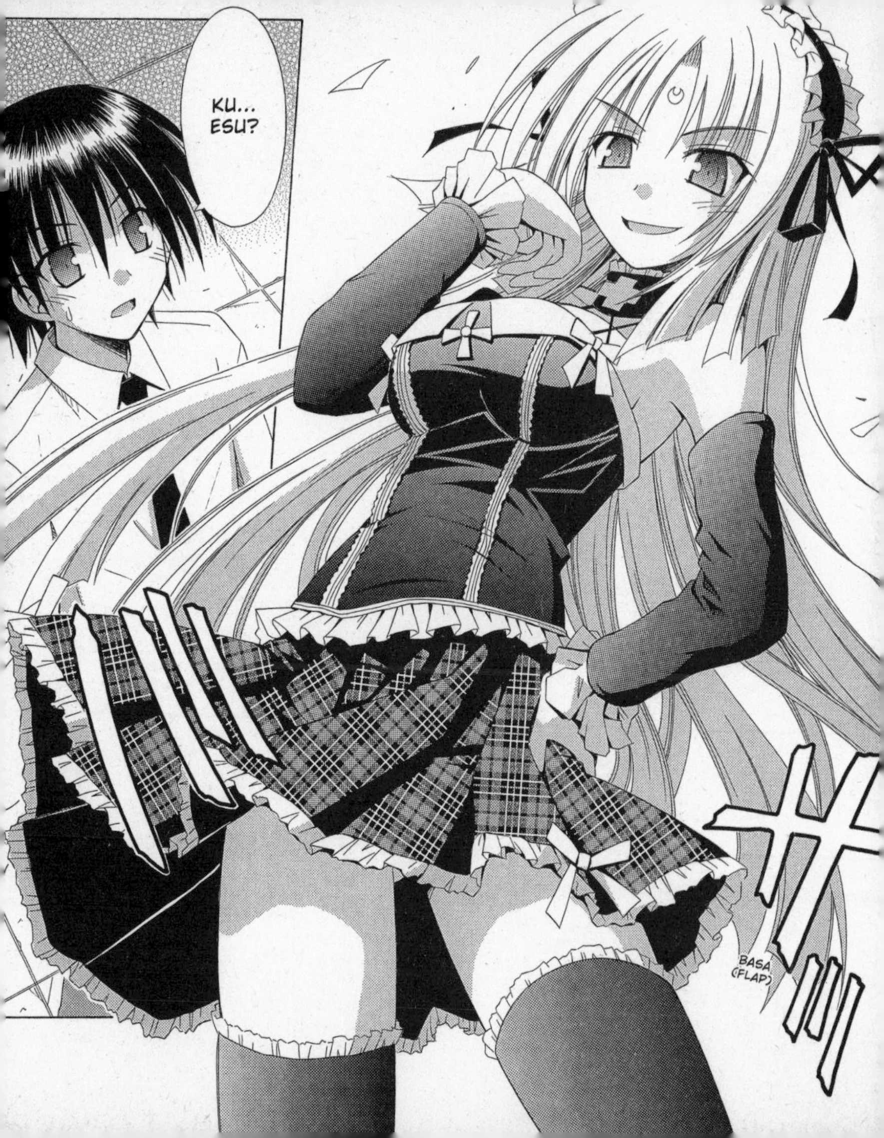
KU... ESU?
BASA (FLAP)

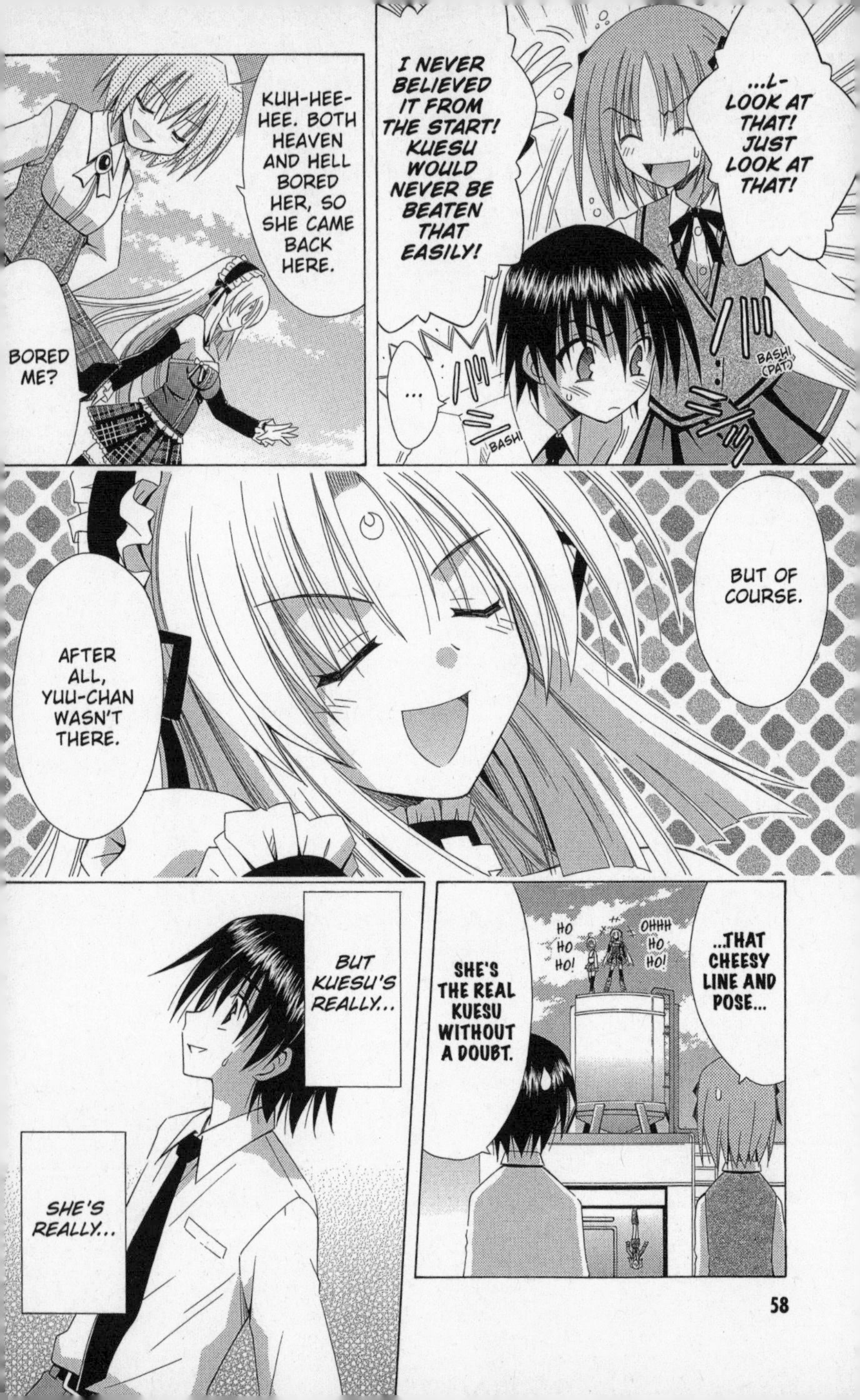

...L- LOOK AT THAT! JUST LOOK AT THAT!
I NEVER BELIEVED IT FROM THE START! KUESU WOULD NEVER BE BEATEN THAT EASILY!
BASH! (PAT)
...
BASH
KUH-HEE-HEE. BOTH HEAVEN AND HELL BORED HER, SO SHE CAME BACK HERE.
BORED ME?
BUT OF COURSE.
AFTER ALL, YUU-CHAN WASN'T THERE.
...THAT CHEESY LINE AND POSE...
OHHH HO HO!
HO HO HO!
SHE'S THE REAL KUESU WITHOUT A DOUBT.
BUT KUESU'S REALLY...
SHE'S REALLY...

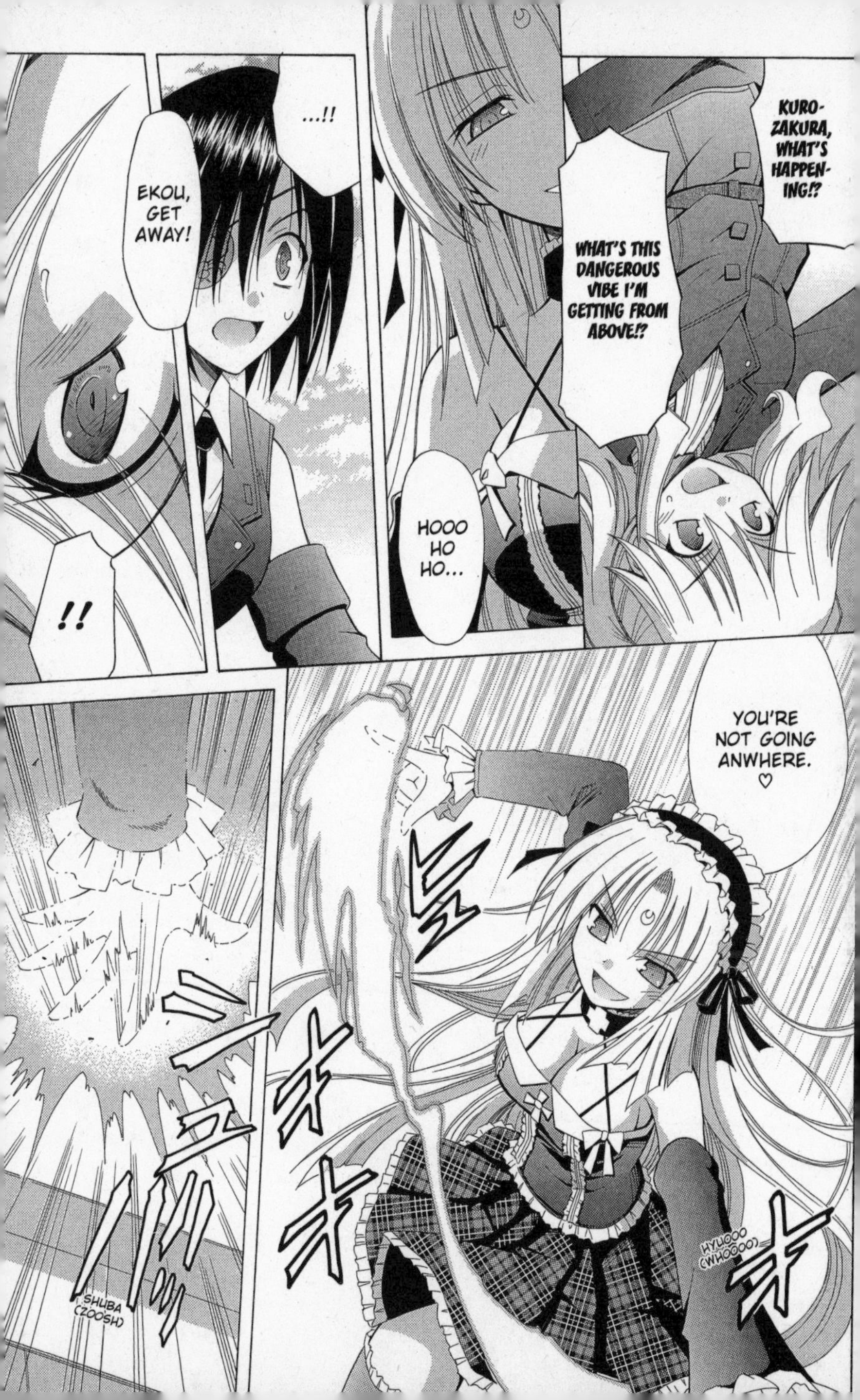
KURO-ZAKURA, WHAT'S HAPPEN-ING!?
WHAT'S THIS DANGEROUS VIBE I'M GETTING FROM ABOVE!?
HOOO HO HO...
...!!
EKOU, GET AWAY!
!!
YOU'RE NOT GOING ANWHERE. ♡
HYUOOO (WHOOOOH)
SHUBA (ZOOSH)

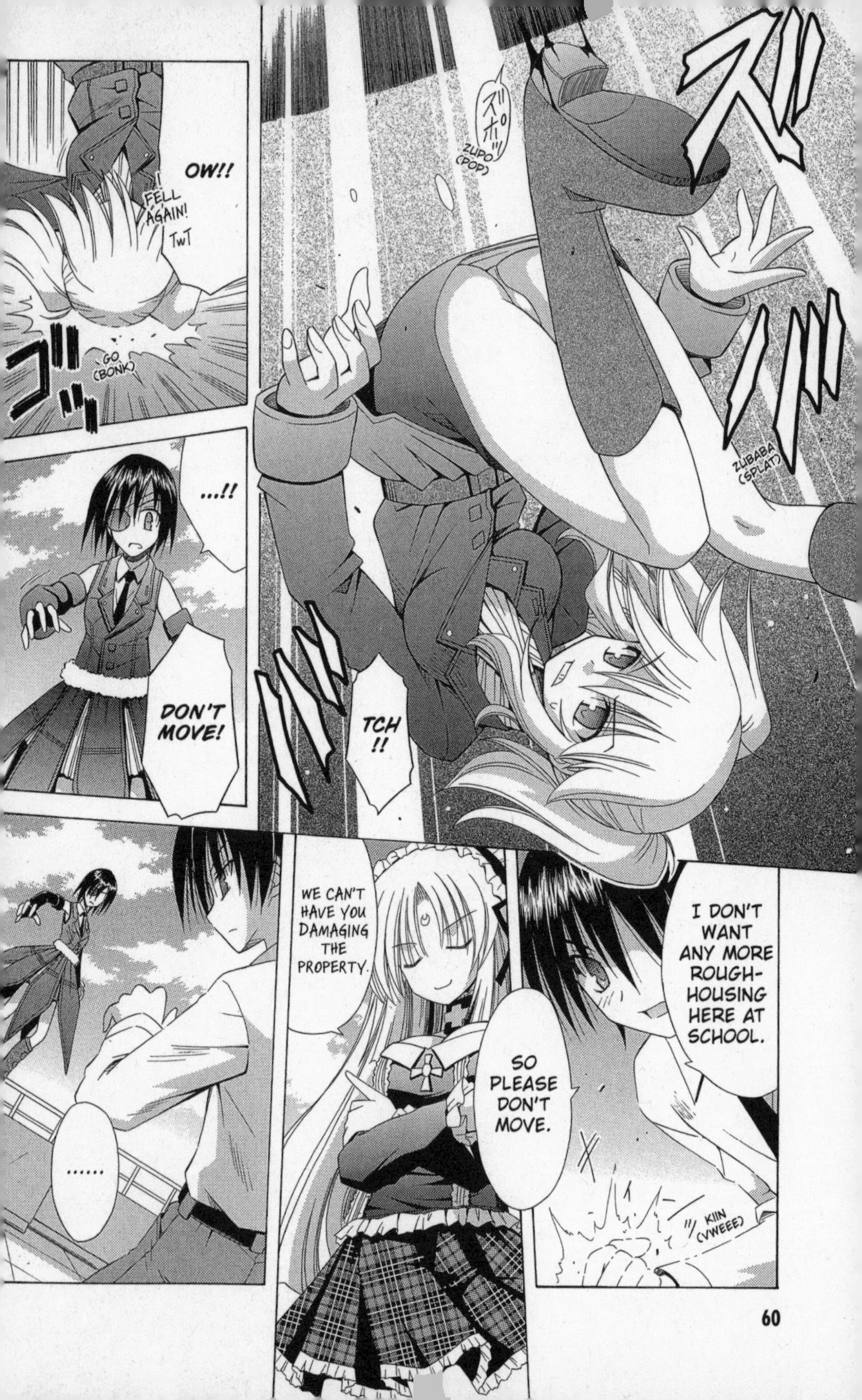
ズボッ
ZUPO (POP)
ZUBABA (SPLAT)
TCH !!
OW!!
I FELL AGAIN! TwT
GO (BONK)
...!!
DON'T MOVE!
I DON'T WANT ANY MORE ROUGH-HOUSING HERE AT SCHOOL.
SO PLEASE DON'T MOVE.
KIIN (VWEEE)
WE CAN'T HAVE YOU DAMAGING THE PROPERTY.
......

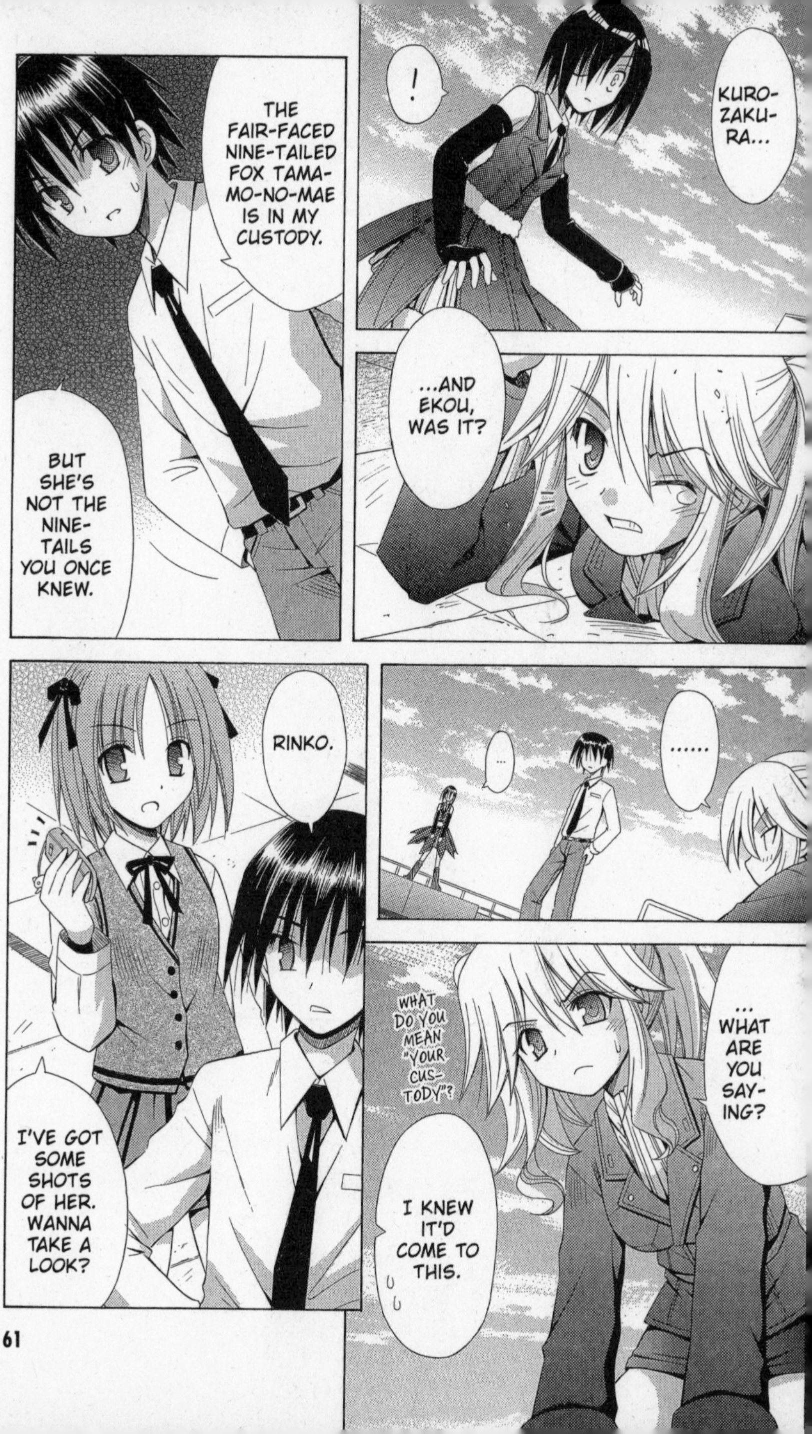
KURO-ZAKU-RA...
!
...AND EKOU, WAS IT?
THE FAIR-FACED NINE-TAILED FOX TAMA-MO-NO-MAE IS IN MY CUSTODY.
BUT SHE'S NOT THE NINE-TAILS YOU ONCE KNEW.
......
...
...WHAT ARE YOU SAY-ING?
WHAT DO YOU MEAN "YOUR CUS-TODY"?
I KNEW IT'D COME TO THIS.
RINKO.
I'VE GOT SOME SHOTS OF HER. WANNA TAKE A LOOK?

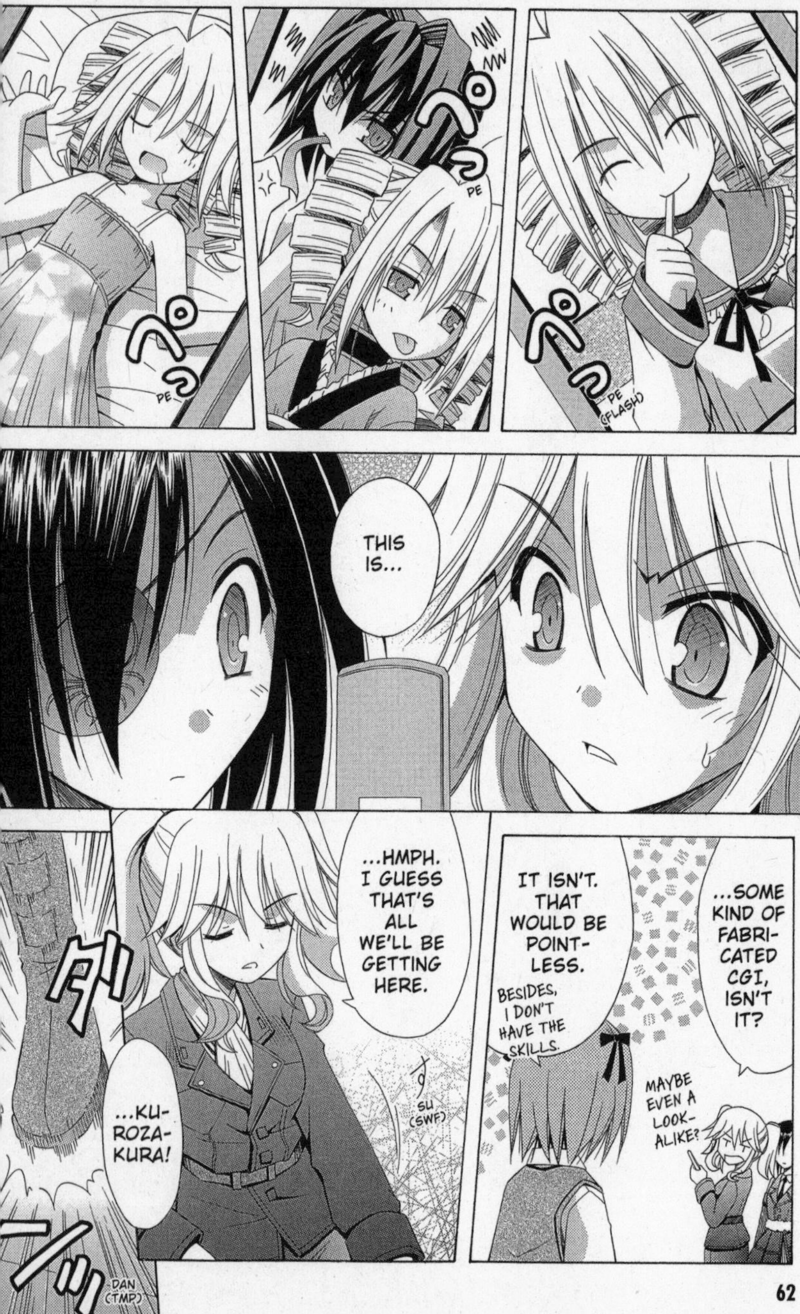
PE (FLASH)
PE
PE
THIS IS...
...SOME KIND OF FABRICATED CGI, ISN'T IT?
IT ISN'T. THAT WOULD BE POINTLESS.
BESIDES, I DON'T HAVE THE SKILLS.
MAYBE EVEN A LOOK-ALIKE?
...HMPH. I GUESS THAT'S ALL WE'LL BE GETTING HERE.
SU (SWF)
...KUROZAKURA!
DAN (TMP)

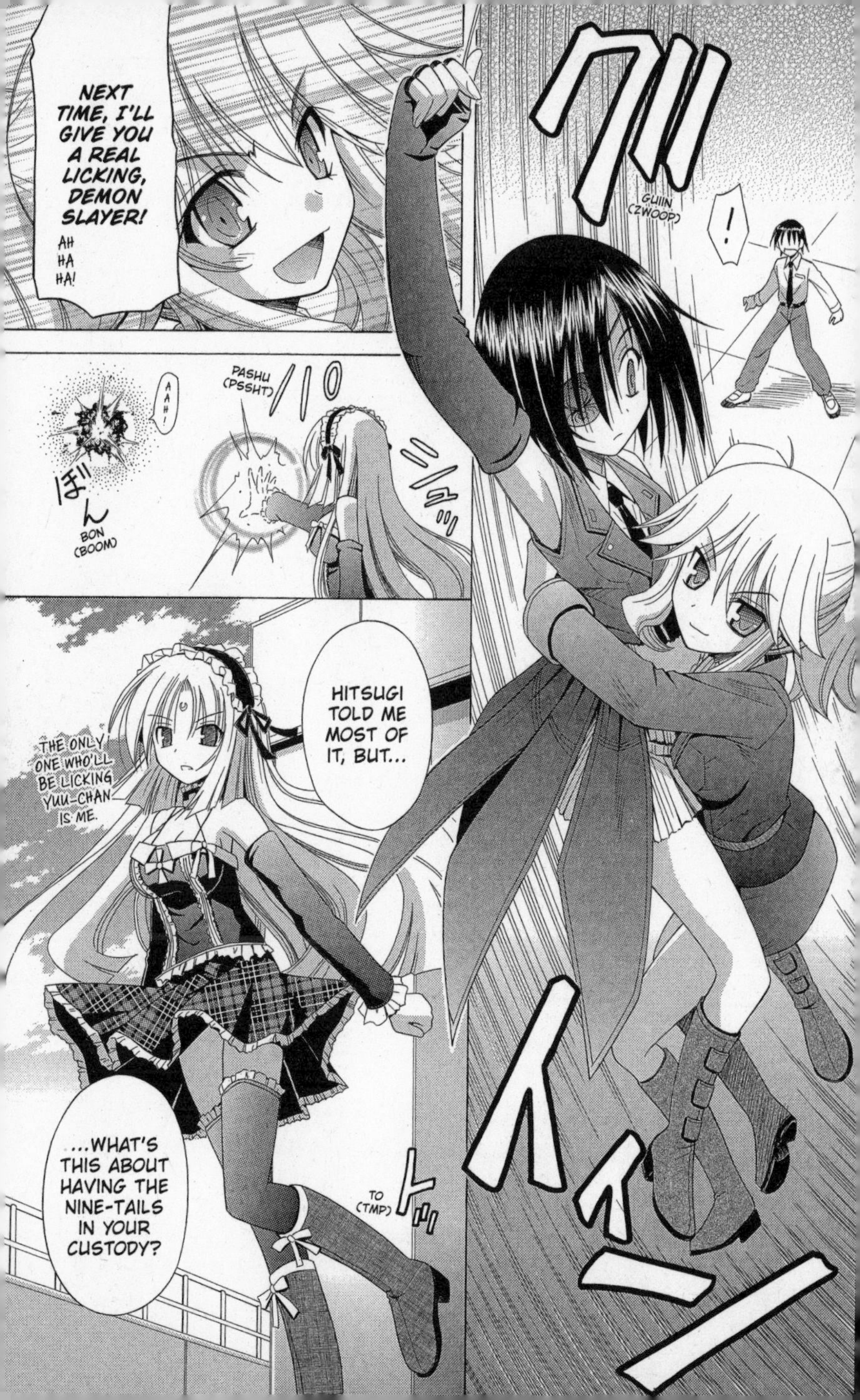
GUIIN (ZWOOP)
!
NEXT TIME, I'LL GIVE YOU A REAL LICKING, DEMON SLAYER!
AH HA HA!
PASHU (PSSHT)
AAH!
BON (BOOM)
HITSUGI TOLD ME MOST OF IT, BUT...
THE ONLY ONE WHO'LL BE LICKING YUU-CHAN IS ME.
...WHAT'S THIS ABOUT HAVING THE NINE-TAILS IN YOUR CUSTODY?
TO (TMP)

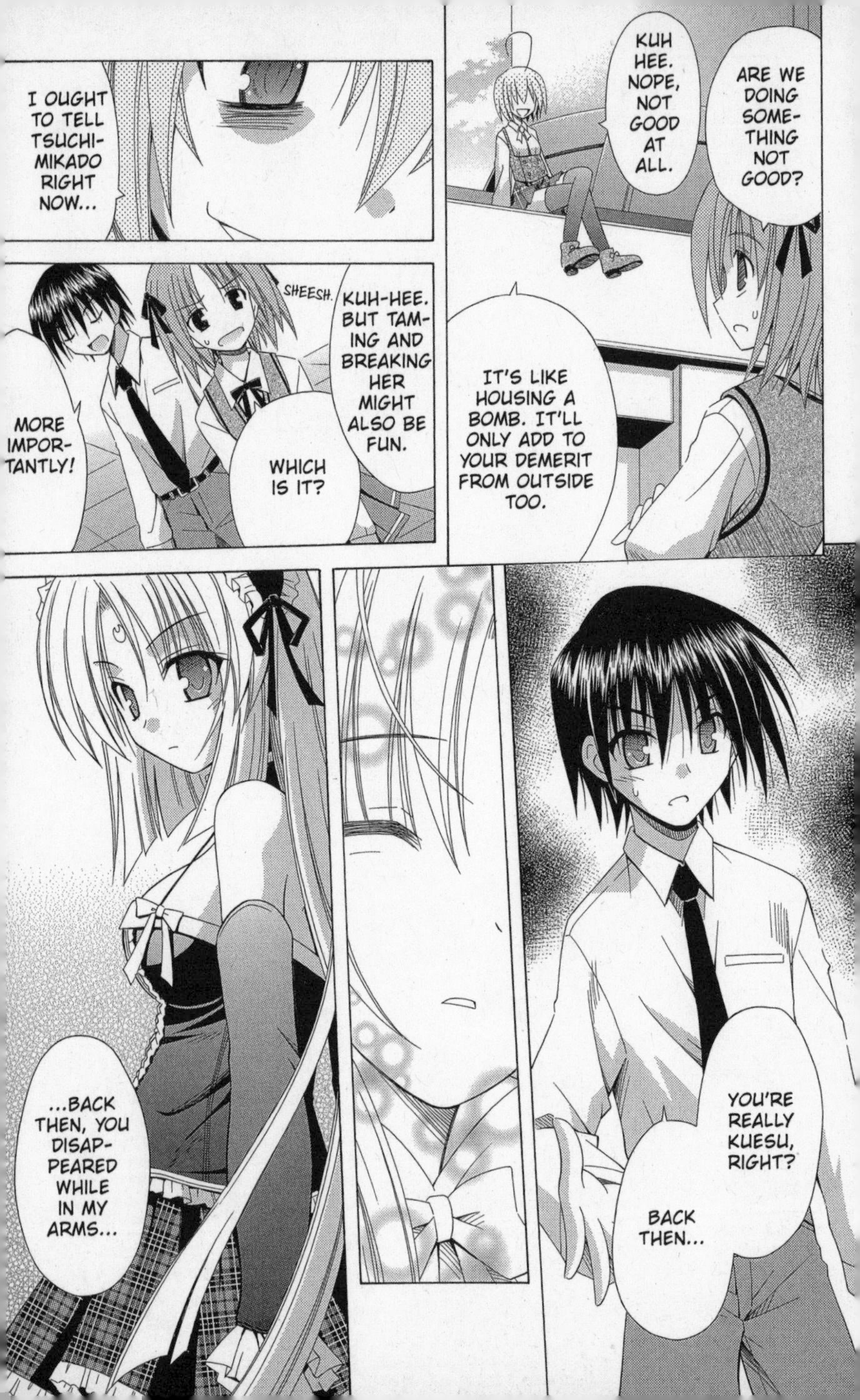
ARE WE DOING SOME-THING NOT GOOD?
KUH HEE. NOPE, NOT GOOD AT ALL.
IT'S LIKE HOUSING A BOMB. IT'LL ONLY ADD TO YOUR DEMERIT FROM OUTSIDE TOO.
I OUGHT TO TELL TSUCHI-MIKADO RIGHT NOW...
SHEESH.
KUH-HEE. BUT TAM-ING AND BREAKING HER MIGHT ALSO BE FUN.
WHICH IS IT?
MORE IMPOR-TANTLY!
YOU'RE REALLY KUESU, RIGHT?
BACK THEN...
...BACK THEN, YOU DISAP-PEARED WHILE IN MY ARMS...

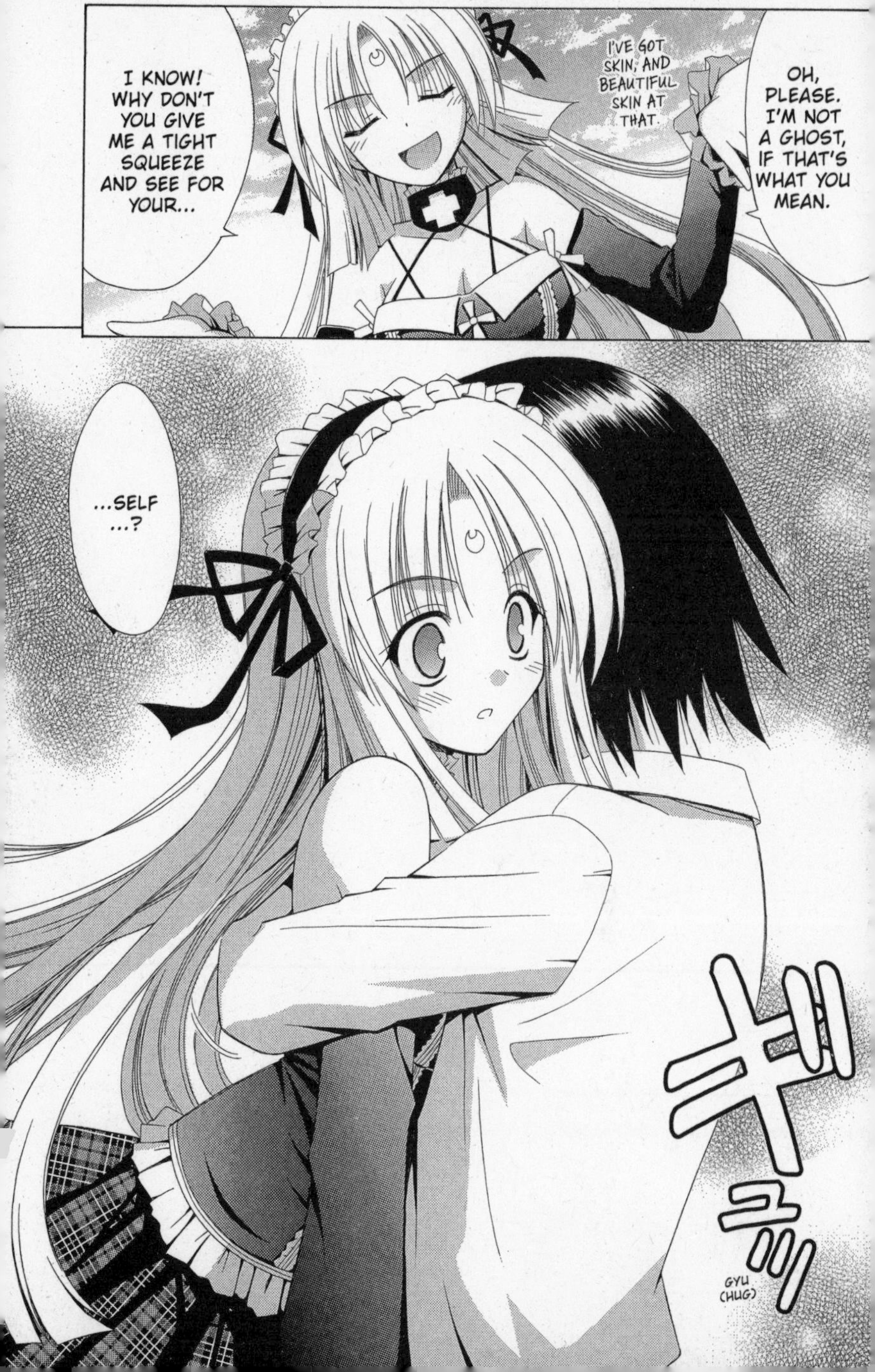
OH, PLEASE. I'M NOT A GHOST, IF THAT'S WHAT YOU MEAN.
I'VE GOT SKIN, AND BEAUTIFUL SKIN AT THAT.
I KNOW! WHY DON'T YOU GIVE ME A TIGHT SQUEEZE AND SEE FOR YOUR...
...SELF ...?
ギュッ
GYU (HUG)

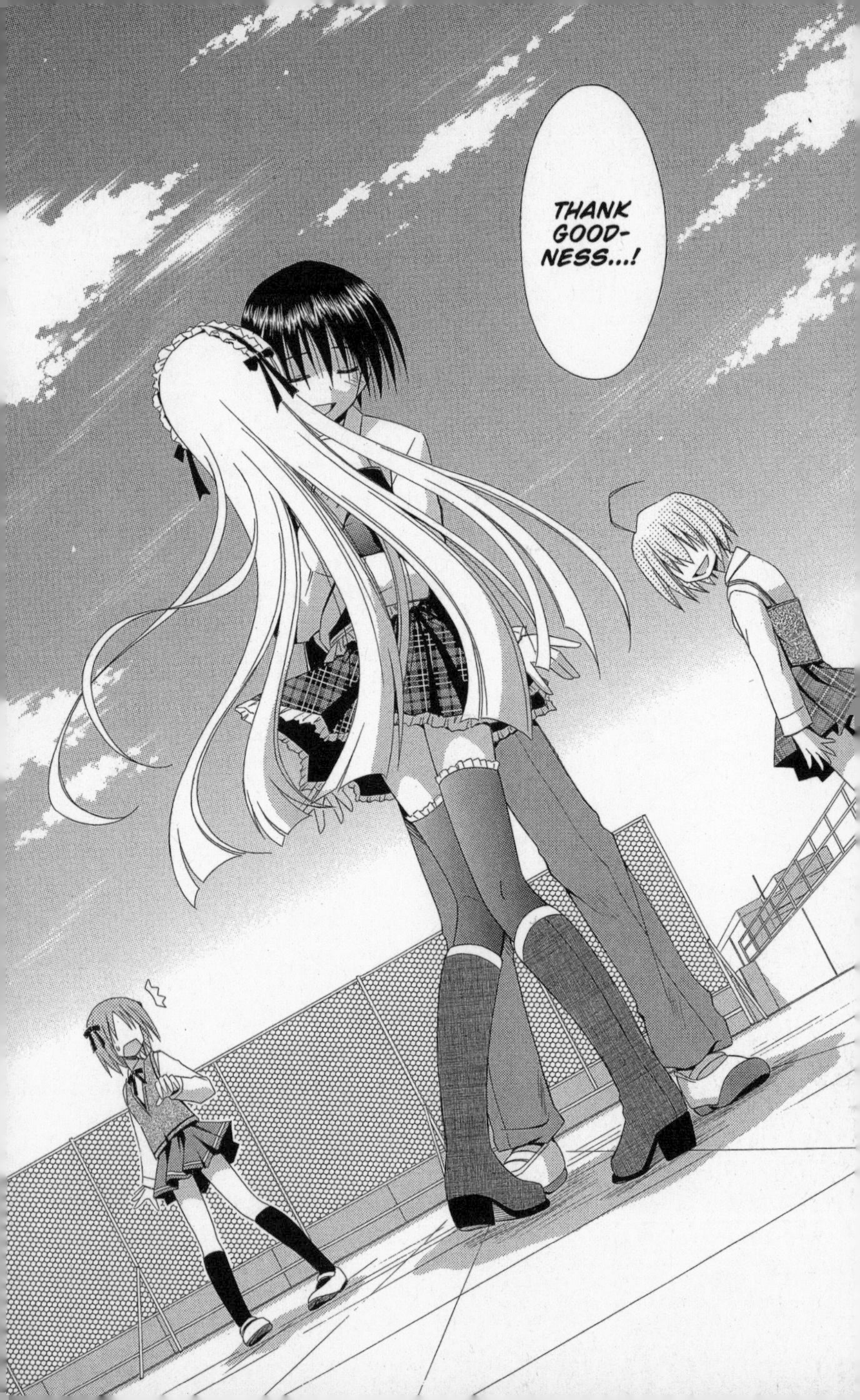
THANK GOOD-NESS...!

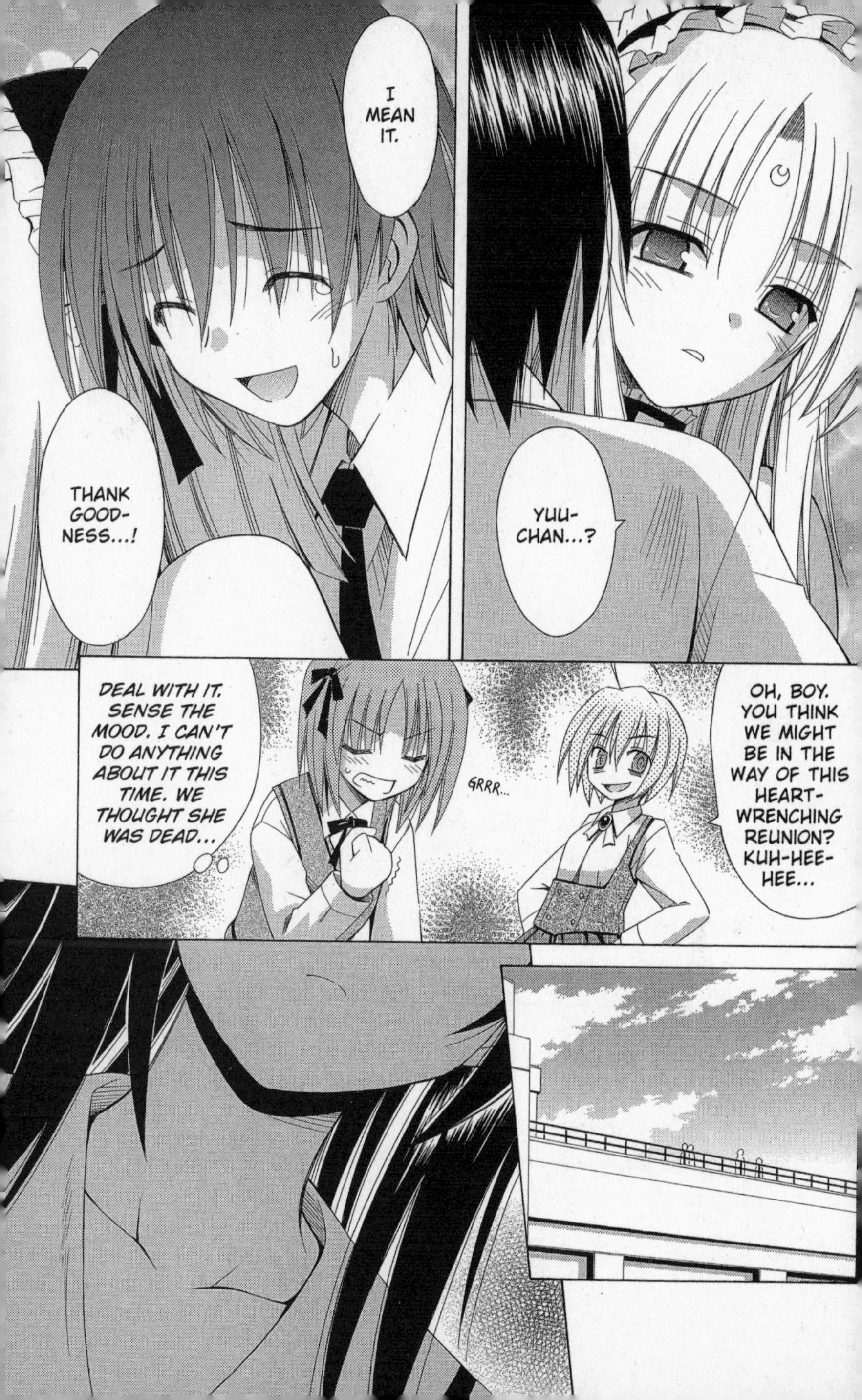
YUU-CHAN...?
I MEAN IT.
THANK GOODNESS...!
OH, BOY. YOU THINK WE MIGHT BE IN THE WAY OF THIS HEART-WRENCHING REUNION? KUH-HEE-HEE...
GRRR...
DEAL WITH IT. SENSE THE MOOD. I CAN'T DO ANYTHING ABOUT IT THIS TIME. WE THOUGHT SHE WAS DEAD...

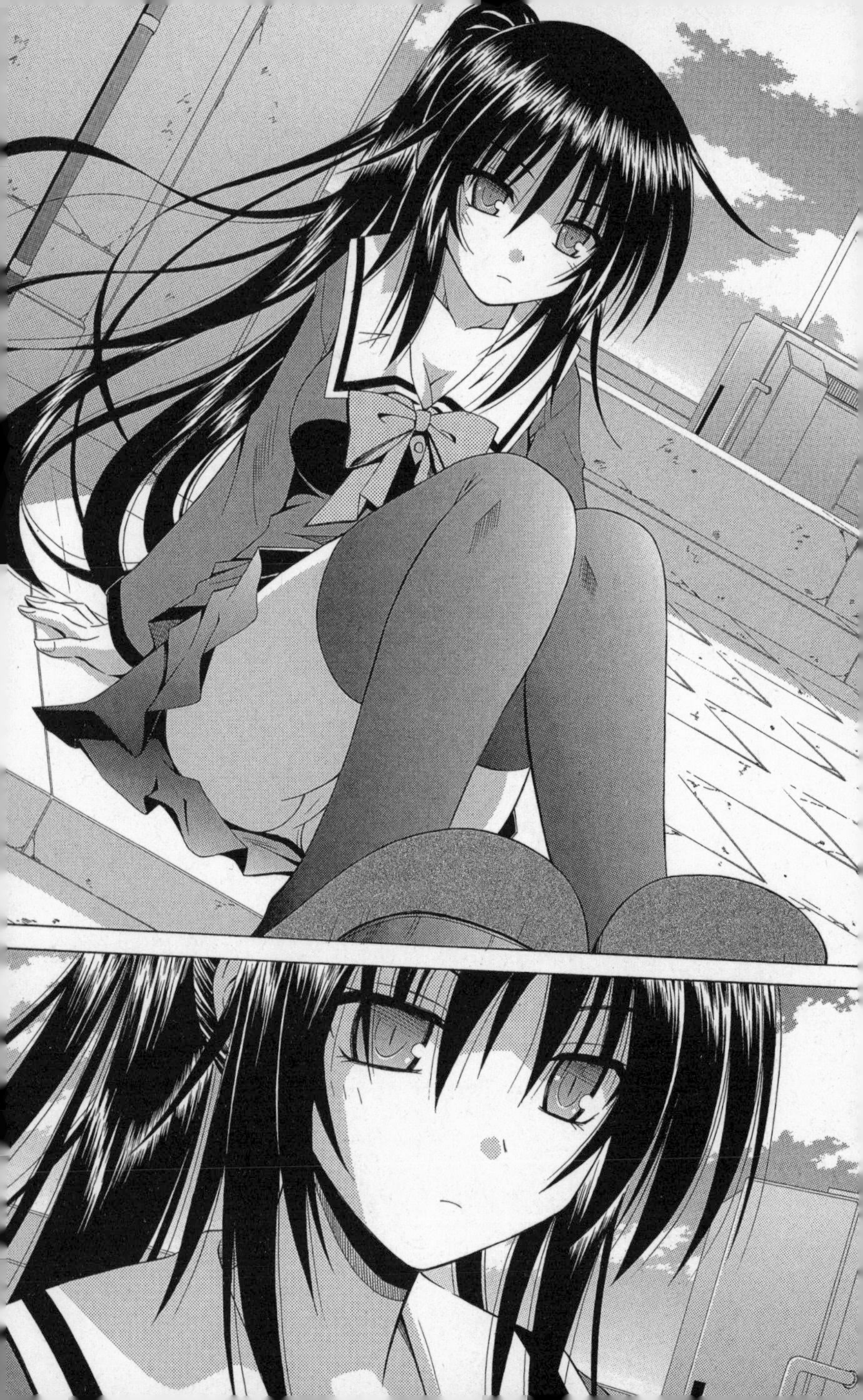

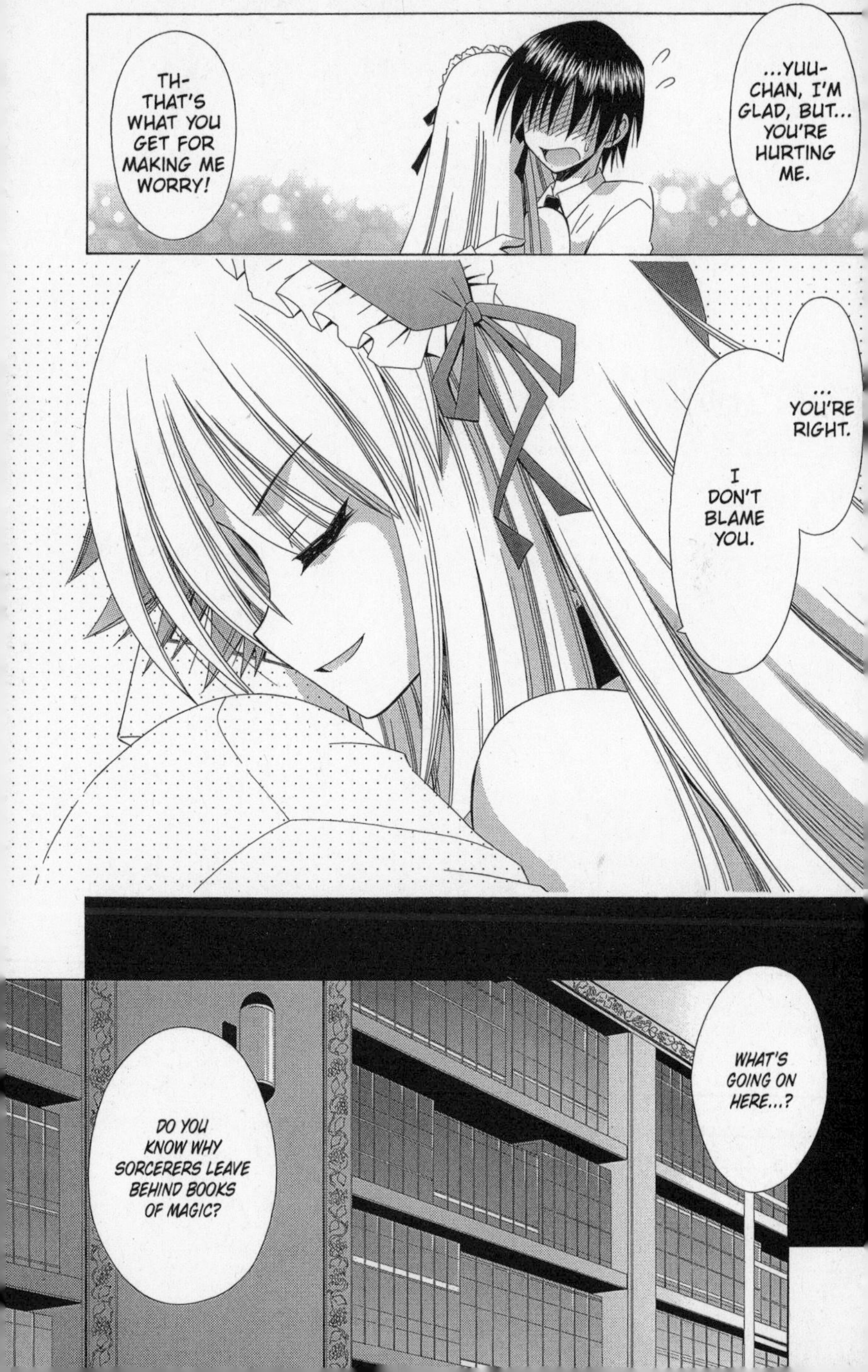
...YUU-CHAN, I'M GLAD, BUT... YOU'RE HURTING ME.
TH-THAT'S WHAT YOU GET FOR MAKING ME WORRY!
... YOU'RE RIGHT.
I DON'T BLAME YOU.
WHAT'S GOING ON HERE...?
DO YOU KNOW WHY SORCERERS LEAVE BEHIND BOOKS OF MAGIC?

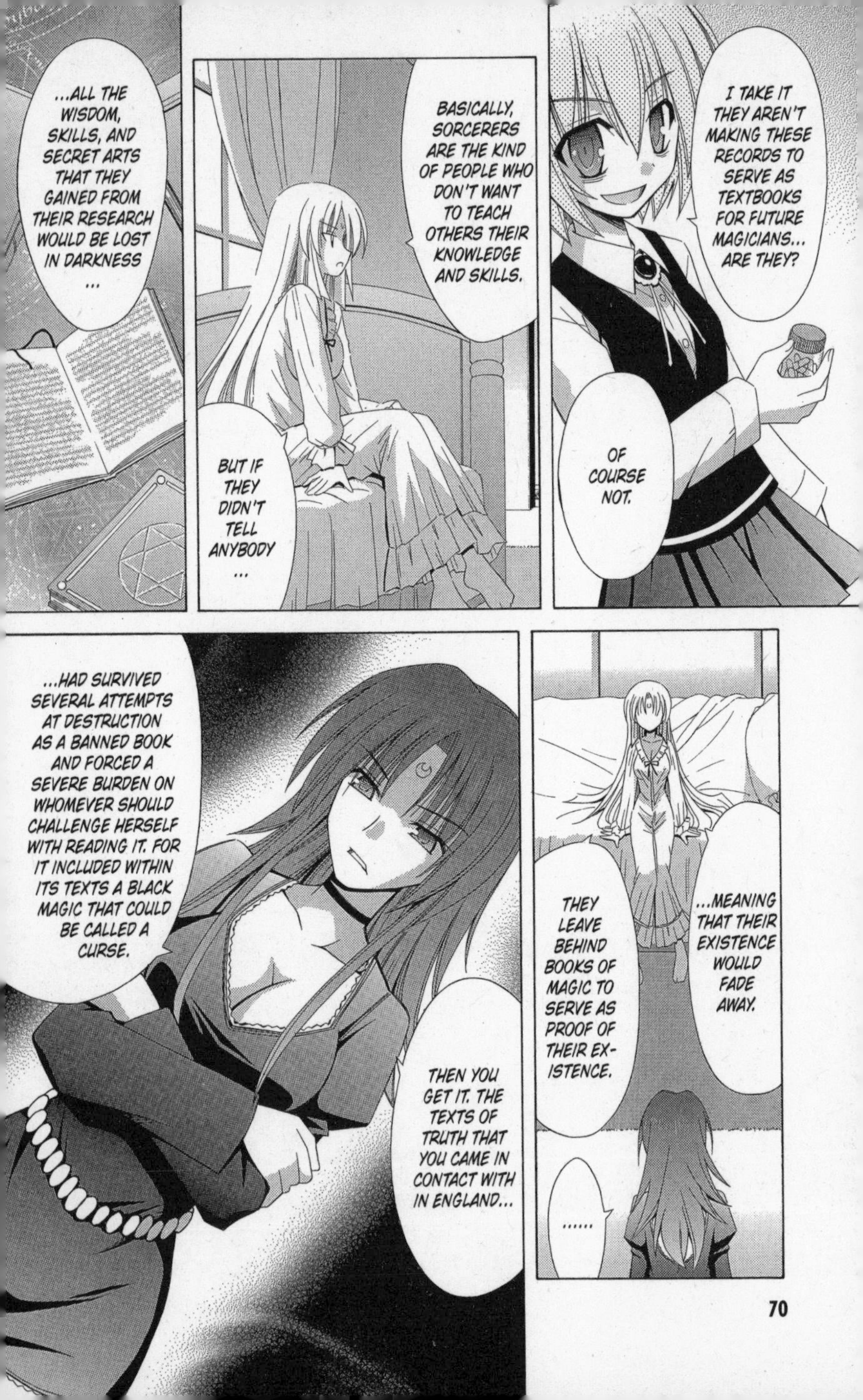
I TAKE IT THEY AREN'T MAKING THESE RECORDS TO SERVE AS TEXTBOOKS FOR FUTURE MAGICIANS... ARE THEY?
OF COURSE NOT.
BASICALLY, SORCERERS ARE THE KIND OF PEOPLE WHO DON'T WANT TO TEACH OTHERS THEIR KNOWLEDGE AND SKILLS.
BUT IF THEY DIDN'T TELL ANYBODY...
...ALL THE WISDOM, SKILLS, AND SECRET ARTS THAT THEY GAINED FROM THEIR RESEARCH WOULD BE LOST IN DARKNESS...
...MEANING THAT THEIR EXISTENCE WOULD FADE AWAY.
THEY LEAVE BEHIND BOOKS OF MAGIC TO SERVE AS PROOF OF THEIR EX-ISTENCE.
......
THEN YOU GET IT. THE TEXTS OF TRUTH THAT YOU CAME IN CONTACT WITH IN ENGLAND...
...HAD SURVIVED SEVERAL ATTEMPTS AT DESTRUCTION AS A BANNED BOOK AND FORCED A SEVERE BURDEN ON WHOMEVER SHOULD CHALLENGE HERSELF WITH READING IT. FOR IT INCLUDED WITHIN ITS TEXTS A BLACK MAGIC THAT COULD BE CALLED A CURSE.

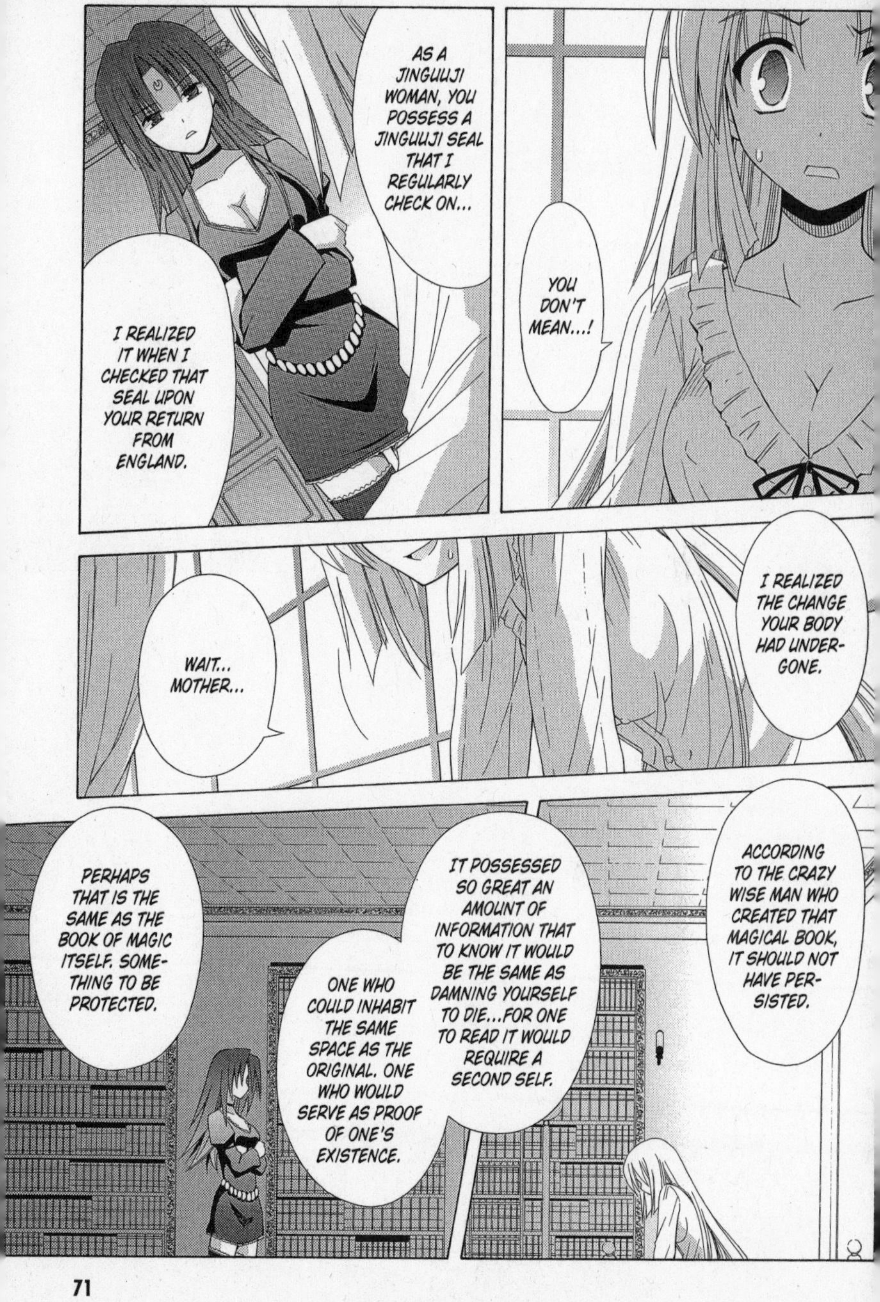
YOU DON'T MEAN...!
AS A JINGUUJI WOMAN, YOU POSSESS A JINGUUJI SEAL THAT I REGULARLY CHECK ON...
I REALIZED IT WHEN I CHECKED THAT SEAL UPON YOUR RETURN FROM ENGLAND.
I REALIZED THE CHANGE YOUR BODY HAD UNDER-GONE.
WAIT... MOTHER...
ACCORDING TO THE CRAZY WISE MAN WHO CREATED THAT MAGICAL BOOK, IT SHOULD NOT HAVE PER-SISTED.
IT POSSESSED SO GREAT AN AMOUNT OF INFORMATION THAT TO KNOW IT WOULD BE THE SAME AS DAMNING YOURSELF TO DIE...FOR ONE TO READ IT WOULD REQUIRE A SECOND SELF.
ONE WHO COULD INHABIT THE SAME SPACE AS THE ORIGINAL. ONE WHO WOULD SERVE AS PROOF OF ONE'S EXISTENCE.
PERHAPS THAT IS THE SAME AS THE BOOK OF MAGIC ITSELF. SOME-THING TO BE PROTECTED.

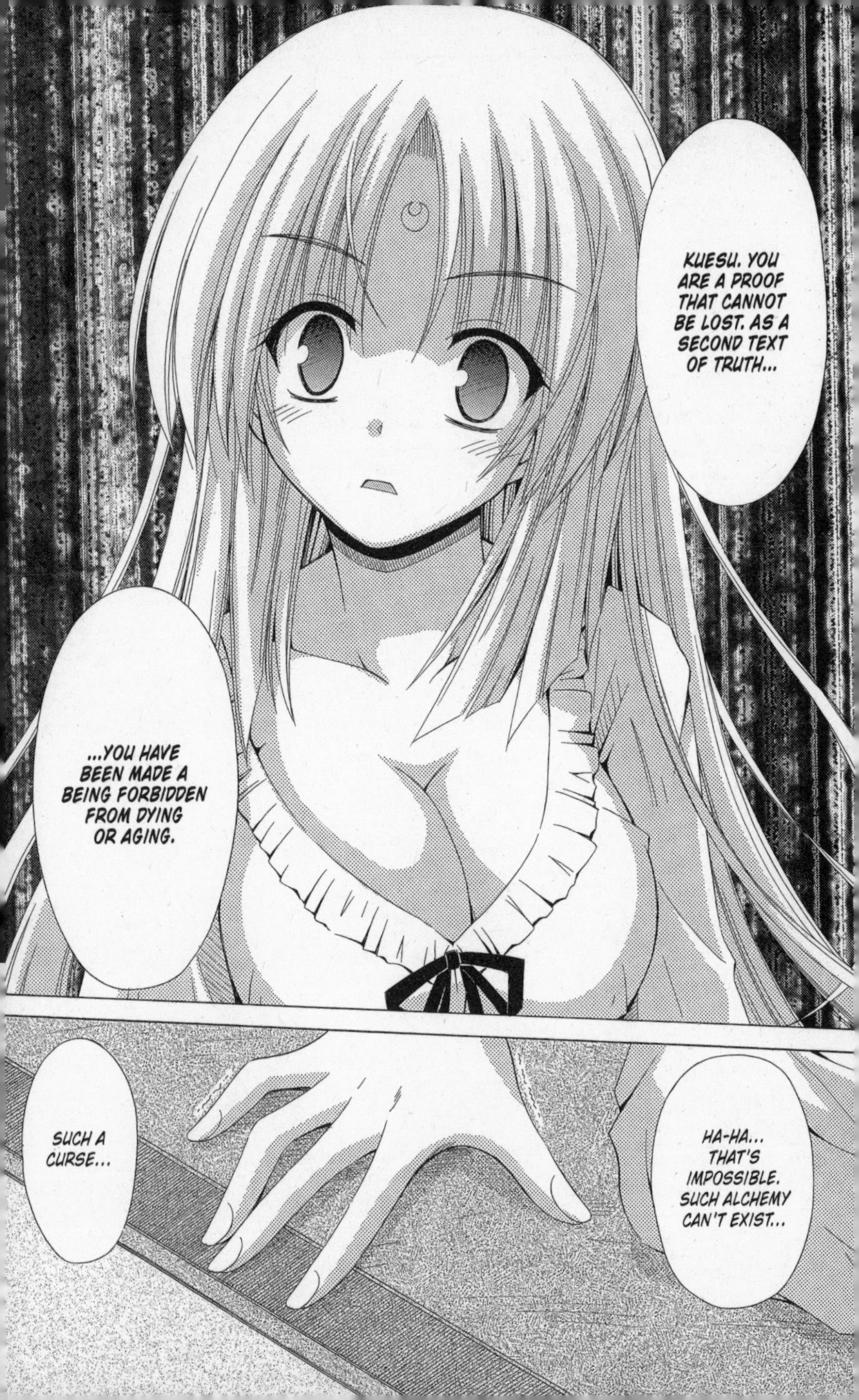
KUESU. YOU ARE A PROOF THAT CANNOT BE LOST. AS A SECOND TEXT OF TRUTH...
...YOU HAVE BEEN MADE A BEING FORBIDDEN FROM DYING OR AGING.
HA-HA... THAT'S IMPOSSIBLE. SUCH ALCHEMY CAN'T EXIST...
SUCH A CURSE...

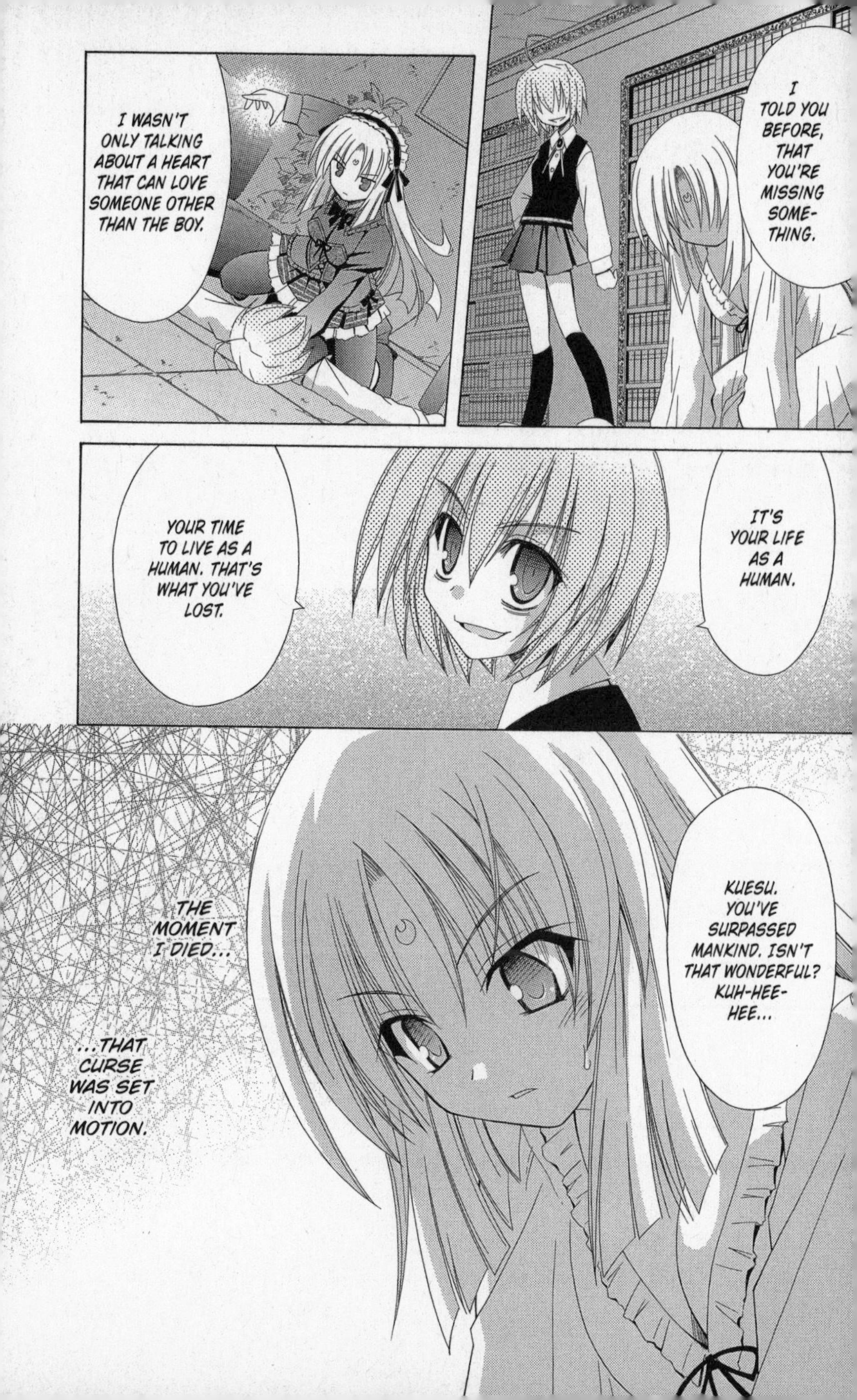
I TOLD YOU BEFORE, THAT YOU'RE MISSING SOME-THING.
I WASN'T ONLY TALKING ABOUT A HEART THAT CAN LOVE SOMEONE OTHER THAN THE BOY.
IT'S YOUR LIFE AS A HUMAN.
YOUR TIME TO LIVE AS A HUMAN. THAT'S WHAT YOU'VE LOST.
KUESU. YOU'VE SURPASSED MANKIND. ISN'T THAT WONDERFUL? KUH-HEE-HEE...
THE MOMENT I DIED...
...THAT CURSE WAS SET INTO MOTION.

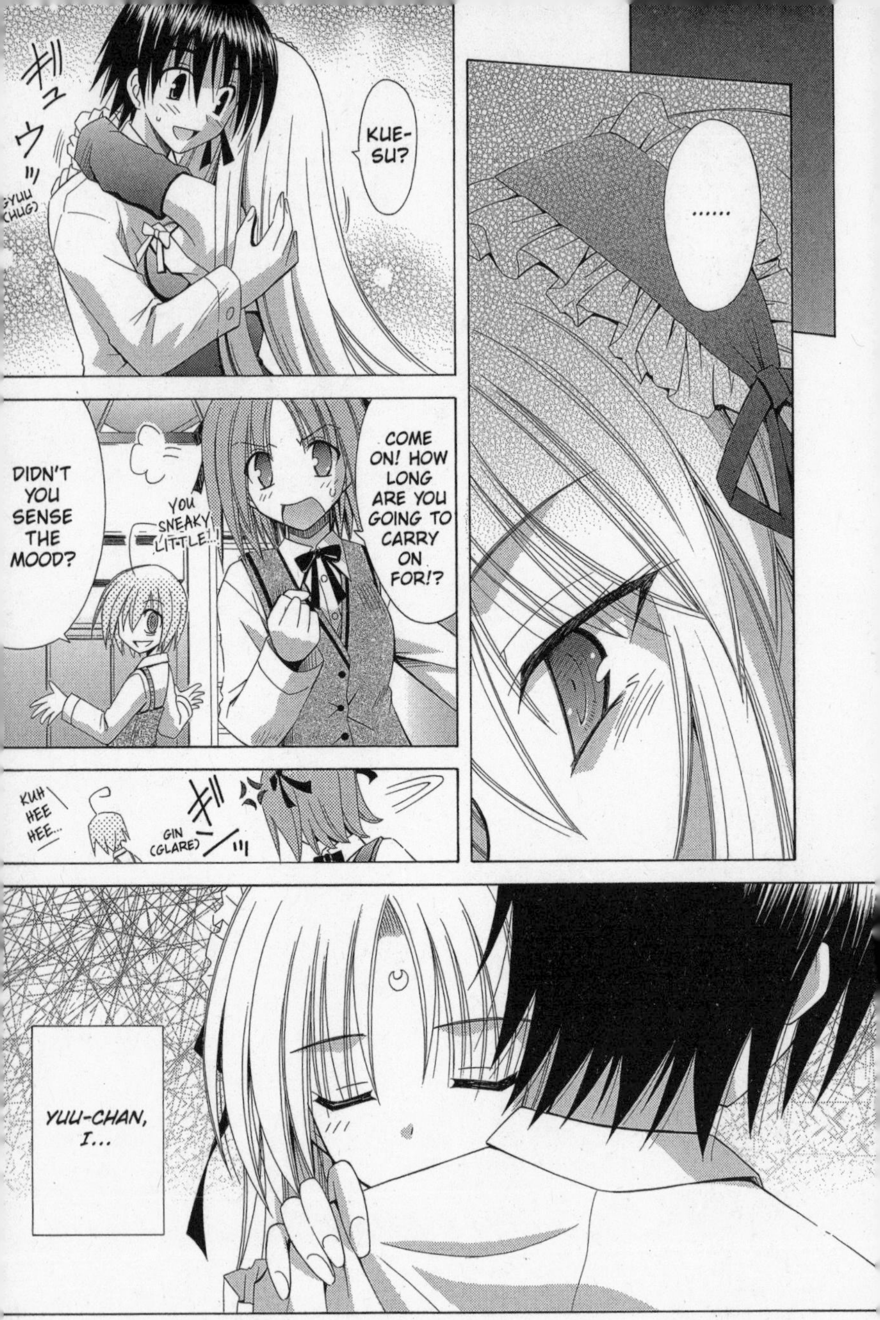
GYUU (HUG)
KUE-SU?
......
COME ON! HOW LONG ARE YOU GOING TO CARRY ON FOR!?
YOU SNEAKY LITTLE...!
DIDN'T YOU SENSE THE MOOD?
GIN (GLARE)
KUH HEE HEE...
YUU-CHAN, I...

OMAMORI HIMARI

OMAMORI HIMARI

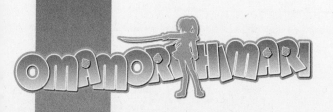

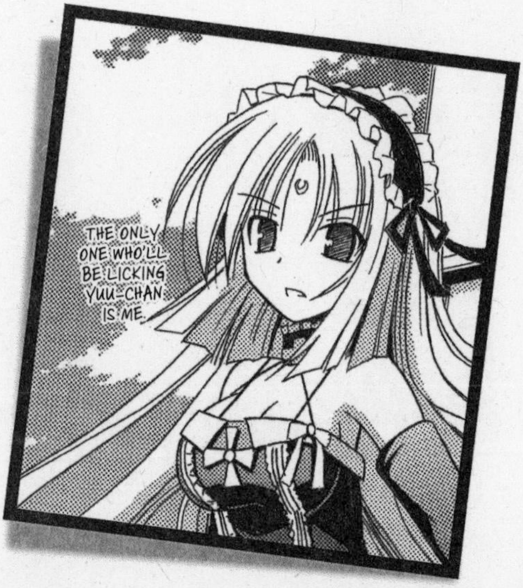
THE ONLY ONE WHO'LL BE LICKING YUU-CHAN IS ME.

MENAGERIE 66: THE TRIGGER TO THE CAT'S ACCIDENTAL FIRING

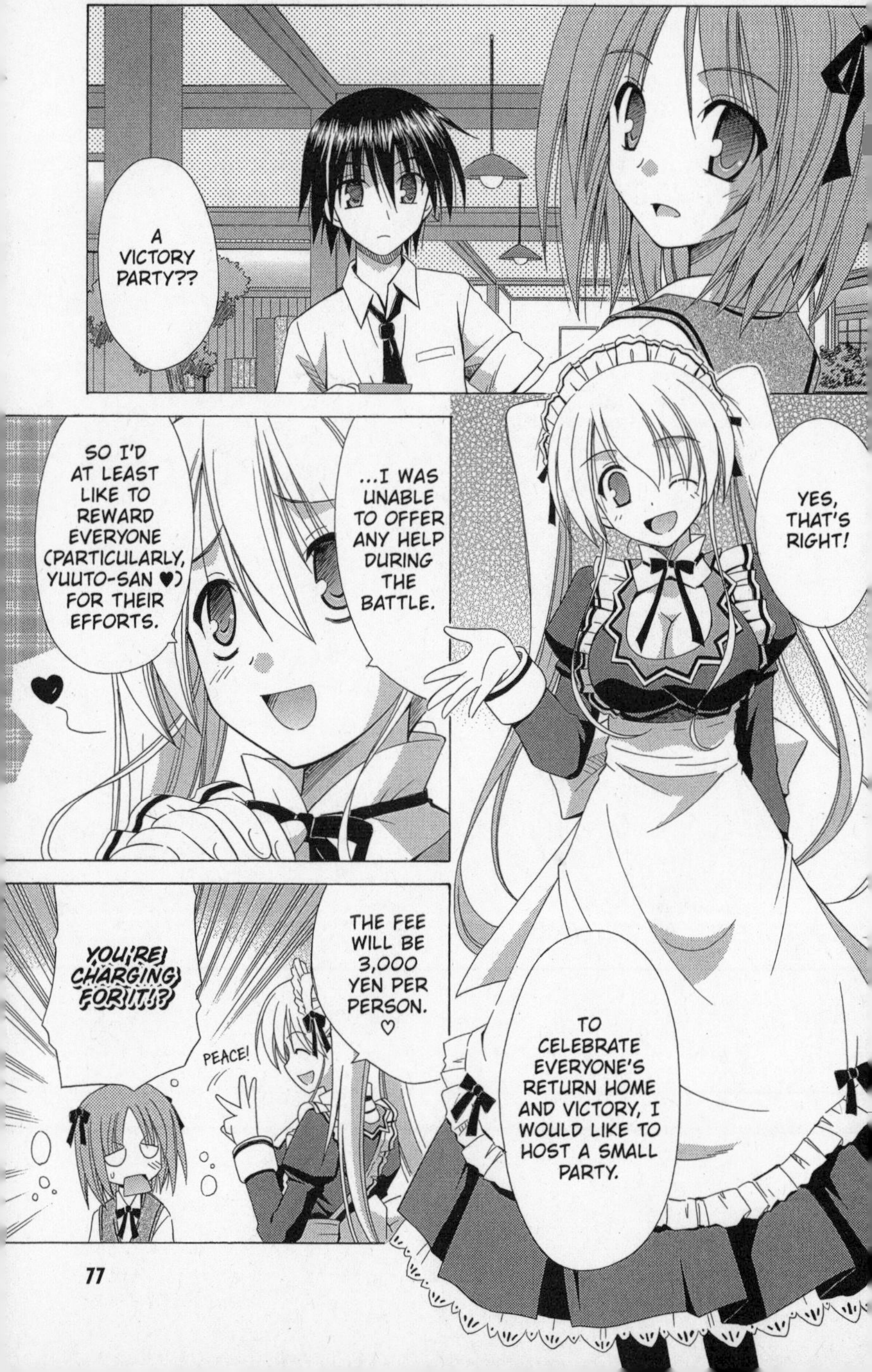
A VICTORY PARTY??
YES, THAT'S RIGHT!
TO CELEBRATE EVERYONE'S RETURN HOME AND VICTORY, I WOULD LIKE TO HOST A SMALL PARTY.
...I WAS UNABLE TO OFFER ANY HELP DURING THE BATTLE.
SO I'D AT LEAST LIKE TO REWARD EVERYONE (PARTICULARLY, YUUTO-SAN ♥) FOR THEIR EFFORTS.
THE FEE WILL BE 3,000 YEN PER PERSON. ♡
PEACE!
YOU'RE CHARGING FOR IT!?

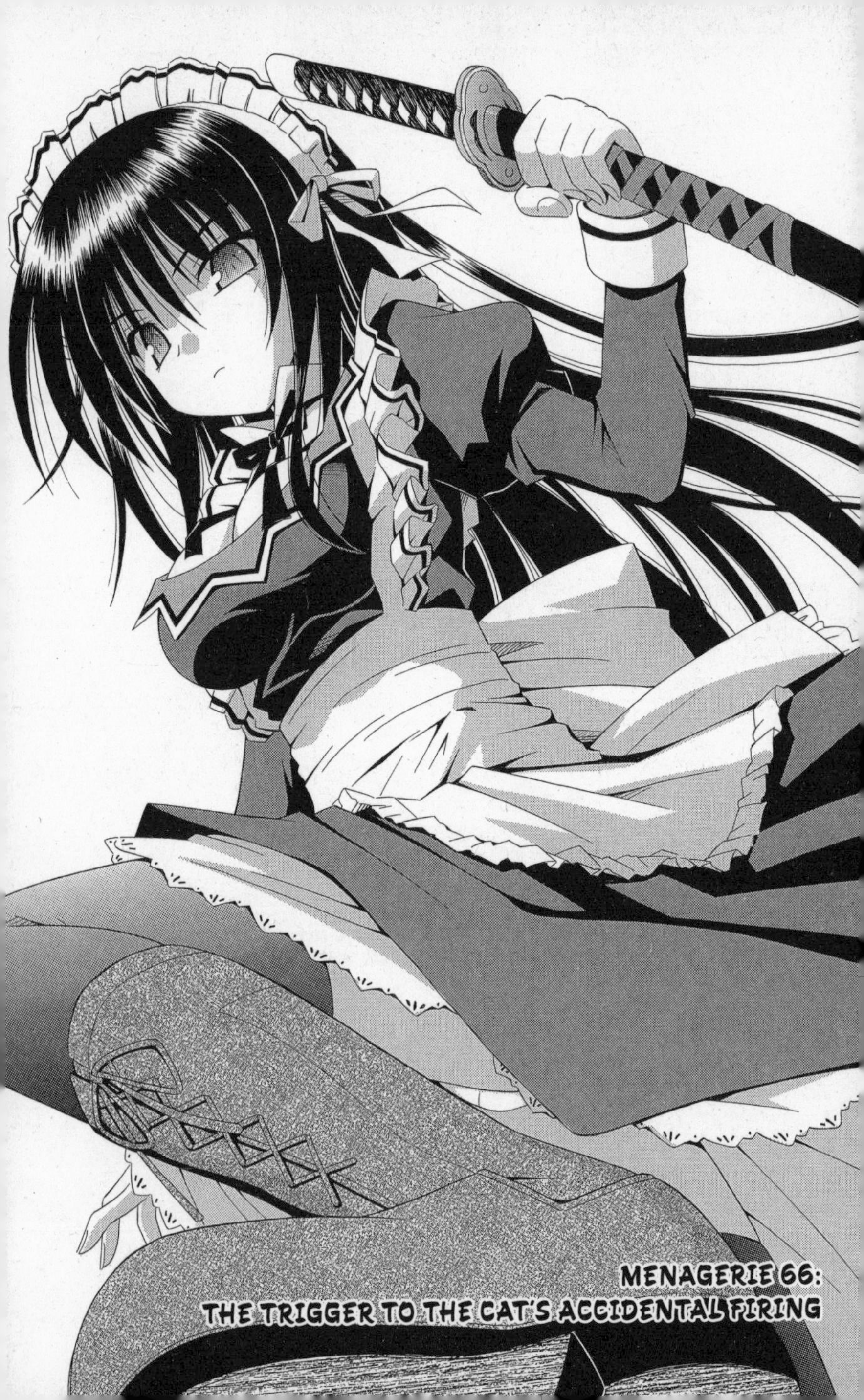
MENAGERIE 66:
THE TRIGGER TO THE CAT'S ACCIDENTAL FIRING

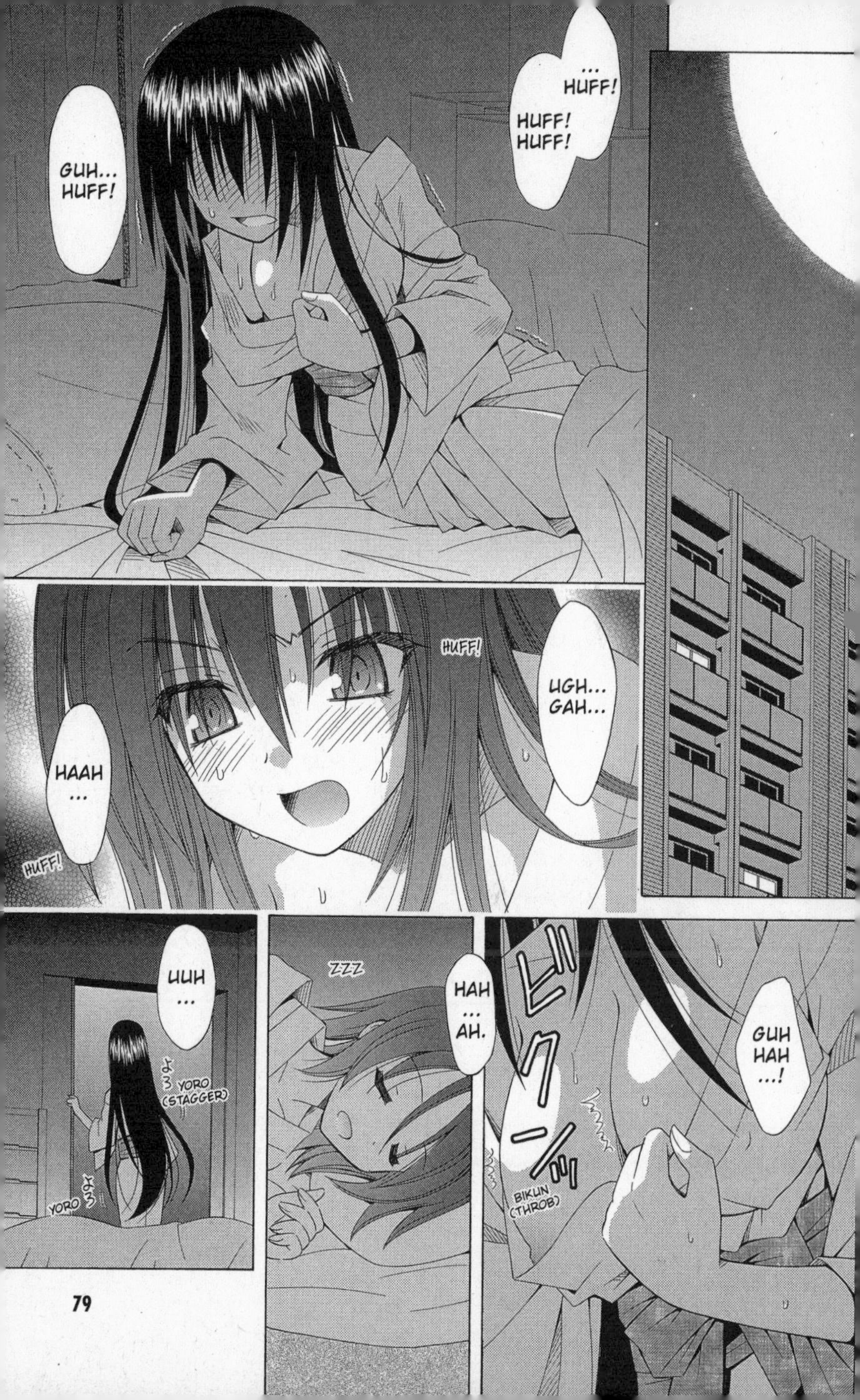

... HUFF! HUFF! HUFF!
GUH... HUFF!
HUFF!
UGH... GAH...
HAAH ...
HUFF!
GUH HAH ...!
HAH ... AH.
BIKUN (THROB)
Z-Z-Z
UUH ...
よろ YORO (STAGGER)
YORO よろ

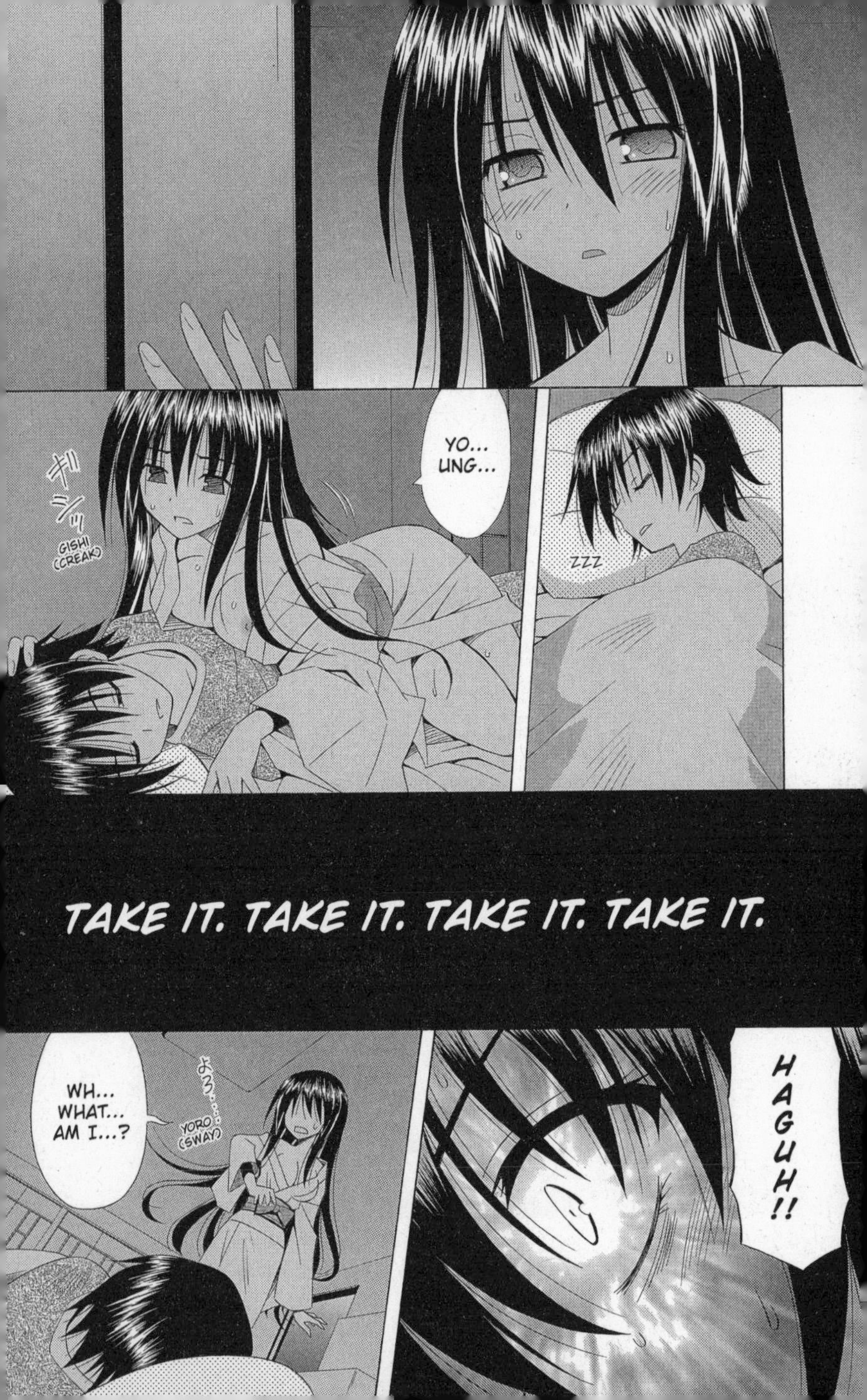
ZZZ
YO... UNG...
ギシッ
GISHI (CREAK)
TAKE IT. TAKE IT. TAKE IT. TAKE IT.
HAGUH!!
よろ...
YORO (SWAY)
WH... WHAT... AM I...?

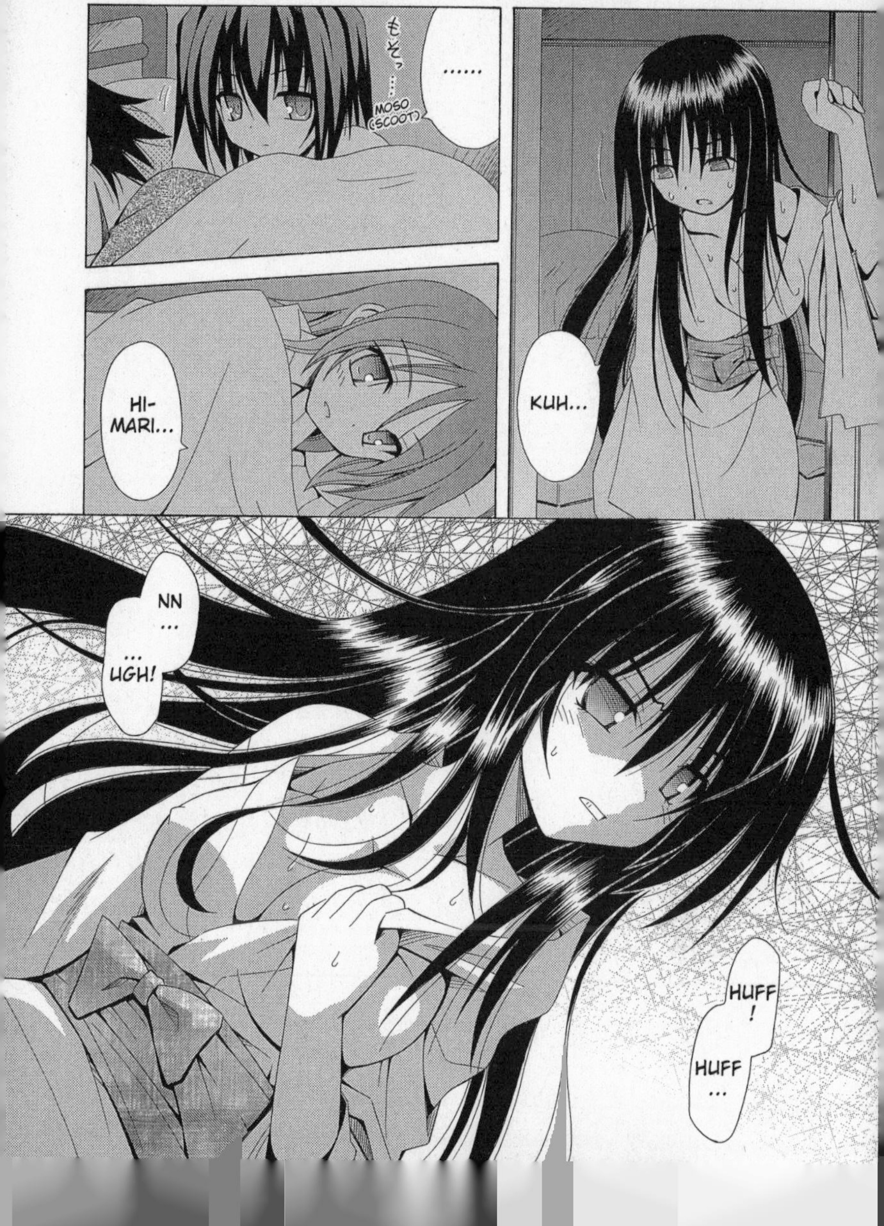
KUH...
......
もぞっ…
MOSO (SCOOT)
HI-MARI...
NN... ...UGH!
HUFF! HUFF...

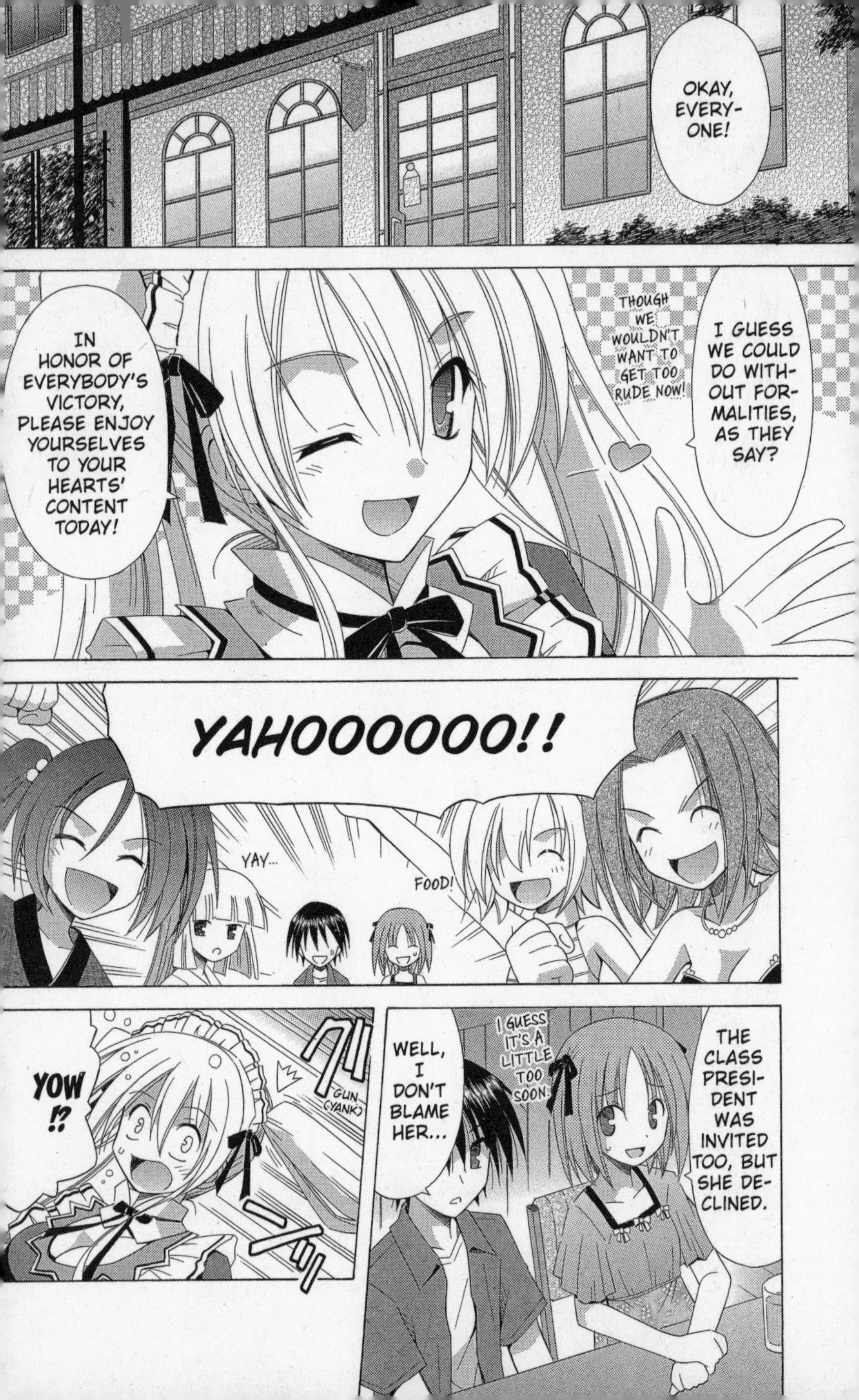
OKAY, EVERYONE!
I GUESS WE COULD DO WITHOUT FORMALITIES, AS THEY SAY?
THOUGH WE WOULDN'T WANT TO GET TOO RUDE NOW!
IN HONOR OF EVERYBODY'S VICTORY, PLEASE ENJOY YOURSELVES TO YOUR HEARTS' CONTENT TODAY!
YAHOOOOOOO!!
FOOD!
YAY...
THE CLASS PRESIDENT WAS INVITED TOO, BUT SHE DECLINED.
I GUESS IT'S A LITTLE TOO SOON.
WELL, I DON'T BLAME HER...
GUN (YANK)
YOW !?

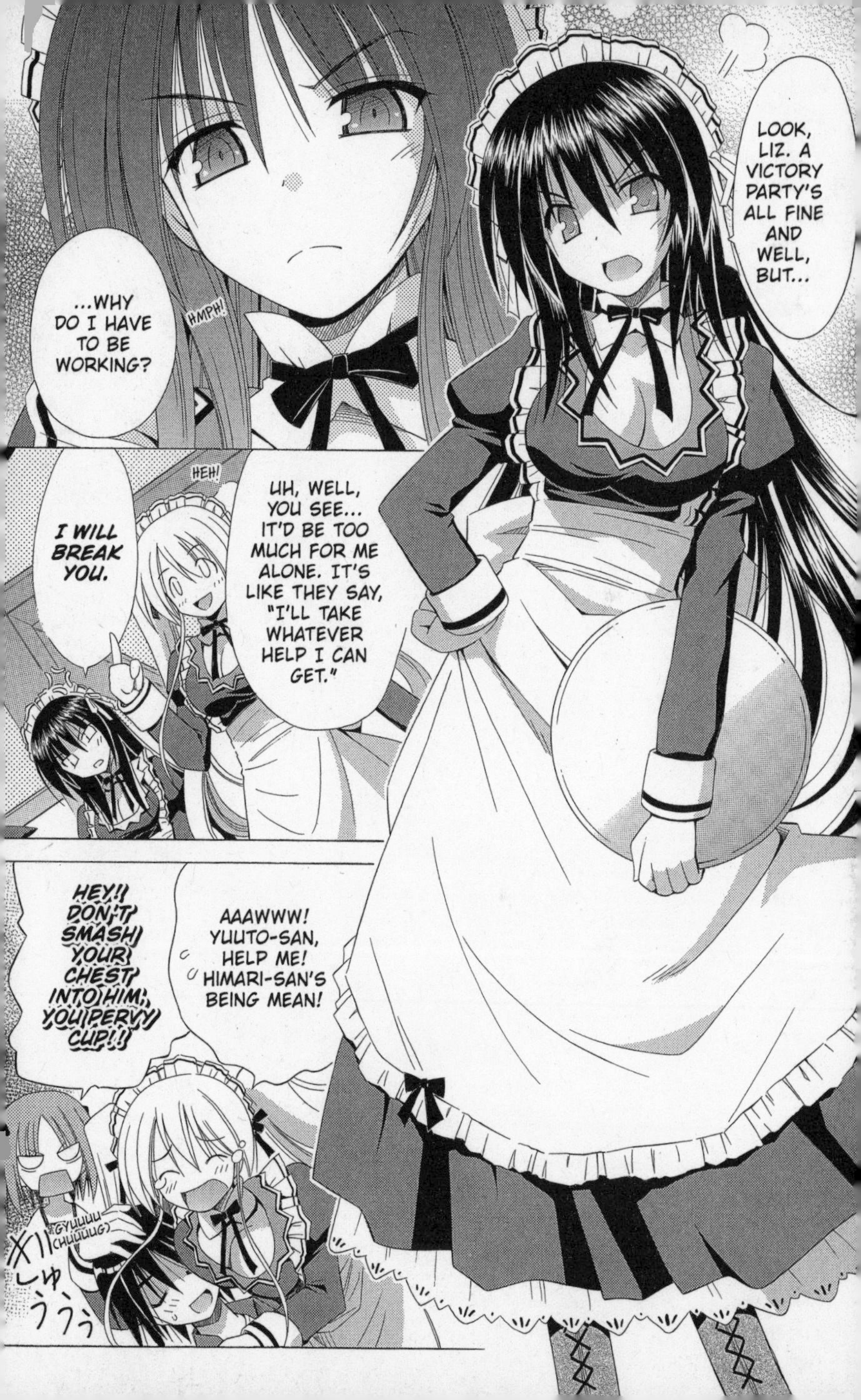
LOOK, LIZ. A VICTORY PARTY'S ALL FINE AND WELL, BUT...
...WHY DO I HAVE TO BE WORKING?
HMPH!
UH, WELL, YOU SEE... IT'D BE TOO MUCH FOR ME ALONE. IT'S LIKE THEY SAY, "I'LL TAKE WHATEVER HELP I CAN GET."
HEH!
I WILL BREAK YOU.
AAAWWW! YUUTO-SAN, HELP ME! HIMARI-SAN'S BEING MEAN!
HEY!! DON'T SMASH YOUR CHEST INTO HIM, YOU PERVY CUP!!
ぎゅううぅ
GYUUUU (CHUUUUG)

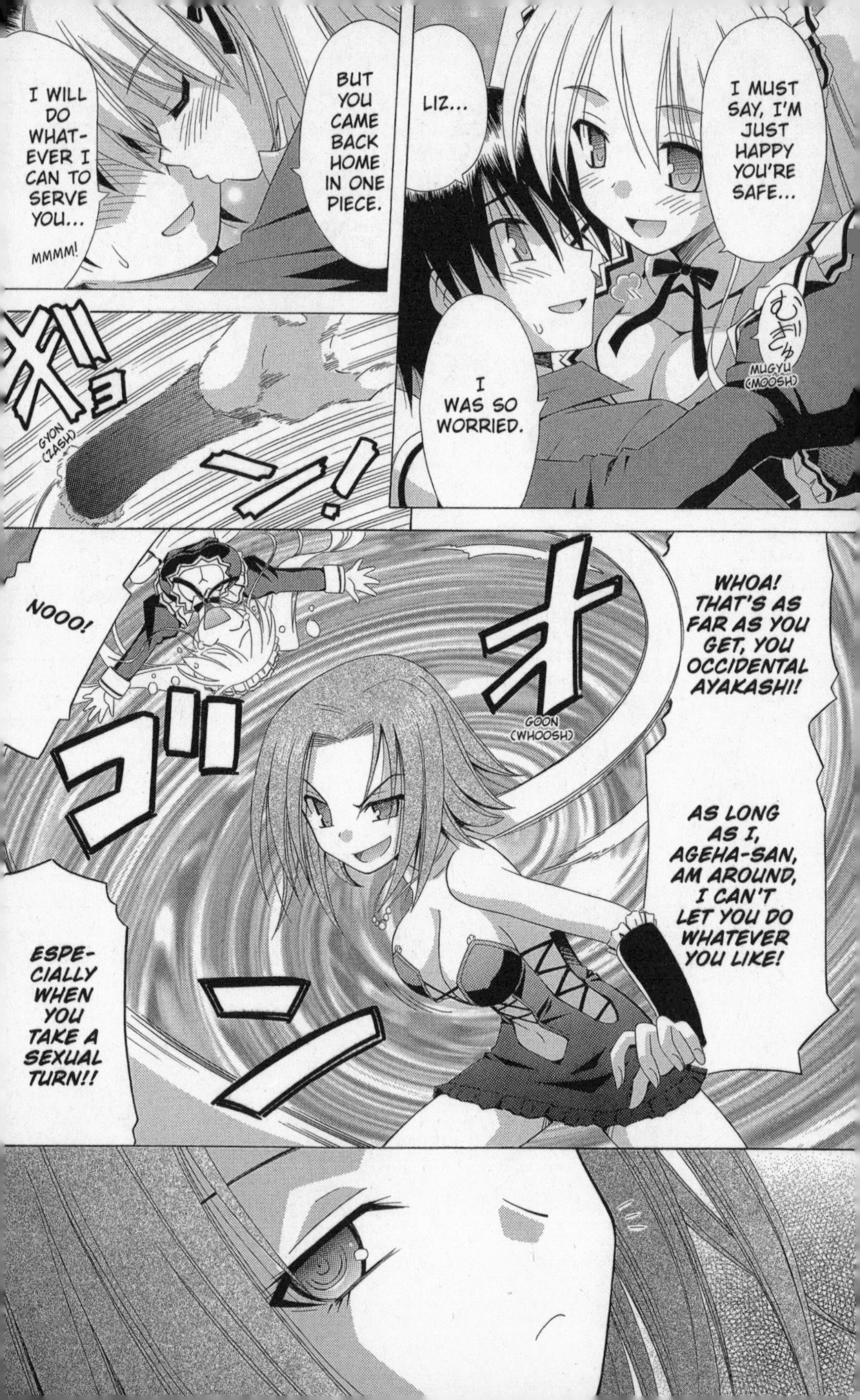
I MUST SAY, I'M JUST HAPPY YOU'RE SAFE...
LIZ...
MUGYU (MOOSH)
I WAS SO WORRIED.
BUT YOU CAME BACK HOME IN ONE PIECE.
I WILL DO WHAT-EVER I CAN TO SERVE YOU...
MMMM!
GYON (ZASH)
WHOA! THAT'S AS FAR AS YOU GET, YOU OCCIDENTAL AYAKASHI!
AS LONG AS I, AGEHA-SAN, AM AROUND, I CAN'T LET YOU DO WHATEVER YOU LIKE!
GOON (WHOOSH)
NOOO!
ESPE-CIALLY WHEN YOU TAKE A SEXUAL TURN!!

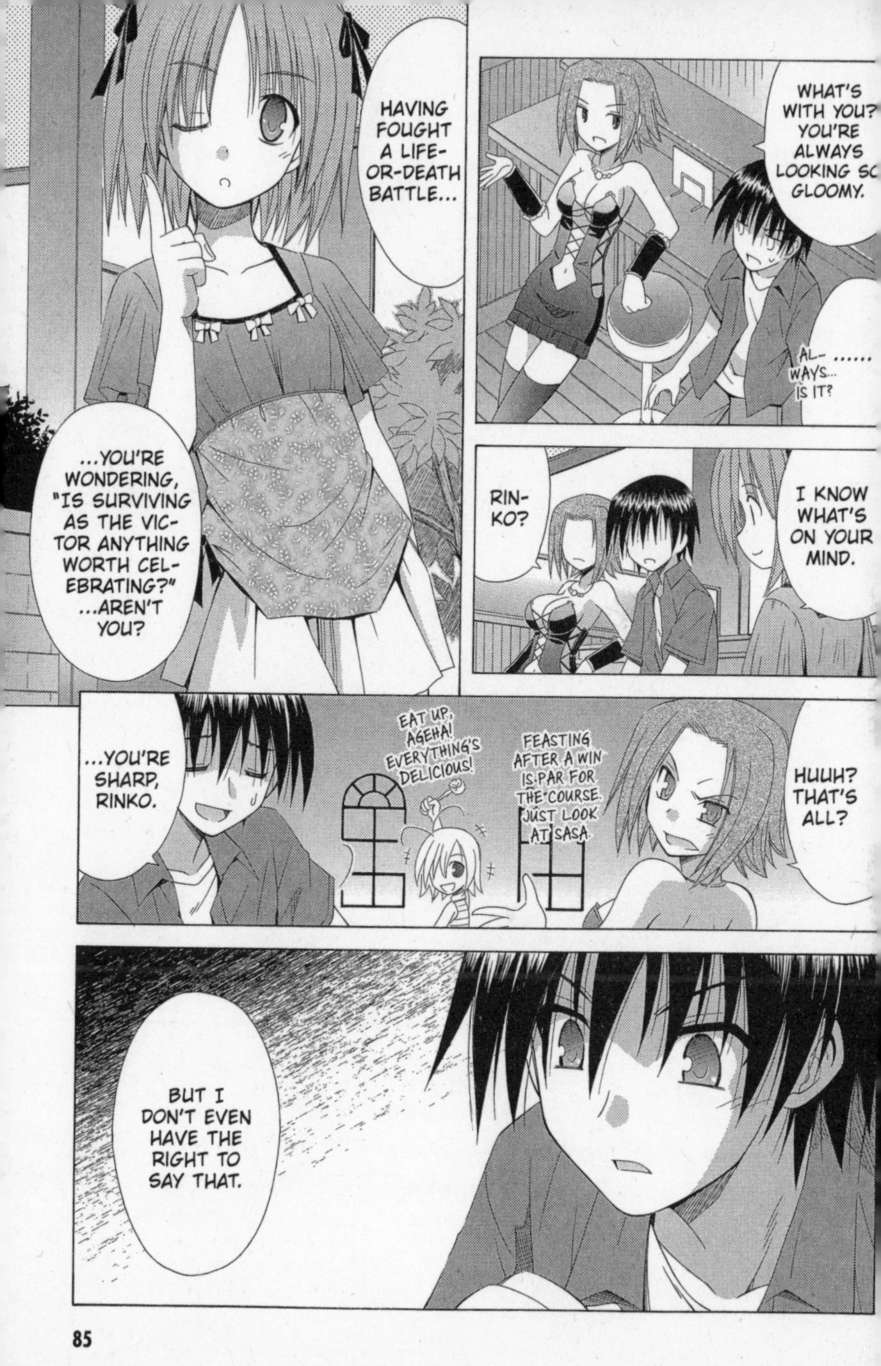
WHAT'S WITH YOU? YOU'RE ALWAYS LOOKING SO GLOOMY.
......
AL-WAYS... IS IT?
I KNOW WHAT'S ON YOUR MIND.
RIN-KO?
HAVING FOUGHT A LIFE-OR-DEATH BATTLE...
...YOU'RE WONDERING, "IS SURVIVING AS THE VIC-TOR ANYTHING WORTH CEL-EBRATING?" ...AREN'T YOU?
HUUH? THAT'S ALL?
FEASTING AFTER A WIN IS PAR FOR THE COURSE. JUST LOOK AT SASA.
EAT UP, AGEHA! EVERYTHING'S DELICIOUS!
...YOU'RE SHARP, RINKO.
BUT I DON'T EVEN HAVE THE RIGHT TO SAY THAT.

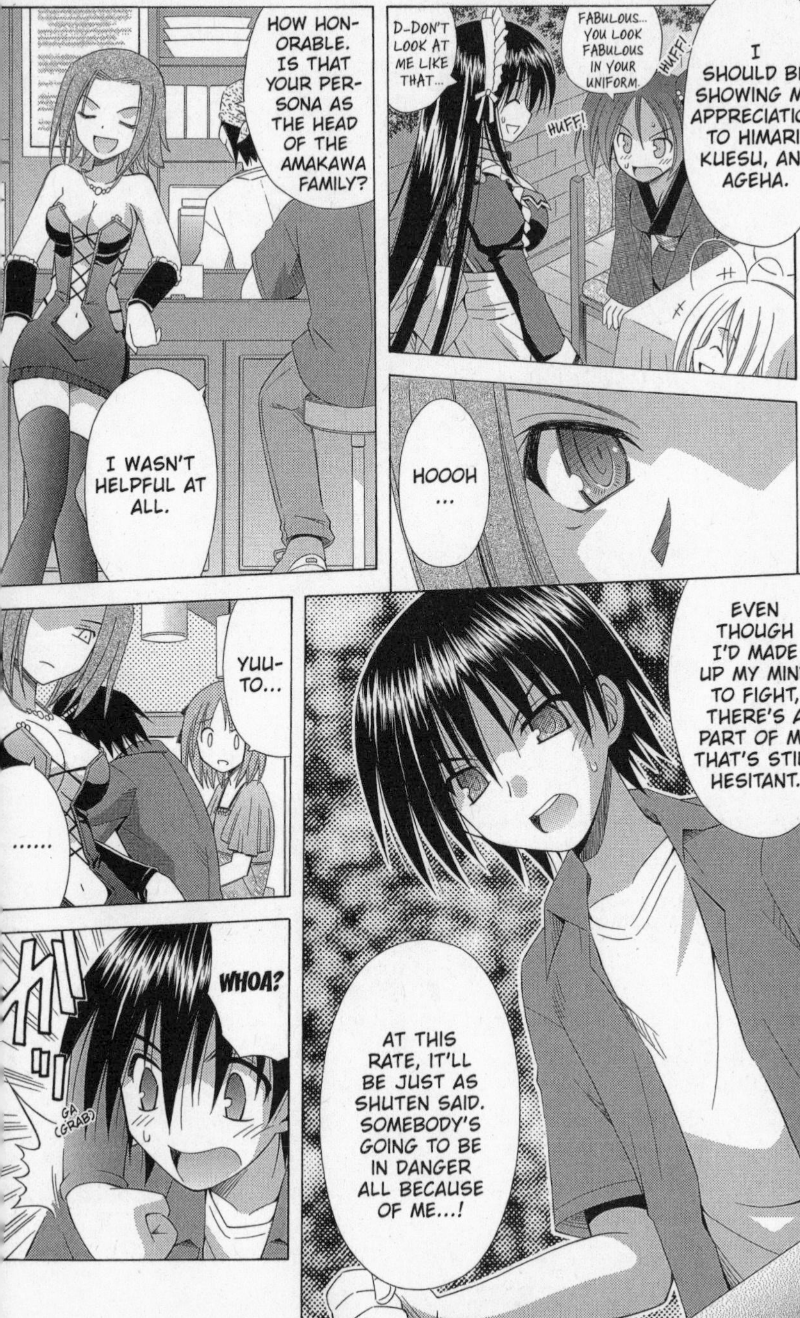
I SHOULD BE SHOWING MY APPRECIATION TO HIMARI, KUESU, AND AGEHA.
HUFF!
FABULOUS... YOU LOOK FABULOUS IN YOUR UNIFORM.
HUFF!
D-DON'T LOOK AT ME LIKE THAT...
HOOOH ...
HOW HON-ORABLE. IS THAT YOUR PER-SONA AS THE HEAD OF THE AMAKAWA FAMILY?
I WASN'T HELPFUL AT ALL.
EVEN THOUGH I'D MADE UP MY MIND TO FIGHT, THERE'S A PART OF ME THAT'S STILL HESITANT.
AT THIS RATE, IT'LL BE JUST AS SHUTEN SAID. SOMEBODY'S GOING TO BE IN DANGER ALL BECAUSE OF ME...!
YUU-TO...
......
WHOA?
GA (GRAB)

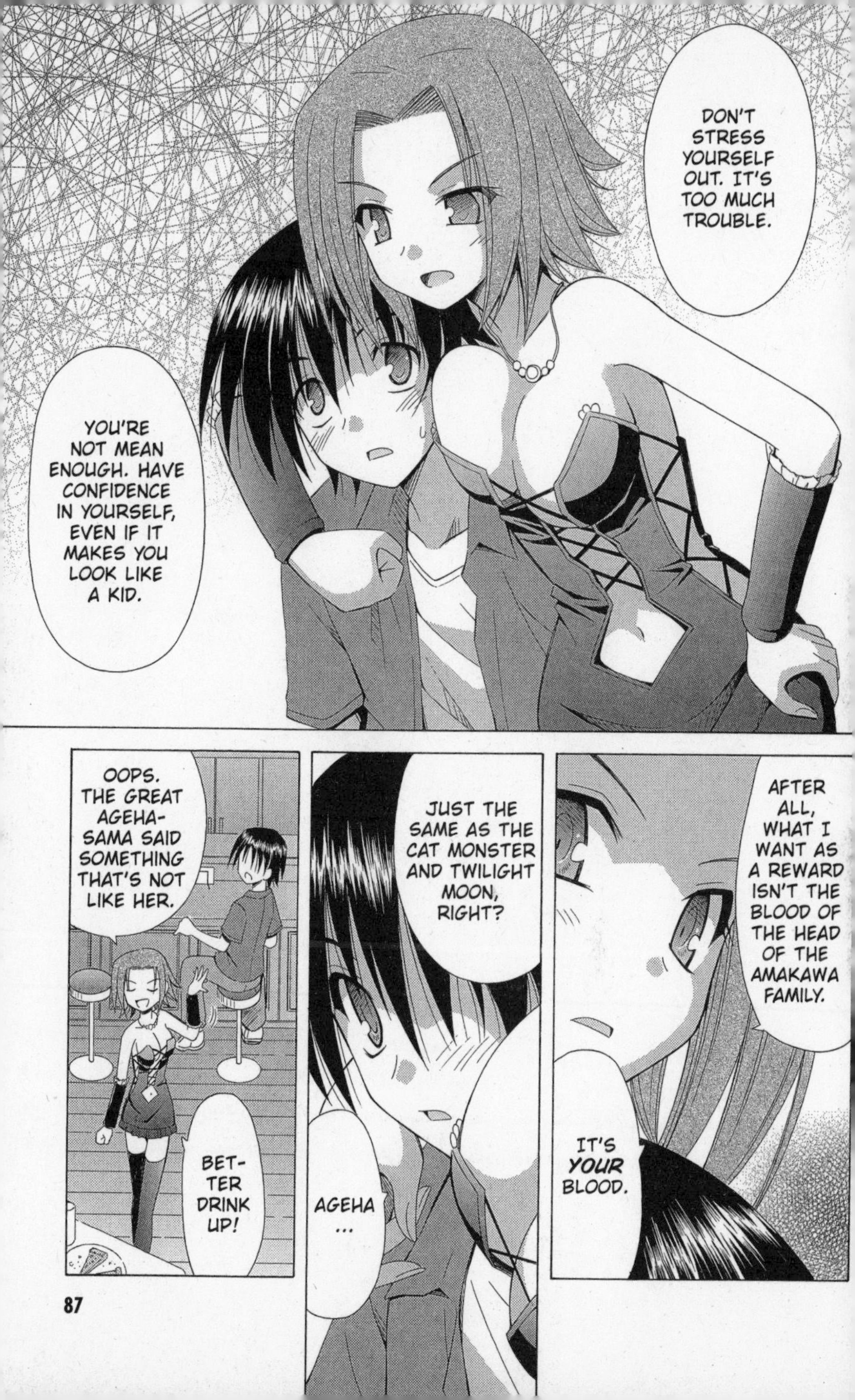
DON'T STRESS YOURSELF OUT. IT'S TOO MUCH TROUBLE.
YOU'RE NOT MEAN ENOUGH. HAVE CONFIDENCE IN YOURSELF, EVEN IF IT MAKES YOU LOOK LIKE A KID.
AFTER ALL, WHAT I WANT AS A REWARD ISN'T THE BLOOD OF THE HEAD OF THE AMAKAWA FAMILY.
IT'S *YOUR* BLOOD.
JUST THE SAME AS THE CAT MONSTER AND TWILIGHT MOON, RIGHT?
AGEHA...
OOPS. THE GREAT AGEHA-SAMA SAID SOMETHING THAT'S NOT LIKE HER.
BET-TER DRINK UP!

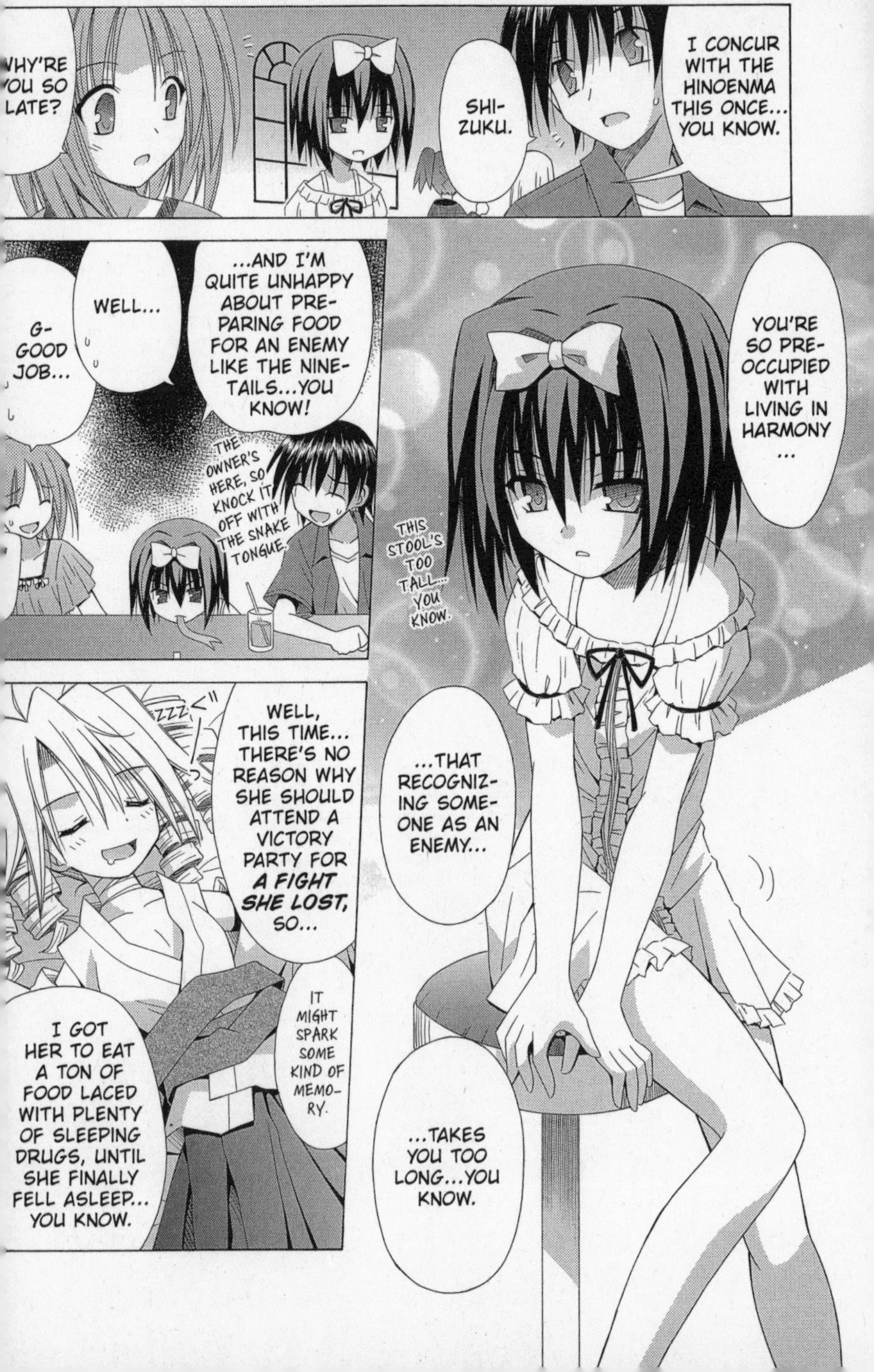
I CONCUR WITH THE HINOENMA THIS ONCE... YOU KNOW.
SHI-ZUKU.
WHY'RE YOU SO LATE?
YOU'RE SO PRE-OCCUPIED WITH LIVING IN HARMONY...
THIS STOOL'S TOO TALL... YOU KNOW.
...THAT RECOGNIZING SOMEONE AS AN ENEMY...
...TAKES YOU TOO LONG...YOU KNOW.
...AND I'M QUITE UNHAPPY ABOUT PREPARING FOOD FOR AN ENEMY LIKE THE NINE-TAILS...YOU KNOW!
WELL...
G-GOOD JOB...
THE OWNER'S HERE, SO KNOCK IT OFF WITH THE SNAKE TONGUE.
WELL, THIS TIME... THERE'S NO REASON WHY SHE SHOULD ATTEND A VICTORY PARTY FOR ***A FIGHT SHE LOST,*** SO...
ZZZ
IT MIGHT SPARK SOME KIND OF MEMORY.
I GOT HER TO EAT A TON OF FOOD LACED WITH PLENTY OF SLEEPING DRUGS, UNTIL SHE FINALLY FELL ASLEEP... YOU KNOW.

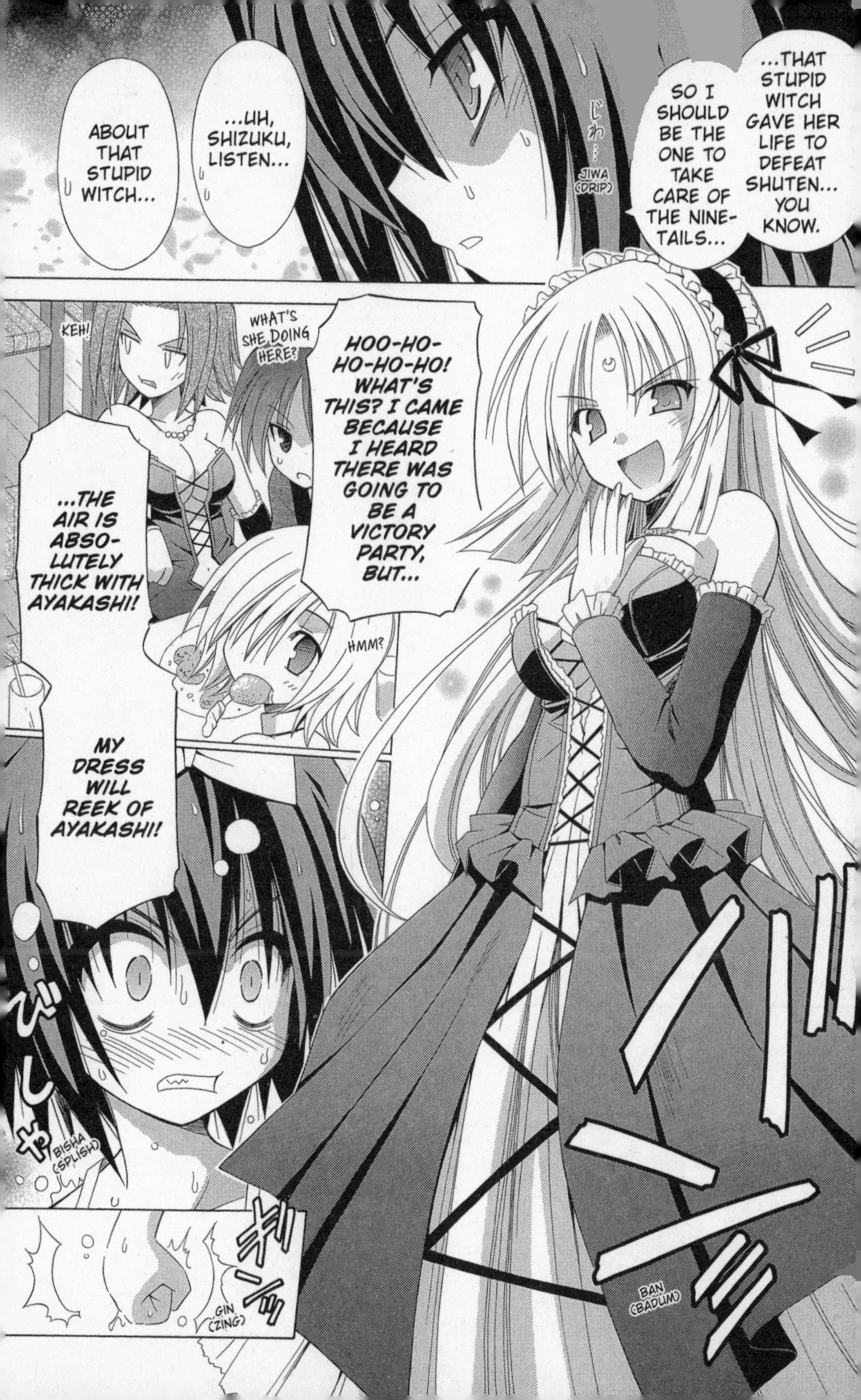
...THAT STUPID WITCH GAVE HER LIFE TO DEFEAT SHUTEN... YOU KNOW.
SO I SHOULD BE THE ONE TO TAKE CARE OF THE NINE-TAILS...
じわ…
JIWA (DRIP)
...UH, SHIZUKU, LISTEN...
ABOUT THAT STUPID WITCH...
HOO-HO-HO-HO-HO! WHAT'S THIS? I CAME BECAUSE I HEARD THERE WAS GOING TO BE A VICTORY PARTY, BUT...
WHAT'S SHE DOING HERE?
KEH!
...THE AIR IS ABSOLUTELY THICK WITH AYAKASHI!
HMM?
MY DRESS WILL REEK OF AYAKASHI!
BAN (BADUM)
びしゃ
BISHA (SPLISH)
ギリ
GIN (ZING)

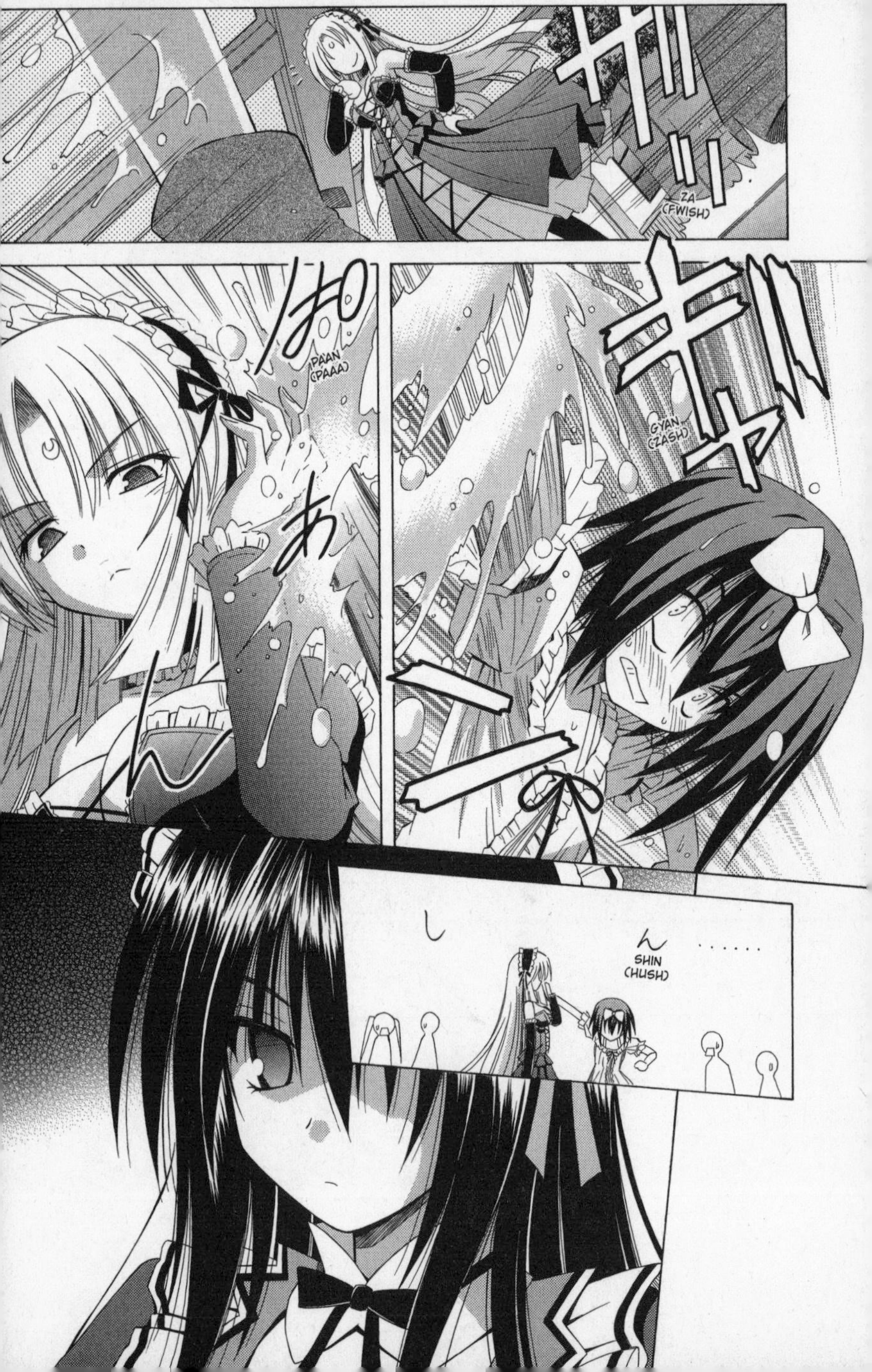
ZA
(FWISH)
GYAN
(ZASH)
PAAN
(PAAA)
SHIN
(HUSH)
......

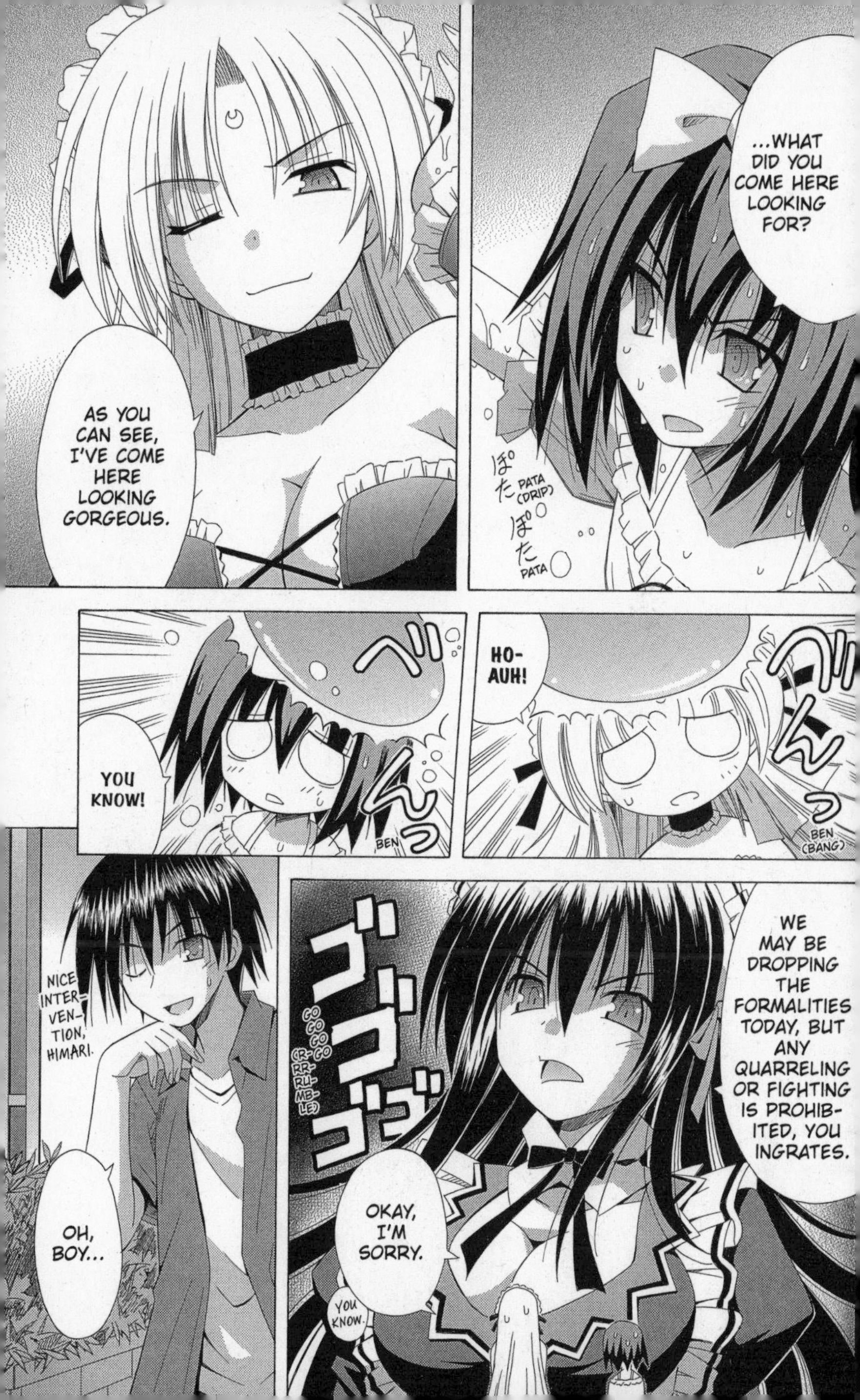
...WHAT DID YOU COME HERE LOOKING FOR?
ぽた PATA (DRIP)
ぽた PATA
AS YOU CAN SEE, I'VE COME HERE LOOKING GORGEOUS.
HO-AUH!
BEN (BANG)
YOU KNOW!
BEN
ゴゴゴ GO GO GO (R-GO RR-RU-MB-LE)
WE MAY BE DROPPING THE FORMALITIES TODAY, BUT ANY QUARRELING OR FIGHTING IS PROHIB-ITED, YOU INGRATES.
OKAY, I'M SORRY.
YOU KNOW.
NICE INTER-VEN-TION, HIMARI.
OH, BOY...

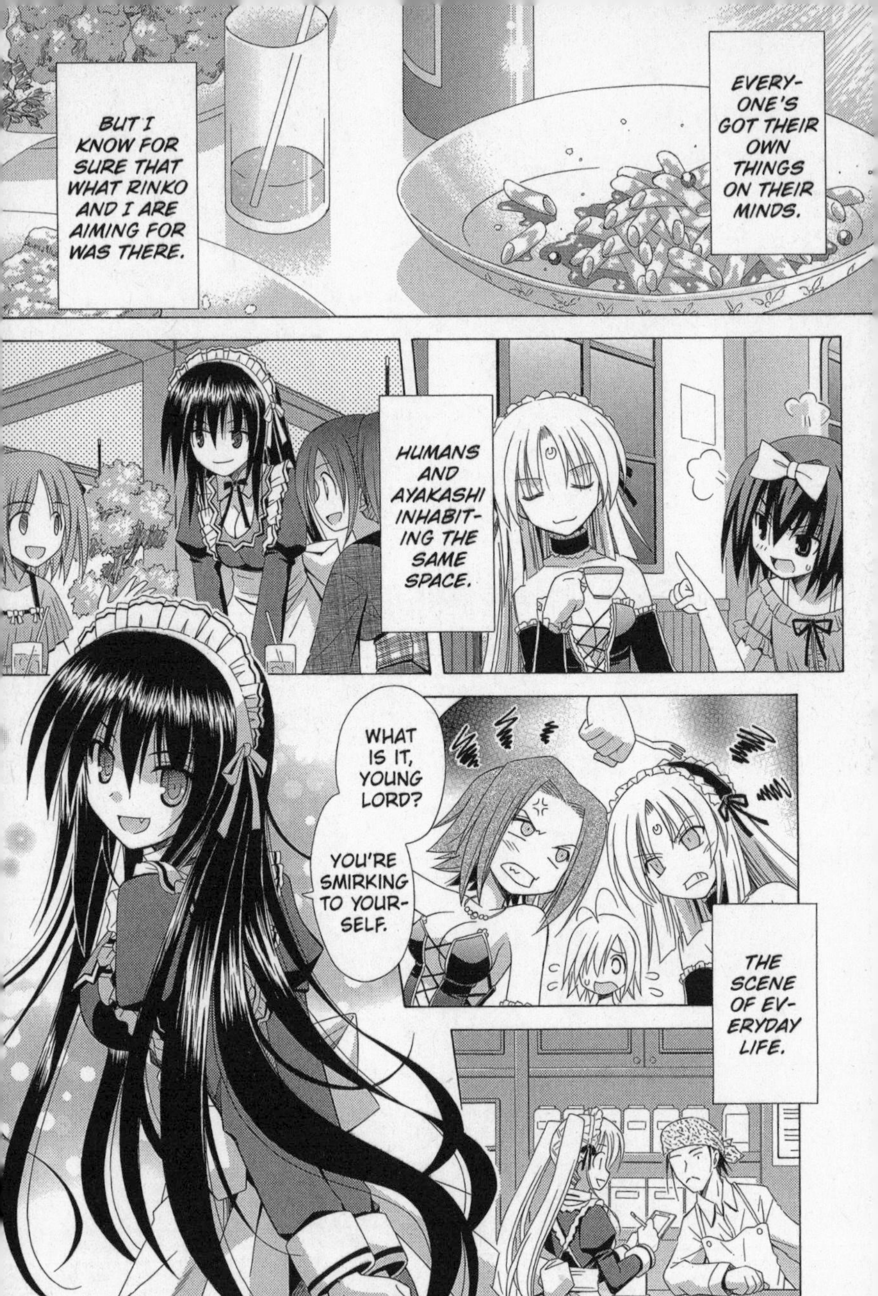
EVERYONE'S GOT THEIR OWN THINGS ON THEIR MINDS.
BUT I KNOW FOR SURE THAT WHAT RINKO AND I ARE AIMING FOR WAS THERE.
HUMANS AND AYAKASHI INHABITING THE SAME SPACE.
WHAT IS IT, YOUNG LORD?
YOU'RE SMIRKING TO YOURSELF.
THE SCENE OF EVERYDAY LIFE.

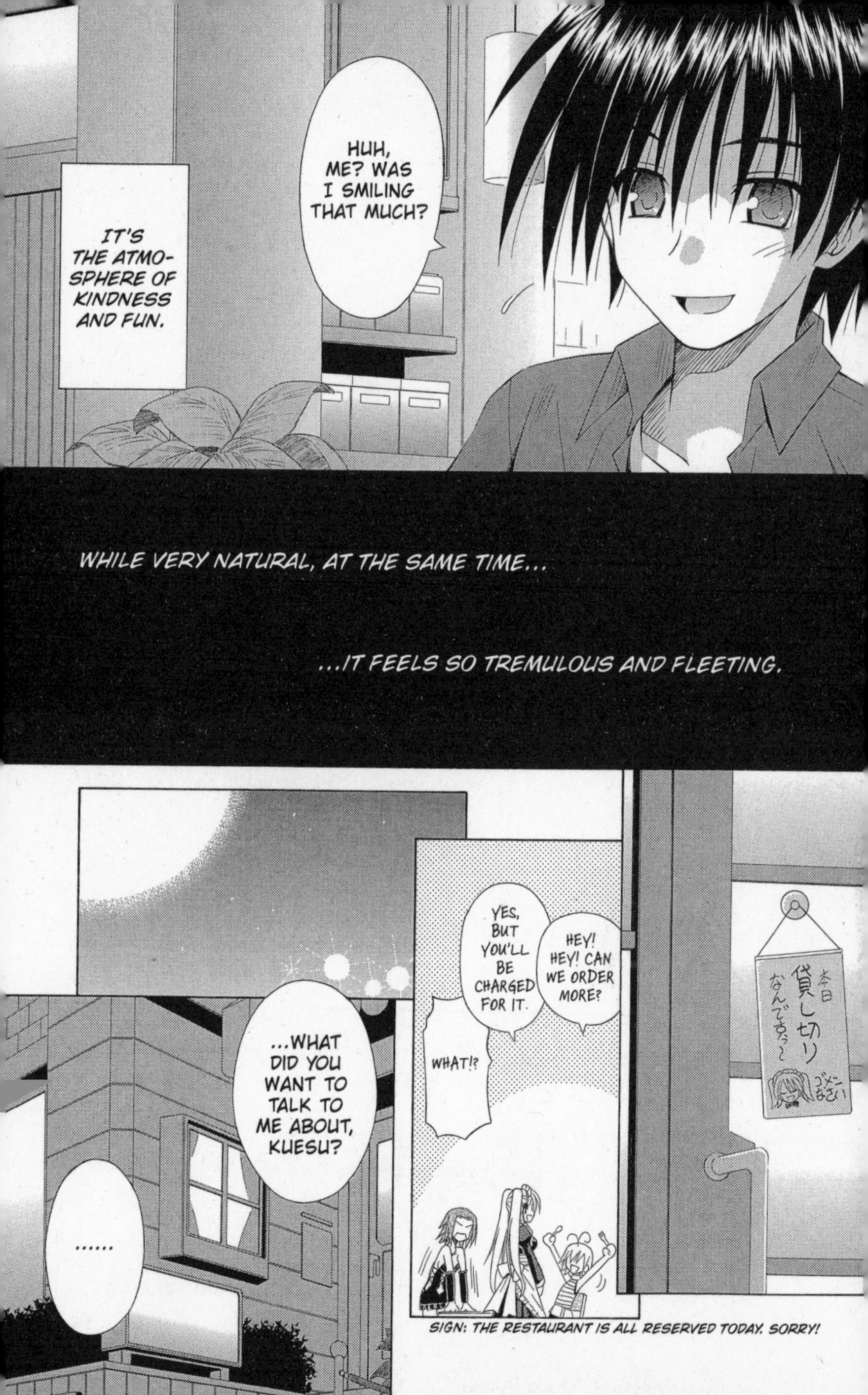
HUH, ME? WAS I SMILING THAT MUCH?
IT'S THE ATMOSPHERE OF KINDNESS AND FUN.
WHILE VERY NATURAL, AT THE SAME TIME...
...IT FEELS SO TREMULOUS AND FLEETING.
本日 貸し切り なんです～
ゴメンなさい
HEY! HEY! CAN WE ORDER MORE?
YES, BUT YOU'LL BE CHARGED FOR IT.
WHAT!?
...WHAT DID YOU WANT TO TALK TO ME ABOUT, KUESU?
......

SIGN: THE RESTAURANT IS ALL RESERVED TODAY. SORRY!

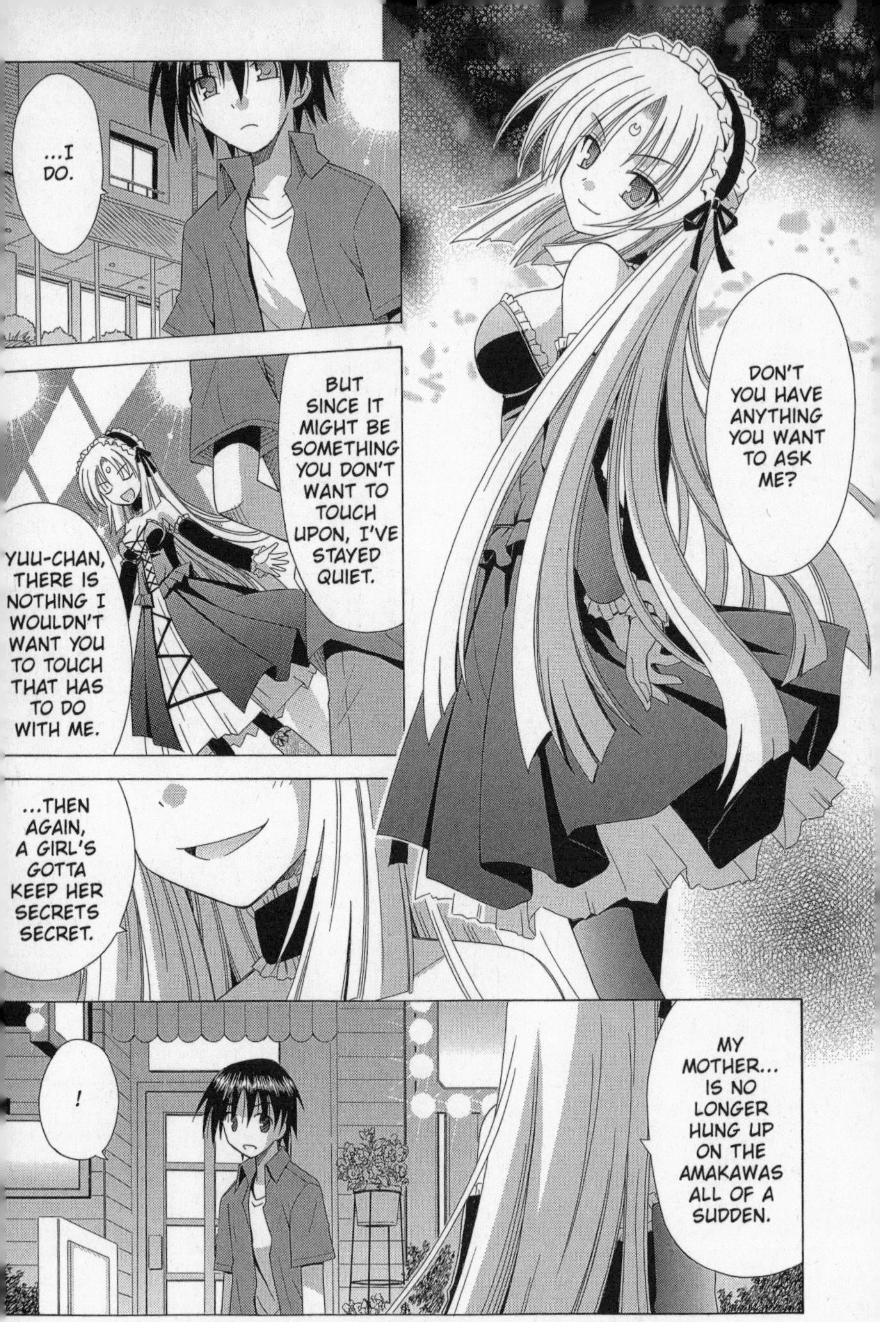
DON'T YOU HAVE ANYTHING YOU WANT TO ASK ME?
...I DO.
BUT SINCE IT MIGHT BE SOMETHING YOU DON'T WANT TO TOUCH UPON, I'VE STAYED QUIET.
YUU-CHAN, THERE IS NOTHING I WOULDN'T WANT YOU TO TOUCH THAT HAS TO DO WITH ME.
...THEN AGAIN, A GIRL'S GOTTA KEEP HER SECRETS SECRET.
MY MOTHER... IS NO LONGER HUNG UP ON THE AMAKAWAS ALL OF A SUDDEN.
!

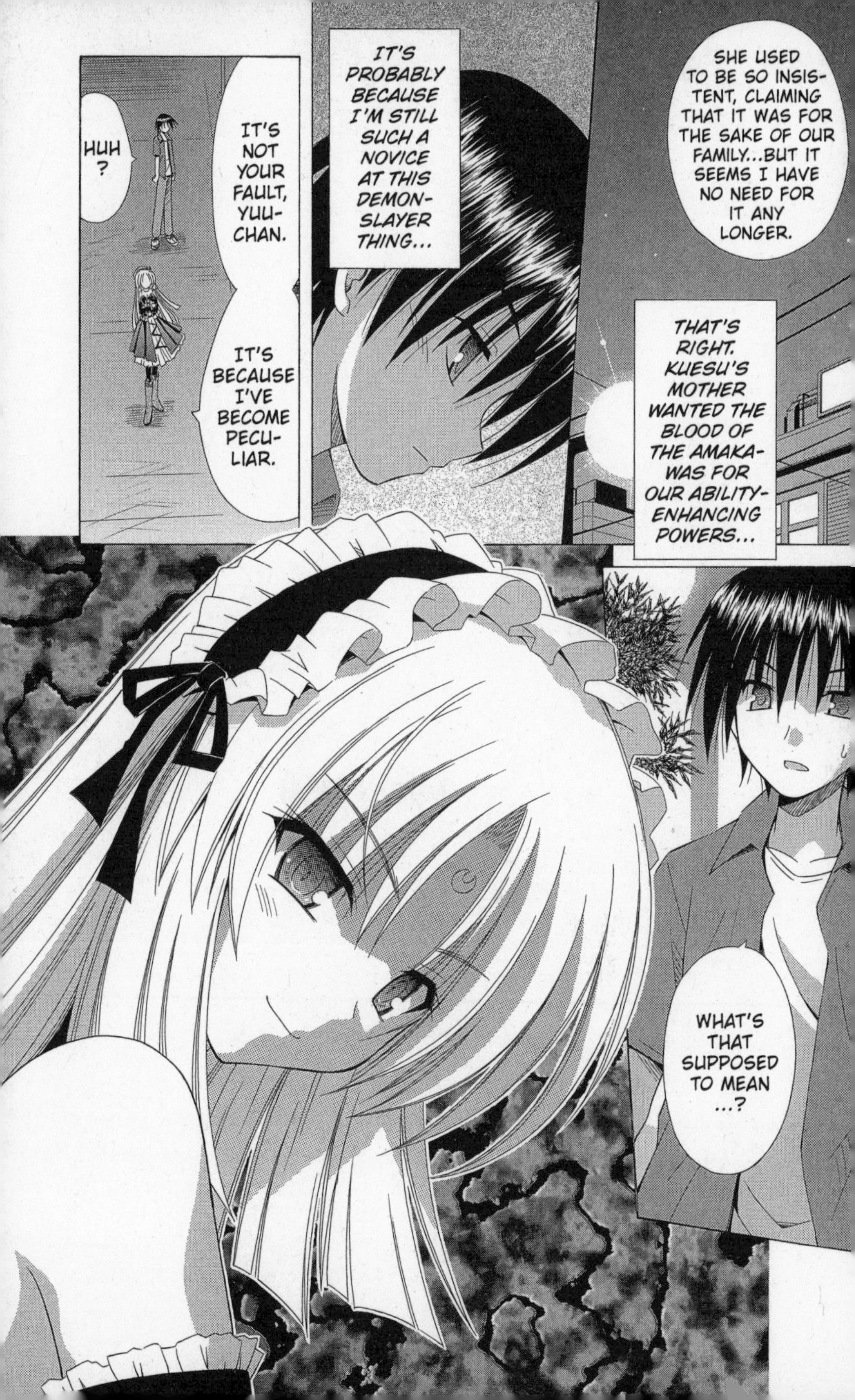
SHE USED TO BE SO INSISTENT, CLAIMING THAT IT WAS FOR THE SAKE OF OUR FAMILY...BUT IT SEEMS I HAVE NO NEED FOR IT ANY LONGER.
THAT'S RIGHT. KUESU'S MOTHER WANTED THE BLOOD OF THE AMAKAWAS FOR OUR ABILITY-ENHANCING POWERS...
IT'S PROBABLY BECAUSE I'M STILL SUCH A NOVICE AT THIS DEMON-SLAYER THING...
IT'S NOT YOUR FAULT, YUU-CHAN.
HUH?
IT'S BECAUSE I'VE BECOME PECULIAR.
WHAT'S THAT SUPPOSED TO MEAN ...?

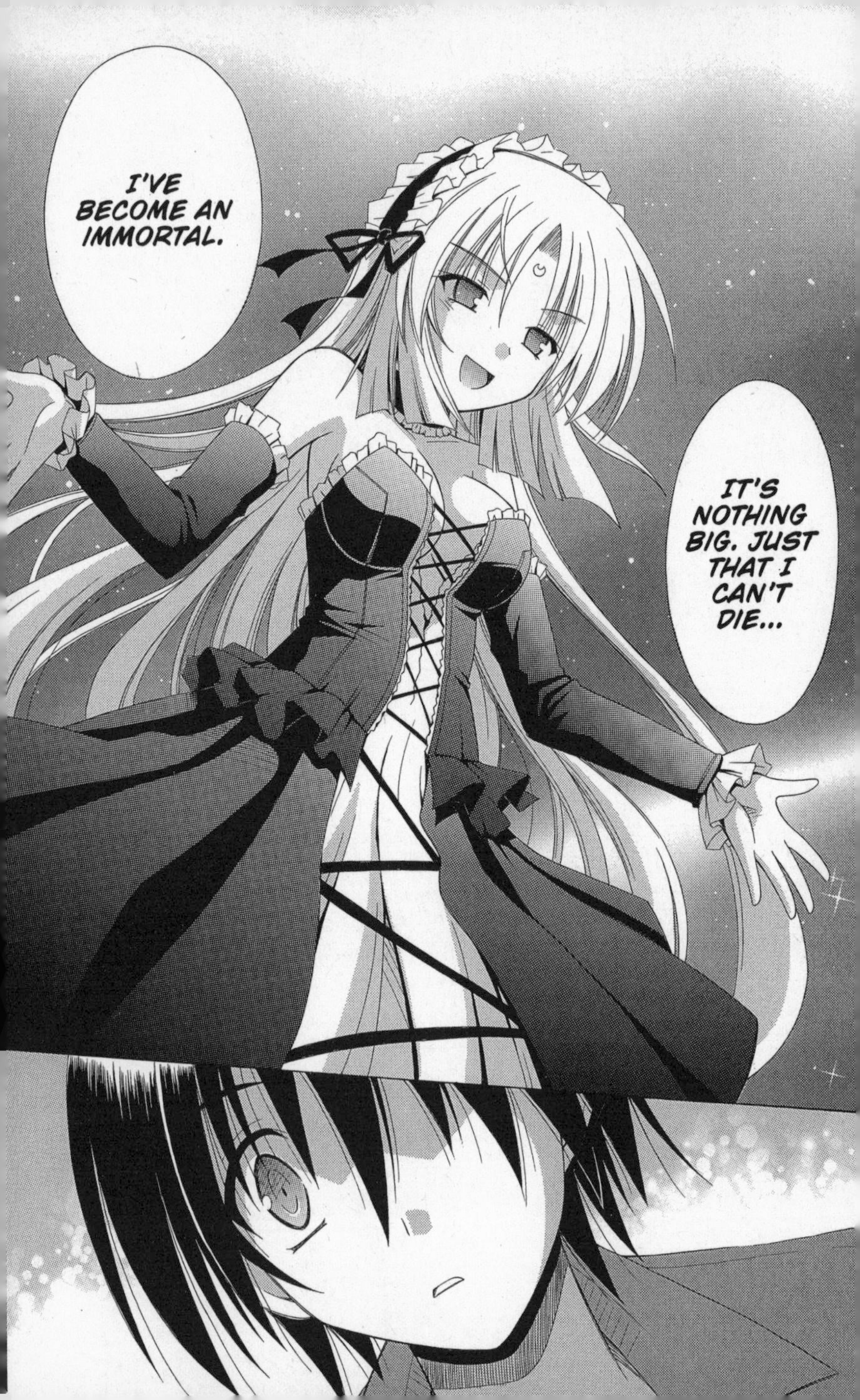
IT'S NOTHING BIG. JUST THAT I CAN'T DIE...
I'VE BECOME AN IMMORTAL.

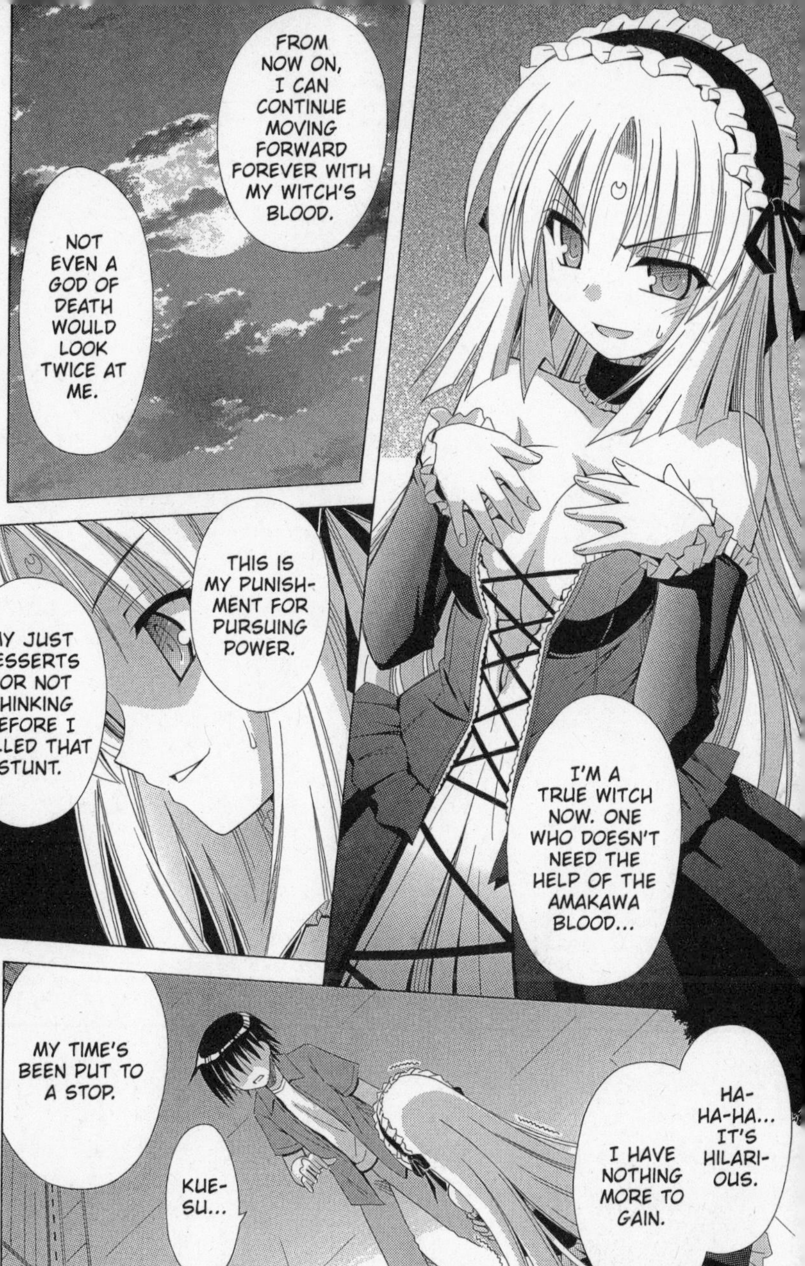
I'M A TRUE WITCH NOW. ONE WHO DOESN'T NEED THE HELP OF THE AMAKAWA BLOOD...
FROM NOW ON, I CAN CONTINUE MOVING FORWARD FOREVER WITH MY WITCH'S BLOOD.
NOT EVEN A GOD OF DEATH WOULD LOOK TWICE AT ME.
THIS IS MY PUNISHMENT FOR PURSUING POWER.
MY JUST DESSERTS FOR NOT THINKING BEFORE I PULLED THAT STUNT.
HA-HA-HA... IT'S HILARIOUS.
I HAVE NOTHING MORE TO GAIN.
MY TIME'S BEEN PUT TO A STOP.
KUE-SU...

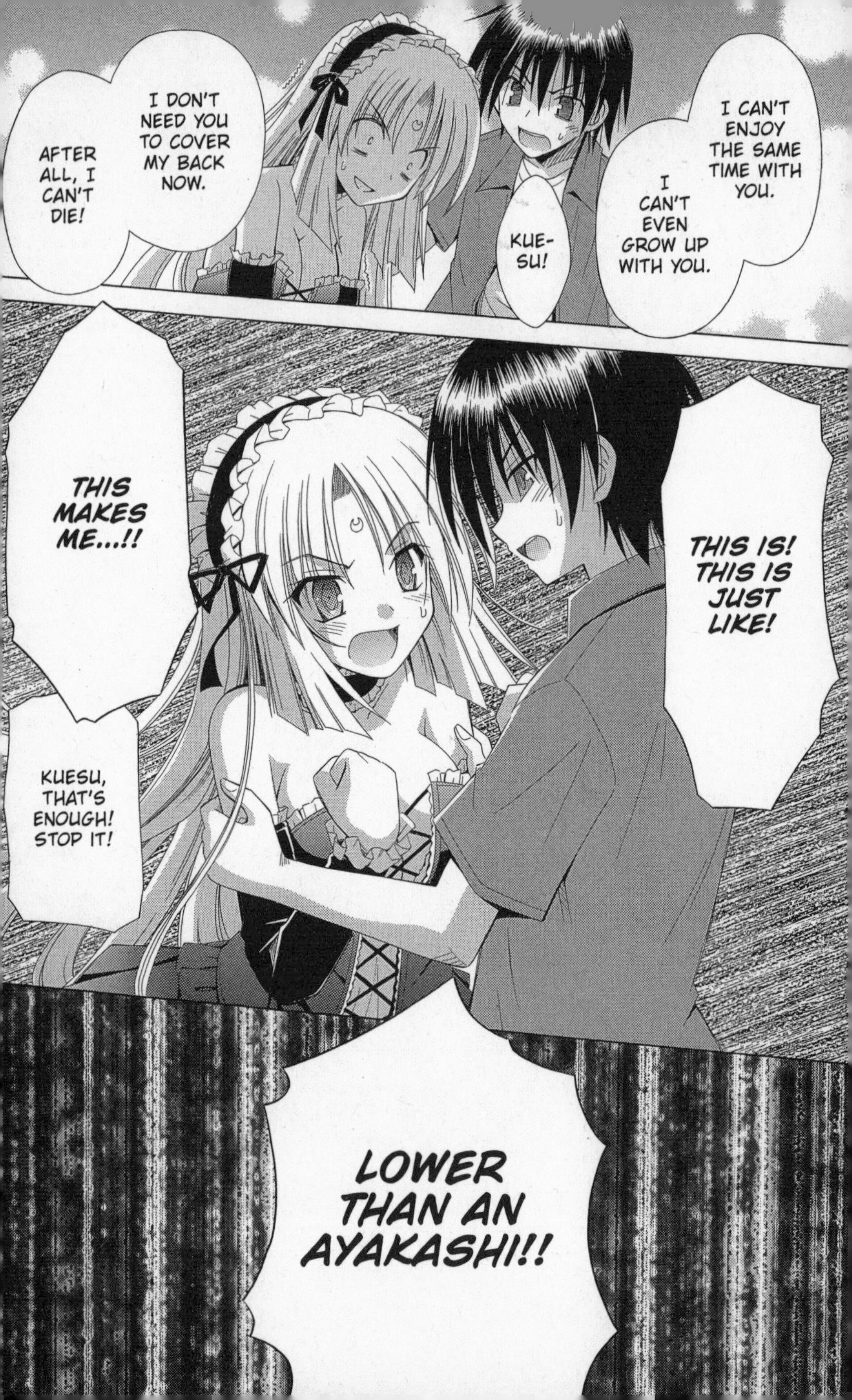
I CAN'T ENJOY THE SAME TIME WITH YOU.
I CAN'T EVEN GROW UP WITH YOU.
KUE-SU!
I DON'T NEED YOU TO COVER MY BACK NOW.
AFTER ALL, I CAN'T DIE!
THIS IS! THIS IS JUST LIKE!
THIS MAKES ME...!!
KUESU, THAT'S ENOUGH! STOP IT!
LOWER THAN AN AYAKASHI!!

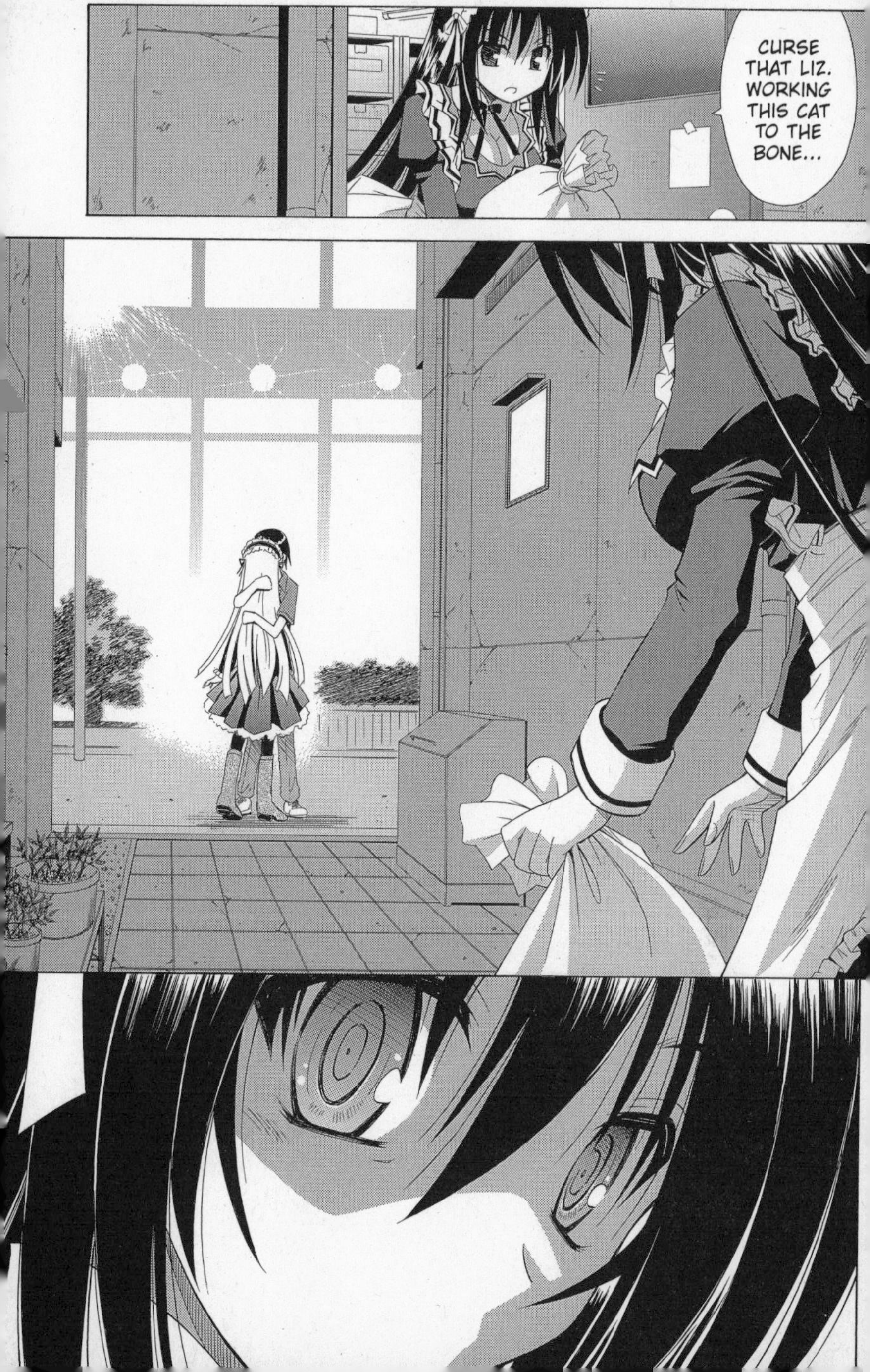
CURSE THAT LIZ. WORKING THIS CAT TO THE BONE...

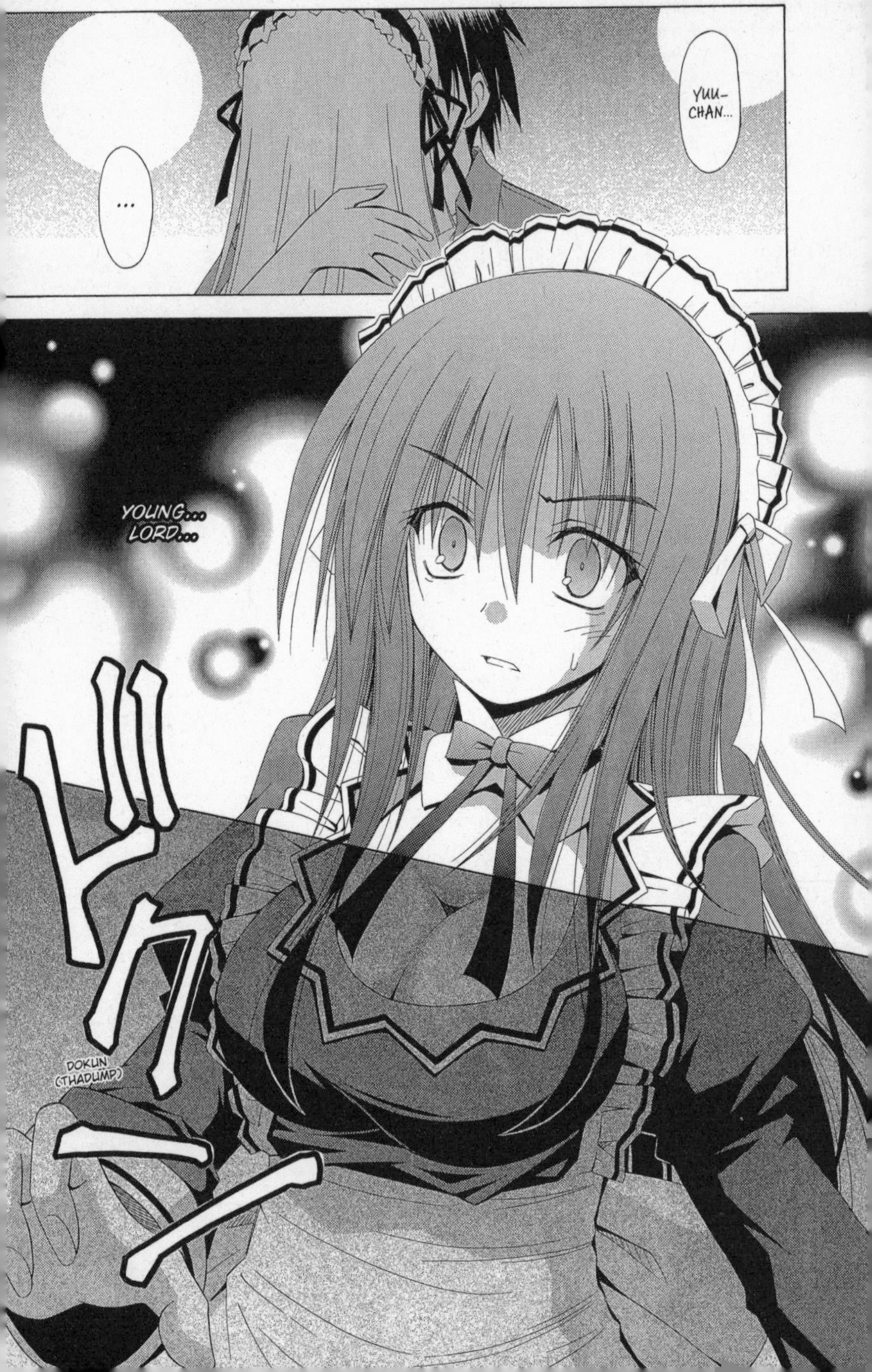
YUU-CHAN...
...
YOUNG... LORD...
DOKUN (THADUMP)

MENAGERIE 67: THE TRIGGER TO THE END OF THE CAT'S CONFUSION

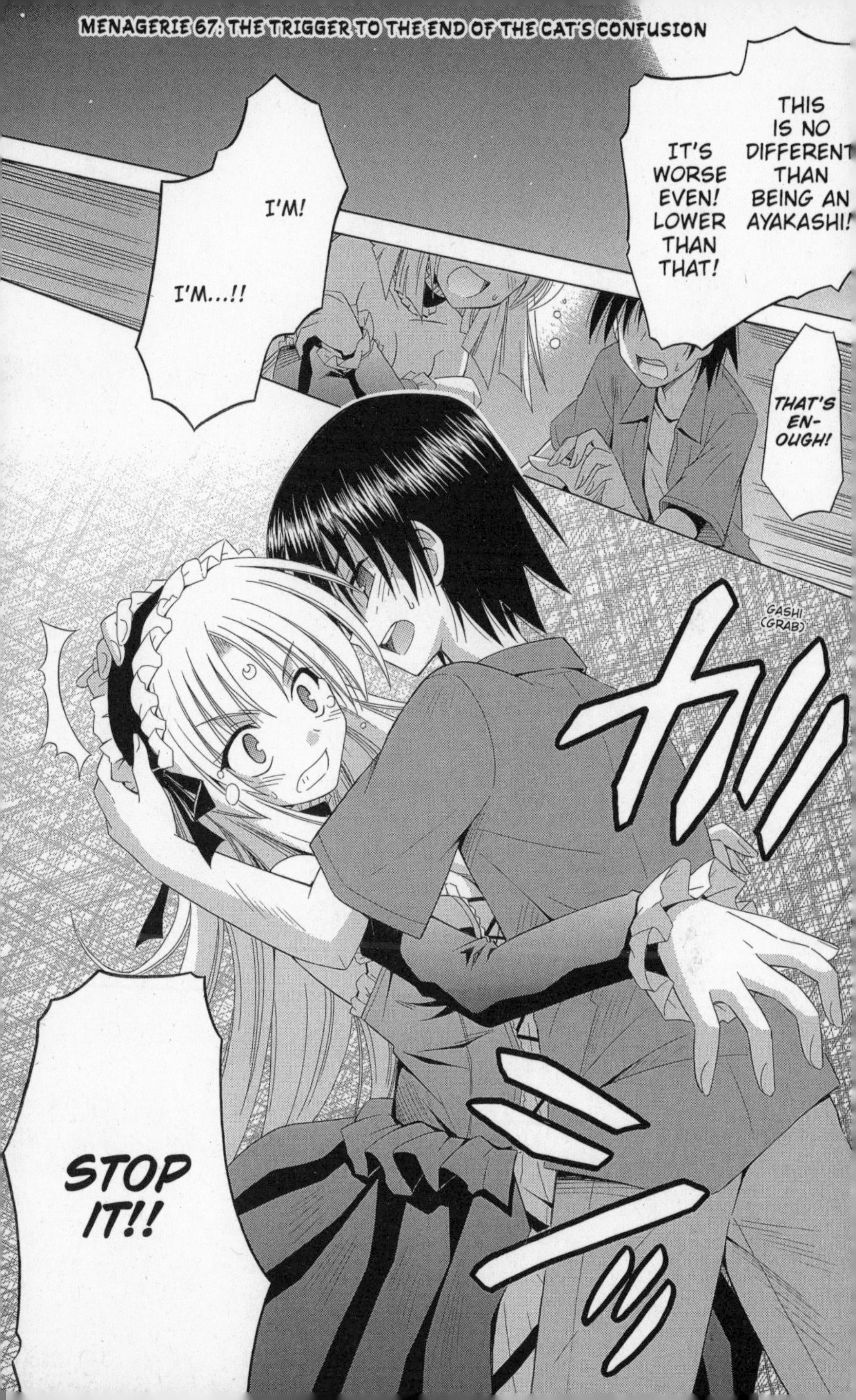
THIS IS NO DIFFERENT THAN BEING AN AYAKASHI!
IT'S WORSE EVEN! LOWER THAN THAT!
I'M!
I'M...!!
THAT'S EN-OUGH!
GASHI (GRAB)
STOP IT!!

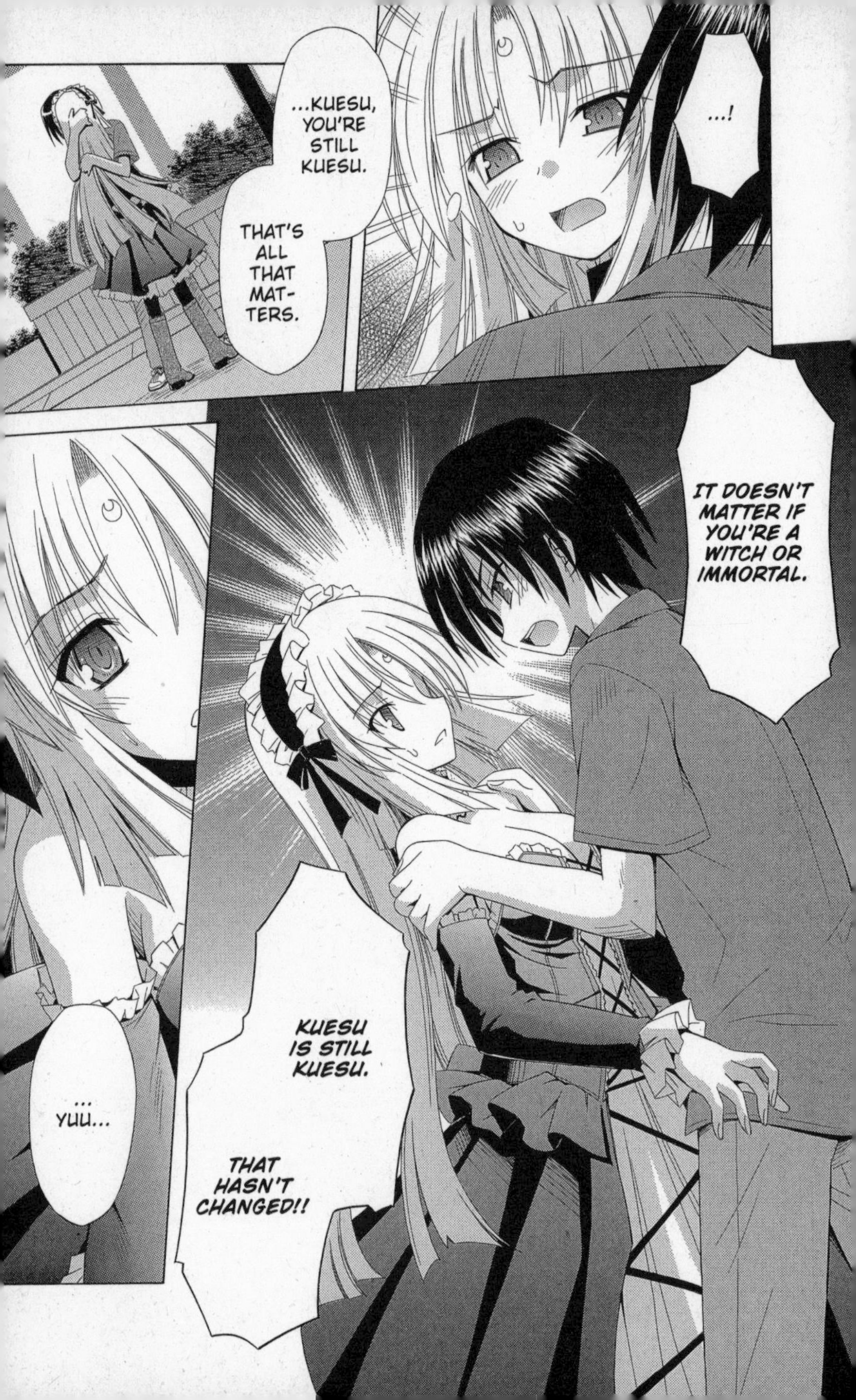
...!
...KUESU, YOU'RE STILL KUESU.
THAT'S ALL THAT MAT-TERS.
IT DOESN'T MATTER IF YOU'RE A WITCH OR IMMORTAL.
KUESU IS STILL KUESU.
THAT HASN'T CHANGED!!
... YUU...

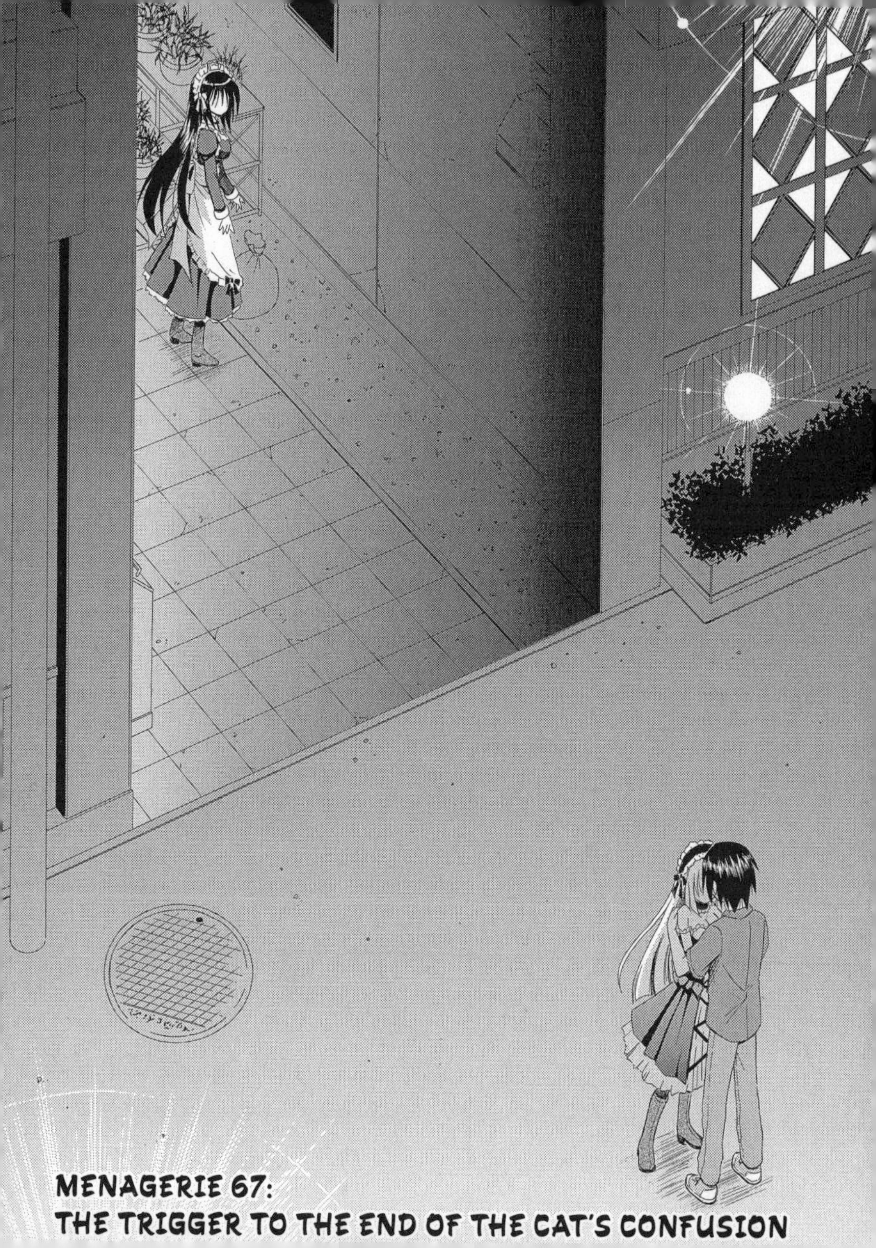

MENAGERIE 67:
THE TRIGGER TO THE END OF THE CAT'S CONFUSION

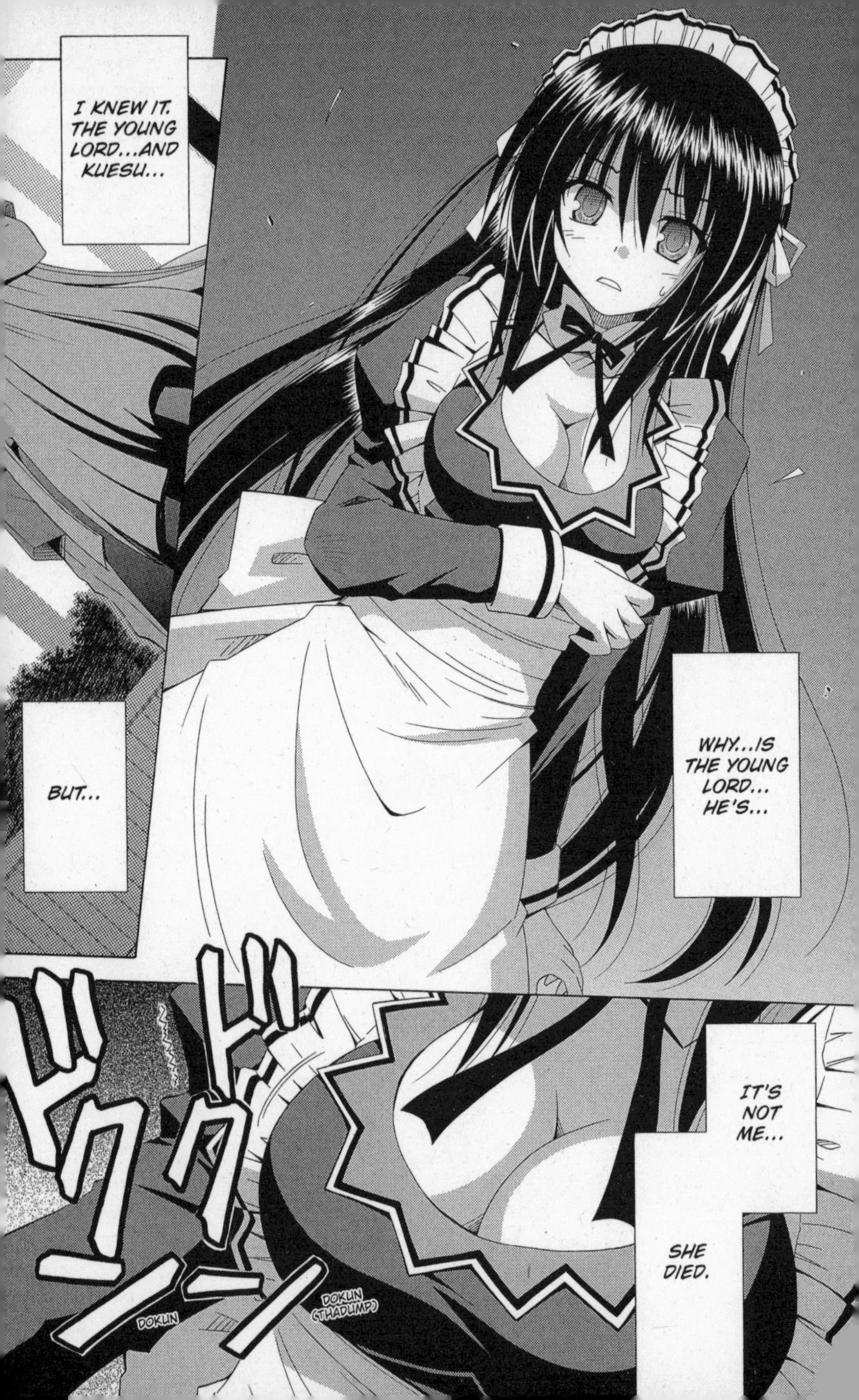
I KNEW IT. THE YOUNG LORD...AND KUESU...
WHY...IS THE YOUNG LORD... HE'S...
BUT...
IT'S NOT ME...
SHE DIED.
DOKUN (THADUMP)
DOKUN

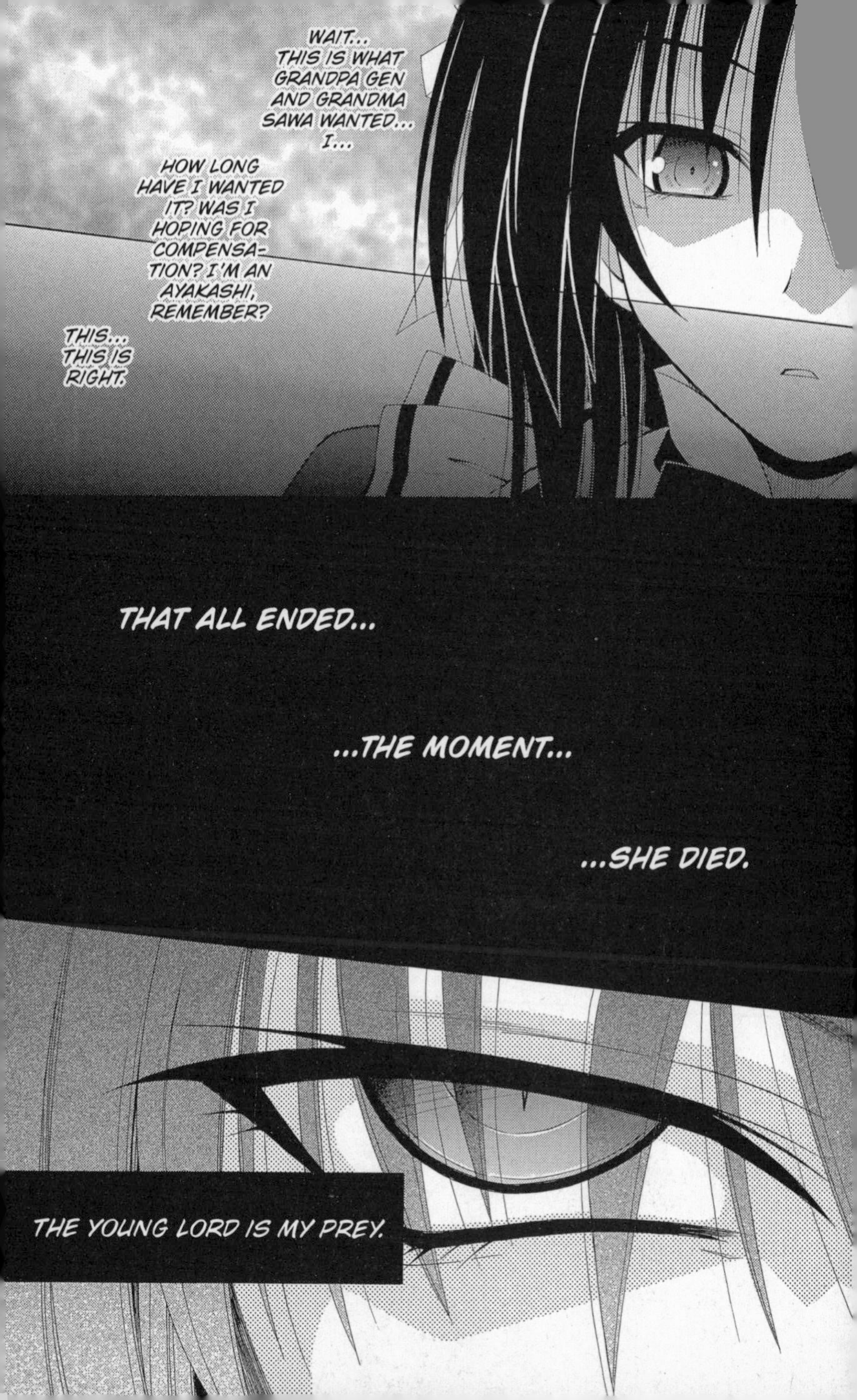
WAIT... THIS IS WHAT GRANDPA GEN AND GRANDMA SAWA WANTED... I...
HOW LONG HAVE I WANTED IT? WAS I HOPING FOR COMPENSA-TION? I'M AN AYAKASHI, REMEMBER?
THIS... THIS IS RIGHT.
THAT ALL ENDED...
...THE MOMENT...
...SHE DIED.
THE YOUNG LORD IS MY PREY.

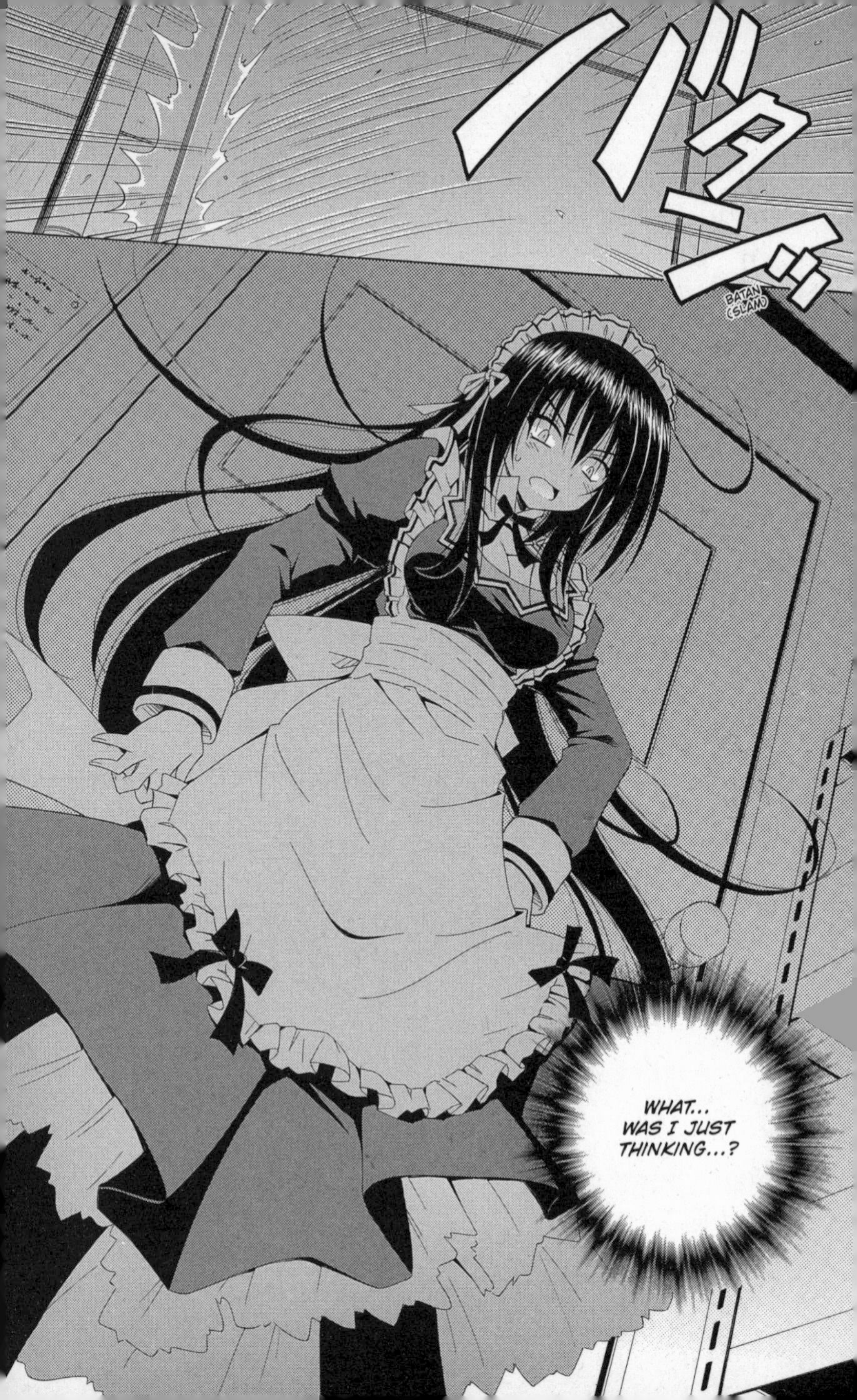
BATAN (SLAM)
WHAT... WAS I JUST THINKING...?

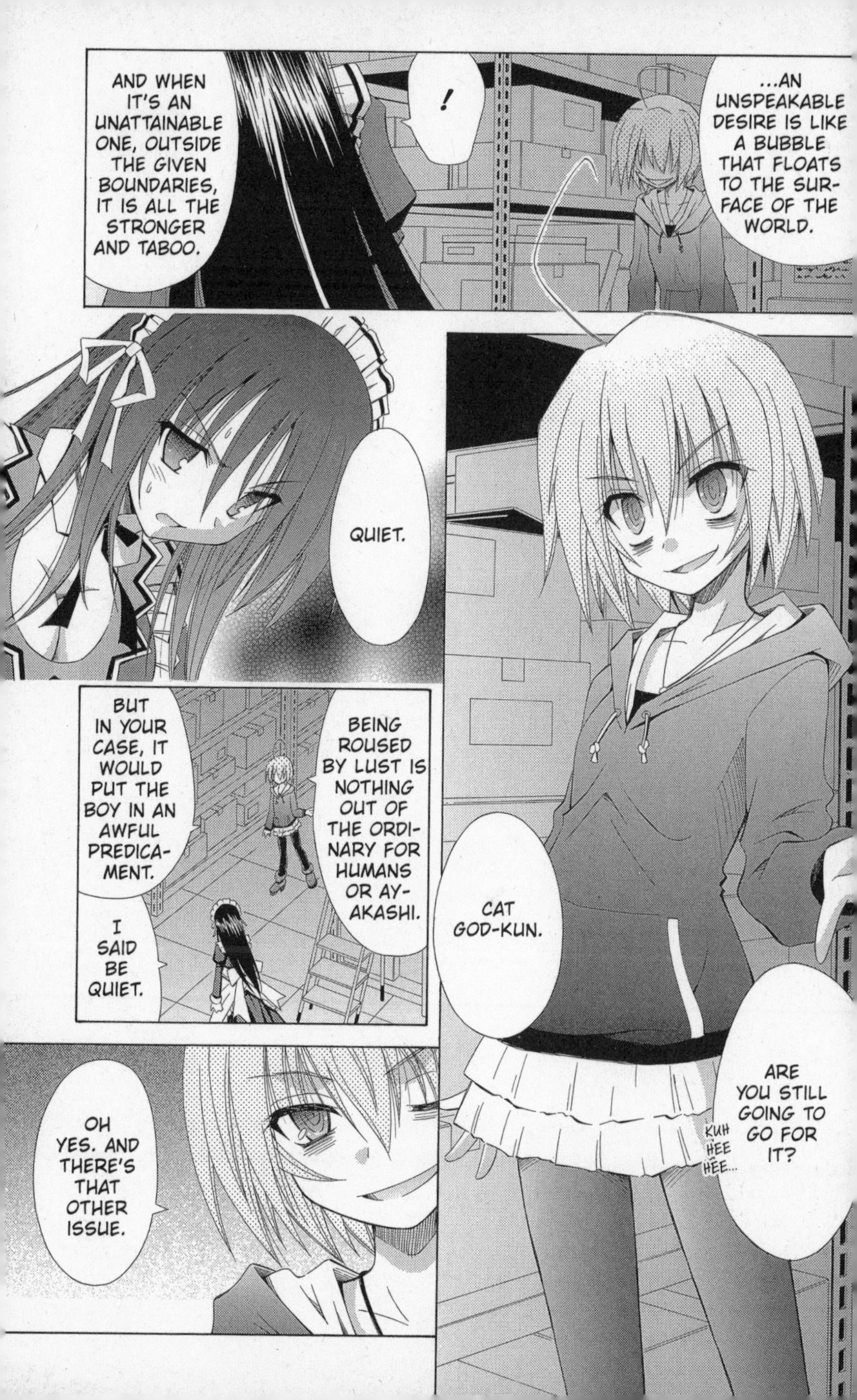
...AN UNSPEAKABLE DESIRE IS LIKE A BUBBLE THAT FLOATS TO THE SURFACE OF THE WORLD.
!
AND WHEN IT'S AN UNATTAINABLE ONE, OUTSIDE THE GIVEN BOUNDARIES, IT IS ALL THE STRONGER AND TABOO.
CAT GOD-KUN.
ARE YOU STILL GOING TO GO FOR IT?
KUH HEE HEE...
QUIET.
BEING ROUSED BY LUST IS NOTHING OUT OF THE ORDINARY FOR HUMANS OR AYAKASHI.
BUT IN YOUR CASE, IT WOULD PUT THE BOY IN AN AWFUL PREDICAMENT.
I SAID BE QUIET.
OH YES. AND THERE'S THAT OTHER ISSUE.

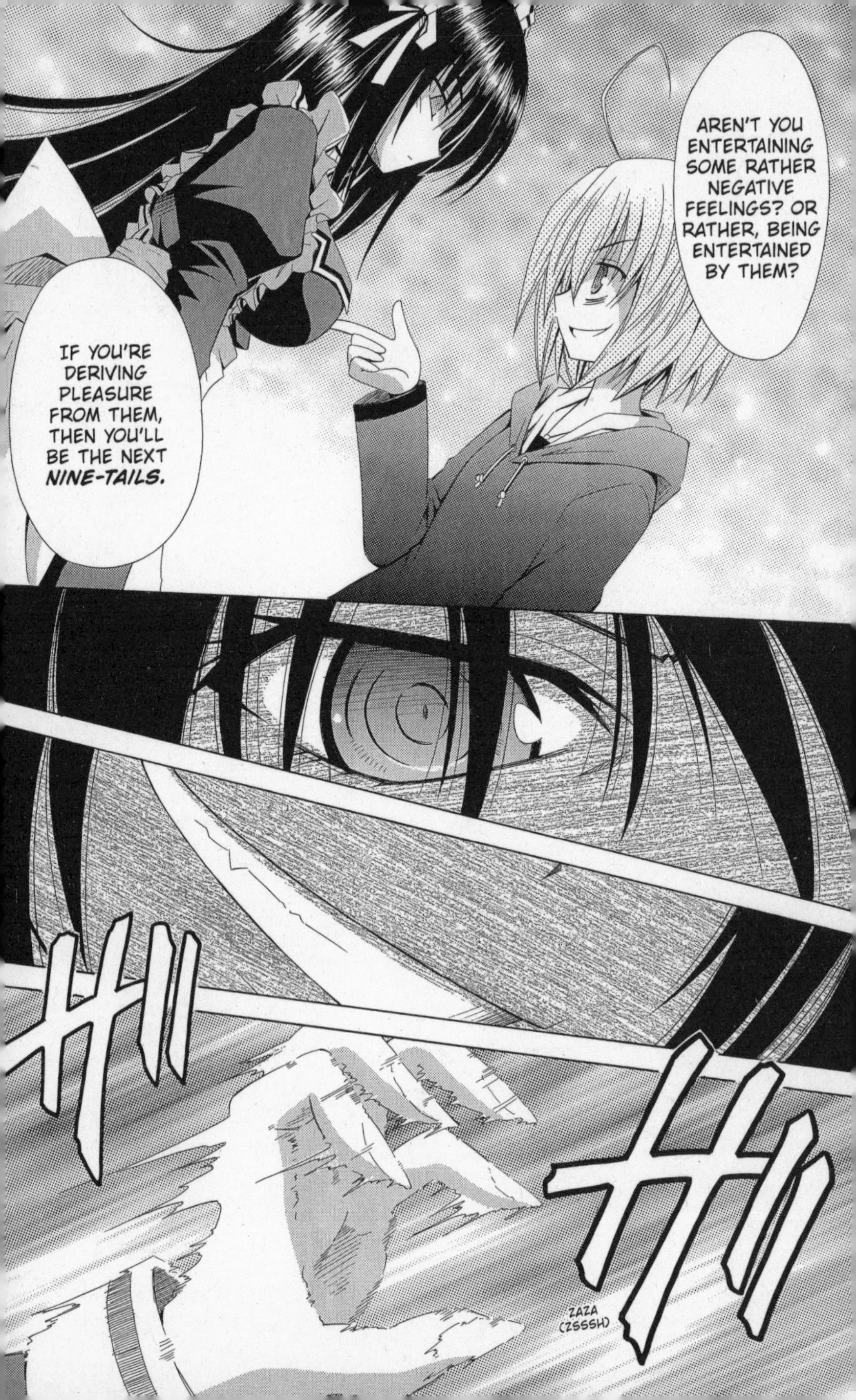
AREN'T YOU ENTERTAINING SOME RATHER NEGATIVE FEELINGS? OR RATHER, BEING ENTERTAINED BY THEM?
IF YOU'RE DERIVING PLEASURE FROM THEM, THEN YOU'LL BE THE NEXT *NINE-TAILS.*
ZAZA (ZSSSH)

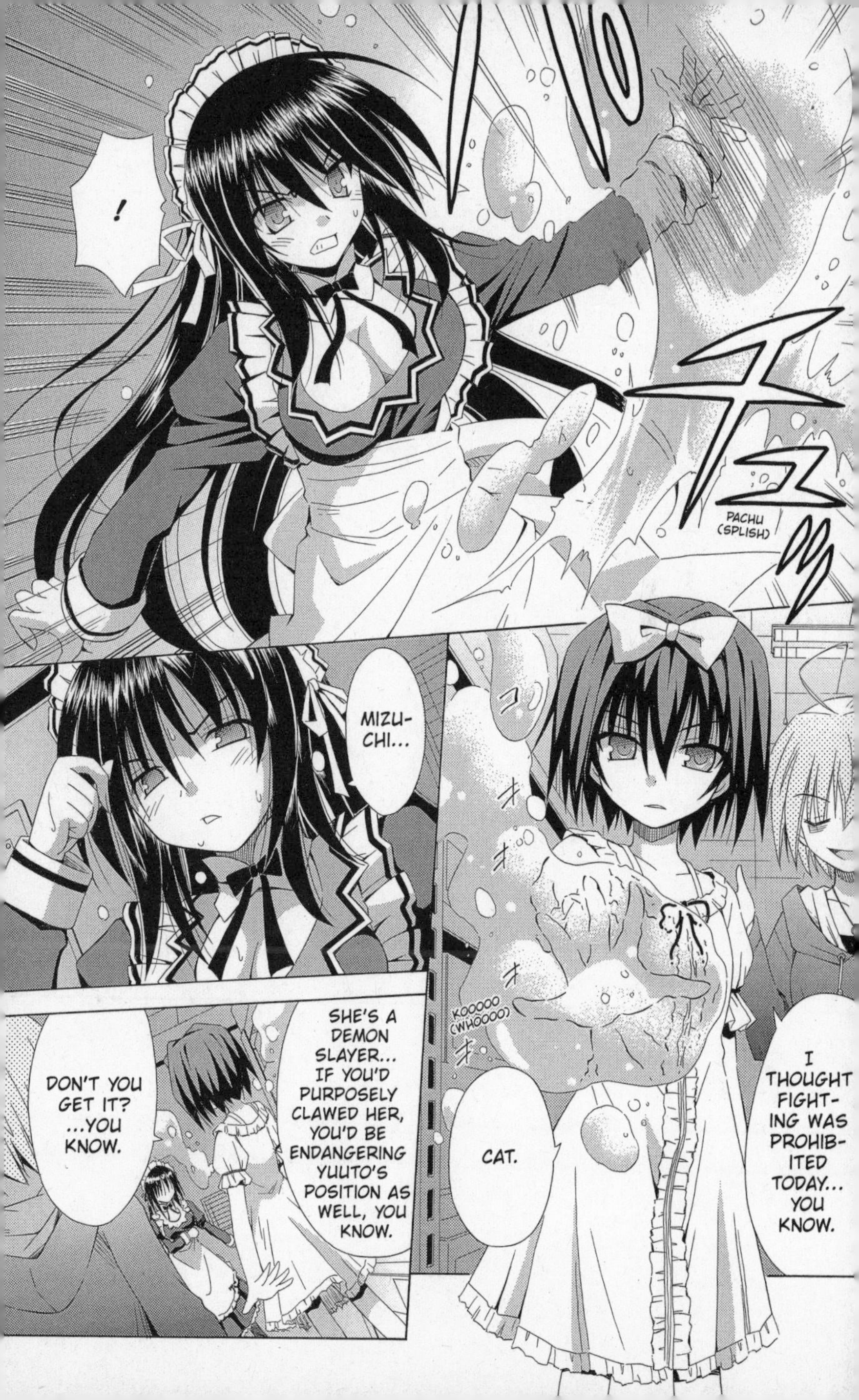

PACHU (SPLISH)
!
I THOUGHT FIGHTING WAS PROHIBITED TODAY... YOU KNOW.
KOOOOO (WHOOOO)
CAT.
MIZU-CHI...
SHE'S A DEMON SLAYER... IF YOU'D PURPOSELY CLAWED HER, YOU'D BE ENDANGERING YUUTO'S POSITION AS WELL, YOU KNOW.
DON'T YOU GET IT? ...YOU KNOW.

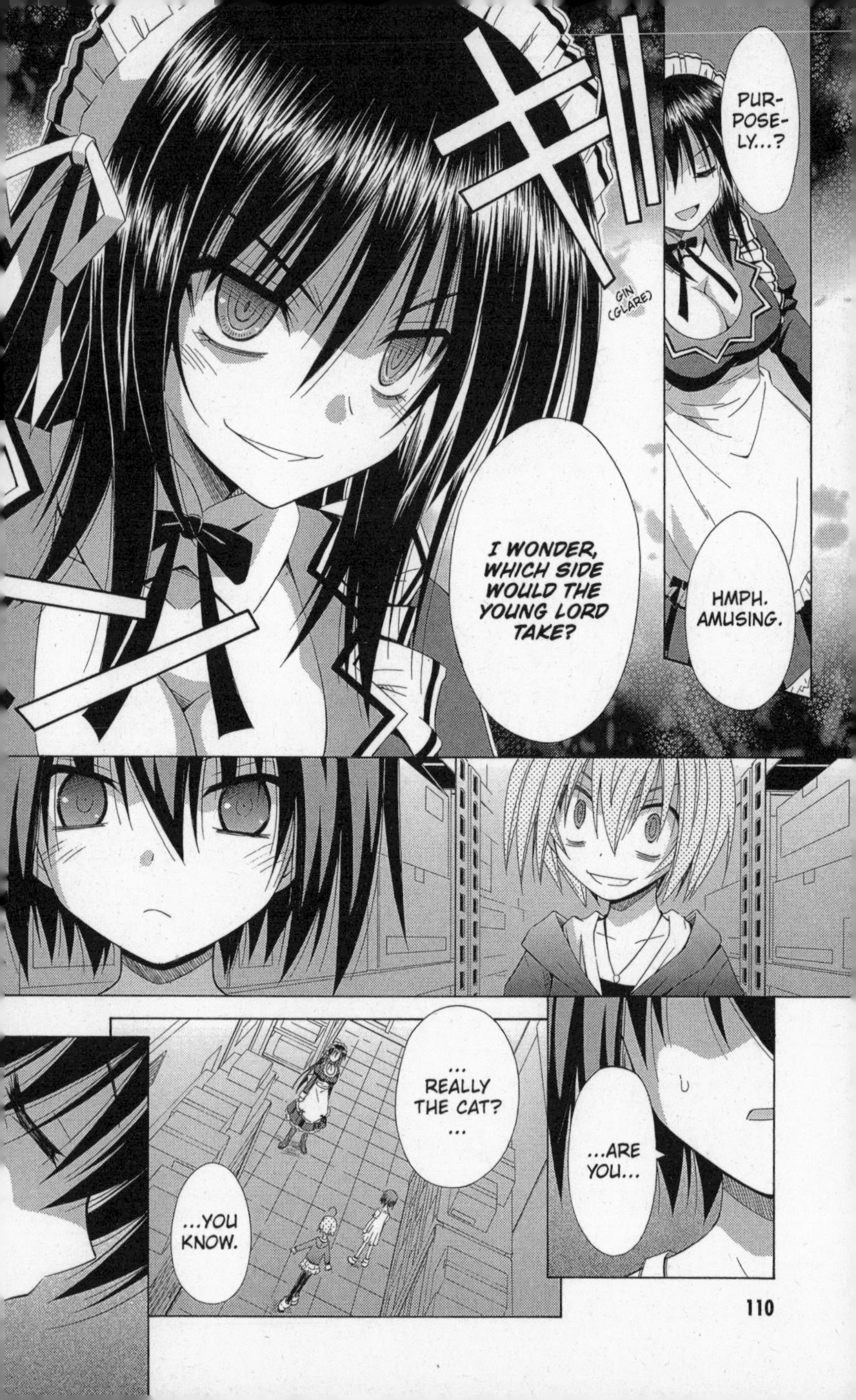
PUR-POSE-LY...?
HMPH. AMUSING.
GIN (GLARE)
I WONDER, WHICH SIDE WOULD THE YOUNG LORD TAKE?
...ARE YOU...
...REALLY THE CAT? ...
...YOU KNOW.

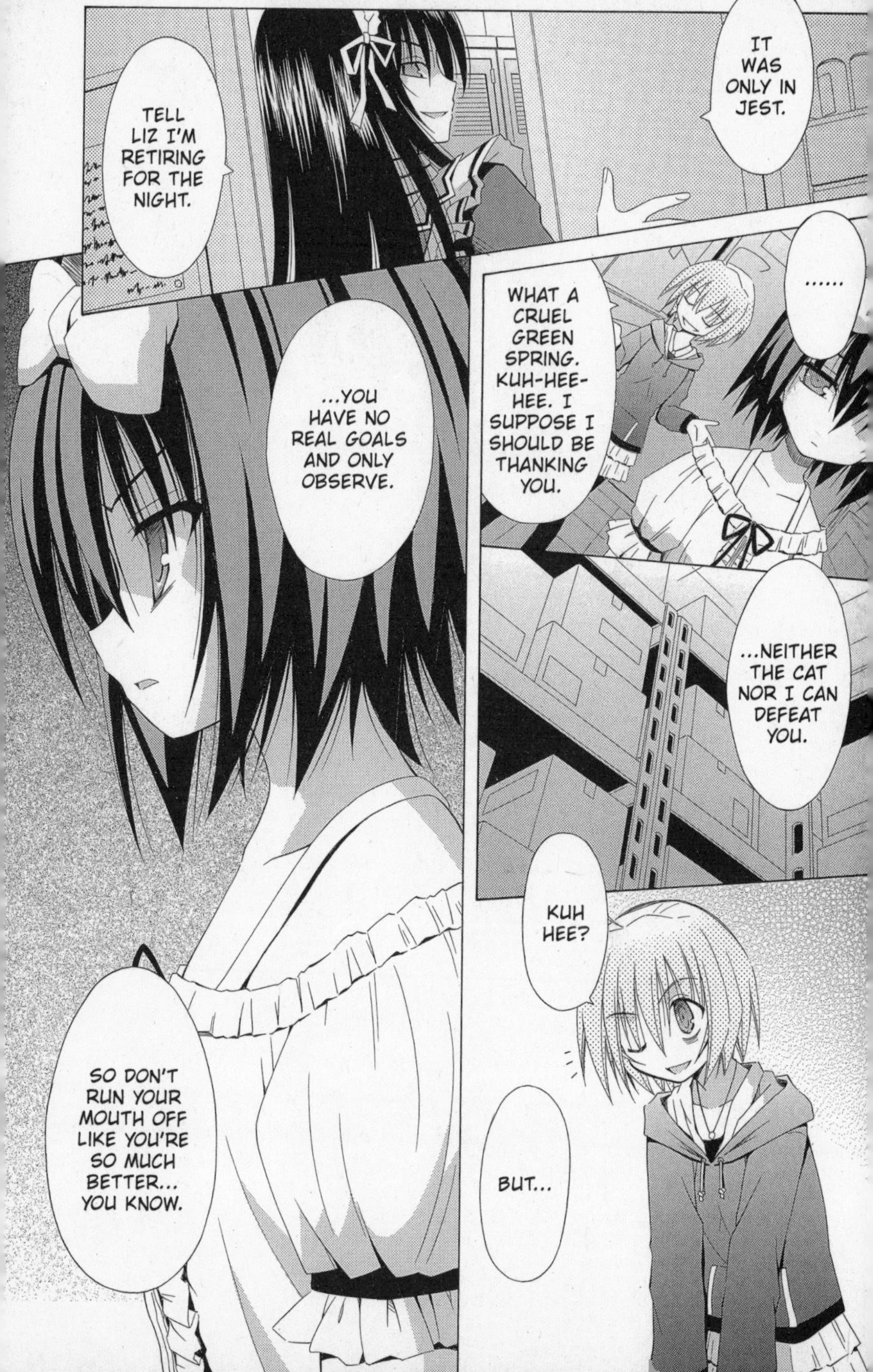
IT WAS ONLY IN JEST.
TELL LIZ I'M RETIRING FOR THE NIGHT.
......
WHAT A CRUEL GREEN SPRING. KUH-HEE-HEE. I SUPPOSE I SHOULD BE THANKING YOU.
...NEITHER THE CAT NOR I CAN DEFEAT YOU.
KUH HEE?
BUT...
...YOU HAVE NO REAL GOALS AND ONLY OBSERVE.
SO DON'T RUN YOUR MOUTH OFF LIKE YOU'RE SO MUCH BETTER... YOU KNOW.

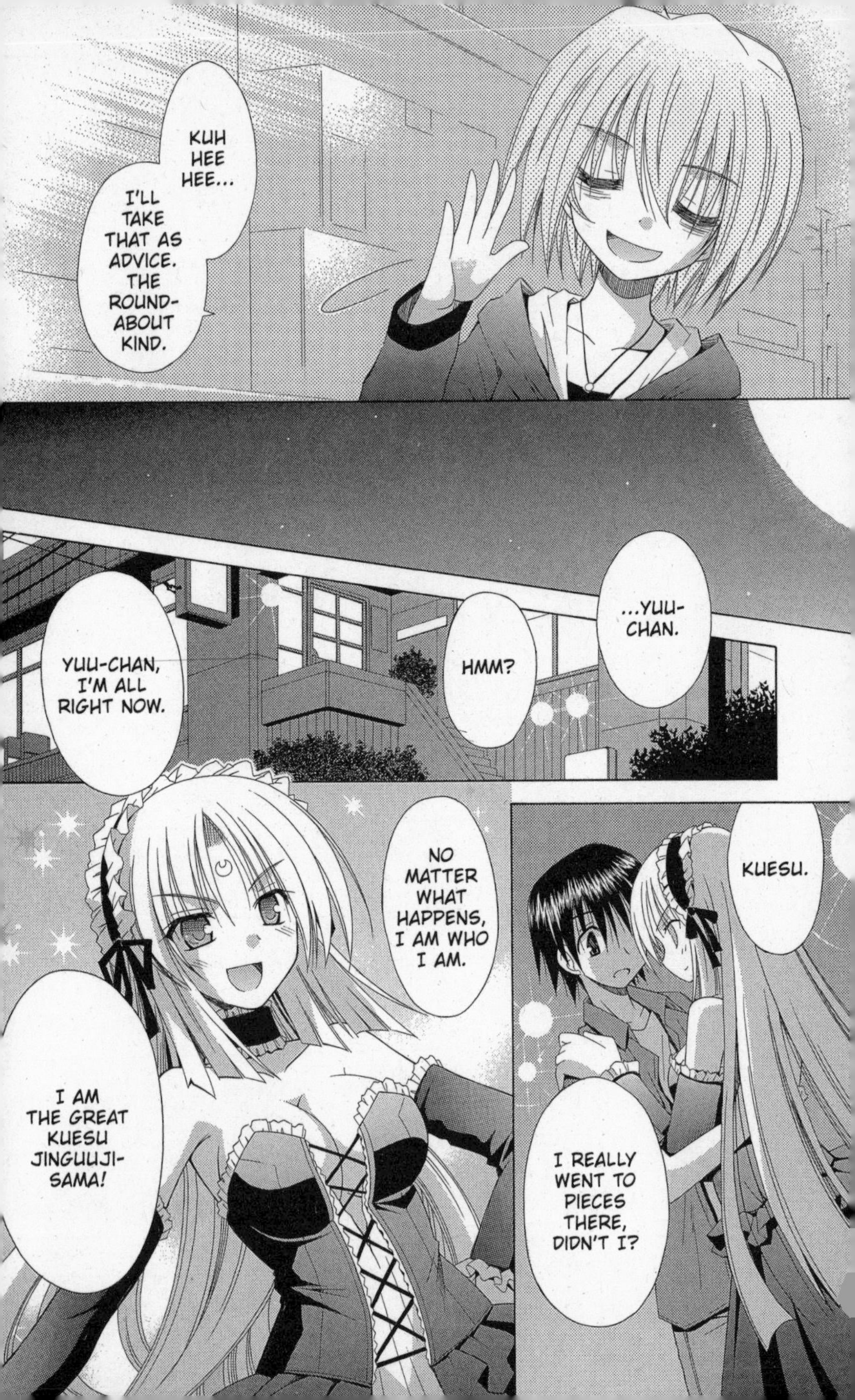
KUH HEE HEE... I'LL TAKE THAT AS ADVICE. THE ROUND-ABOUT KIND.
...YUU-CHAN.
HMM?
YUU-CHAN, I'M ALL RIGHT NOW.
KUESU.
I REALLY WENT TO PIECES THERE, DIDN'T I?
NO MATTER WHAT HAPPENS, I AM WHO I AM.
I AM THE GREAT KUESU JINGUUJI-SAMA!

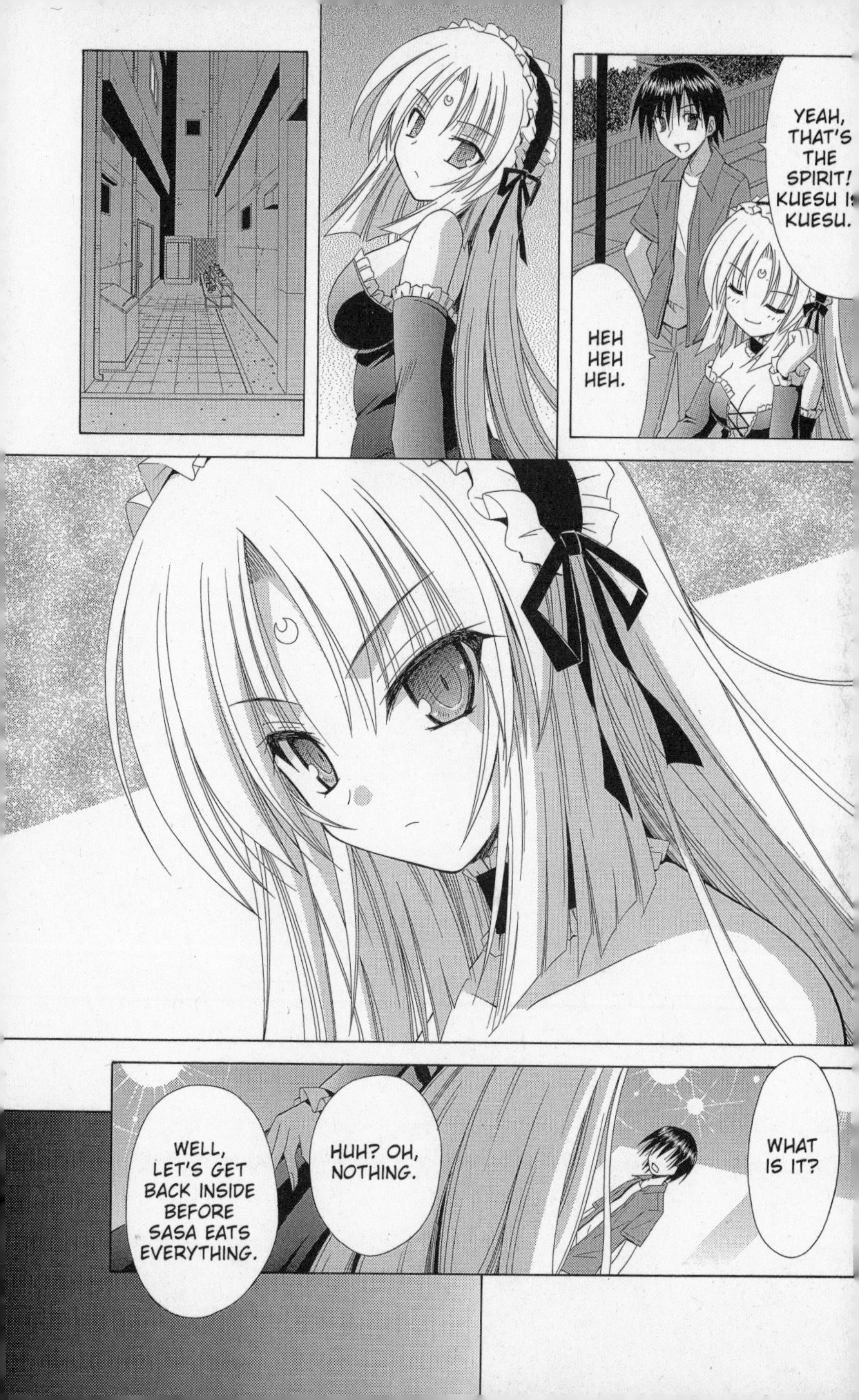

YEAH, THAT'S THE SPIRIT! KUESU I KUESU.
HEH HEH HEH.
WHAT IS IT?
HUH? OH, NOTHING.
WELL, LET'S GET BACK INSIDE BEFORE SASA EATS EVERYTHING.

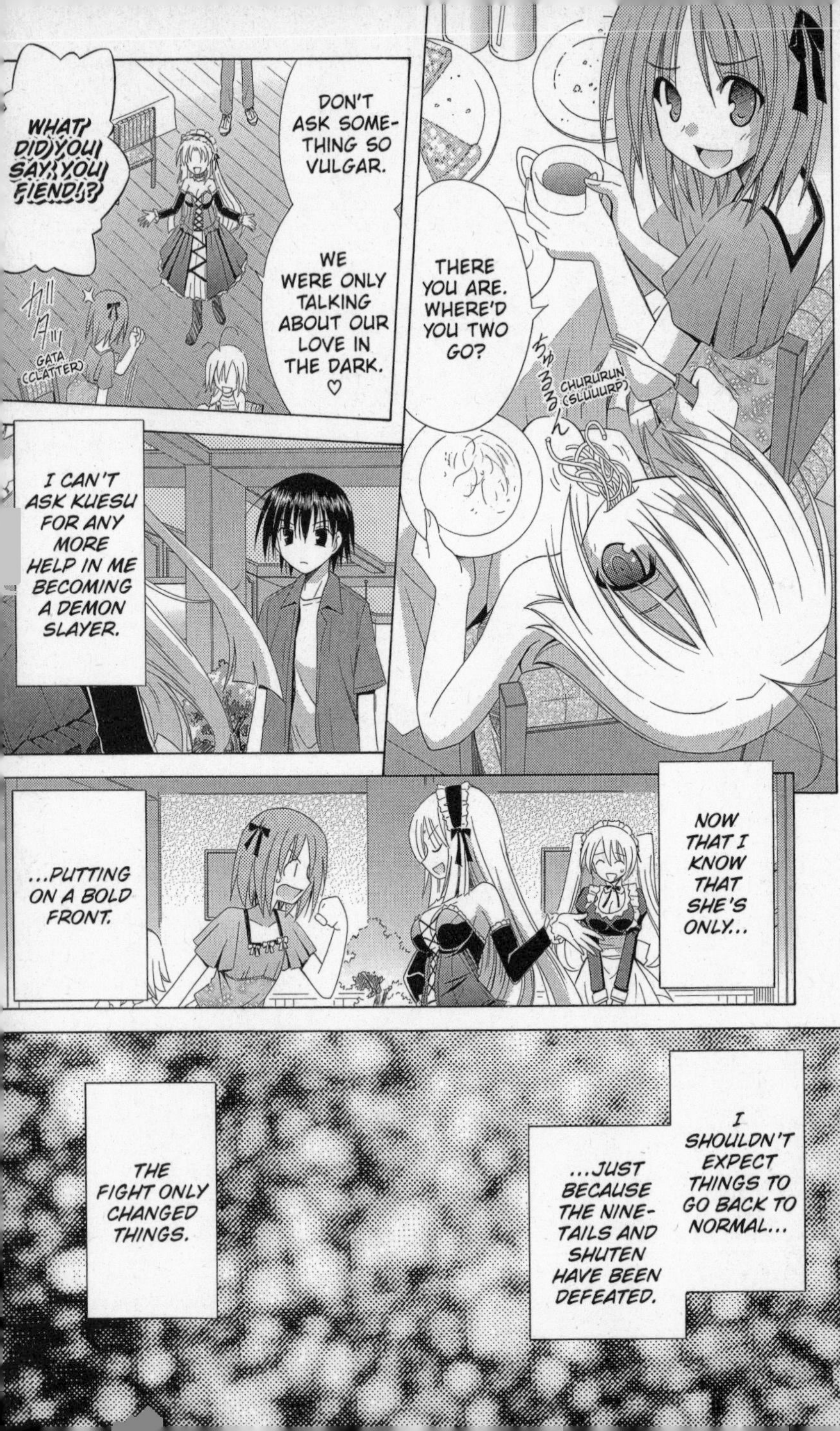
THERE YOU ARE. WHERE'D YOU TWO GO?
ちゅるるん
CHURURUN (SLUUURP)
DON'T ASK SOME-THING SO VULGAR.
WE WERE ONLY TALKING ABOUT OUR LOVE IN THE DARK. ♥
WHAT DID YOU SAY, YOU FIEND!?
ガタッ
GATA (CLATTER)
I CAN'T ASK KUESU FOR ANY MORE HELP IN ME BECOMING A DEMON SLAYER.
NOW THAT I KNOW THAT SHE'S ONLY...
...PUTTING ON A BOLD FRONT.
I SHOULDN'T EXPECT THINGS TO GO BACK TO NORMAL...
...JUST BECAUSE THE NINE-TAILS AND SHUTEN HAVE BEEN DEFEATED.
THE FIGHT ONLY CHANGED THINGS.

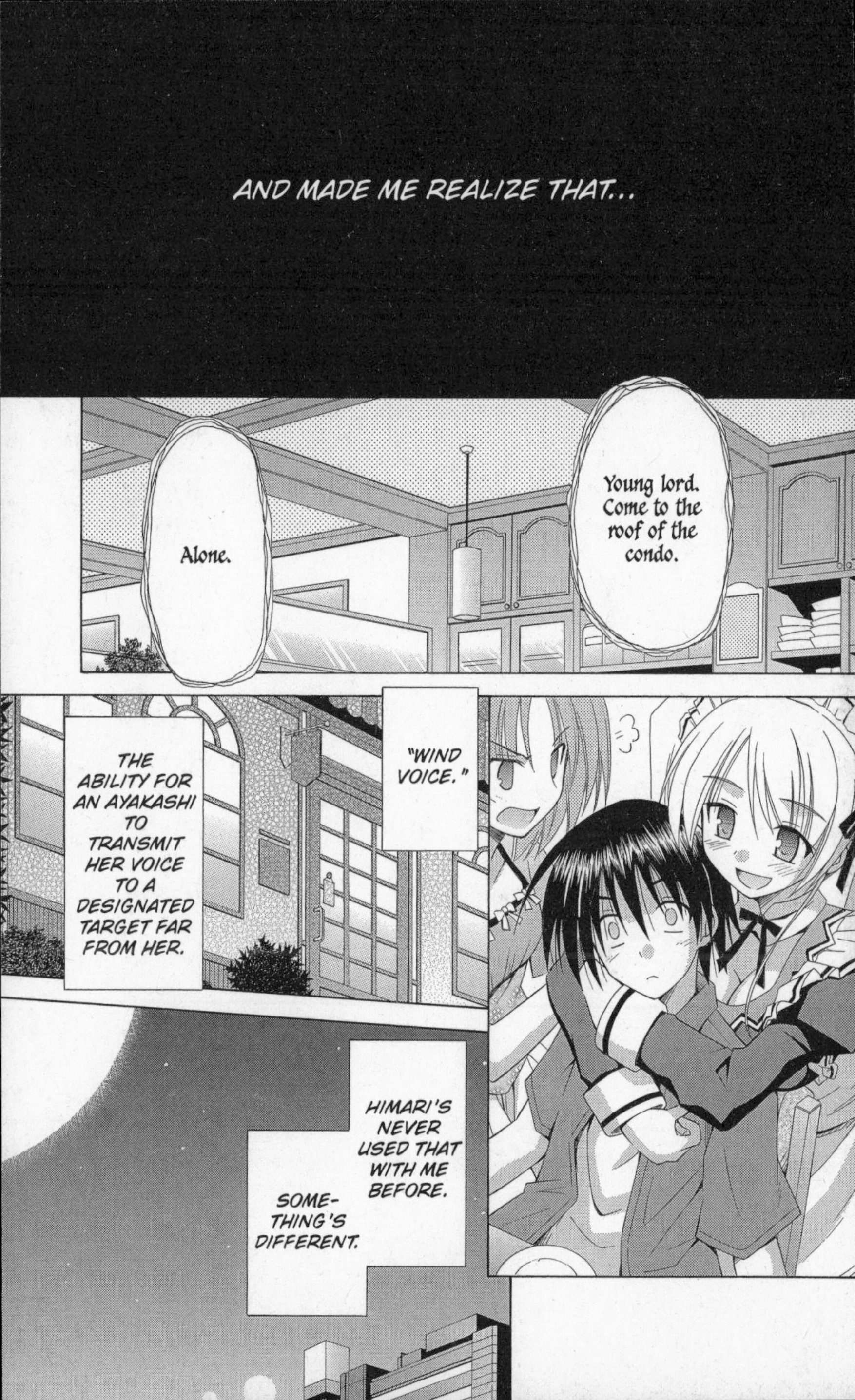

AND MADE ME REALIZE THAT...
Young lord. Come to the roof of the condo.
Alone.
"WIND VOICE."
THE ABILITY FOR AN AYAKASHI TO TRANSMIT HER VOICE TO A DESIGNATED TARGET FAR FROM HER.
HIMARI'S NEVER USED THAT WITH ME BEFORE.
SOME-THING'S DIFFERENT.

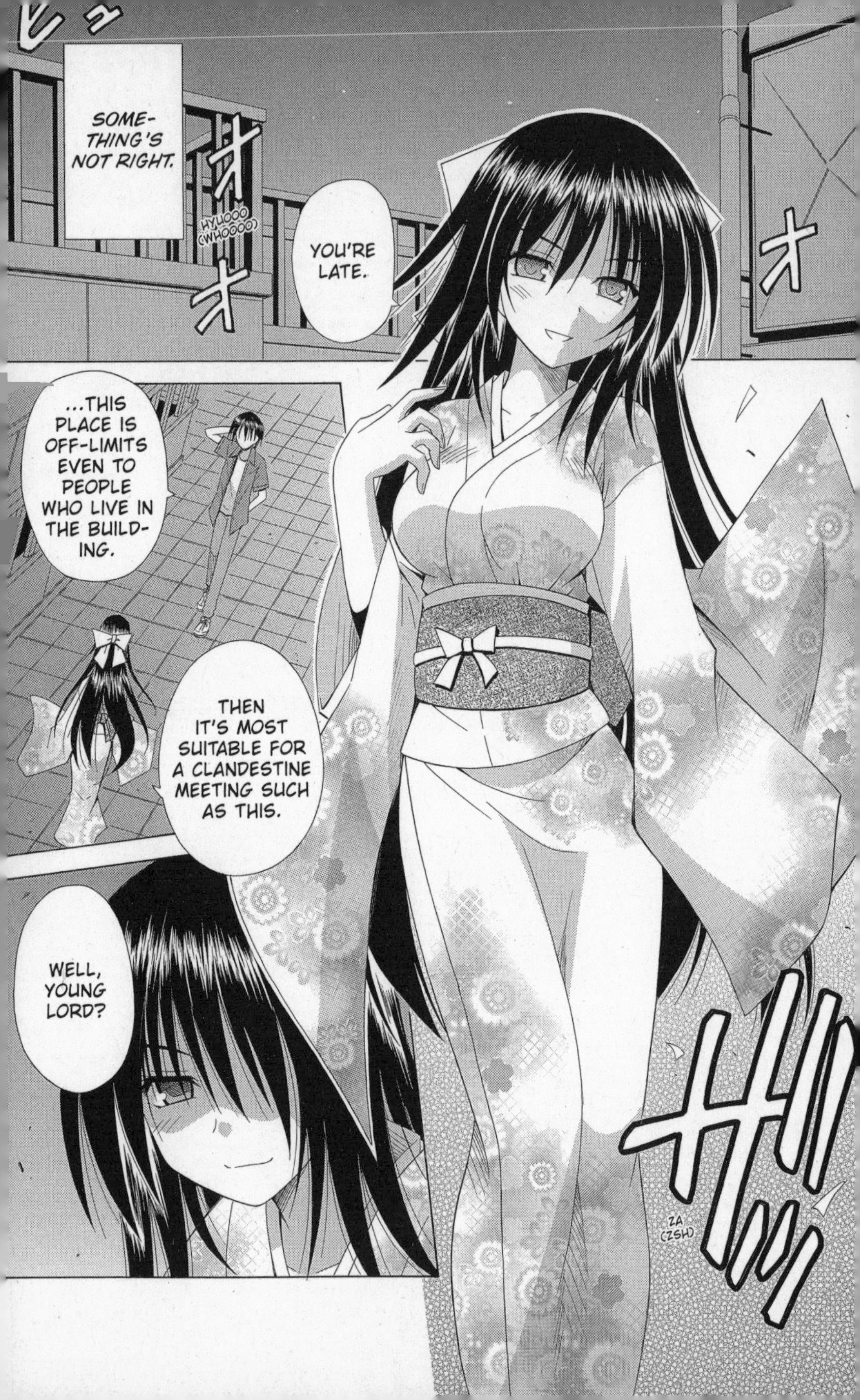
SOME-THING'S NOT RIGHT.
HYUOOO (WHOOOO)
YOU'RE LATE.
...THIS PLACE IS OFF-LIMITS EVEN TO PEOPLE WHO LIVE IN THE BUILD-ING.
THEN IT'S MOST SUITABLE FOR A CLANDESTINE MEETING SUCH AS THIS.
WELL, YOUNG LORD?
ZA (ZSH)

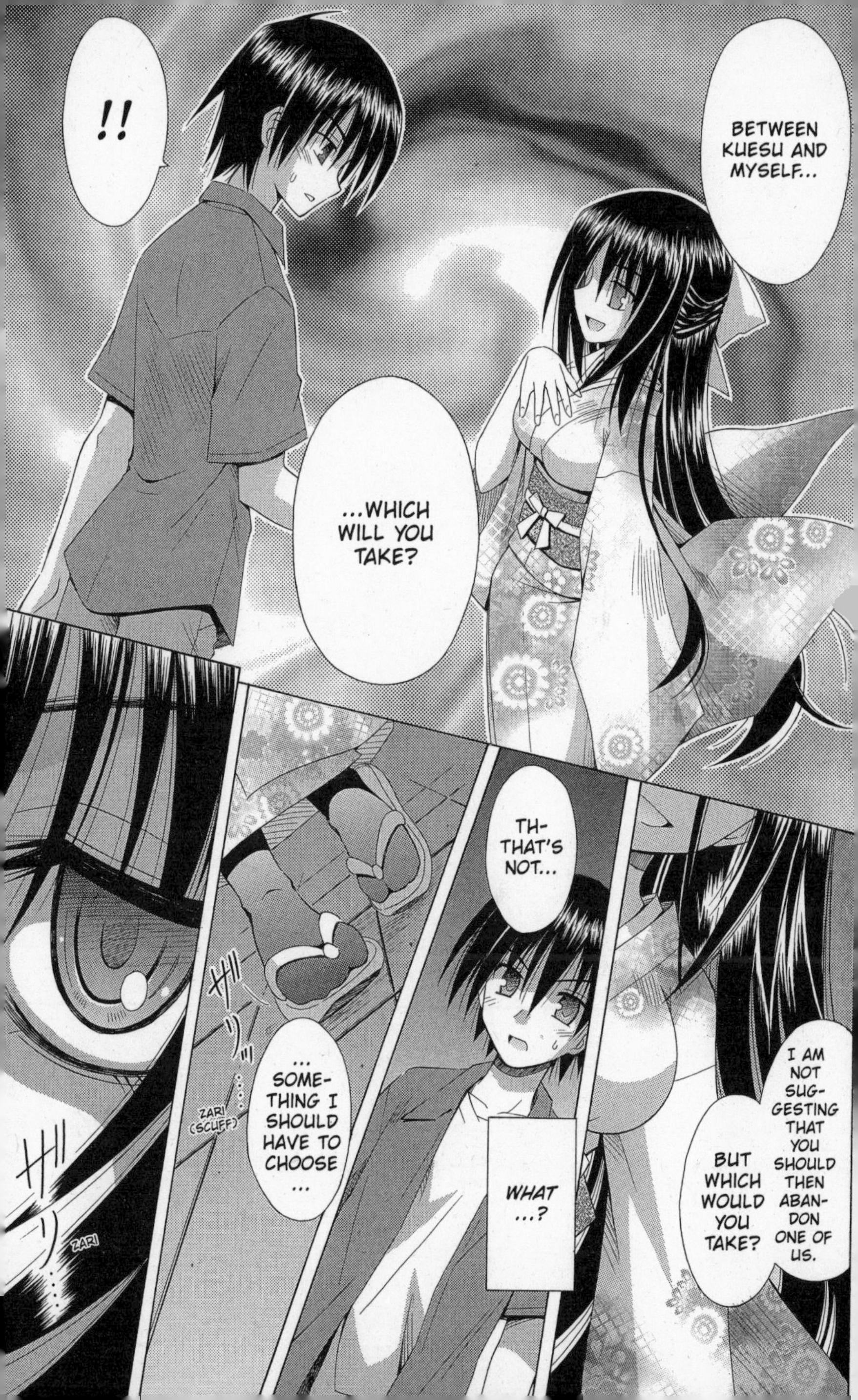
BETWEEN KUESU AND MYSELF...
...WHICH WILL YOU TAKE?
!!
I AM NOT SUGGESTING THAT YOU SHOULD THEN ABANDON ONE OF US.
BUT WHICH WOULD YOU TAKE?
TH- THAT'S NOT...
WHAT ...?
... SOMETHING I SHOULD HAVE TO CHOOSE ...
ZARI (SCUFF)
ZARI

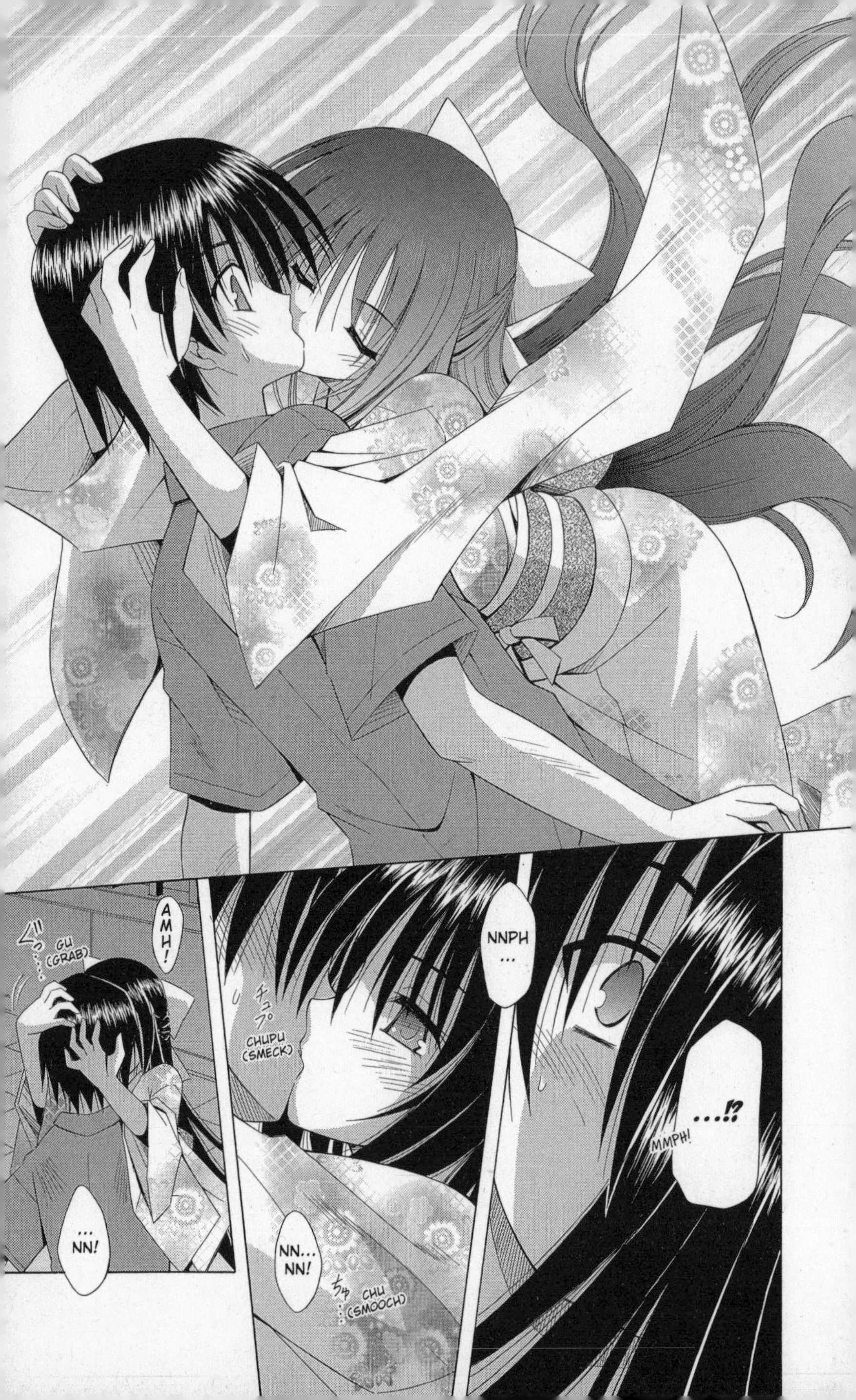
NNPH ...
...!?
MMPH!
チュプ
CHUPU (SMECK)
NN... NN!
ちゅ...
CHU (SMOOCH)
AMH!
GU (GRAB)
... NN!

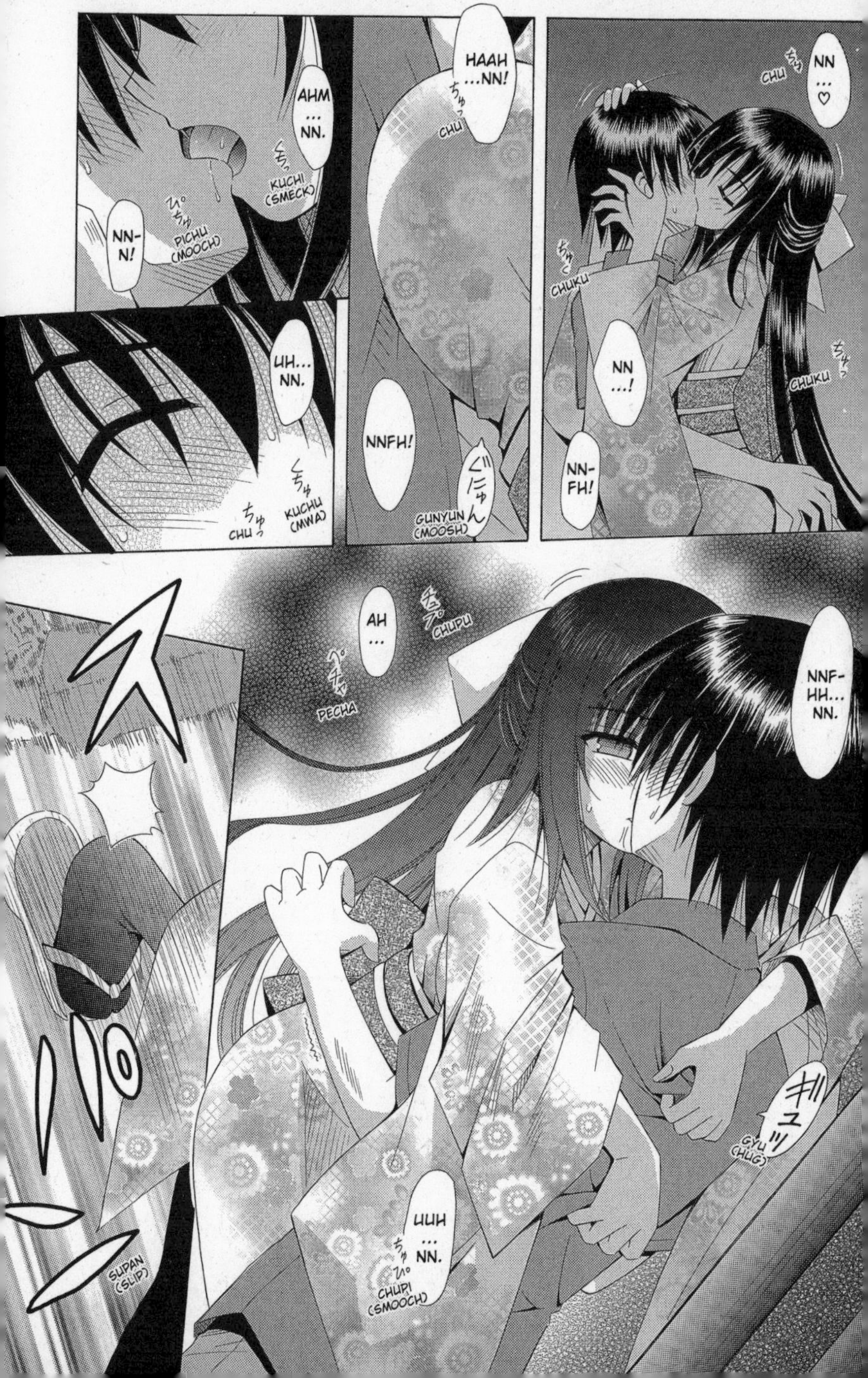
NN … ♡
CHU
CHUKU
CHUKU
NN …!
NN-FH!
HAAH …NN!
CHU
NNFH!
GUNYUN (MOOSH)
AHM … NN.
KUCHI (SMECK)
PICHU (MOOCH)
NN-N!
UH… NN.
KUCHU (MWA)
CHU
NNF-HH… NN.
CHUPU
AH …
PECHA
GYU (HUG)
UUH … NN.
CHUPI (SMOOCH)
SUPAN (SLIP)

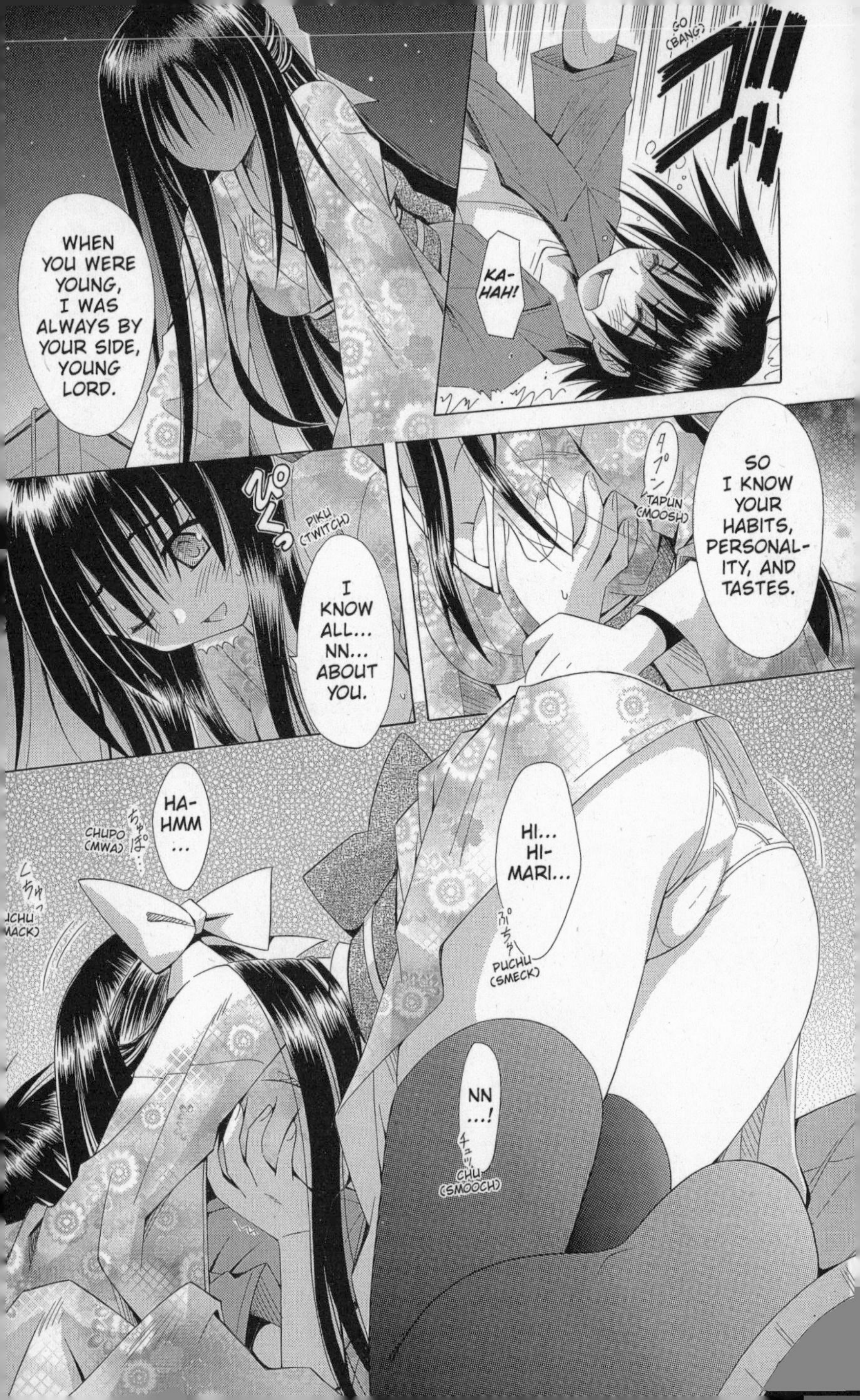
GO (BANG)
KA-HAH!
WHEN YOU WERE YOUNG, I WAS ALWAYS BY YOUR SIDE, YOUNG LORD.
TAPUN (MOOSH)
SO I KNOW YOUR HABITS, PERSONAL-ITY, AND TASTES.
PIKU (TWITCH)
I KNOW ALL... NN... ABOUT YOU.
HI... HI-MARI...
PUCHU (SMECK)
HA-HMM...
CHUPO (MWA)
NN...!
CHU (SMOOCH)

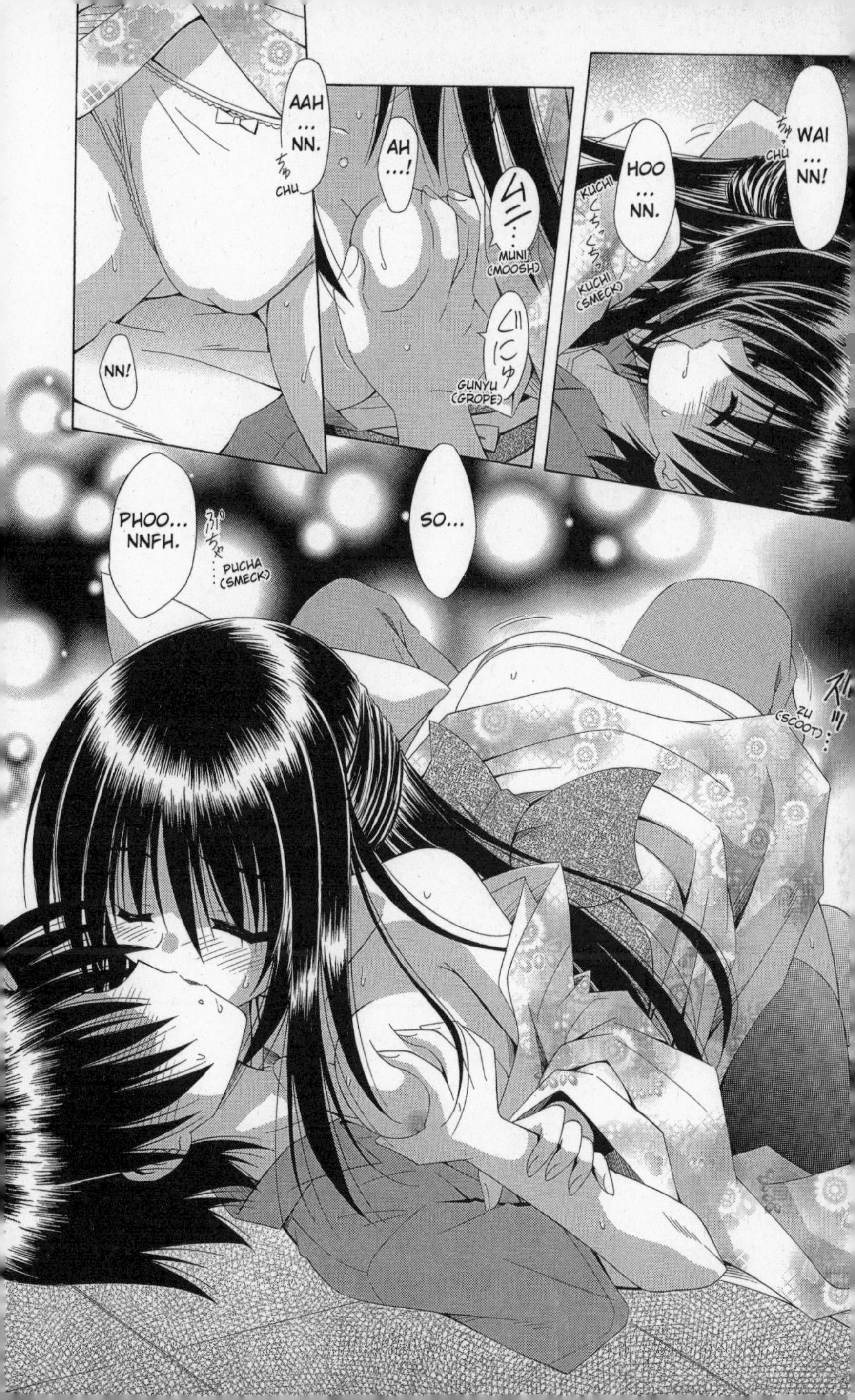

WAI ... NN!
ちゅ CHU
HOO ... NN.
KUCHI くちゅくちゅ KUCHI (SMECK)
AH ...!
ムニ… MUNI (MOOSH)
ぐにゅ GUNYU (GROPE)
AAH ... NN.
ちゅ CHU
NN!
ズッ… ZU (SCOOT)
SO...
PHOO... NNFH.
ぷちゅ… PUCHA (SMECK)

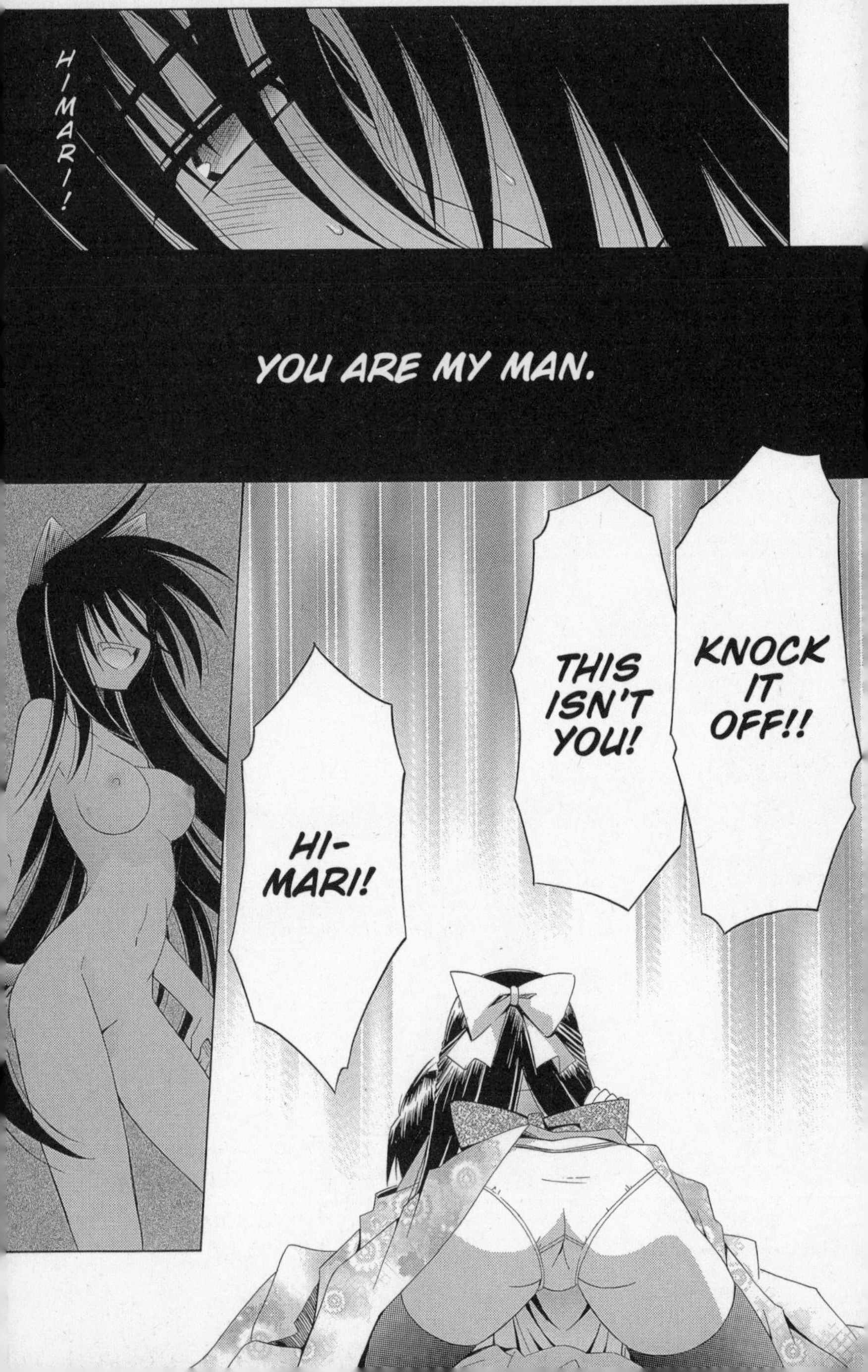
HIMARI!!
YOU ARE MY MAN.
KNOCK IT OFF!!
THIS ISN'T YOU!
HI-MARI!

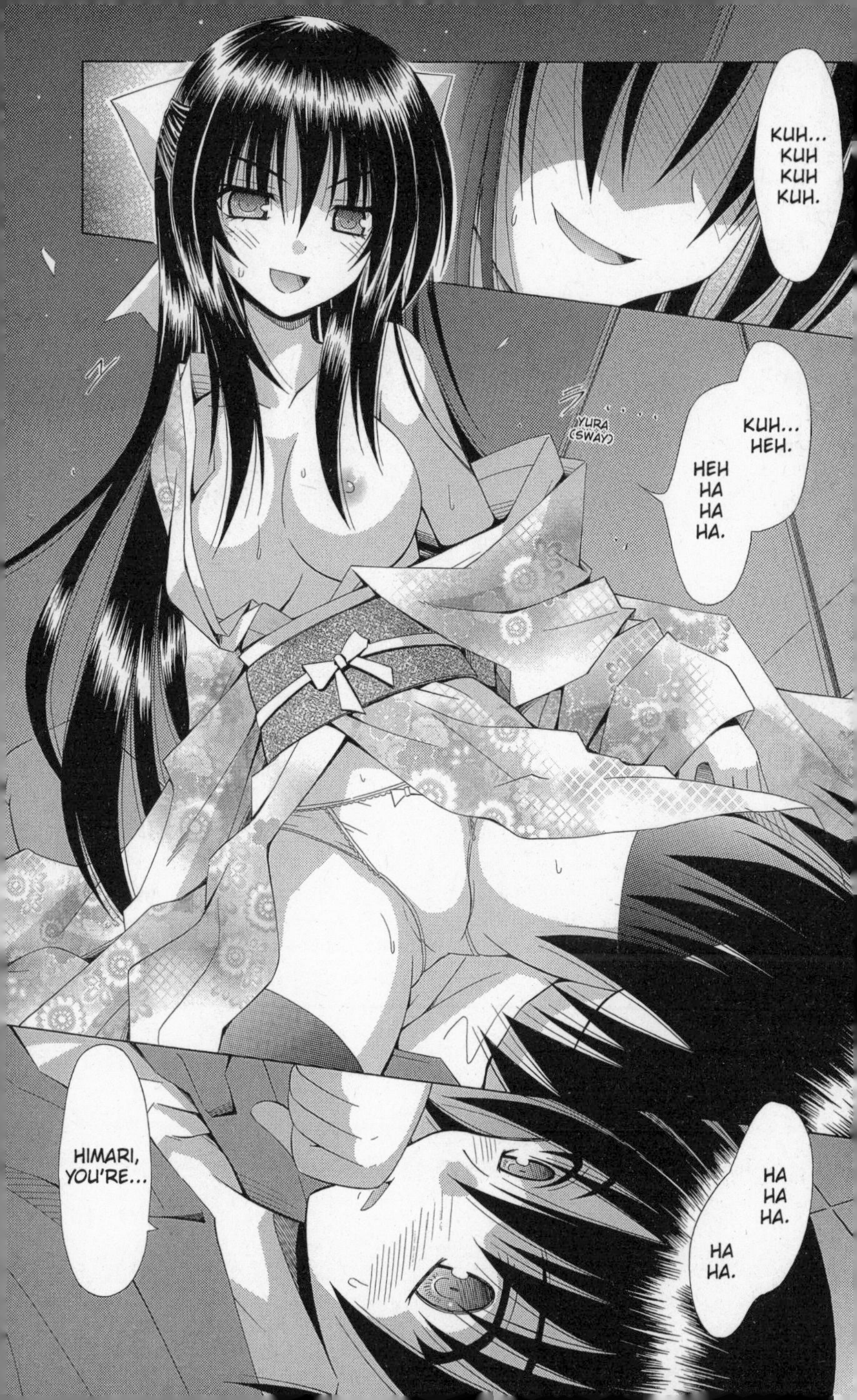
KUH... KUH KUH KUH.
KUH... HEH. HEH HA HA HA.
YURA (SWAY)
HA HA HA. HA HA.
HIMARI, YOU'RE...

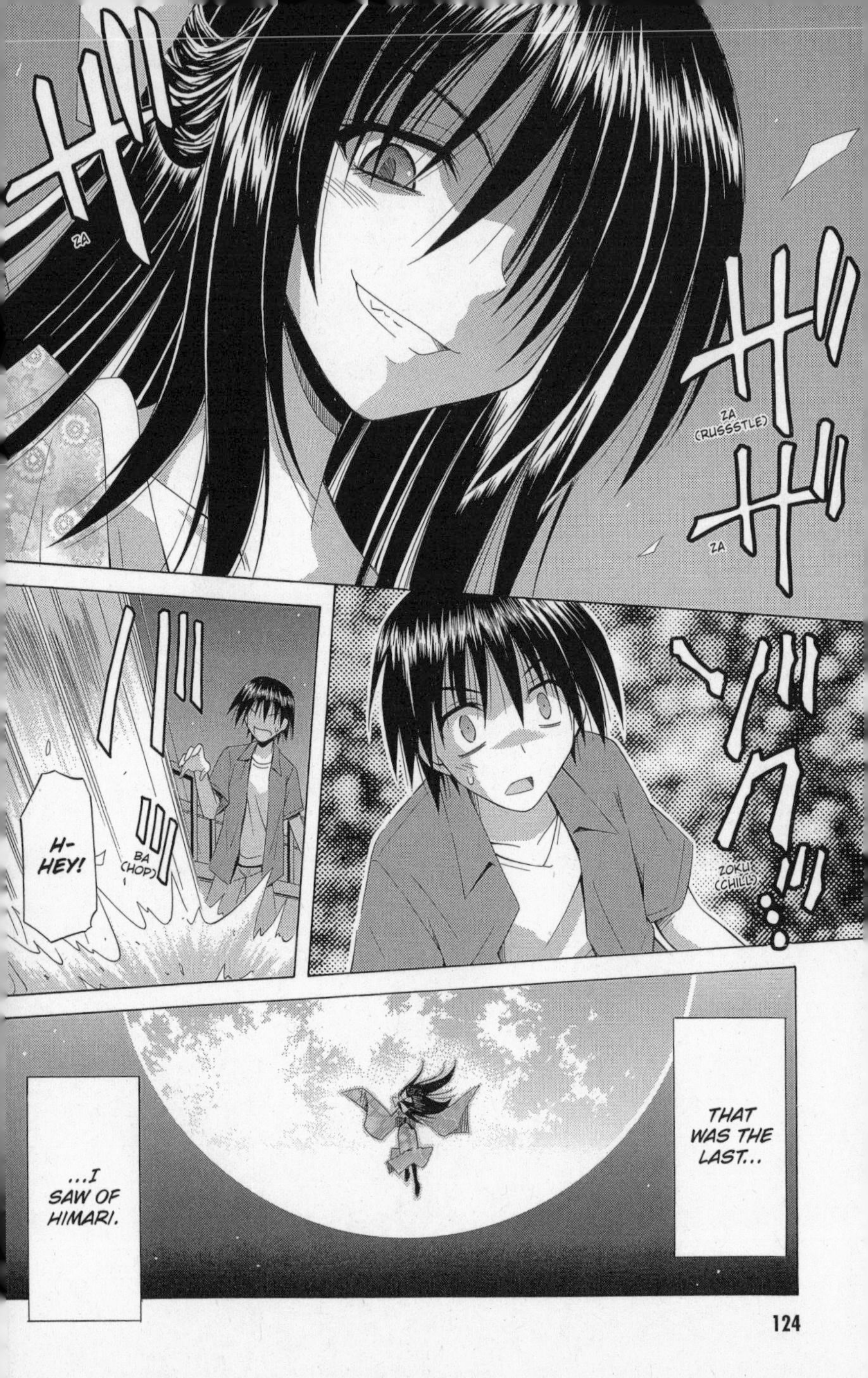
ZA (RUSSSTLE)
ZA
ZA
ZOKU (CHILL)
BA (HOP)
H-HEY!
THAT WAS THE LAST...
...I SAW OF HIMARI.

MENAGERIE 68: ONE OF THE BROKEN CAT'S SHADOWS APPEARS IN THE MIRROR

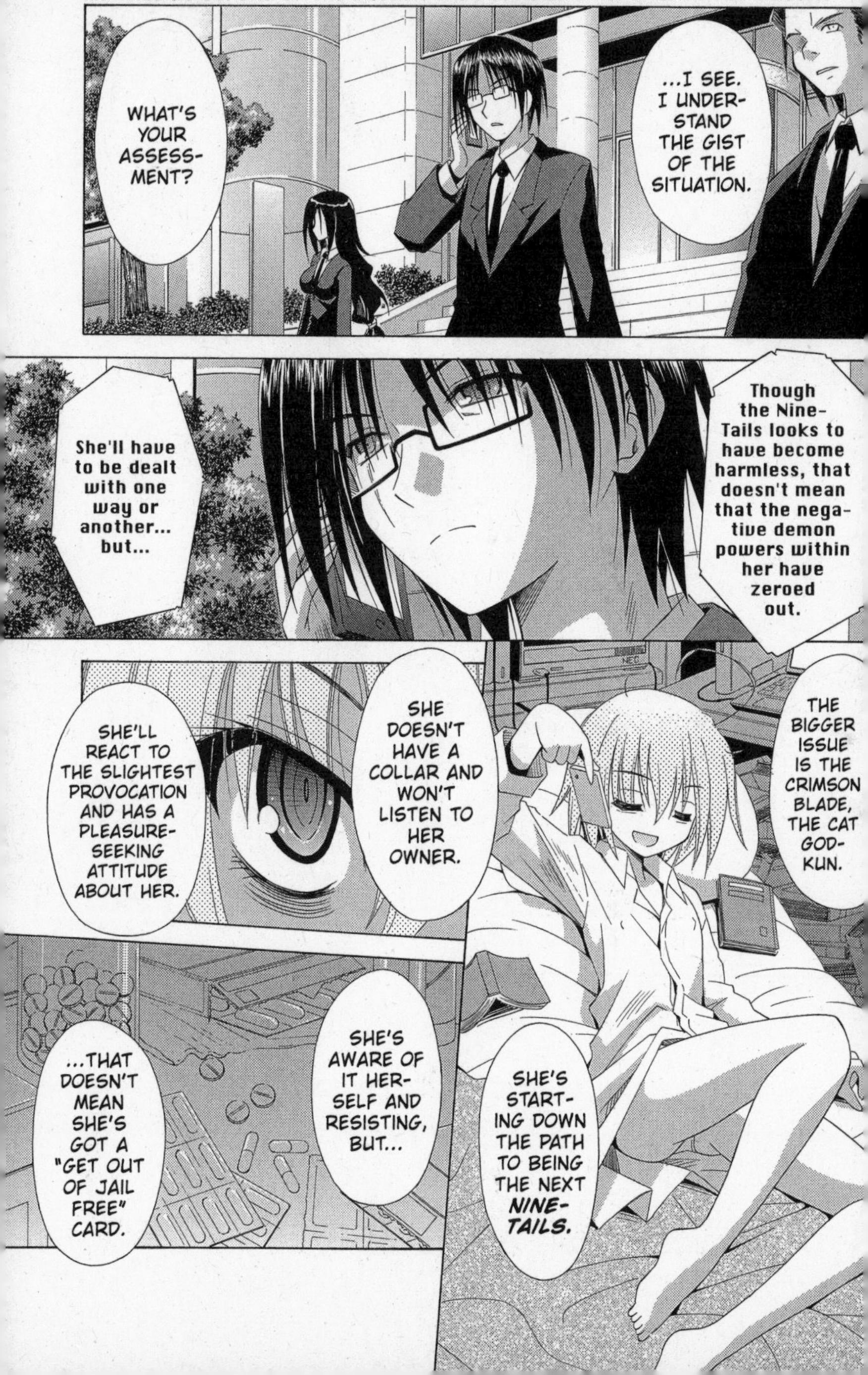
...I SEE. I UNDERSTAND THE GIST OF THE SITUATION.
WHAT'S YOUR ASSESSMENT?
Though the Nine-Tails looks to have become harmless, that doesn't mean that the negative demon powers within her have zeroed out.
She'll have to be dealt with one way or another... but...
THE BIGGER ISSUE IS THE CRIMSON BLADE, THE CAT GOD-KUN.
SHE DOESN'T HAVE A COLLAR AND WON'T LISTEN TO HER OWNER.
SHE'LL REACT TO THE SLIGHTEST PROVOCATION AND HAS A PLEASURE-SEEKING ATTITUDE ABOUT HER.
SHE'S AWARE OF IT HERSELF AND RESISTING, BUT...
...THAT DOESN'T MEAN SHE'S GOT A "GET OUT OF JAIL FREE" CARD.
SHE'S STARTING DOWN THE PATH TO BEING THE NEXT NINE-TAILS.

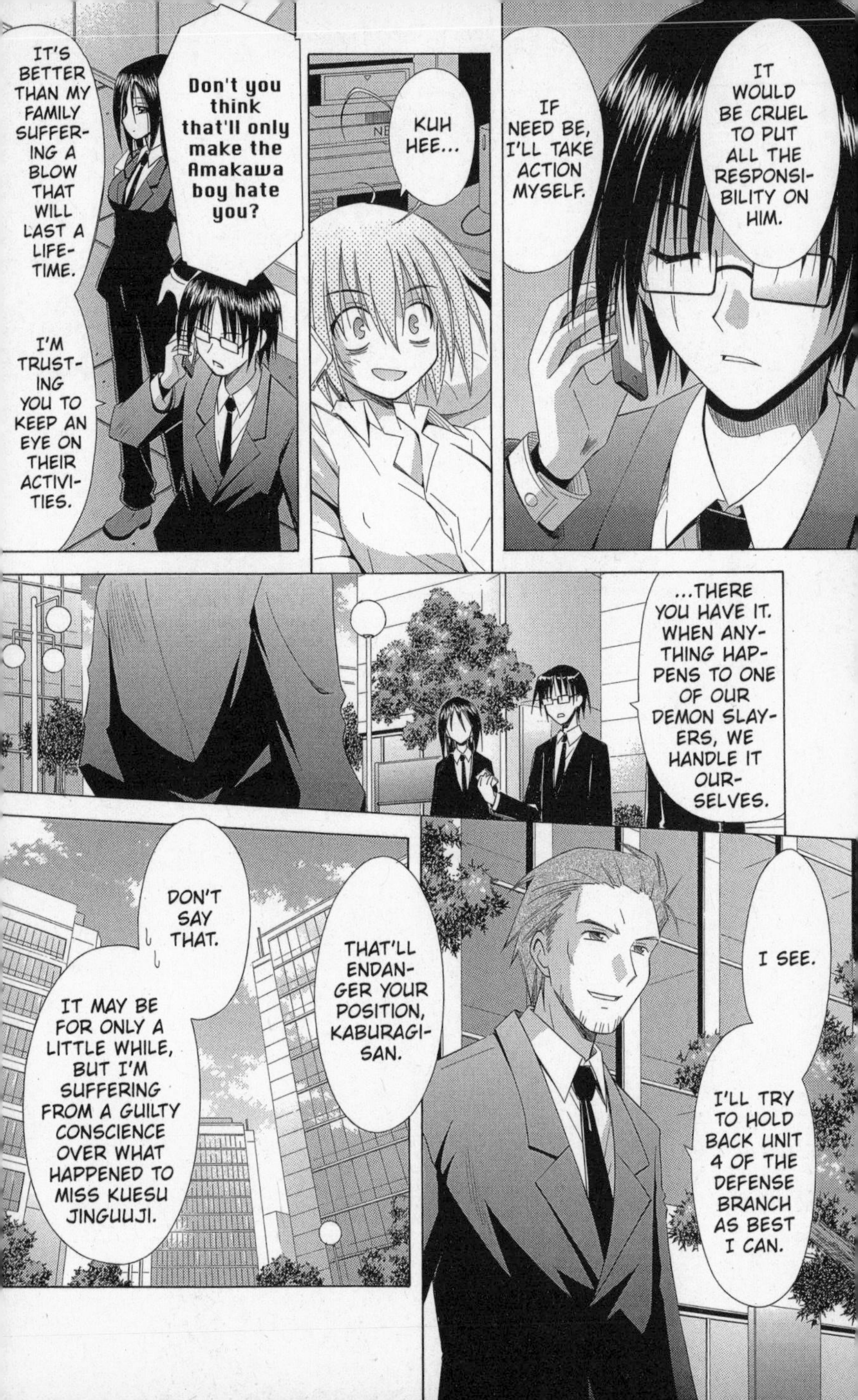
IT WOULD BE CRUEL TO PUT ALL THE RESPONSIBILITY ON HIM.
IF NEED BE, I'LL TAKE ACTION MYSELF.
KUH HEE...
Don't you think that'll only make the Amakawa boy hate you?
IT'S BETTER THAN MY FAMILY SUFFERING A BLOW THAT WILL LAST A LIFETIME.
I'M TRUSTING YOU TO KEEP AN EYE ON THEIR ACTIVITIES.
...THERE YOU HAVE IT. WHEN ANYTHING HAPPENS TO ONE OF OUR DEMON SLAYERS, WE HANDLE IT OURSELVES.
I SEE.
I'LL TRY TO HOLD BACK UNIT 4 OF THE DEFENSE BRANCH AS BEST I CAN.
THAT'LL ENDANGER YOUR POSITION, KABURAGI-SAN.
DON'T SAY THAT.
IT MAY BE FOR ONLY A LITTLE WHILE, BUT I'M SUFFERING FROM A GUILTY CONSCIENCE OVER WHAT HAPPENED TO MISS KUESU JINGUUJI.

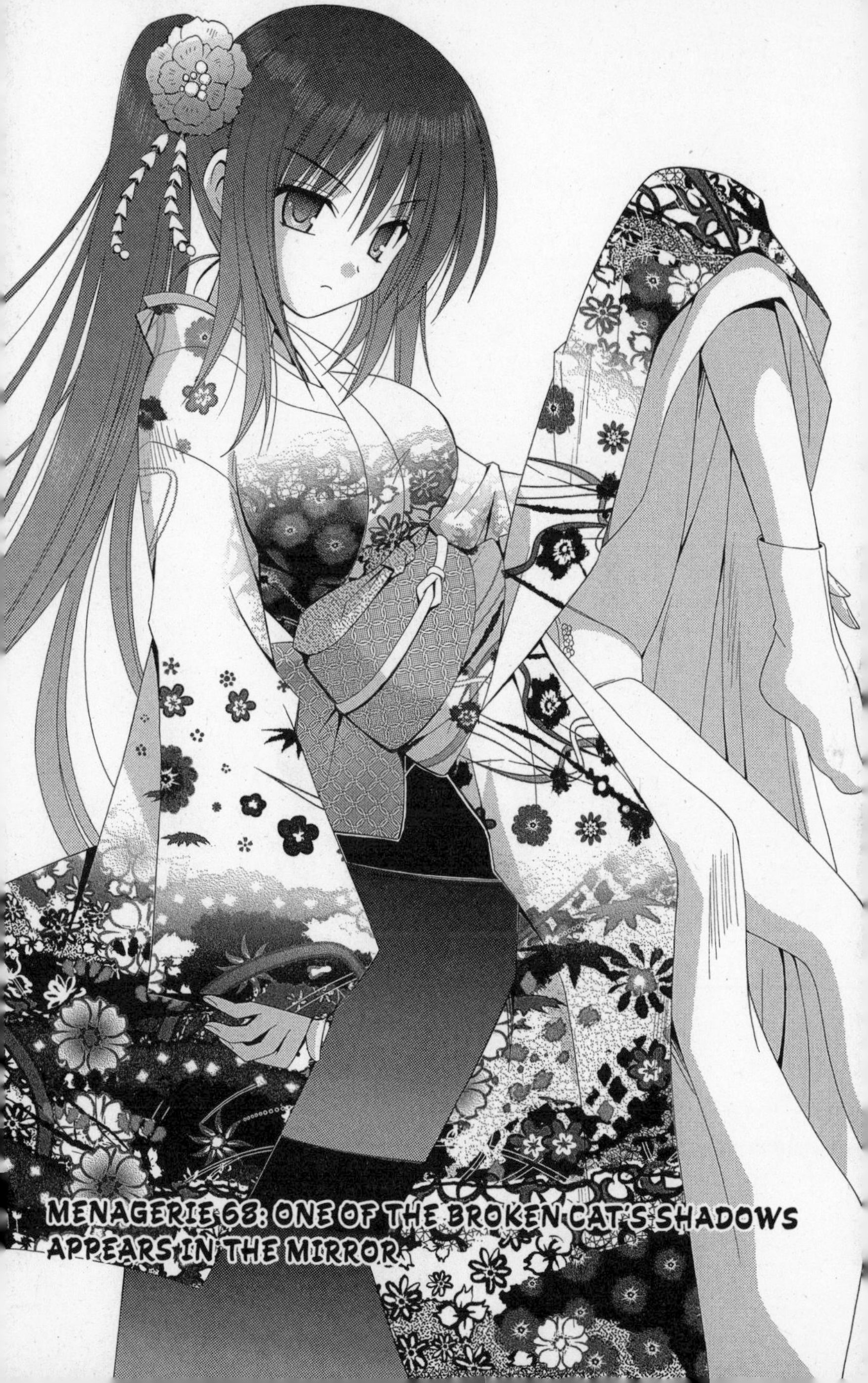

MENAGERIE 68: ONE OF THE BROKEN CAT'S SHADOWS APPEARS IN THE MIRROR

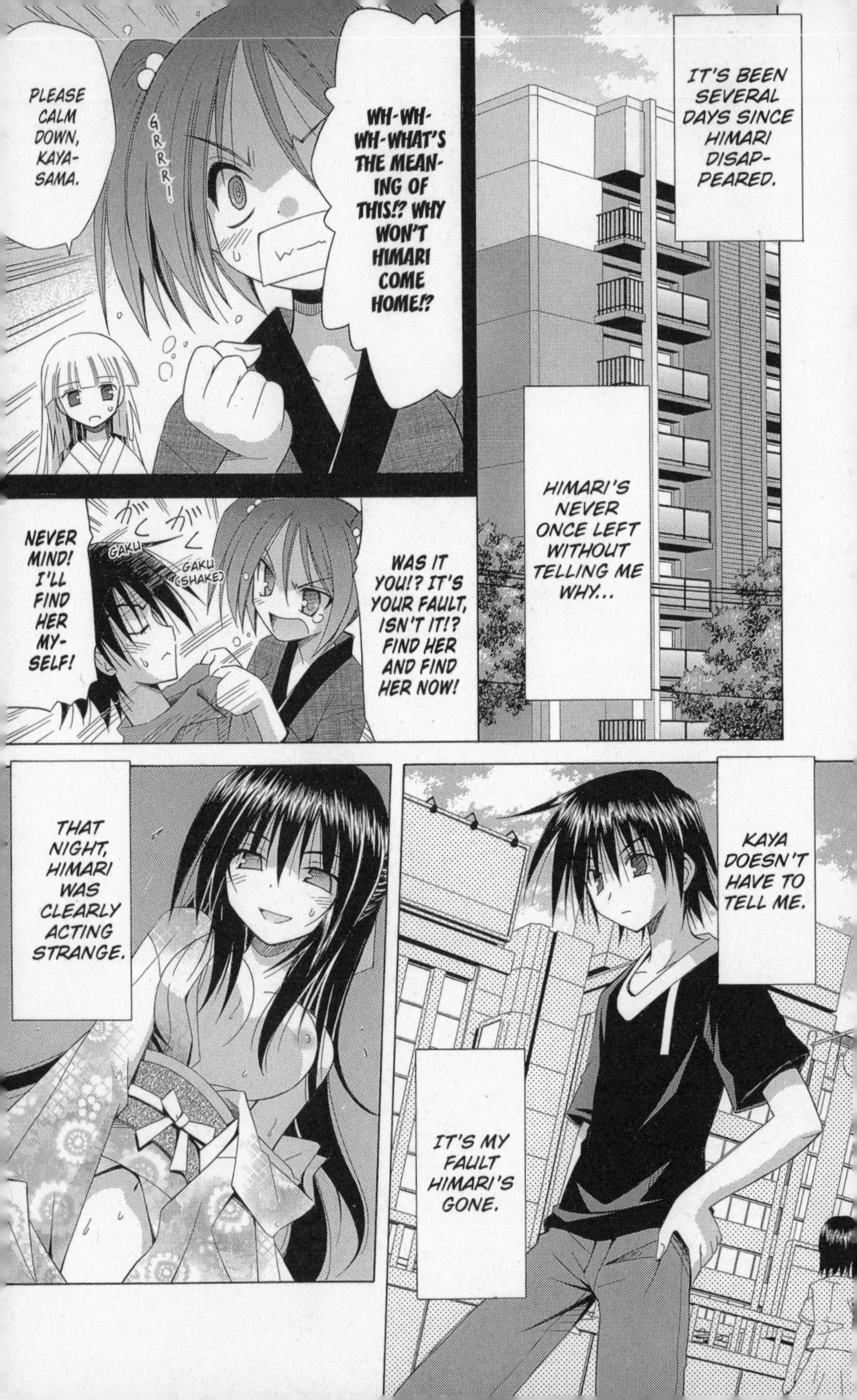
IT'S BEEN SEVERAL DAYS SINCE HIMARI DISAPPEARED.
HIMARI'S NEVER ONCE LEFT WITHOUT TELLING ME WHY...
WH-WH-WH-WHAT'S THE MEANING OF THIS!? WHY WON'T HIMARI COME HOME!?
GRRR!
PLEASE CALM DOWN, KAYA-SAMA.
WAS IT YOU!? IT'S YOUR FAULT, ISN'T IT!? FIND HER AND FIND HER NOW!
がく がく
GAKU
GAKU (SHAKE)
NEVER MIND! I'LL FIND HER MYSELF!
KAYA DOESN'T HAVE TO TELL ME.
IT'S MY FAULT HIMARI'S GONE.
THAT NIGHT, HIMARI WAS CLEARLY ACTING STRANGE.

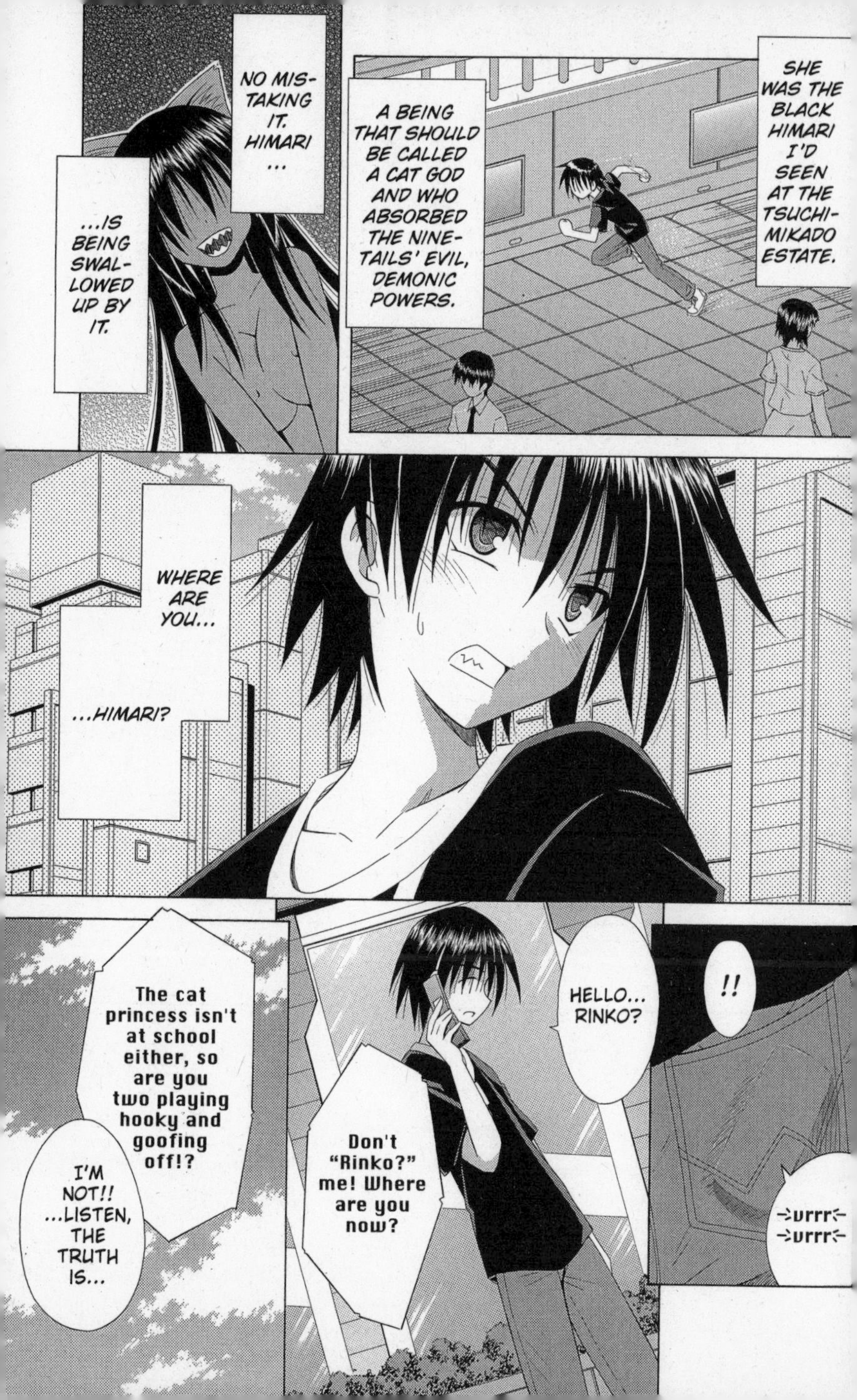
SHE WAS THE BLACK HIMARI I'D SEEN AT THE TSUCHIMIKADO ESTATE.
A BEING THAT SHOULD BE CALLED A CAT GOD AND WHO ABSORBED THE NINE-TAILS' EVIL, DEMONIC POWERS.
NO MISTAKING IT. HIMARI...
...IS BEING SWALLOWED UP BY IT.
WHERE ARE YOU...
...HIMARI?
!!
~vrrr~ ~vrrr~
HELLO... RINKO?
Don't "Rinko?" me! Where are you now?
The cat princess isn't at school either, so are you two playing hooky and goofing off!?
I'M NOT!! ...LISTEN, THE TRUTH IS...

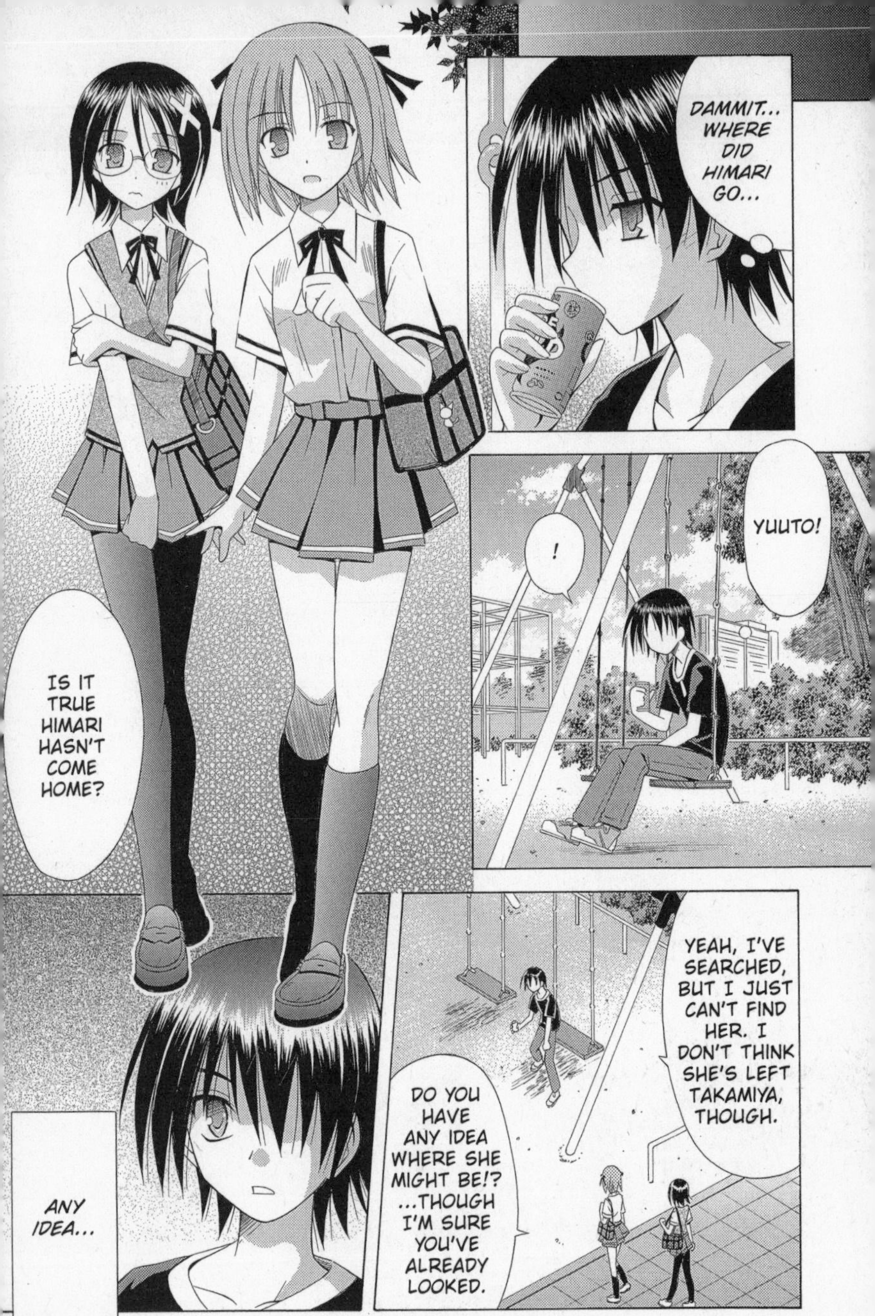
DAMMIT... WHERE DID HIMARI GO...
YUUTO!
!
IS IT TRUE HIMARI HASN'T COME HOME?
YEAH, I'VE SEARCHED, BUT I JUST CAN'T FIND HER. I DON'T THINK SHE'S LEFT TAKAMIYA, THOUGH.
DO YOU HAVE ANY IDEA WHERE SHE MIGHT BE!? ...THOUGH I'M SURE YOU'VE ALREADY LOOKED.
ANY IDEA...

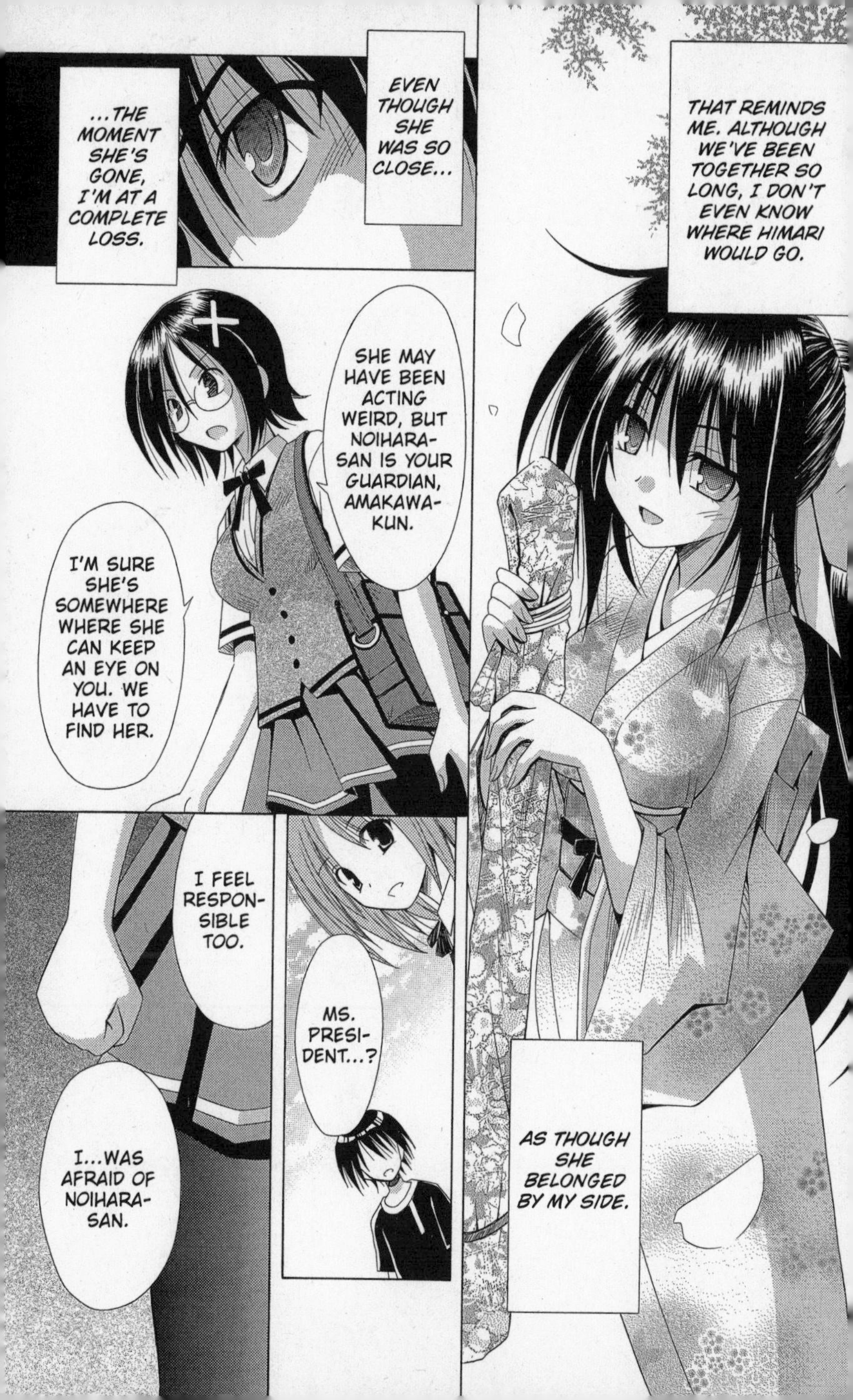
THAT REMINDS ME. ALTHOUGH WE'VE BEEN TOGETHER SO LONG, I DON'T EVEN KNOW WHERE HIMARI WOULD GO.
AS THOUGH SHE BELONGED BY MY SIDE.
EVEN THOUGH SHE WAS SO CLOSE...
...THE MOMENT SHE'S GONE, I'M AT A COMPLETE LOSS.
SHE MAY HAVE BEEN ACTING WEIRD, BUT NOIHARA-SAN IS YOUR GUARDIAN, AMAKAWA-KUN.
I'M SURE SHE'S SOMEWHERE WHERE SHE CAN KEEP AN EYE ON YOU. WE HAVE TO FIND HER.
MS. PRESIDENT...?
I FEEL RESPONSIBLE TOO.
I...WAS AFRAID OF NOIHARA-SAN.

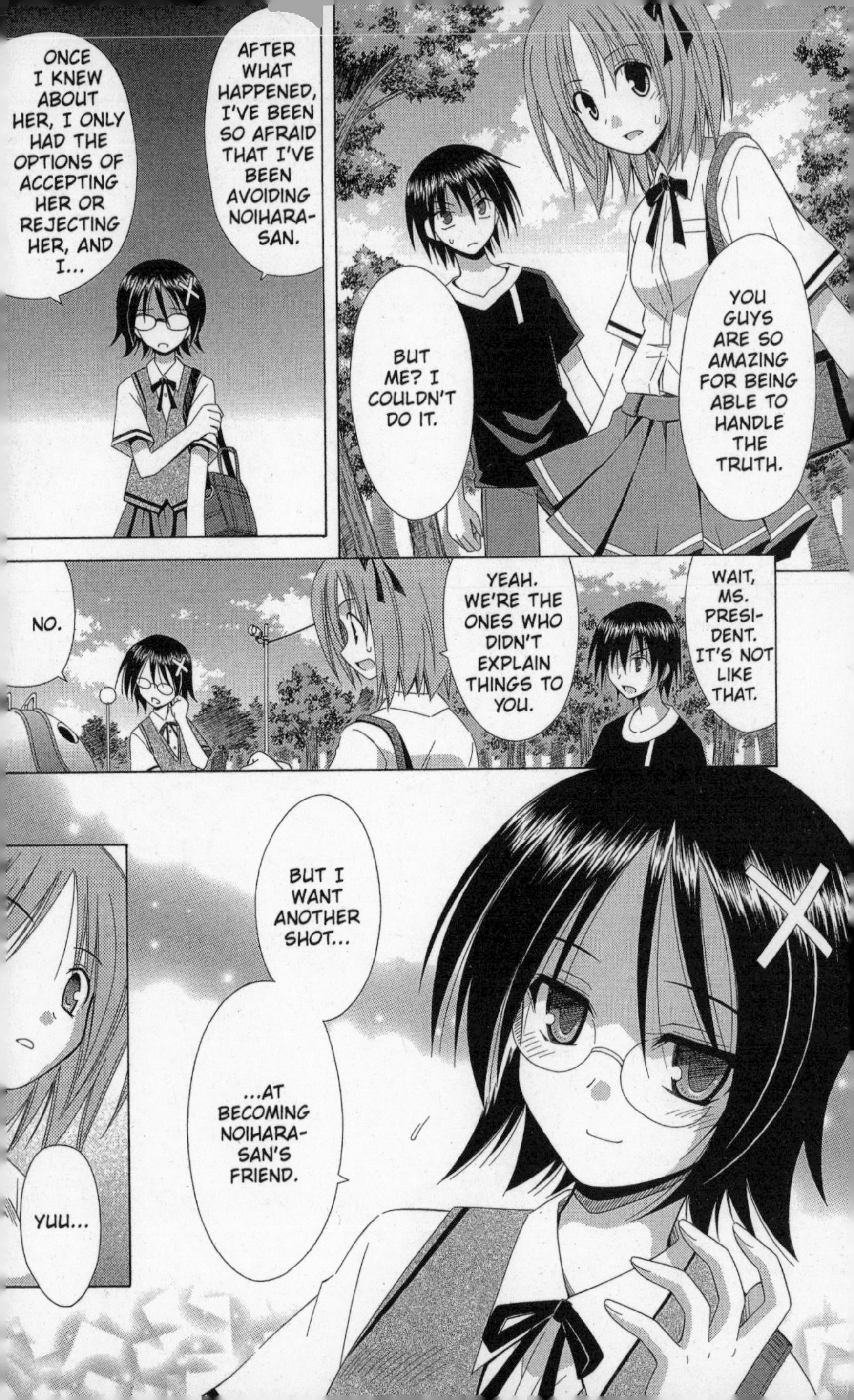
YOU GUYS ARE SO AMAZING FOR BEING ABLE TO HANDLE THE TRUTH.
BUT ME? I COULDN'T DO IT.
AFTER WHAT HAPPENED, I'VE BEEN SO AFRAID THAT I'VE BEEN AVOIDING NOIHARA-SAN.
ONCE I KNEW ABOUT HER, I ONLY HAD THE OPTIONS OF ACCEPTING HER OR REJECTING HER, AND I...
WAIT, MS. PRESIDENT. IT'S NOT LIKE THAT.
YEAH. WE'RE THE ONES WHO DIDN'T EXPLAIN THINGS TO YOU.
NO.
BUT I WANT ANOTHER SHOT...
...AT BECOMING NOIHARA-SAN'S FRIEND.
YUU...

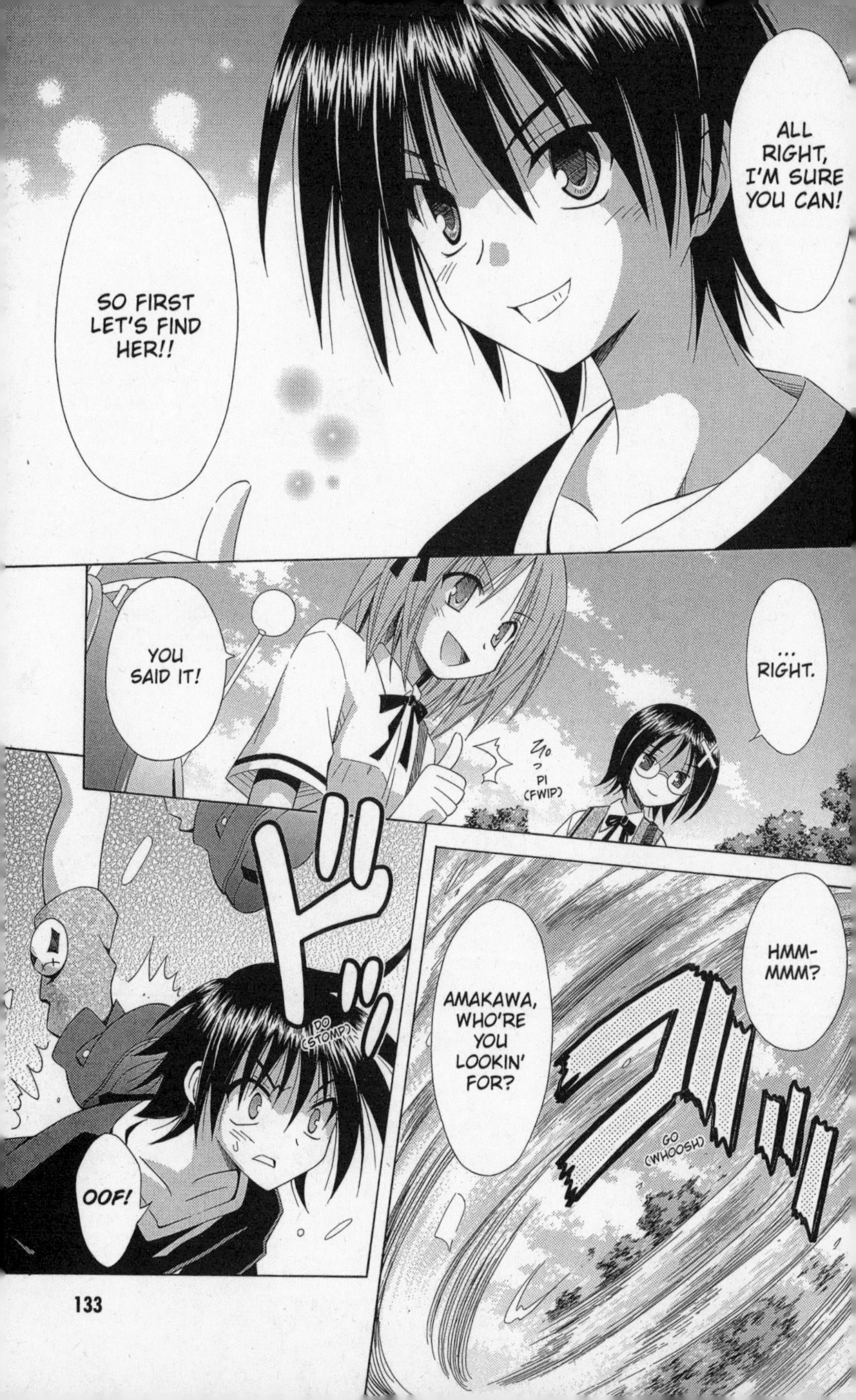
ALL RIGHT, I'M SURE YOU CAN!
SO FIRST LET'S FIND HER!!
... RIGHT.
PI (FWIP)
YOU SAID IT!
HMM-MMM?
AMAKAWA, WHO'RE YOU LOOKIN' FOR?
GO (WHOOSH)
DO (STOMP)
OOF!

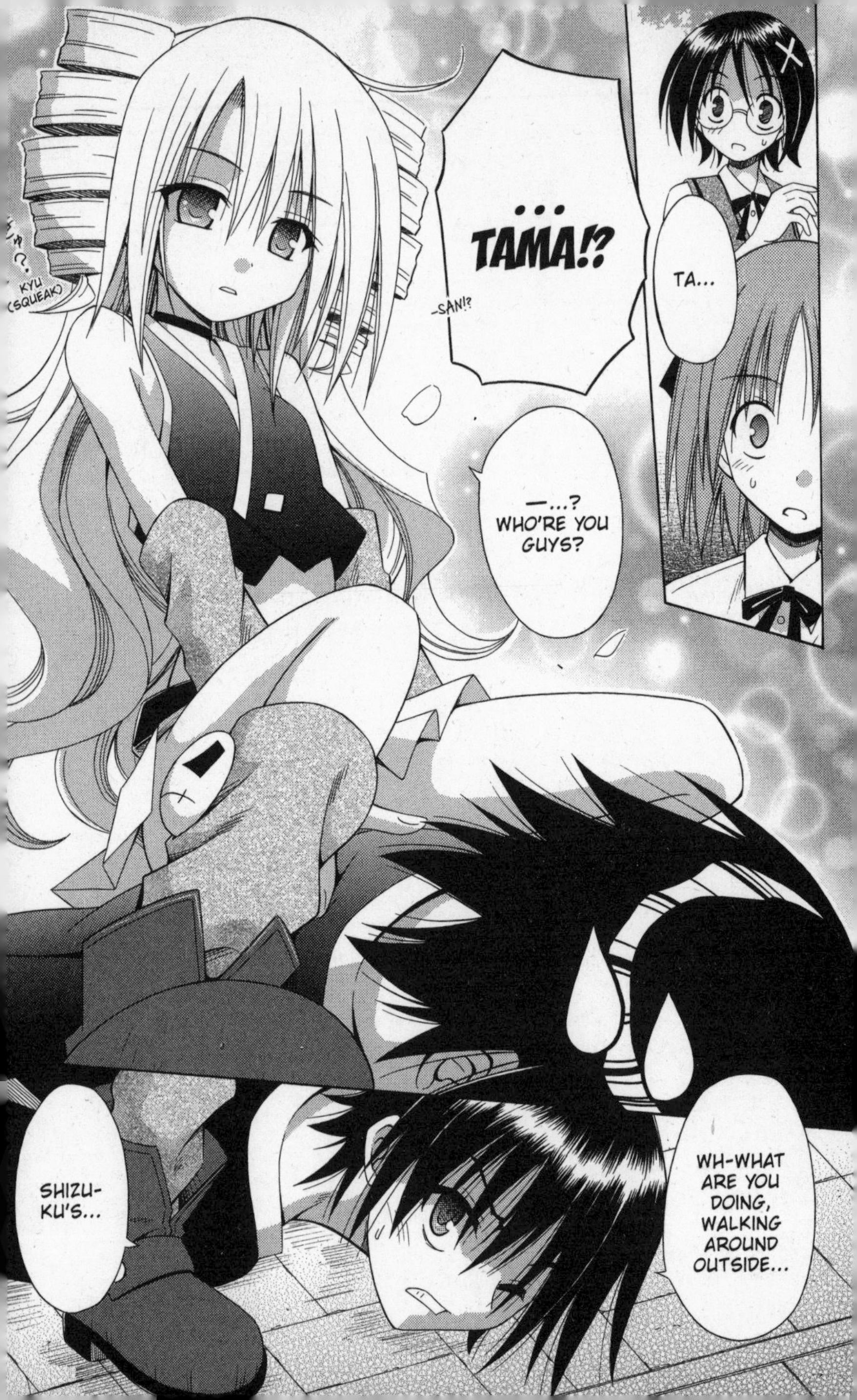
TA...
...TAMA!?
-SAN!?
—...? WHO'RE YOU GUYS?
KYU (SQUEAK)
WH-WHAT ARE YOU DOING, WALKING AROUND OUTSIDE...
SHIZU-KU'S...

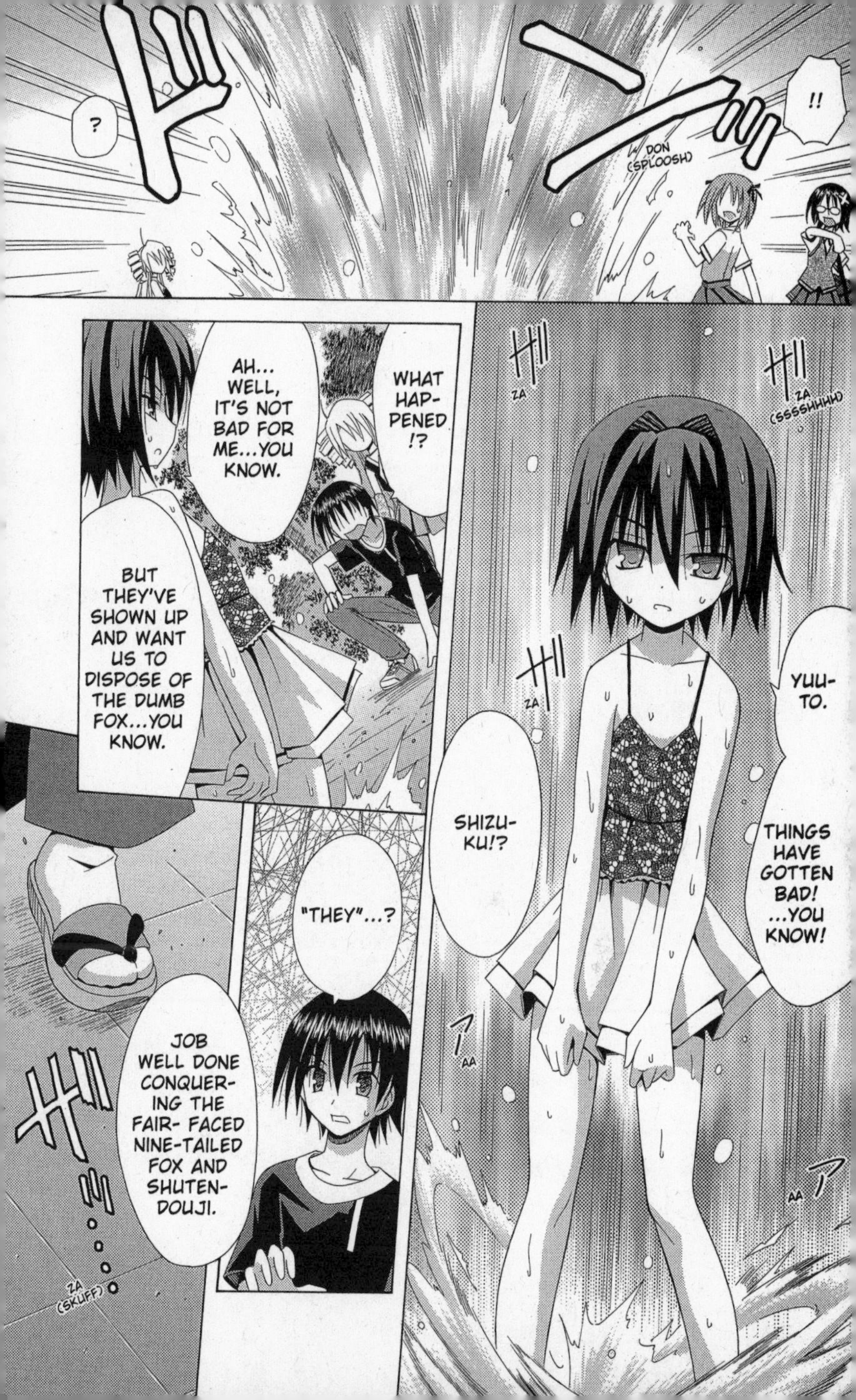
!!
DON (SPLOOSH)
?
ZA (SSSSHHHH)
ZA
ZA
YUU-TO.
THINGS HAVE GOTTEN BAD! ...YOU KNOW!
SHIZU-KU!?
AA
AA
WHAT HAP-PENED !?
AH... WELL, IT'S NOT BAD FOR ME...YOU KNOW.
BUT THEY'VE SHOWN UP AND WANT US TO DISPOSE OF THE DUMB FOX...YOU KNOW.
"THEY"...?
JOB WELL DONE CONQUER-ING THE FAIR- FACED NINE-TAILED FOX AND SHUTEN-DOUJI.
ZA (SKUFF)

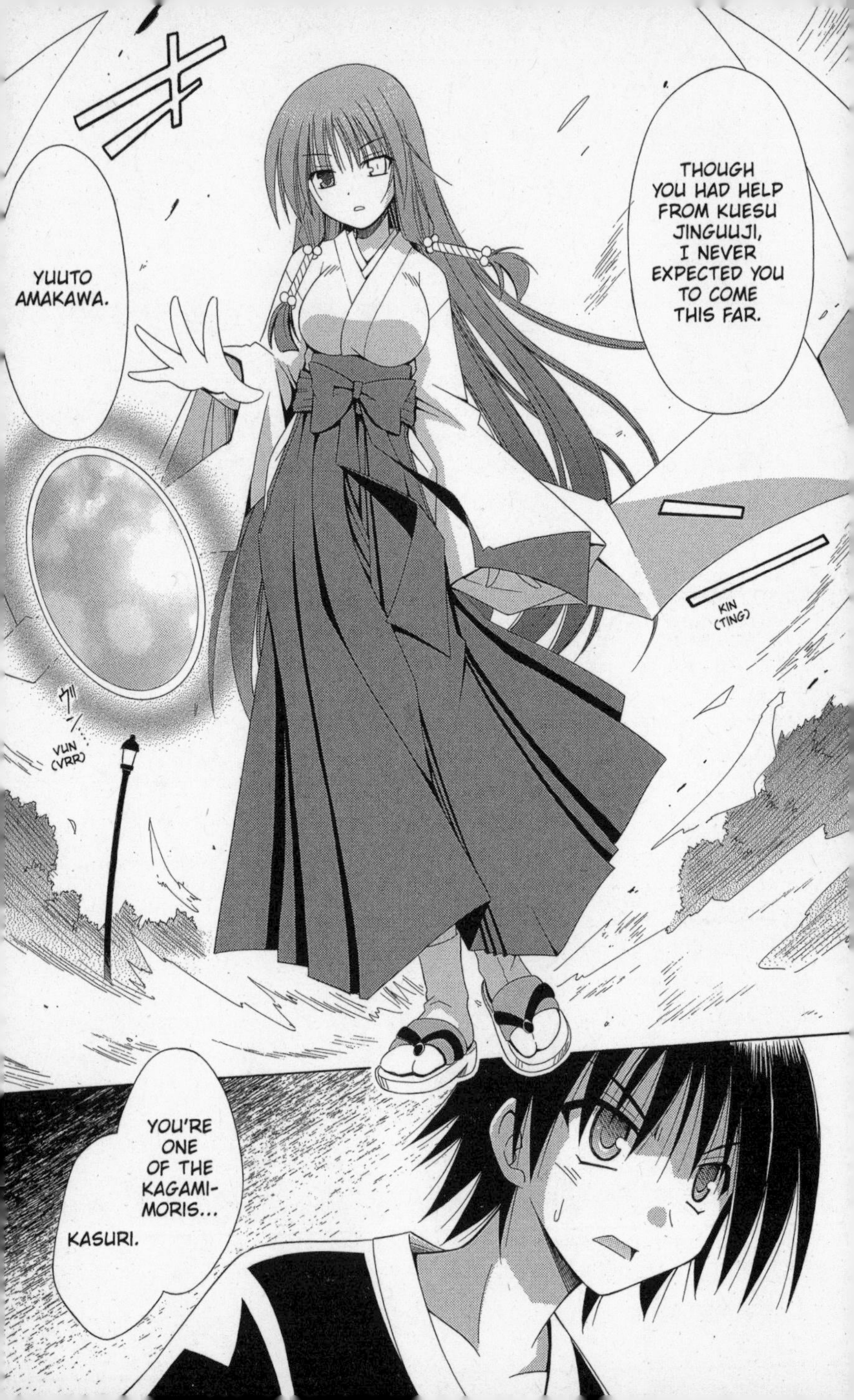
THOUGH YOU HAD HELP FROM KUESU JINGUUJI, I NEVER EXPECTED YOU TO COME THIS FAR.
YUUTO AMAKAWA.
KIN (TING)
VUN (VRR)
YOU'RE ONE OF THE KAGAMI-MORIS...
KASURI.

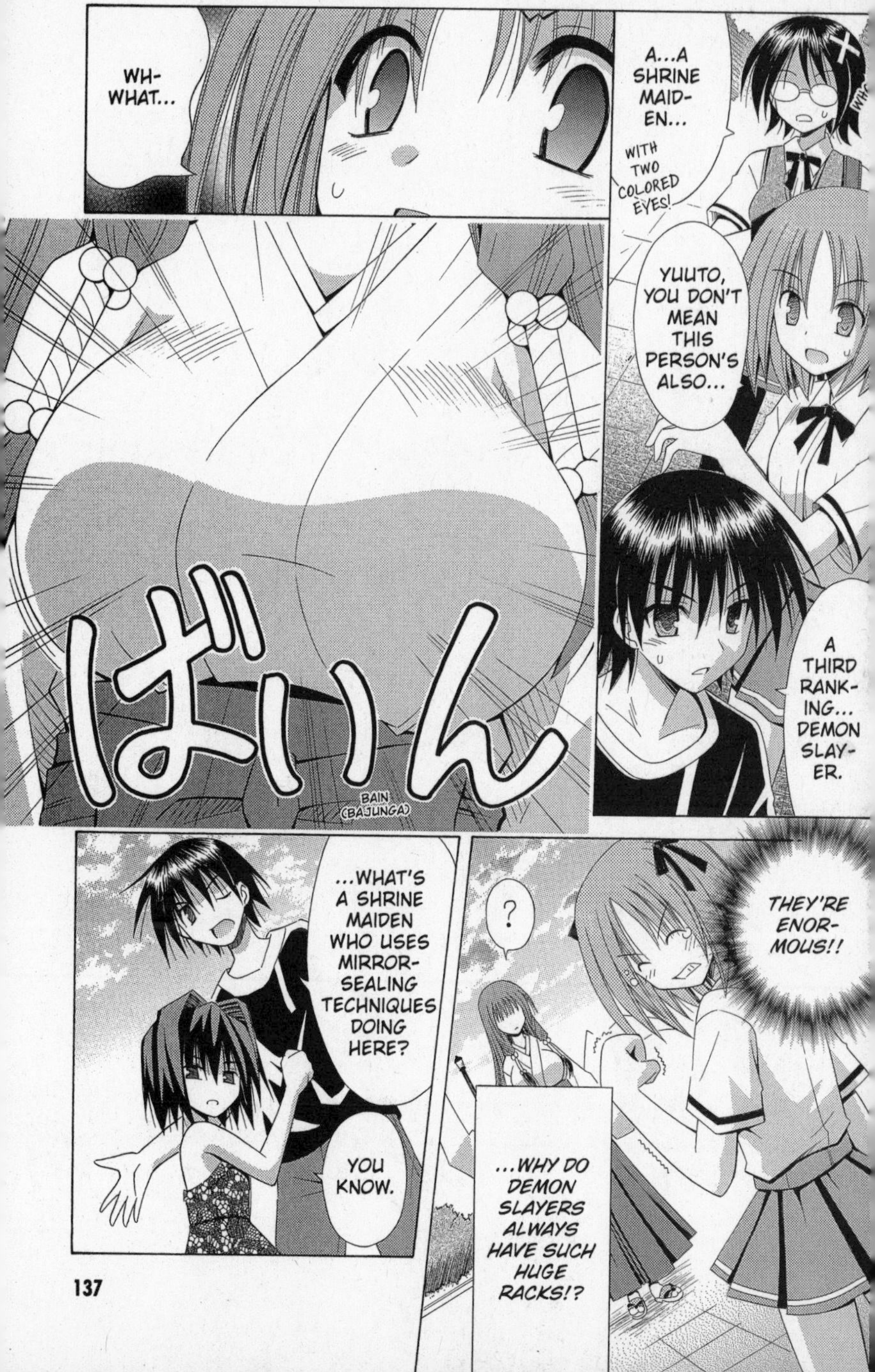
A...A SHRINE MAIDEN...
WITH TWO COLORED EYES!
YUUTO, YOU DON'T MEAN THIS PERSON'S ALSO...
A THIRD RANKING... DEMON SLAYER.
WH-WHAT...
ばいん
BAIN (BAJUNGA)
THEY'RE ENORMOUS!!
?
...WHY DO DEMON SLAYERS ALWAYS HAVE SUCH HUGE RACKS!?
...WHAT'S A SHRINE MAIDEN WHO USES MIRROR-SEALING TECHNIQUES DOING HERE?
YOU KNOW.

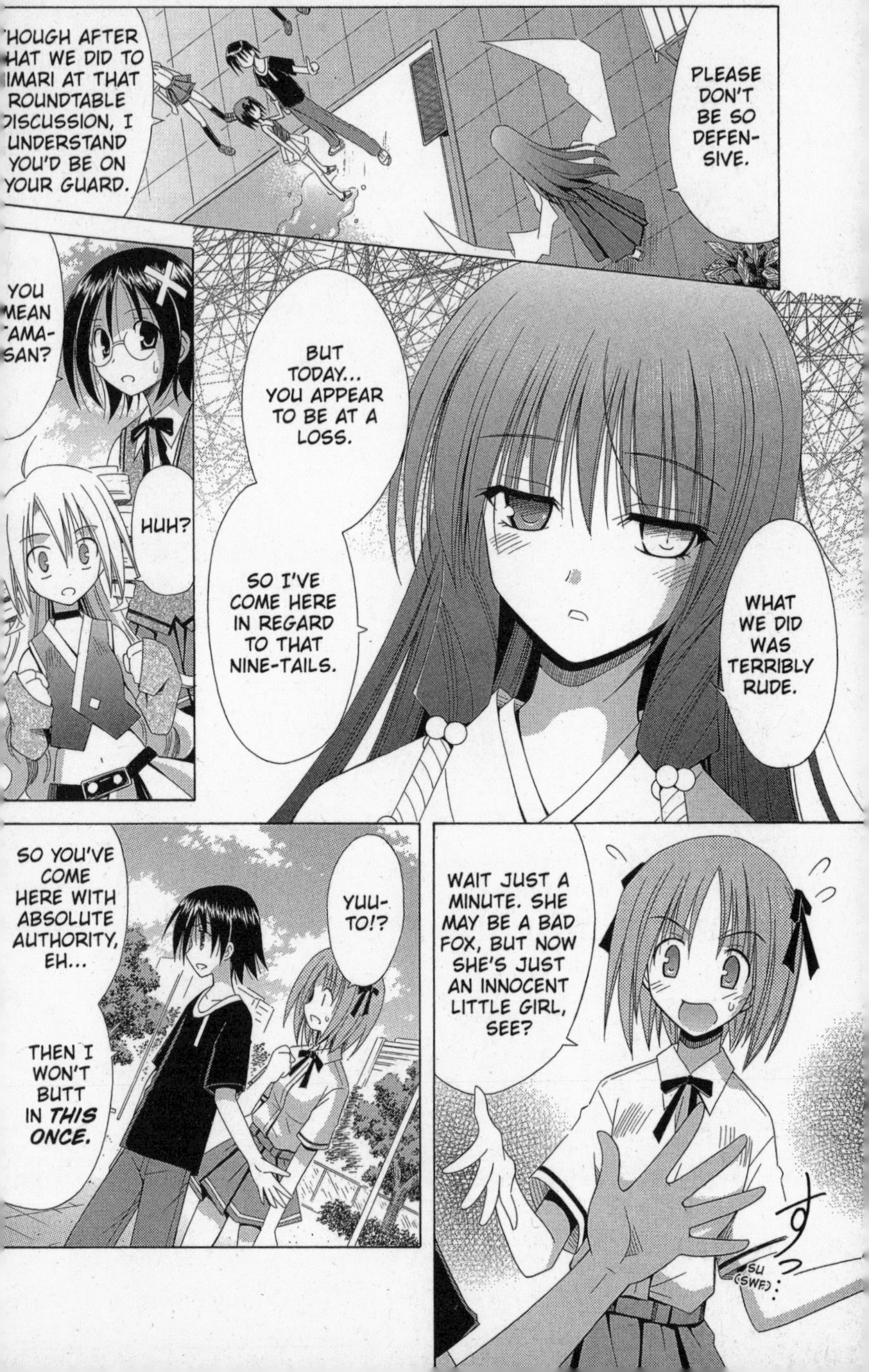
PLEASE DON'T BE SO DEFENSIVE.
THOUGH AFTER WHAT WE DID TO IMARI AT THAT ROUNDTABLE DISCUSSION, I UNDERSTAND YOU'D BE ON YOUR GUARD.
WHAT WE DID WAS TERRIBLY RUDE.
BUT TODAY... YOU APPEAR TO BE AT A LOSS.
SO I'VE COME HERE IN REGARD TO THAT NINE-TAILS.
YOU MEAN TAMA-SAN?
HUH?
WAIT JUST A MINUTE. SHE MAY BE A BAD FOX, BUT NOW SHE'S JUST AN INNOCENT LITTLE GIRL, SEE?
SU (SWF)
YUU-TO!?
SO YOU'VE COME HERE WITH ABSOLUTE AUTHORITY, EH...
THEN I WON'T BUTT IN *THIS ONCE*.

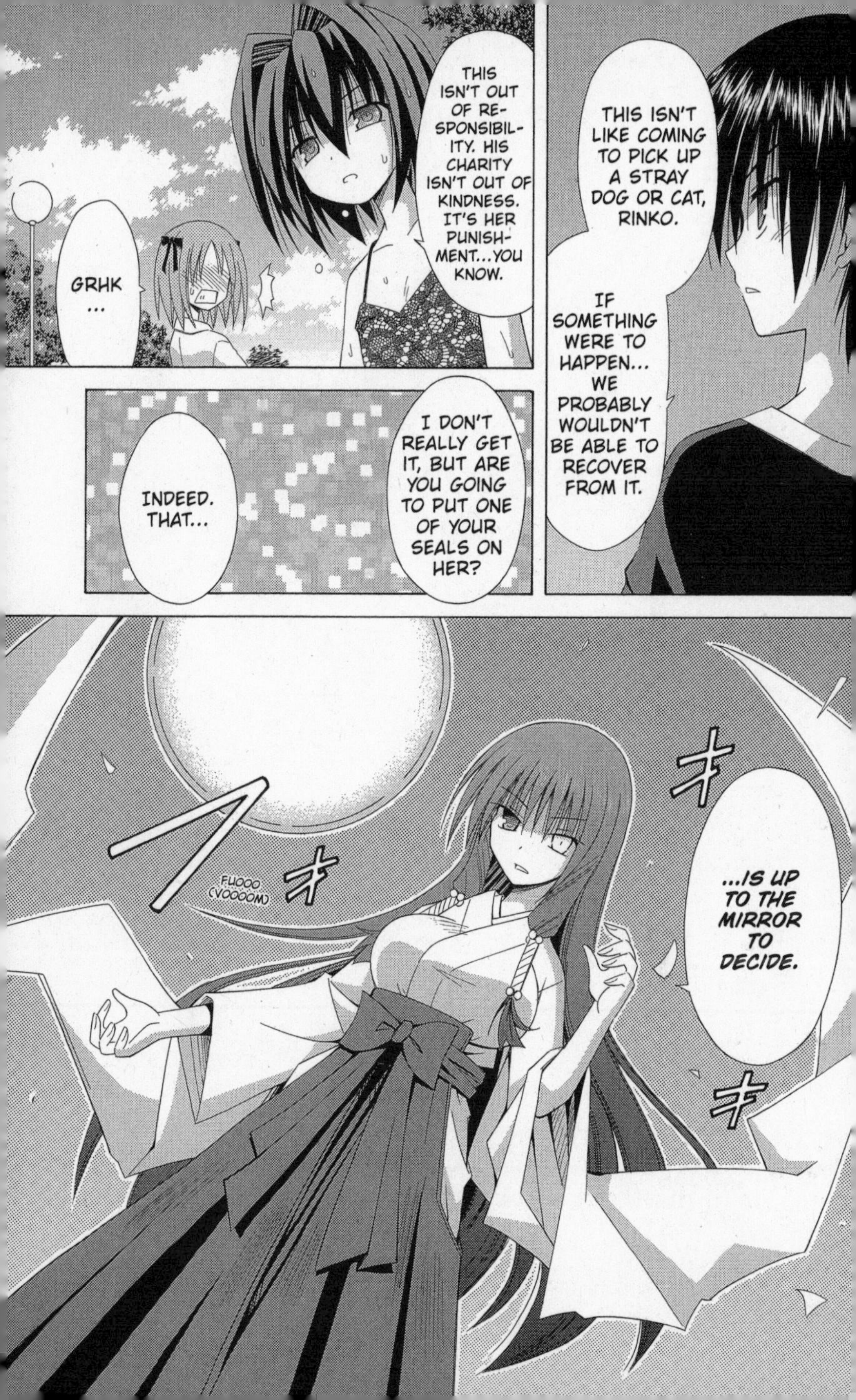
THIS ISN'T LIKE COMING TO PICK UP A STRAY DOG OR CAT, RINKO.
IF SOMETHING WERE TO HAPPEN... WE PROBABLY WOULDN'T BE ABLE TO RECOVER FROM IT.
THIS ISN'T OUT OF RE-SPONSIBIL-ITY. HIS CHARITY ISN'T OUT OF KINDNESS. IT'S HER PUNISH-MENT...YOU KNOW.
GRHK ...
I DON'T REALLY GET IT, BUT ARE YOU GOING TO PUT ONE OF YOUR SEALS ON HER?
INDEED. THAT...
...IS UP TO THE MIRROR TO DECIDE.
FUOOO (VOOOOM)

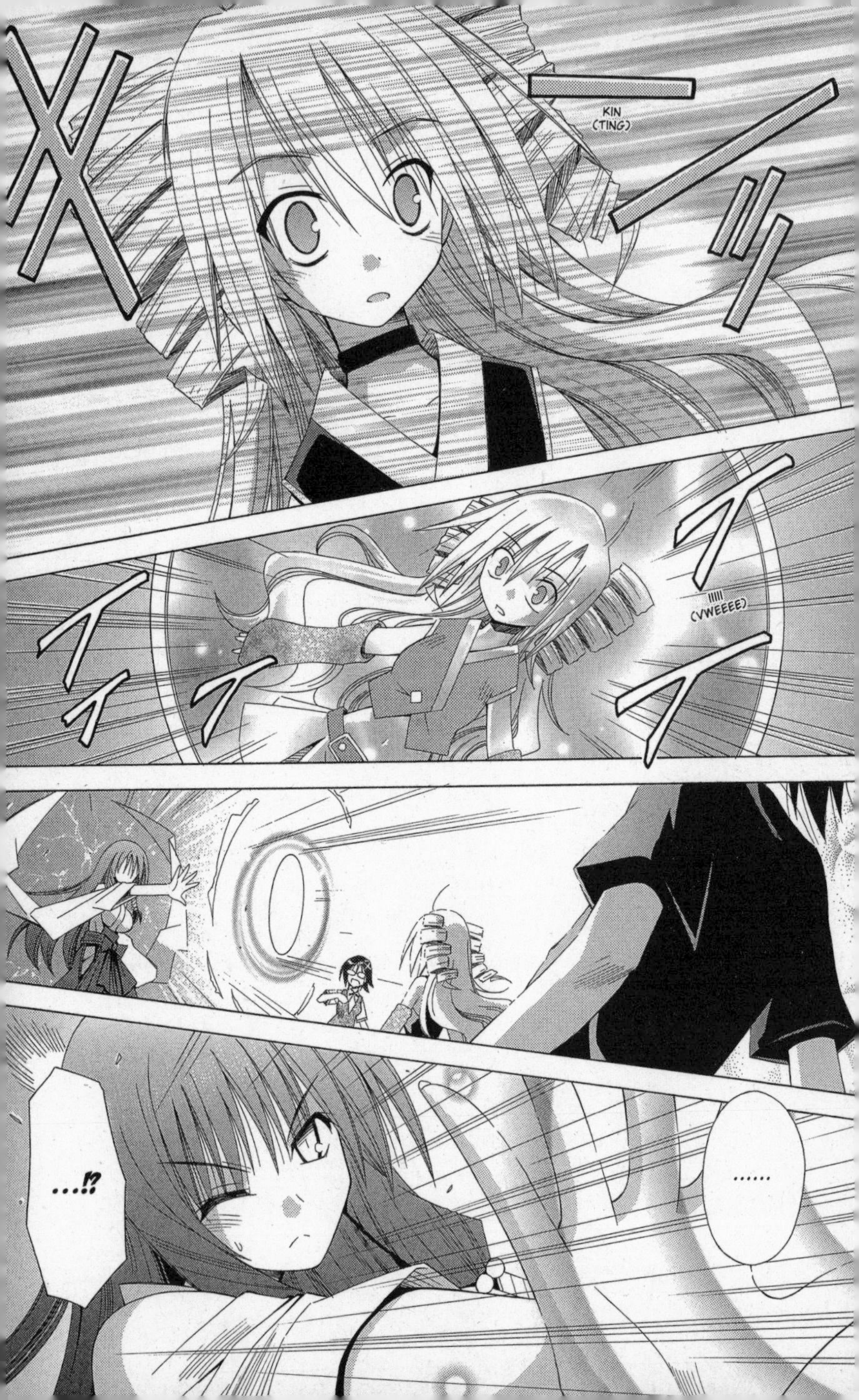
KIN
(TING)
(VWEEEE)
......
...!?

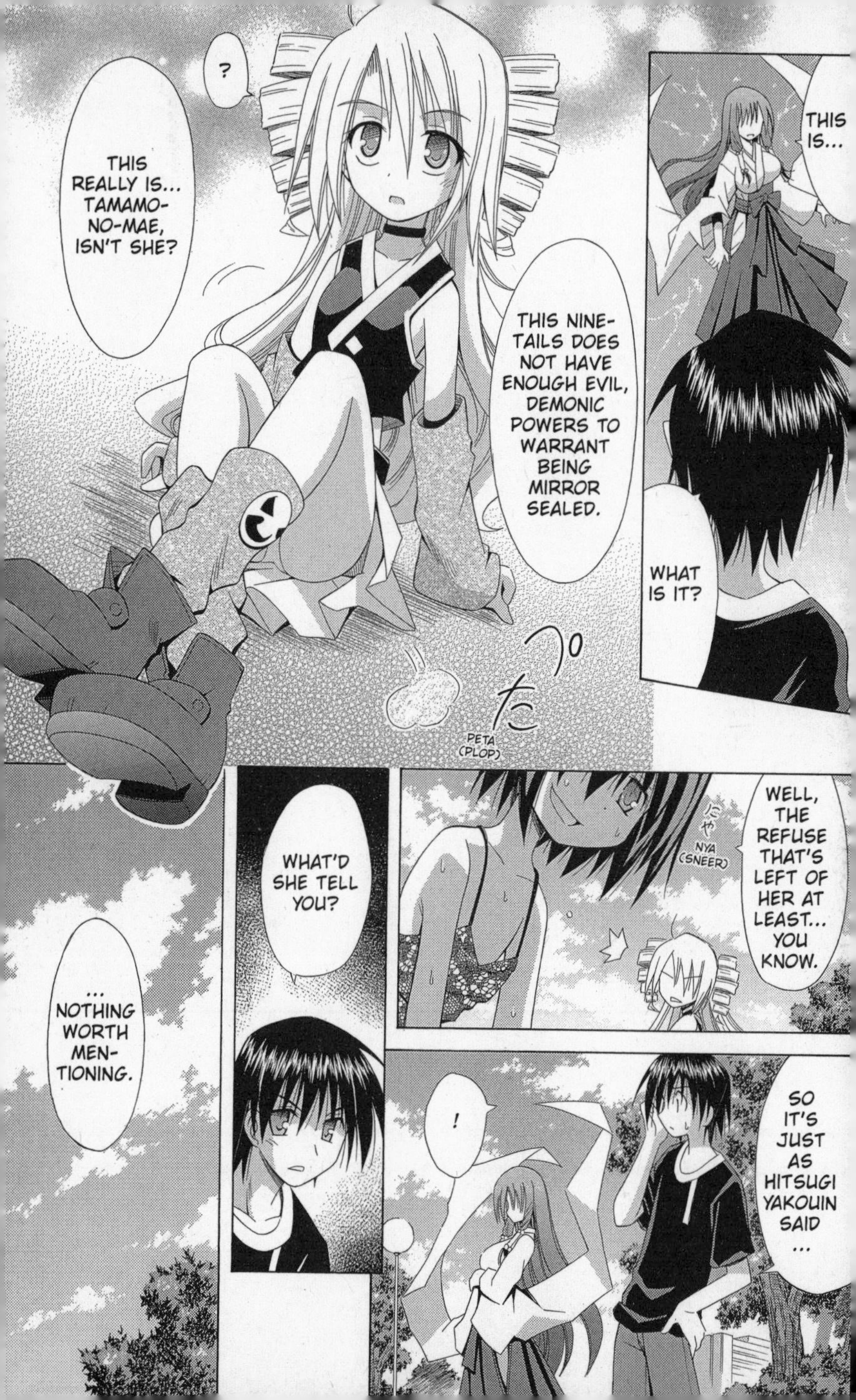
THIS IS...
WHAT IS IT?
THIS NINE-TAILS DOES NOT HAVE ENOUGH EVIL, DEMONIC POWERS TO WARRANT BEING MIRROR SEALED.
?
THIS REALLY IS... TAMAMO-NO-MAE, ISN'T SHE?
PETA (PLOP)
NYA (SNEER)
WELL, THE REFUSE THAT'S LEFT OF HER AT LEAST... YOU KNOW.
WHAT'D SHE TELL YOU?
... NOTHING WORTH MEN-TIONING.
SO IT'S JUST AS HITSUGI YAKOUIN SAID ...
!

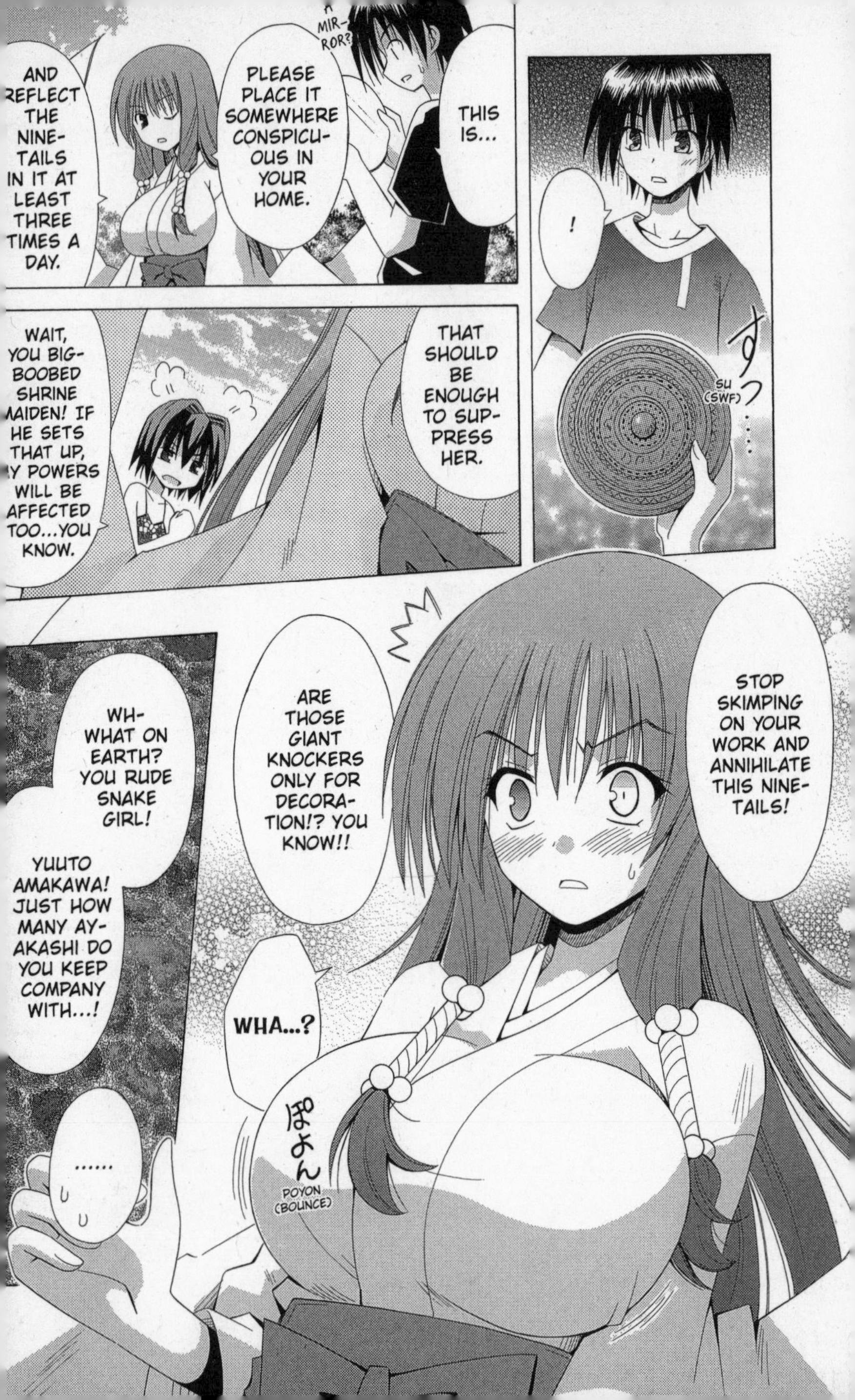
!
すっ
SU (SWF)
THIS IS...
A MIRROR?
PLEASE PLACE IT SOMEWHERE CONSPICUOUS IN YOUR HOME.
AND REFLECT THE NINE-TAILS IN IT AT LEAST THREE TIMES A DAY.
THAT SHOULD BE ENOUGH TO SUPPRESS HER.
WAIT, YOU BIG-BOOBED SHRINE MAIDEN! IF HE SETS THAT UP, MY POWERS WILL BE AFFECTED TOO...YOU KNOW.
STOP SKIMPING ON YOUR WORK AND ANNIHILATE THIS NINE-TAILS!
ARE THOSE GIANT KNOCKERS ONLY FOR DECORATION!? YOU KNOW!!
WH-WHAT ON EARTH? YOU RUDE SNAKE GIRL!
YUUTO AMAKAWA! JUST HOW MANY AYAKASHI DO YOU KEEP COMPANY WITH...!
WHA...?
ぽよん
POYON (BOUNCE)
......

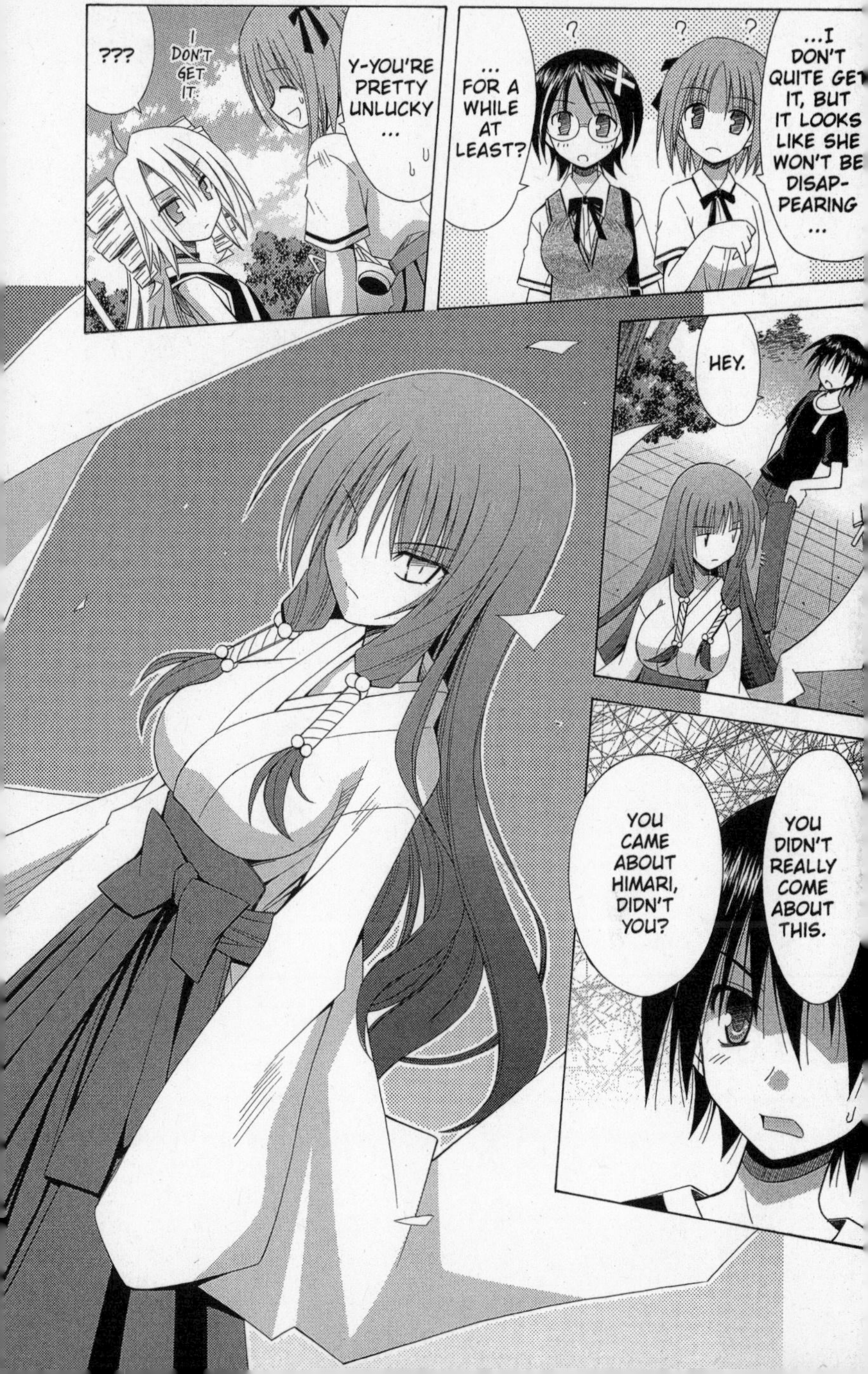
...I DON'T QUITE GET IT, BUT IT LOOKS LIKE SHE WON'T BE DISAPPEARING ...
... FOR A WHILE AT LEAST?
Y-YOU'RE PRETTY UNLUCKY ...
I DON'T GET IT.
???
HEY.
YOU DIDN'T REALLY COME ABOUT THIS.
YOU CAME ABOUT HIMARI, DIDN'T YOU?

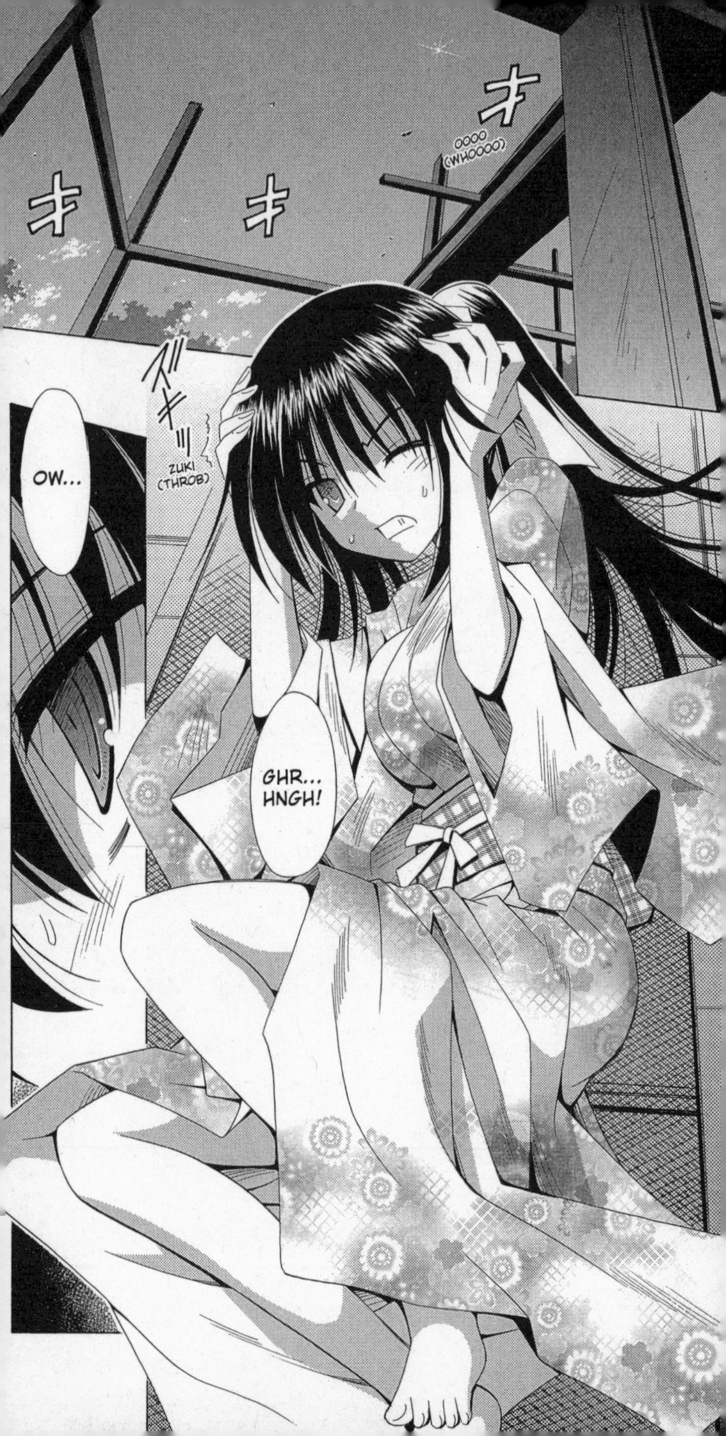
OOOO
(WHOOOO)
ZUKI
(THROB)
GHR... HNGH!
OW...

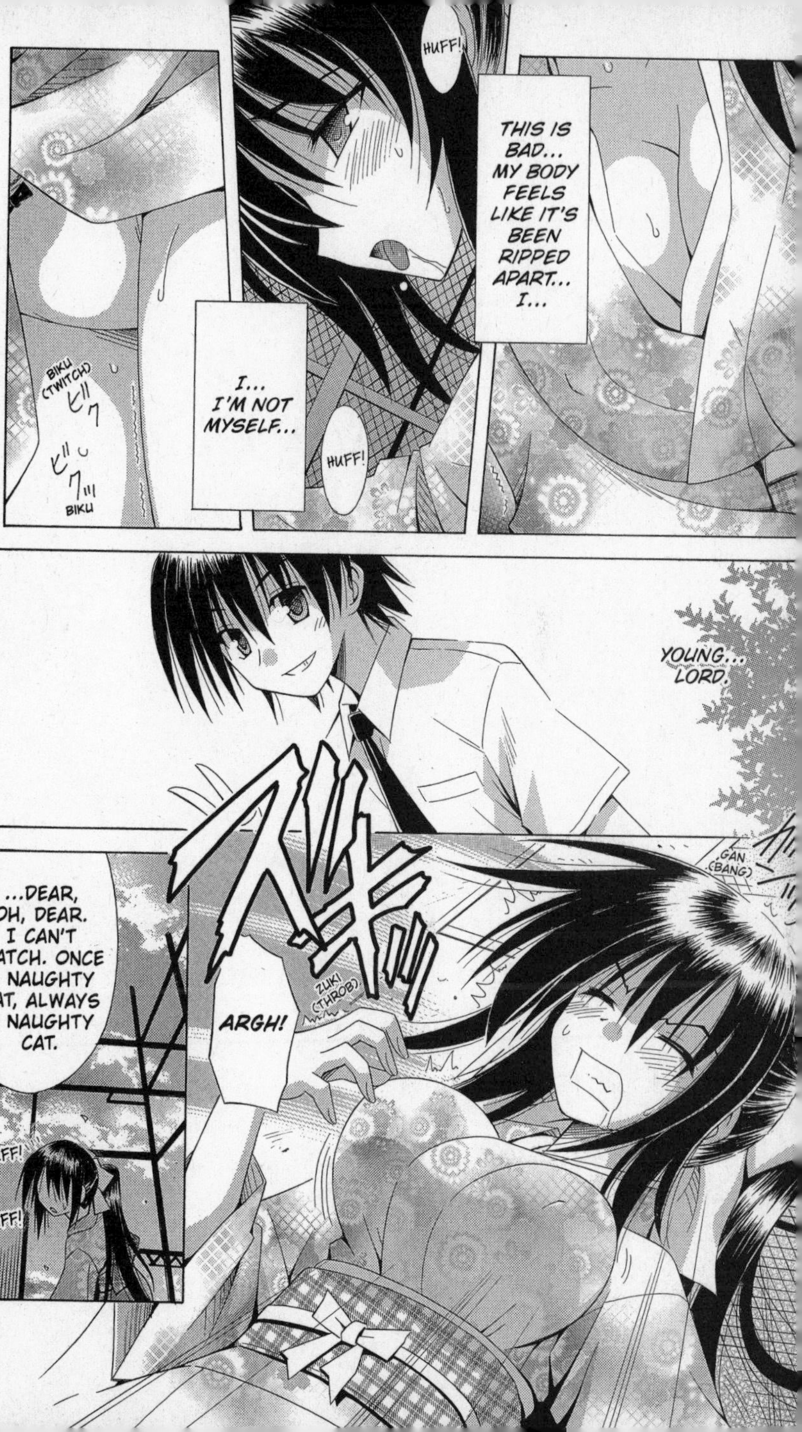
THIS IS BAD... MY BODY FEELS LIKE IT'S BEEN RIPPED APART... I...
HUFF!
I... I'M NOT MYSELF...
HUFF!
BIKU (TWITCH)
BIKU
YOUNG... LORD.
GAN (BANG)
ZUKI (THROB)
ARGH!
...DEAR, OH, DEAR. I CAN'T WATCH. ONCE A NAUGHTY CAT, ALWAYS A NAUGHTY CAT.
HUFF!
HUFF!

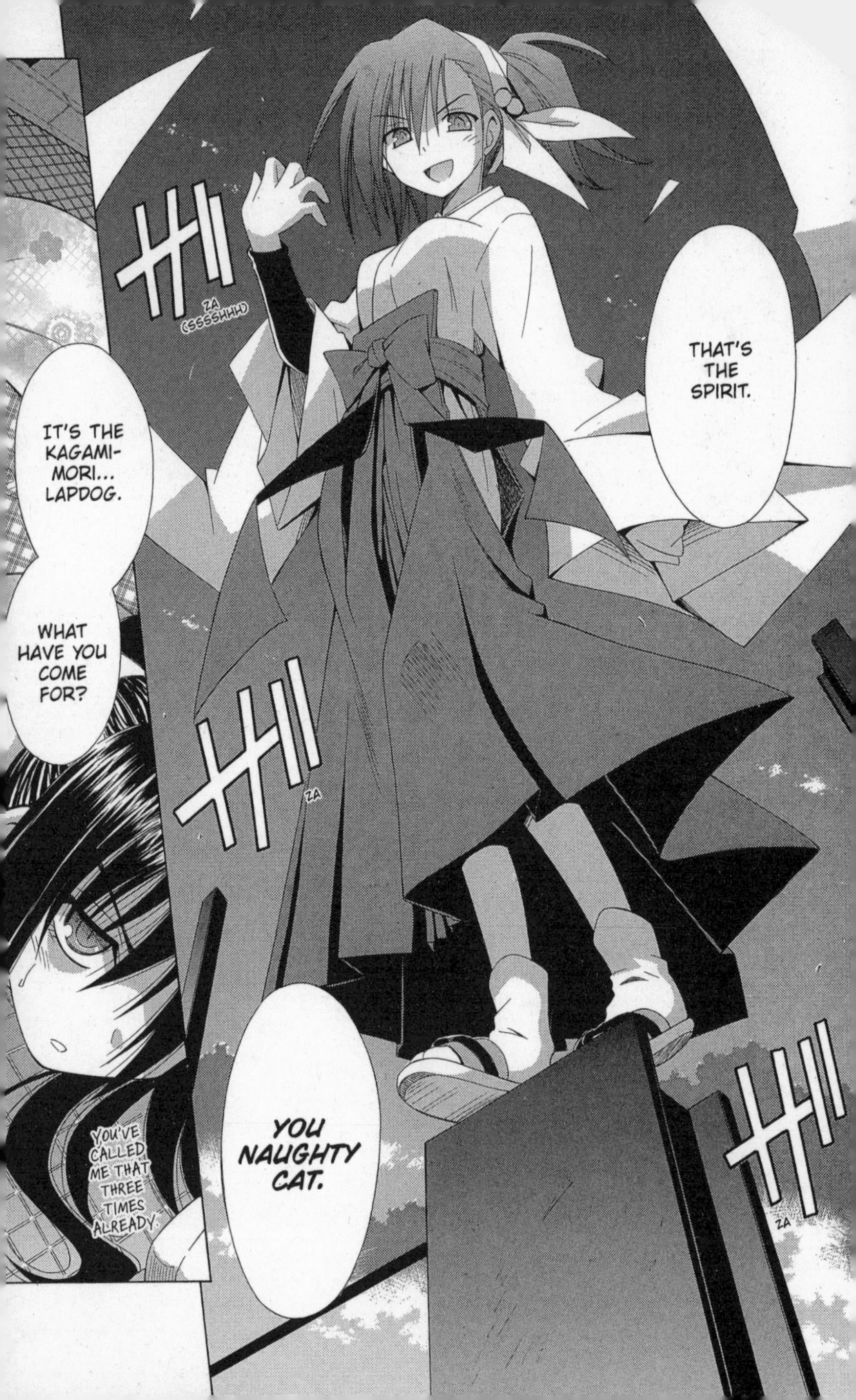
THAT'S THE SPIRIT.
ZA (SSSSHHH)
IT'S THE KAGAMI-MORI... LAPDOG.
WHAT HAVE YOU COME FOR?
ZA
ZA
YOU NAUGHTY CAT.
YOU'VE CALLED ME THAT THREE TIMES ALREADY.

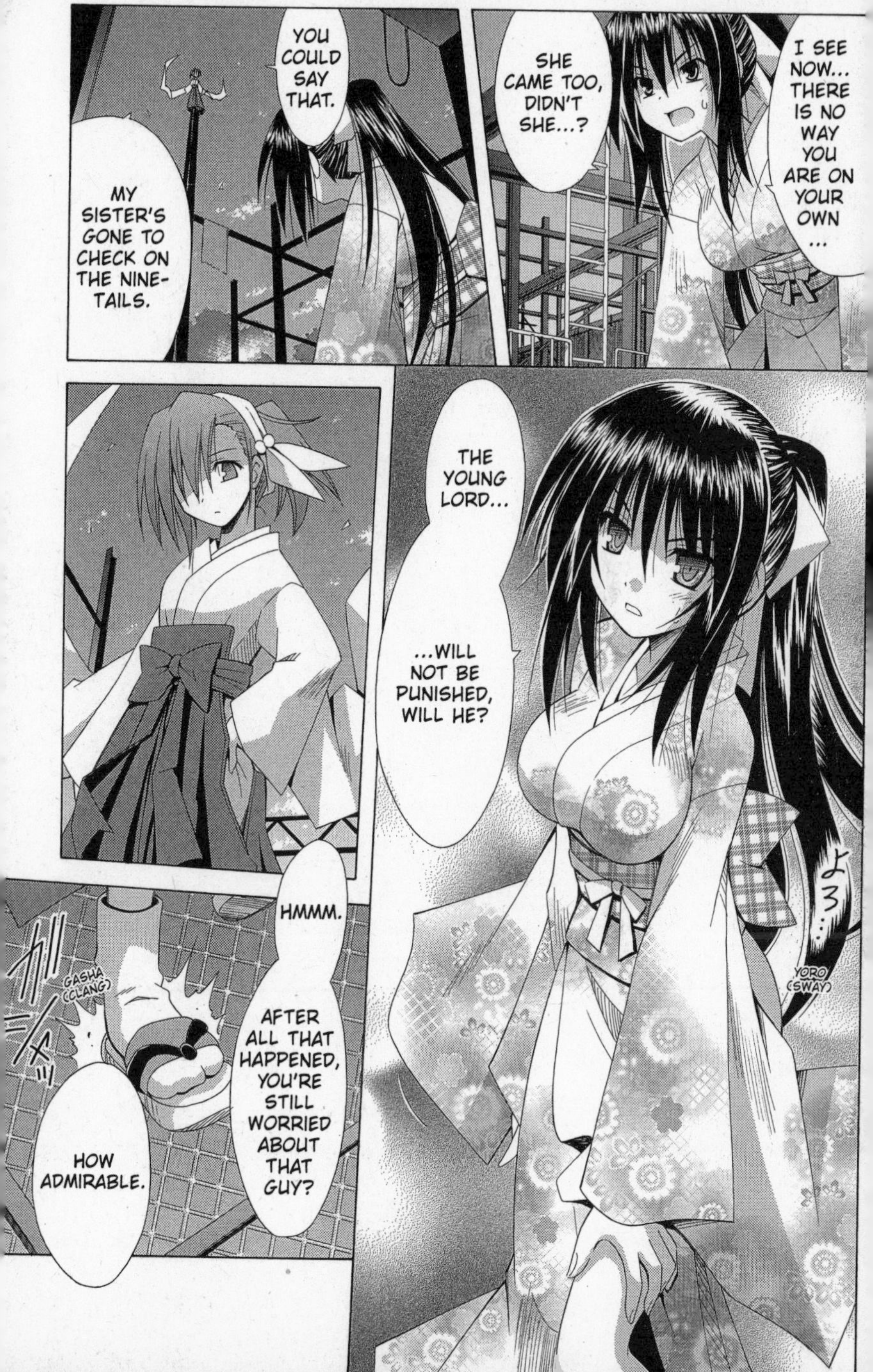
I SEE NOW... THERE IS NO WAY YOU ARE ON YOUR OWN ...
SHE CAME TOO, DIDN'T SHE...?
YOU COULD SAY THAT.
MY SISTER'S GONE TO CHECK ON THE NINE-TAILS.
THE YOUNG LORD...
...WILL NOT BE PUNISHED, WILL HE?
よろ...
YORO (SWAY)
HMMM.
AFTER ALL THAT HAPPENED, YOU'RE STILL WORRIED ABOUT THAT GUY?
HOW ADMIRABLE.
GASHA (CLANG)

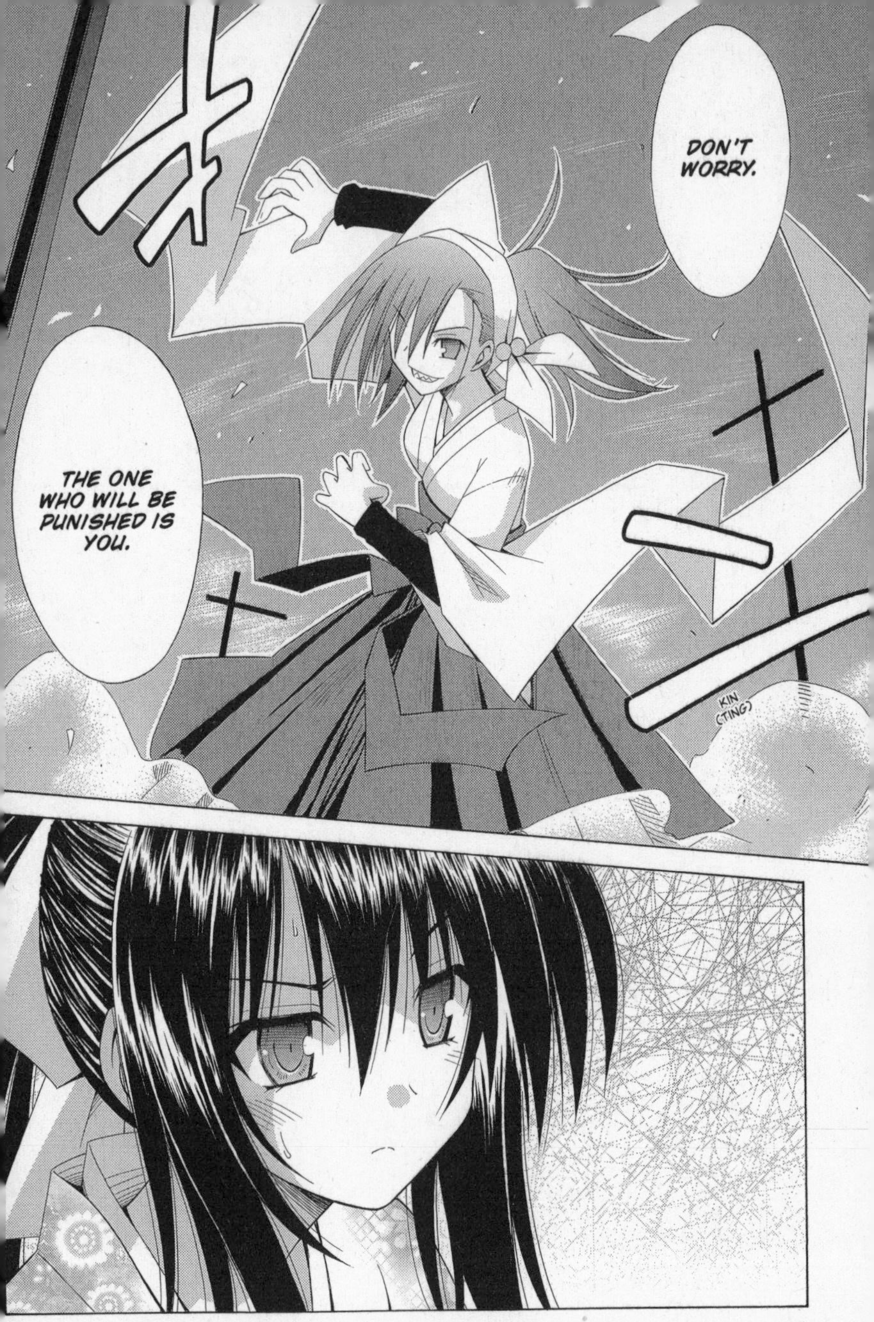
DON'T WORRY.
THE ONE WHO WILL BE PUNISHED IS YOU.
KIN (TING)

OMAMORI HIMARI

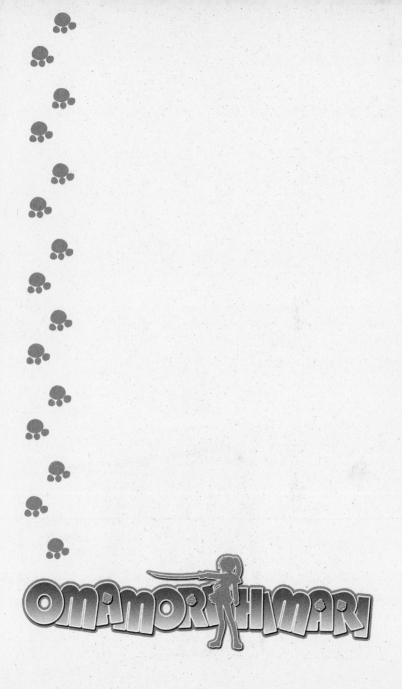

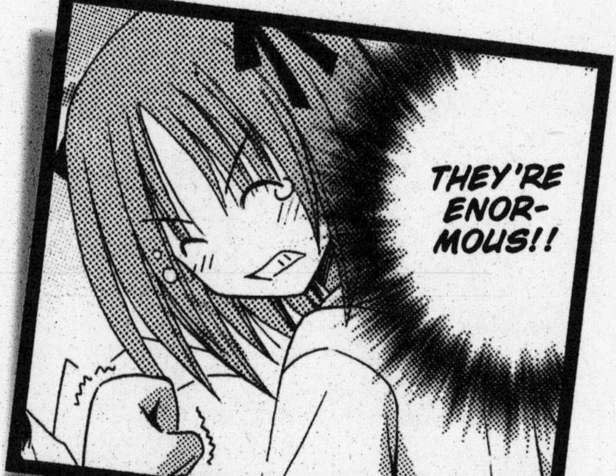
THEY'RE ENOR-MOUS!!

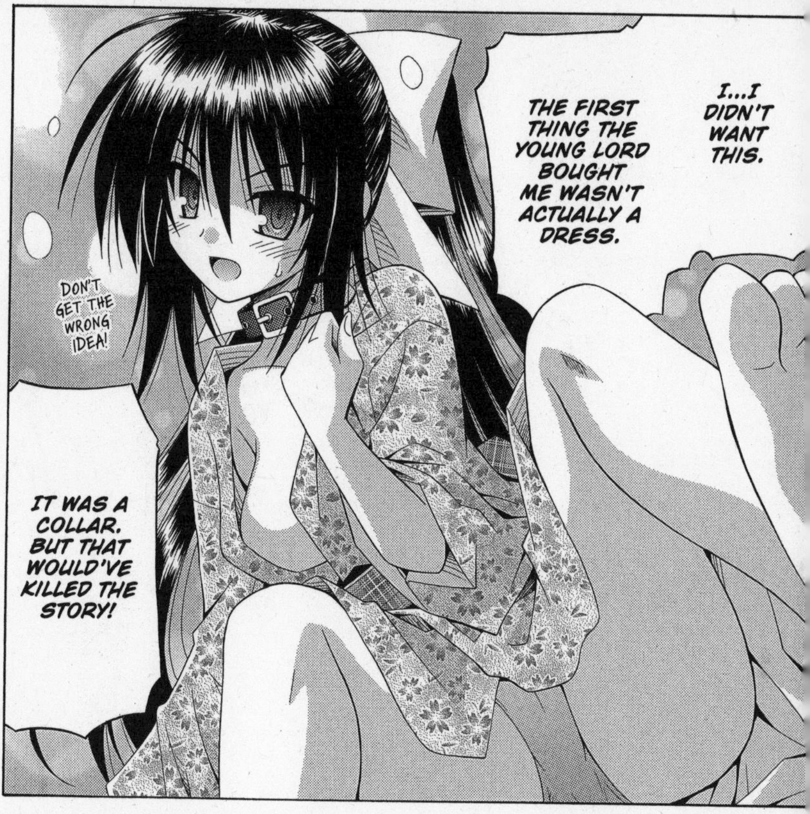
I...I DIDN'T WANT THIS.
THE FIRST THING THE YOUNG LORD BOUGHT ME WASN'T ACTUALLY A DRESS.
DON'T GET THE WRONG IDEA!
IT WAS A COLLAR. BUT THAT WOULD'VE KILLED THE STORY!

MENAGERIE 68.5: THE CAT & COMPANY'S SKETCHBOOK ☆ REVENGE

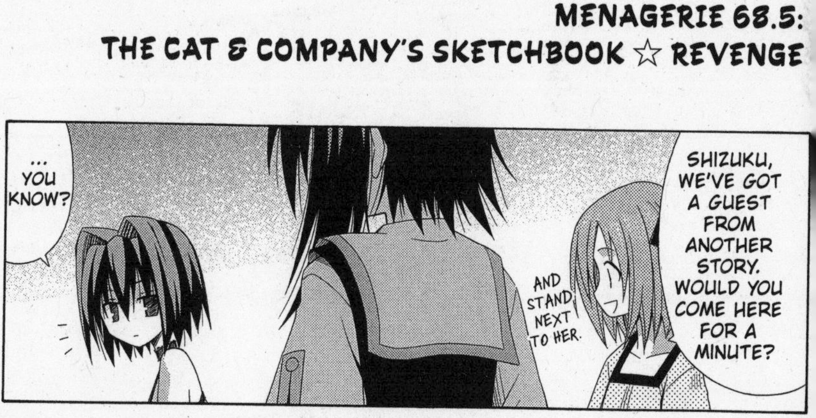
SHIZUKU, WE'VE GOT A GUEST FROM ANOTHER STORY. WOULD YOU COME HERE FOR A MINUTE?
AND STAND NEXT TO HER.
...YOU KNOW?

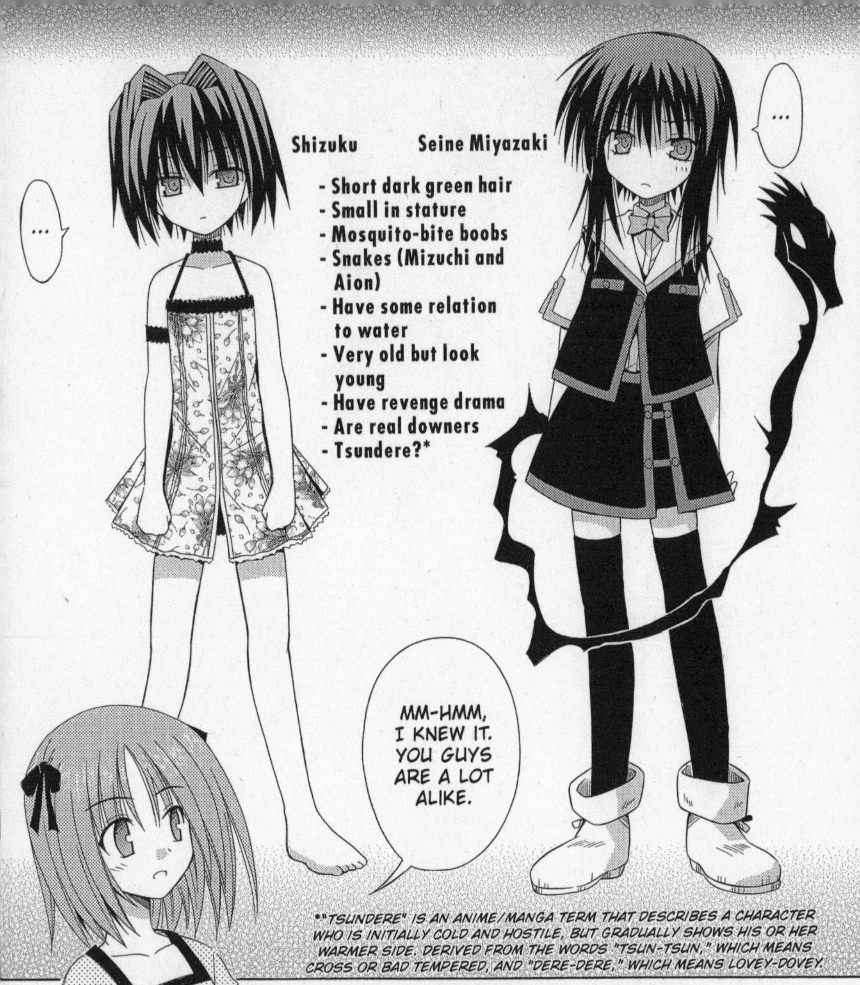
...
Shizuku
Seine Miyazaki
- Short dark green hair
- Small in stature
- Mosquito-bite boobs
- Snakes (Mizuchi and Aion)
- Have some relation to water
- Very old but look young
- Have revenge drama
- Are real downers
- Tsundere?*
...
MM-HMM, I KNEW IT. YOU GUYS ARE A LOT ALIKE.

*"TSUNDERE" IS AN ANIME/MANGA TERM THAT DESCRIBES A CHARACTER WHO IS INITIALLY COLD AND HOSTILE, BUT GRADUALLY SHOWS HIS OR HER WARMER SIDE. DERIVED FROM THE WORDS "TSUN-TSUN," WHICH MEANS CROSS OR BAD TEMPERED, AND "DERE-DERE," WHICH MEANS LOVEY-DOVEY.

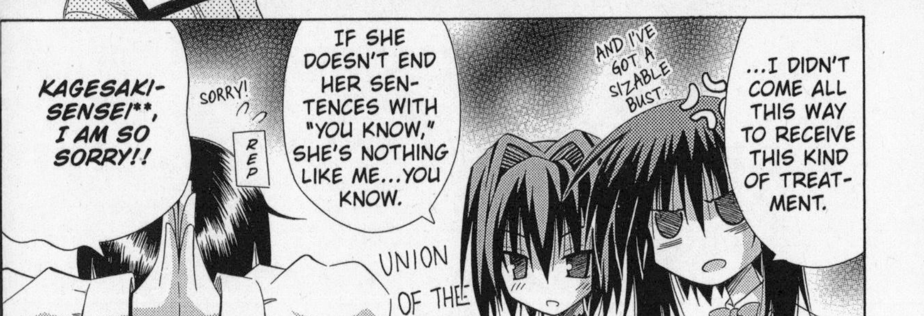
...I DIDN'T COME ALL THIS WAY TO RECEIVE THIS KIND OF TREATMENT.
AND I'VE GOT A SIZABLE BUST.
IF SHE DOESN'T END HER SEN-TENCES WITH "YOU KNOW," SHE'S NOTHING LIKE ME...YOU KNOW.
UNION OF THE SNAKE
SORRY!
REP
KAGESAKI-SENSEI**, I AM SO SORRY!!

**KAGESAKI-SENSEI IS THE CREATOR OF HEKIKAI NO AION THAT SEINE MIYAZAKI COMES FROM.

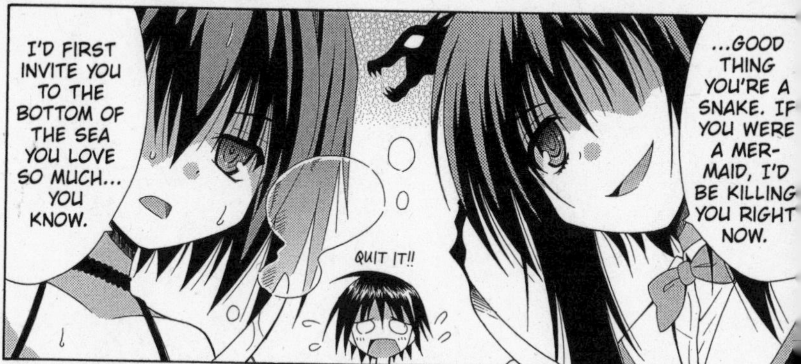
...GOOD THING YOU'RE A SNAKE. IF YOU WERE A MER-MAID, I'D BE KILLING YOU RIGHT NOW.
I'D FIRST INVITE YOU TO THE BOTTOM OF THE SEA YOU LOVE SO MUCH... YOU KNOW.
QUIT IT!!

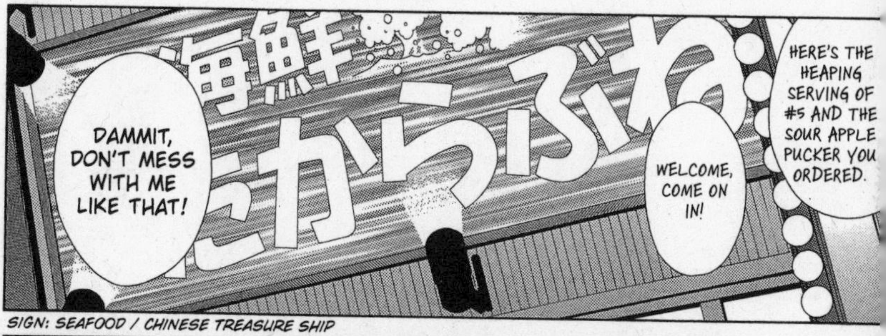
HERE'S THE HEAPING SERVING OF #5 AND THE SOUR APPLE PUCKER YOU ORDERED.
WELCOME, COME ON IN!
海鮮
からぶね
DAMMIT, DON'T MESS WITH ME LIKE THAT!

SIGN: SEAFOOD / CHINESE TREASURE SHIP

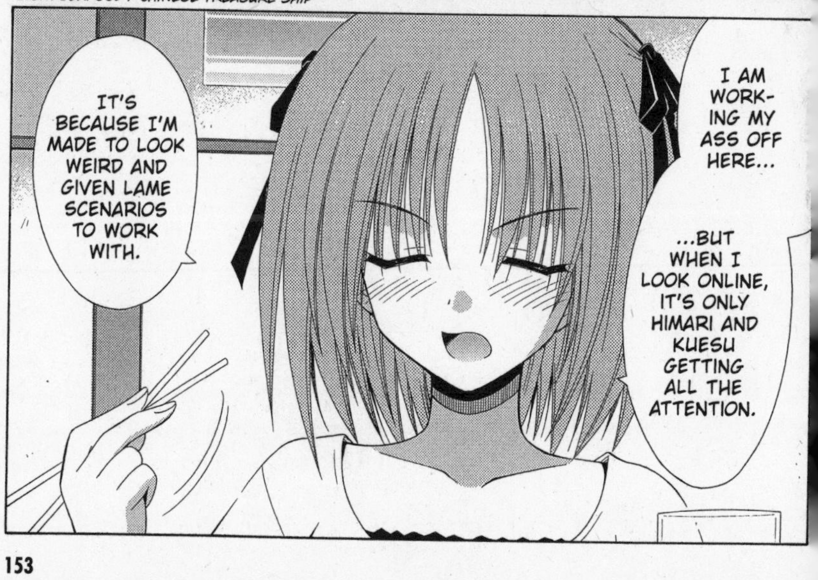
I AM WORK-ING MY ASS OFF HERE...
...BUT WHEN I LOOK ONLINE, IT'S ONLY HIMARI AND KUESU GETTING ALL THE ATTENTION.
IT'S BECAUSE I'M MADE TO LOOK WEIRD AND GIVEN LAME SCENARIOS TO WORK WITH.

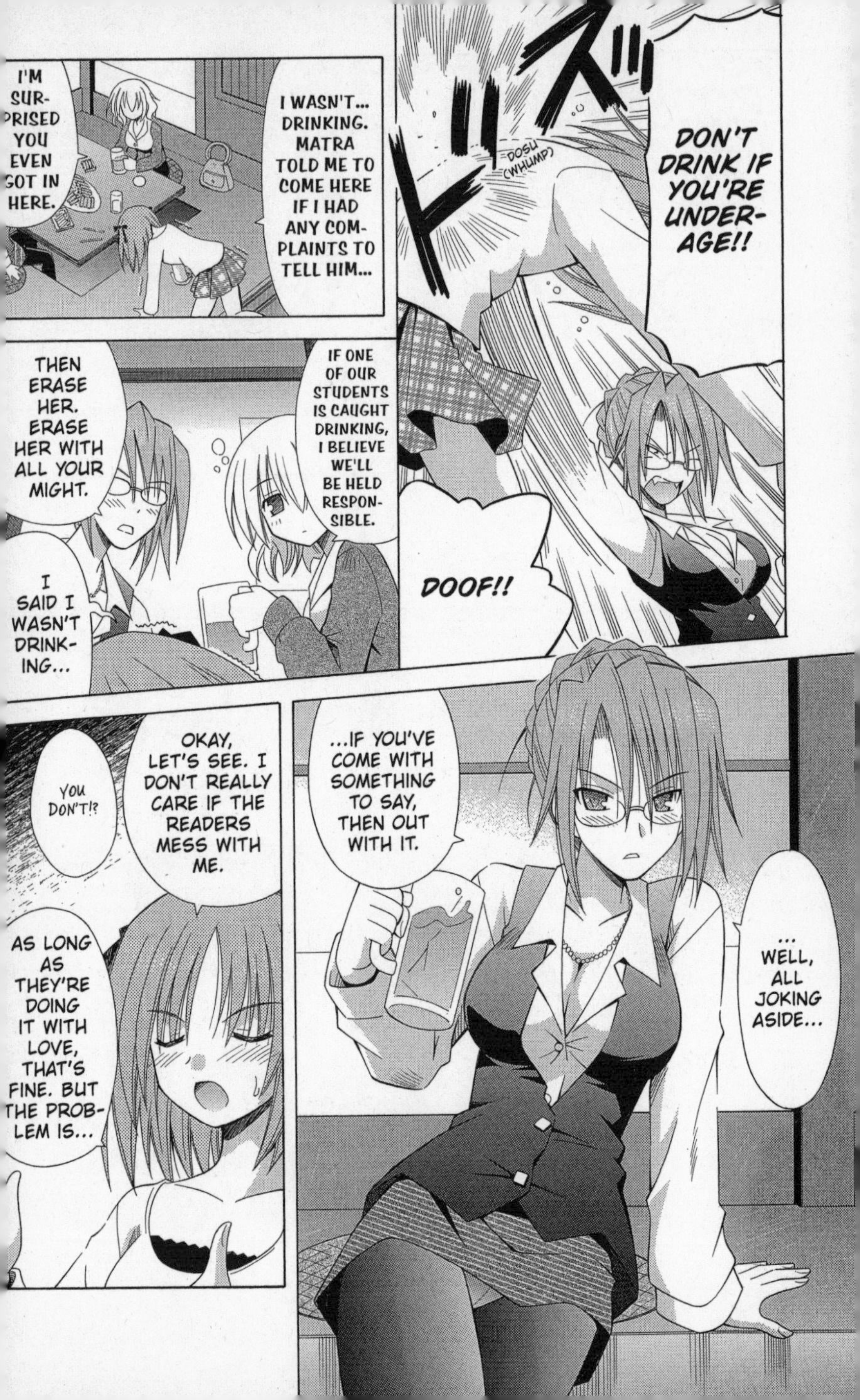
DON'T DRINK IF YOU'RE UNDER-AGE!!
DOSU (WHUMP)
DOOF!!
I WASN'T... DRINKING. MATRA TOLD ME TO COME HERE IF I HAD ANY COM-PLAINTS TO TELL HIM...
I'M SUR-PRISED YOU EVEN GOT IN HERE.
IF ONE OF OUR STUDENTS IS CAUGHT DRINKING, I BELIEVE WE'LL BE HELD RESPON-SIBLE.
THEN ERASE HER. ERASE HER WITH ALL YOUR MIGHT.
I SAID I WASN'T DRINK-ING...
...WELL, ALL JOKING ASIDE...
...IF YOU'VE COME WITH SOMETHING TO SAY, THEN OUT WITH IT.
OKAY, LET'S SEE. I DON'T REALLY CARE IF THE READERS MESS WITH ME.
YOU DON'T!?
AS LONG AS THEY'RE DOING IT WITH LOVE, THAT'S FINE. BUT THE PROB-LEM IS...

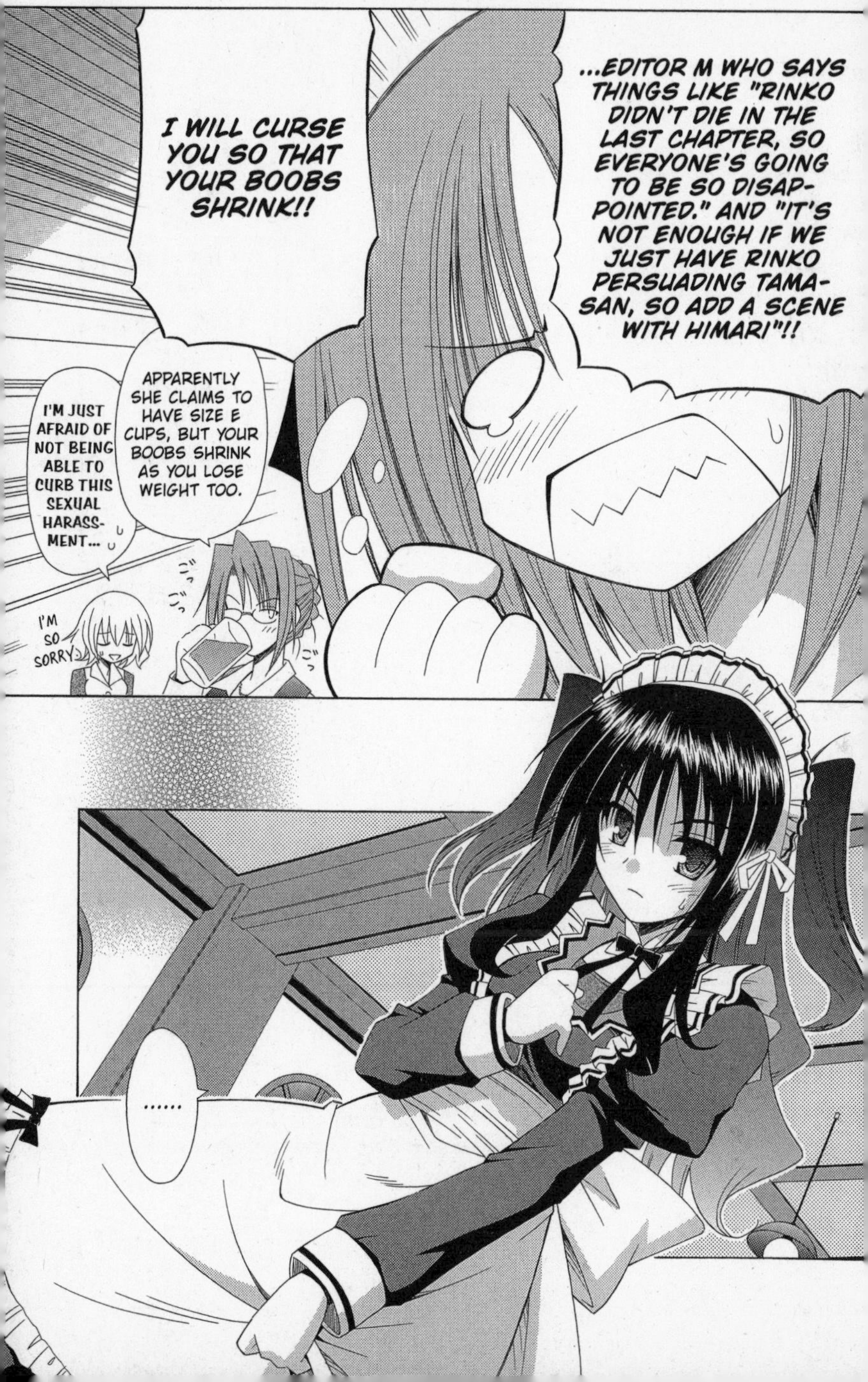
...EDITOR M WHO SAYS THINGS LIKE "RINKO DIDN'T DIE IN THE LAST CHAPTER, SO EVERYONE'S GOING TO BE SO DISAPPOINTED." AND "IT'S NOT ENOUGH IF WE JUST HAVE RINKO PERSUADING TAMA-SAN, SO ADD A SCENE WITH HIMARI"!!
I WILL CURSE YOU SO THAT YOUR BOOBS SHRINK!!
APPARENTLY SHE CLAIMS TO HAVE SIZE E CUPS, BUT YOUR BOOBS SHRINK AS YOU LOSE WEIGHT TOO.
I'M JUST AFRAID OF NOT BEING ABLE TO CURB THIS SEXUAL HARASSMENT...
I'M SO SORRY.
......

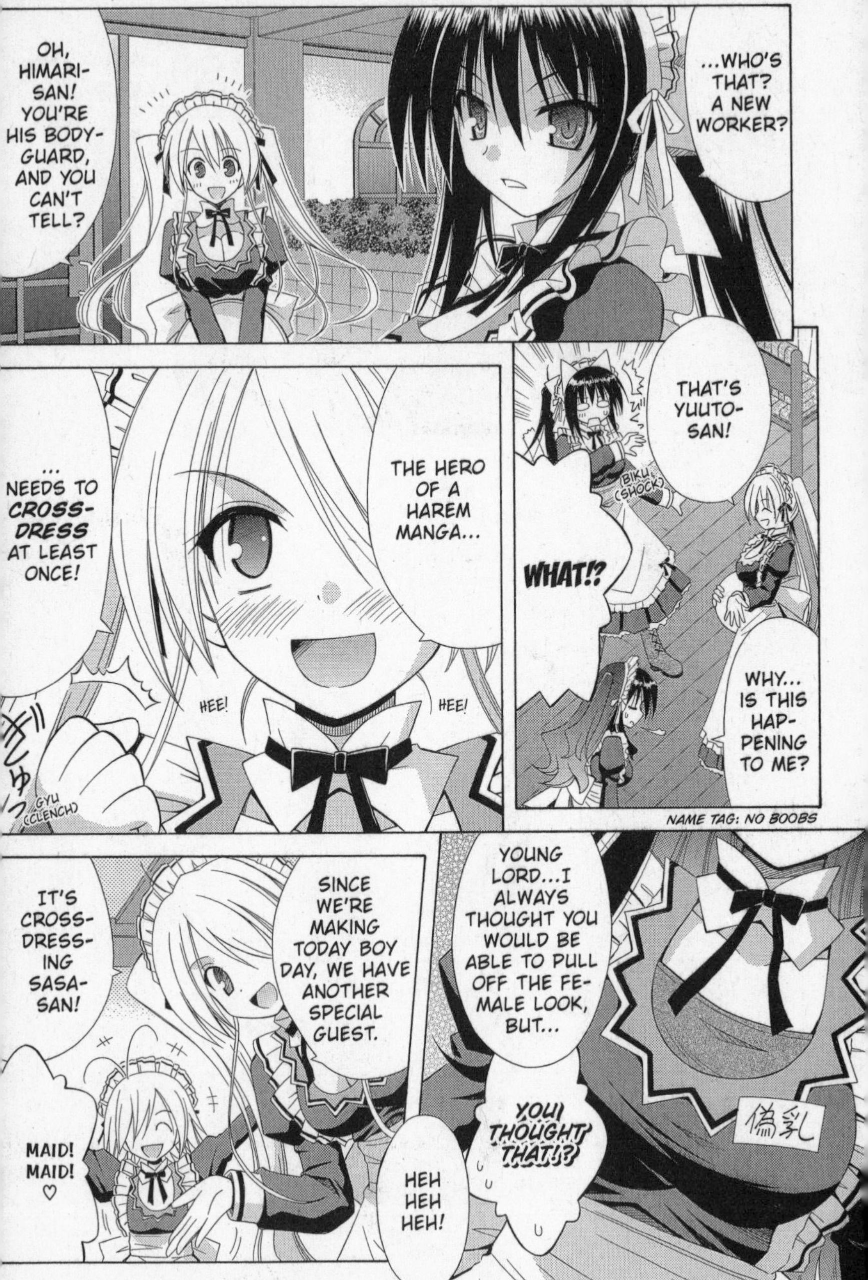
...WHO'S THAT? A NEW WORKER?
OH, HIMARI-SAN! YOU'RE HIS BODY-GUARD, AND YOU CAN'T TELL?
THAT'S YUUTO-SAN!
BIKU (SHOCK)
WHAT!?
WHY... IS THIS HAP-PENING TO ME?
THE HERO OF A HAREM MANGA...
...NEEDS TO CROSS-DRESS AT LEAST ONCE!
HEE!
HEE!
GYU (CLENCH)
NAME TAG: NO BOOBS
YOUNG LORD...I ALWAYS THOUGHT YOU WOULD BE ABLE TO PULL OFF THE FE-MALE LOOK, BUT...
YOU! THOUGHT THAT!?
HEH HEH HEH!
偽乳
SINCE WE'RE MAKING TODAY BOY DAY, WE HAVE ANOTHER SPECIAL GUEST.
IT'S CROSS-DRESSING SASA-SAN!
MAID! MAID! ♡

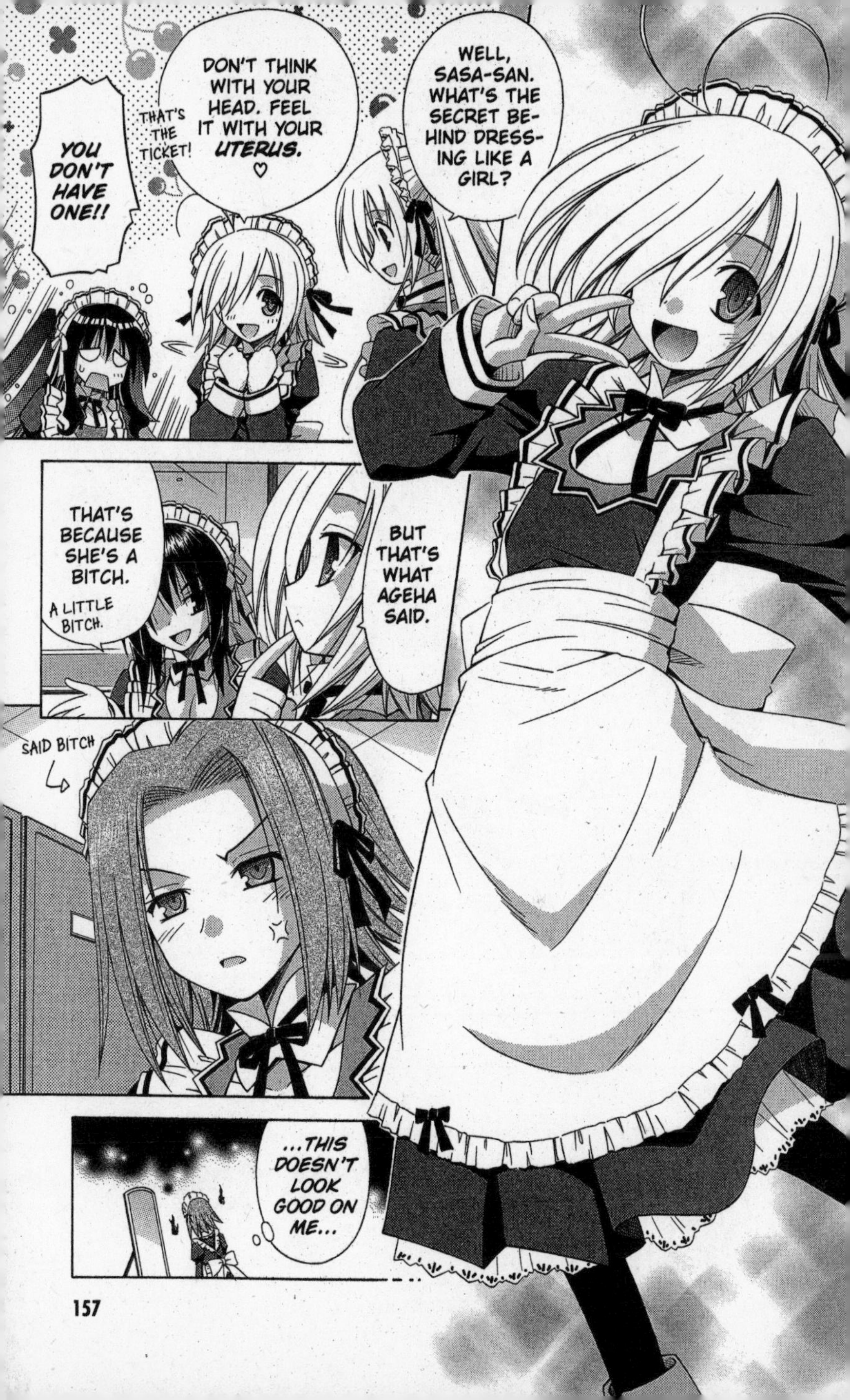
WELL, SASA-SAN. WHAT'S THE SECRET BEHIND DRESSING LIKE A GIRL?
DON'T THINK WITH YOUR HEAD. FEEL IT WITH YOUR UTERUS. ♡
THAT'S THE TICKET!
YOU DON'T HAVE ONE!!
BUT THAT'S WHAT AGEHA SAID.
THAT'S BECAUSE SHE'S A BITCH.
A LITTLE BITCH.
SAID BITCH
...THIS DOESN'T LOOK GOOD ON ME...

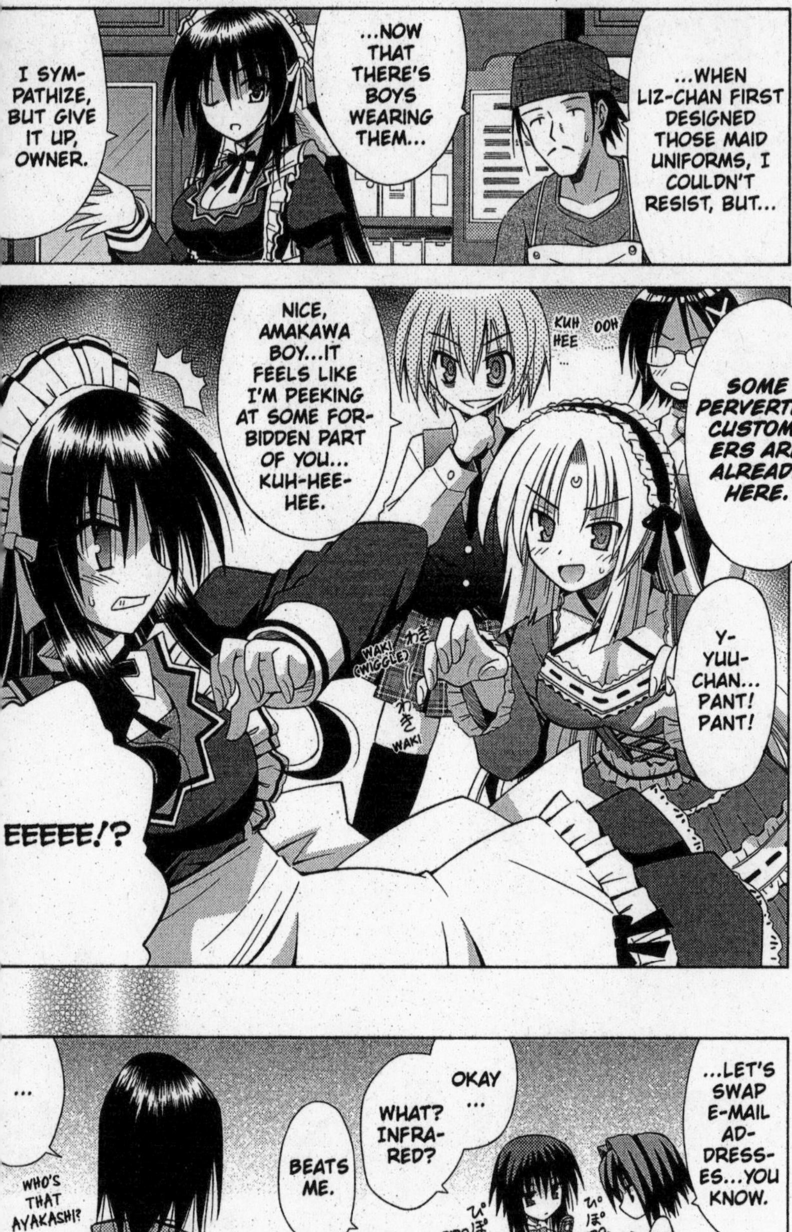
...WHEN LIZ-CHAN FIRST DESIGNED THOSE MAID UNIFORMS, I COULDN'T RESIST, BUT...
...NOW THAT THERE'S BOYS WEARING THEM...
I SYMPATHIZE, BUT GIVE IT UP, OWNER.
SOME PERVERTED CUSTOMERS ARE ALREADY HERE.
OOH...
KUH HEE...
NICE, AMAKAWA BOY...IT FEELS LIKE I'M PEEKING AT SOME FORBIDDEN PART OF YOU... KUH-HEE-HEE.
Y-YUU-CHAN... PANT! PANT!
WAKI (WIGGLE) わき
わき WAKI
EEEEE!?
...LET'S SWAP E-MAIL ADDRESSES...YOU KNOW.
ぴぽ PIPO
OKAY...
WHAT? INFRARED?
BEATS ME.
ぴぽ PIPO (BEEP)
...
WHO'S THAT AYAKASHI?

TO BE CONTINUED.

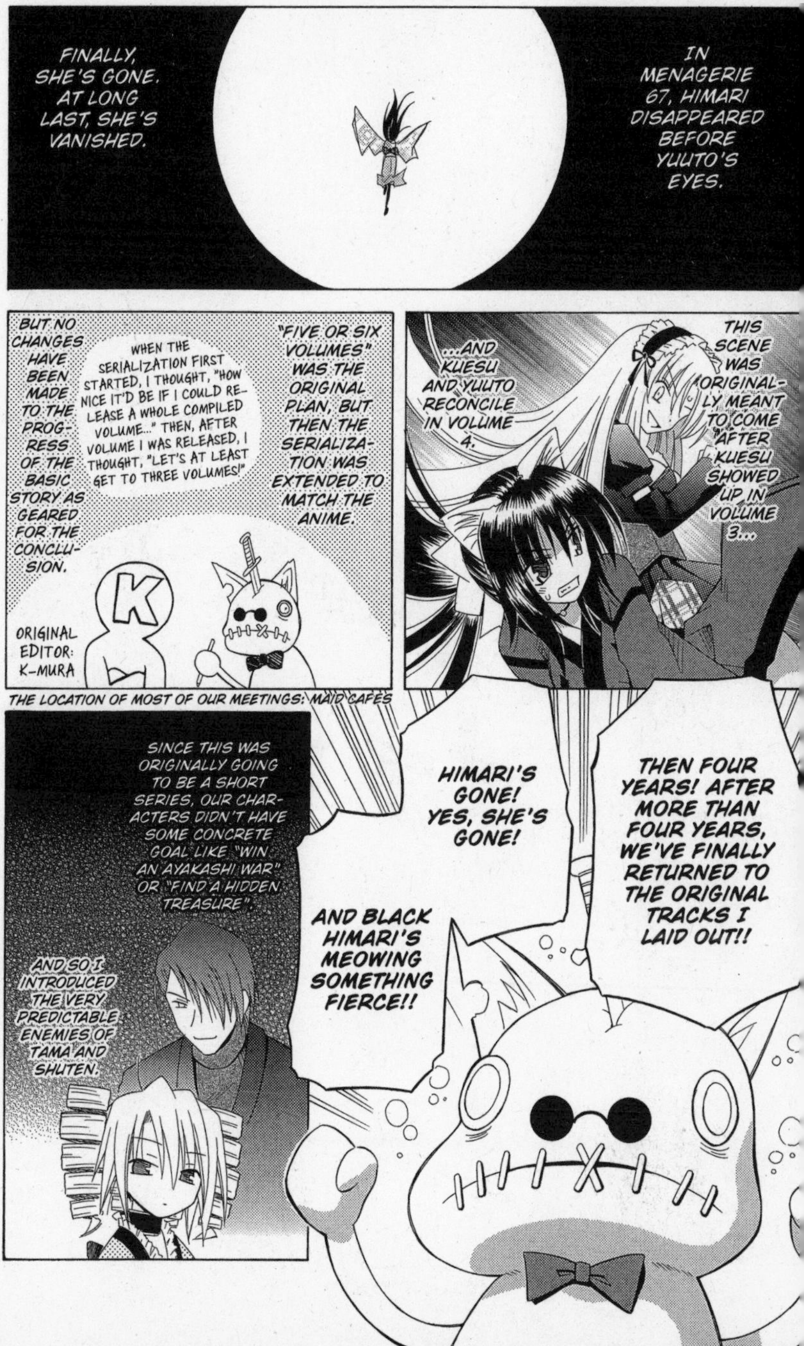
IN MENAGERIE 67, HIMARI DISAPPEARED BEFORE YUUTO'S EYES.
FINALLY, SHE'S GONE. AT LONG LAST, SHE'S VANISHED.
THIS SCENE WAS ORIGINALLY MEANT TO COME AFTER KUESU SHOWED UP IN VOLUME 3...
...AND KUESU AND YUUTO RECONCILE IN VOLUME 4.
"FIVE OR SIX VOLUMES" WAS THE ORIGINAL PLAN, BUT THEN THE SERIALIZATION WAS EXTENDED TO MATCH THE ANIME.
WHEN THE SERIALIZATION FIRST STARTED, I THOUGHT, "HOW NICE IT'D BE IF I COULD RELEASE A WHOLE COMPILED VOLUME..." THEN, AFTER VOLUME I WAS RELEASED, I THOUGHT, "LET'S AT LEAST GET TO THREE VOLUMES!"
BUT NO CHANGES HAVE BEEN MADE TO THE PROGRESS OF THE BASIC STORY AS GEARED FOR THE CONCLUSION.
K
ORIGINAL EDITOR: K-MURA
THE LOCATION OF MOST OF OUR MEETINGS: MAID CAFES
THEN FOUR YEARS! AFTER MORE THAN FOUR YEARS, WE'VE FINALLY RETURNED TO THE ORIGINAL TRACKS I LAID OUT!!
HIMARI'S GONE! YES, SHE'S GONE!
AND BLACK HIMARI'S MEOWING SOMETHING FIERCE!!
SINCE THIS WAS ORIGINALLY GOING TO BE A SHORT SERIES, OUR CHARACTERS DIDN'T HAVE SOME CONCRETE GOAL LIKE "WIN AN AYAKASHI WAR" OR "FIND A HIDDEN TREASURE".
AND SO I INTRODUCED THE VERY PREDICTABLE ENEMIES OF TAMA AND SHUTEN.

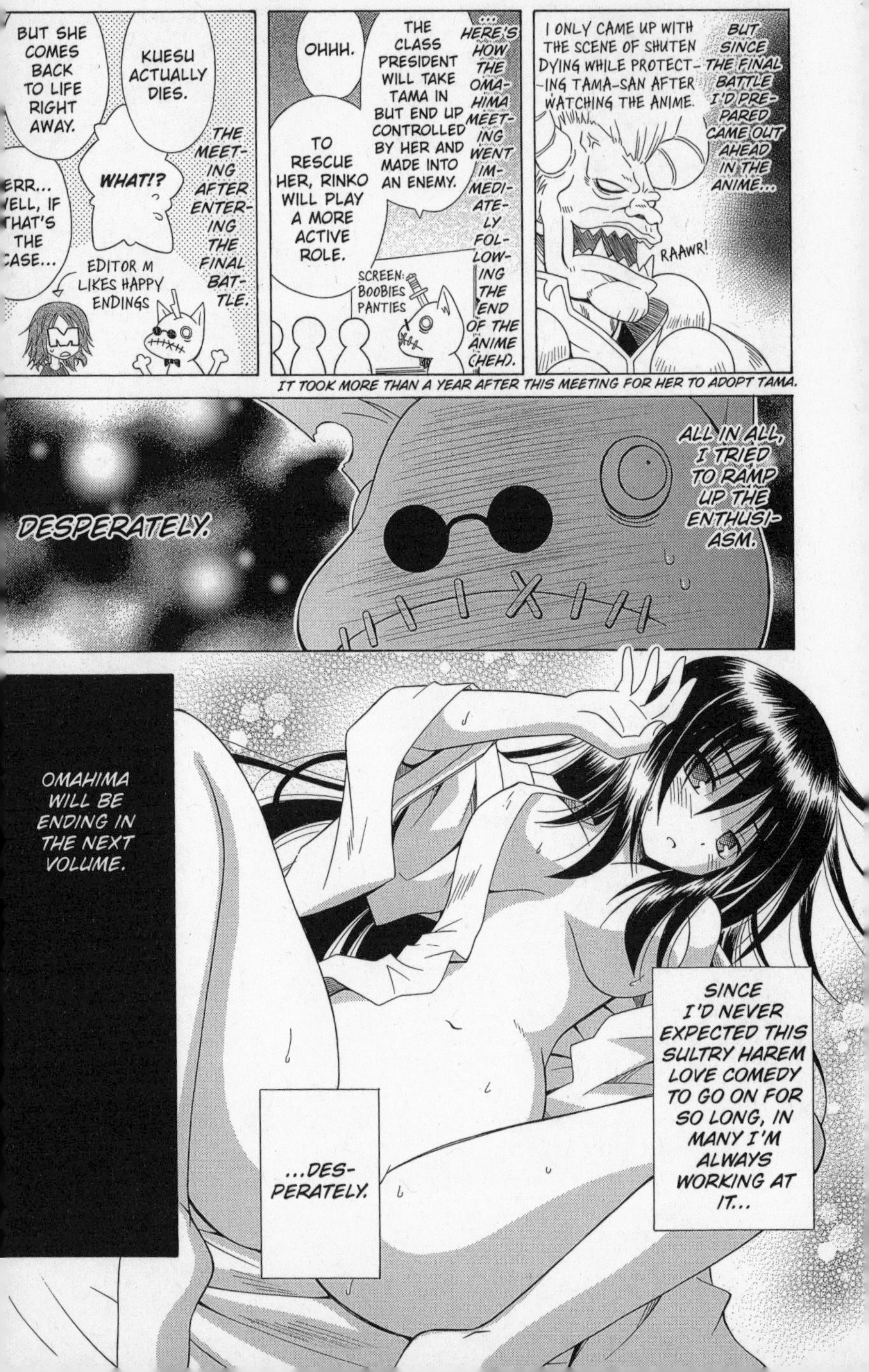
BUT SINCE THE FINAL BATTLE I'D PREPARED CAME OUT AHEAD IN THE ANIME...
I ONLY CAME UP WITH THE SCENE OF SHUTEN DYING WHILE PROTECT-ING TAMA-SAN AFTER WATCHING THE ANIME.
RAAWR!
...HERE'S HOW THE OMAHIMA MEETING WENT IMMEDIATELY FOLLOWING THE END OF THE ANIME (HEH).
THE CLASS PRESIDENT WILL TAKE TAMA IN BUT END UP CONTROLLED BY HER AND MADE INTO AN ENEMY.
OHHH.
TO RESCUE HER, RINKO WILL PLAY A MORE ACTIVE ROLE.
SCREEN: BOOBIES PANTIES
THE MEETING AFTER ENTERING THE FINAL BATTLE.
KUESU ACTUALLY DIES.
BUT SHE COMES BACK TO LIFE RIGHT AWAY.
WHAT!?
ERR... ELL, IF HAT'S THE ASE...
EDITOR M LIKES HAPPY ENDINGS
IT TOOK MORE THAN A YEAR AFTER THIS MEETING FOR HER TO ADOPT TAMA.
ALL IN ALL, I TRIED TO RAMP UP THE ENTHUSIASM.
DESPERATELY.
SINCE I'D NEVER EXPECTED THIS SULTRY HAREM LOVE COMEDY TO GO ON FOR SO LONG, IN MANY I'M ALWAYS WORKING AT IT...
...DESPERATELY.
OMAHIMA WILL BE ENDING IN THE NEXT VOLUME.